Acadia Parish, Louisiana

A History to 1900

by

Mary Alice Fontenot

and

Rev. Paul B. Freeland, D. D.

(map reproduced from Crowley Signal, Oct. 27, 1894)

CLAITOR'S PUBLISHING DIVISION

3165 S. Acadian at I 10, P. O. Box 239
Baton Rouge, Louisiana 70821

Louisiana Literary Award
1976

First printing, 1976
Second printing, 1979

CONTENTS

CHAPTER I

First Inhabitants

The streams and woodlands of Acadia Parish were once the habitat and hunting grounds of the Attakapas Indians. The domain of the Attakapas was roughly from Bayou Teche on the east to the Sabine River on the west, and north from the coastal marshes of the Gulf of Mexico to approximately the northern boundary of Acadia Parish.[1] The entire area of the parish was encompassed within Attakapas territory.

Knowledge of the Attakapas is meagre and vague. The white man was late in coming to territory occupied by the Attakapas; the early French and Spanish explorers avoided the region, either for fear of the Indians or because the Attakapas had little to offer of trade value.[2]

This first chapter of Acadia's history will attempt to bring together the bits and pieces of published information on the Attakapas Indians, the first known inhabitants of the parish.

The first European to report on the Attakapas was the Spanish explorer, Alvar Nunez Cabeza de Vaca, who visited the western sector of Attakapas territory in 1527.[3] He described the Indians as large and well-formed, and skillful with the bow and arrow, their only weapon.

De Vaca reported that the Attakapas were food gatherers, not food growers; they subsisted on roots and fish in winter. When cold weather made it impossible for them to fish or dig, they endured hunger stoically.

Another source says the Attakapas were "semi-agriculturists . . . Their diet was largely supplemented by fish, shellfish, and water birds."[4] Another writer is of the opinion that the abundance of natural food, such as fish, birds, small animals, deer, bear, persimmons, nuts and berries, made consistent agriculture unnecessary.[5] A third writer claims: "They (the Attakapas) were, as a matter of fact, a settled, agricultural people inhabiting one general region."[6]

De Vaca noted that the Indians showed great affection toward their children. A death was mourned for a year; they did not mourn for the

---

1 Sibley: *Louisiana's Ancients of Man,* 184

2 Post: "Some Notes on the Attakapas Indians of Southwest Louisiana," *Louisiana History,* Vol. II, No. 3, 224

3 "The Attakapas Country — Cabeza de Vaca," *Attakapas Gazette,* Vol. II, No. 3, 223

4 Sibley: *Louisiana's Ancients of Man,* 184

5 Post: "Some Notes," etc. *Louisiana History,* Vol. III, No. 3, 223

6 *Louisiana, a Guide to the State,* 33

aged. The men of the tribe went about naked, and ornamented their bodies by wearing a piece of cane in one nipple, sometimes both nipples. The cane was inserted through holes bored in the nipples from side to side. The women partially covered their bodies with Spanish moss, and "damsels" wore deer skin.[7]

In 1698 the Attakapas population in Louisiana was 1,750.[8] The population centers were on the inland streams: the Rivers Vermilion, Mermentau and Calcasieu, also bayou tributaries of the Mermentau, Bayous Queue de Tortue and Plaquemine Brûlée.[9]

Like other Indians of south Louisiana, the Attakapas built houses of cane, reeds or wood, using moss, palmetto leaves or cornhusks for thatching.[10] Their environment was such that few tools or weapons were needed; the unsophisticated tools and weapons that were developed must have been quite adequate for the environment, since these did permit them to work and live autonomously until faced with the overpowering onslaught of the white man.[11]

A document preserved by Martin Duralde, commandant of Poste des Opelousas in 1795, contains all that is known of the mythology of the Attakapas. That portion of Duralde's narrative which pertains to the Attakapas is as follows:

"The Atacapas pretend that they are come out of the sea, that a prophet or man inspired by God laid down the rules of conduct to their first ancestors (pères), which consisted in not doing any evil. They believe in an author of all things: that those who do well go above, and those who do evil descend under the earth into the shades. They speak of a deluge which swallowed up men, animals, and the land, and it was only those who resided along a high land or mountain (that of San Antonio, if we may judge) who escaped this calamity.

"According to their law a man ceases to bear his own name as soon as he has a child born, and he is then called the father of such a boy giving the name of the child. If the child dies, the father again assumes his own name. The women alone are charged with the labors of the field and of the household.

---

7 "The Attakapas Country, Cabeza de Vaca," *Attakapas Gazette*, Vol. II, No. 1, 5
8 Swanton: *Indian Tribes of the Lower Mississippi Valley*, 45
9 Swanton: *Indians of the Southeastern United States*, 93-94
10 Davis: *Louisiana, a Narrative History*, 14
11 Gibson: Jon A., PhD, assoc. prof. anthropology, ch. social studies, University of Southwestern Louisiana

"The mounds, according to them, were intended to elevate and distinguish the dwellings of the chiefs, and were thrown up under their supervision by the women . . . .

"Many years before the discovery of the elephant in the bayou called Carancro an Atacapas savage had informed a man who is at present in my service in the capacity of cow-herd that the ancestors of his nation transmitted (the story) to their descendants that a beast of enormous size had perished either in this bayou or in one of the two water courses a short distance from it without their being able to indicate the true place, the antiquity of the event having without doubt made them forget it. The fact has realized this tradition."[12]

A tradition concerning the Attakapas was recounted by Felix Voorhies:

"The Attakapas Indians were much dreaded by other Indian tribes . . . There is a tradition that the Attakapas Nation becoming more and more aggressive, the neighboring tribes of Chactas (Choctaws), Alibamons, and Opelousas formed a league for the purpose of resisting their aggressions, and to repel their inroads and attacks. A war of extermination ensued. Several severe skirmishes took place. Finally, the hated and blood thirsty Attakapas Indians were almost annihilated in a great battle, fought on the hills three miles west of the town of St. Martinville. Now powerless to do harm, the remnant of the once warlike Attakapas was either incorporated in the victorious tribes, or allowed to remain unmolested in the district . . . From the time of this terrible overthrow the Attakapas ceased to be known and feared as a tribe.

"This occurred shortly before the advent of the white man in Louisiana. The conquered territory was divided among the victors. That part of the district which now forms the parish of St. Landry was allotted to the Opelousas, and went by that name until after the cession of Louisiana to the United States. The Alibamons had for their share of the spoils that part of the district which extends from the Vermilion River to the River Mermentau, whilst the Choctaws took possession of the Teche country. But although they located two or three villages on the Teche and Vermilion Bayous, the immense Attakapas region was by mutual consent reserved as hunting grounds for the three confederated tribes."[13]

It should be noted that Voorhies labels his account of the Indian war as "tradition." Also, the part concerning the distribution of the conquered

12 Swanton: *Indian Tribes, Lower Mississippi Valley*, 363
13 Perrin: *Southwest Louisiana Biographical and Historical*, Part 1, 13

3

Attakapas Indian, detail from a drawing by A. De Batz, about 1735. The original drawing is in the National Anthropological Archives, Smithsonian Institution, Washington, D.C.

territory should be viewed as dubious, since sales of Indian lands in this specific area in the late 1700s show only the Attakapas as land owners.[14]

The Attakapas had the reputation of being cannibals. Early maps label their territory "Wandering Indians and Man-Eaters." Many of the early writers accepted this cannibalistic reputation, some later writers discount it.

The name Attakapas (Atakapa, Atacapas) is a Choctaw word meaning "man-eater." M. Le Page Du Pratz, who spent 16 years in Louisiana, from 1718 to 1734, relates:

"Along the west coast, not far from the sea, inhabit the nation called Atacapas, that is, Man-eaters, being so called by the other nations on account of their detestable custom of eating their enemies, or such as they believe to be their enemies. In this vast country there are no other cannibals to be met with besides the Atacapas; and since the French have gone among them, they have raised in them so great an horror of that abominable practice of devouring creatures of their own species, that they have promised to leave it off; and accordingly for a long time past we have heard of no such barbarity among them."[15]

One white man, a Frenchman, Simars de Belle-Isle, claimed to have witnessed the Attakapas eating human flesh. Historians give divergent accounts of Belle-Isle's story:

C. C. Robin, who traveled in Louisiana 1802-1806, relates:

"And now a deplorable event occurred which strengthened still more the fear of these Indians among the Louisianians. About 1720 a ship of the company of the West Indies missed Balise and was carried by the currents to the west to the Bay of Saint Bernard to the vicinity of the peninsula called today Belle-Isle. Five officers went with the longboat that put ashore to look for water, in order to hunt. The longboat made several trips back and forth, but having waited in vain for the officers, after a time, returned finally to the ship. The captain had the barbarity to weigh anchor and abandon the five officers. They wandered for a long time on those wild and marshy coasts, in the greatest trepidation of meeting the Indians, whose anthropophagic reputation they already know. Four of these unfortunates eventually died of hunger. The fifth, named Belle-Isle, who survived them, buried them with his own hands in order to keep the cadavers from being eaten by wild animals.

---

14 *American State Papers — Public Lands,* Vol. III, 96
15 Du Pratz: *History of Louisiana,* 302

5

"Belle-Isle wandered for several days, sharing what he found to eat with his dog, but the animal was wounded by a wildcat, and his master was obliged to kill him, and afterwards to eat him. At length, almost ready to die of hunger, he came across traces of human beings and followed them to a river, where he found a pirogue. Using this, he crossed the river to the other bank, where he found himself among a group of Indians who were engaged in stripping and drying fish and meat. His thinness frightened them, but they despoiled him of his clothes, which they divided. They at first gave him human meat to eat, but when he refused this horrible meal, they offered him fish. The savages, having decided that he had not come to harm them, but rather as a guest requesting hospitality, did not treat him as an enemy. He was made the slave of a widow. His regular occupation was carrying the bodies of the enemies destined to be eaten. He was soon adopted by the widow and then into the tribe. He went with them to war, where he distinguished himself, but he was never able to get used to eating human flesh, although he observed this odious spectacle daily. Two years went by in this way, when finally a deputation of some of the Indians, who lived near the post of Natchitoches, arrived at the encampment, and by this means he was able to send news of his plight to the commandant of that post, who took measures to deliver him. Back among his own people, Belle-Isle, by his narrative, still further discouraged settlers in the region, and even today Louisianians speak of the bay of St. Bernard with horror."[16]

Robin adds that the Attakapas "gradually became accustomed to going to New Orleans to exchange their furs, and traders there, conversely, began to go among them, and these reciprocal relations softened the customs of the Atakapas."[17]

Fortier also makes mention of Belle-Isle's adventures:

"Simarre de Belle-Isle had had a most romantic career. In 1719, while on board a vessel bound for Louisiana, he went ashore in St. Bernard Bay with four friends in a boat that had been sent out to get drinking water. Having gone hunting, Belle-Isle and his friends were abandoned by the French vessel, and after a few days Belle-Isle alone survived. He wandered about, and finally gave himself up to the Attakapas Indians, who were cannibals. He was saved by a widow who took him for her slave, and after some time he was adopted as a warrior by the tribe. He

16 Robin: *Voyage to Louisiana, 1803-1805,* Landry trans., 188
17 *Ibid*

was rescued by St. Denis, commandant at Natchitoches, who had heard of his plight through some Indians of a white man among the Attakapas. Bienville, who was then governor, received Belle-Isle very kindly, and the former Indian brave soon became again a trusted French officer."[18]

A summary of Belle-Isle's own account of his experiences among the Attakapas gives other details of the incident. The following is a paraphrased, abbreviated version of the summary:

The ship ran aground, due to the incompetence of the ship's officers, and Belle-Isle and his companions decided to take their chances of reaching their destination on foot. They wandered around in the marshy terrain and endured many hardships before four of the Frenchmen died. Two weeks afterward, Belle-Isle saw human beings again: three Indians. They took him captive, made him strip off his clothing and took his belongings. That night, Belle-Isle, still naked, had to stand in the water up to his neck because of the mosquitoes.

Next day other members of the tribe screamed when they saw Belle-Isle, but he was given a meal of boiled roots. Two days later more Indians arrived in two pirogues, and they also greeted the white man with screams. Belle-Isle noted that the aborigines resorted to screaming from "both pleasure and pain."

The captive Frenchman spent the summer with the tribe, wandering from place to place in search of food. In good weather the Indians killed bison and deer, and the women dug for roots. During bad weather no effort was made to find food. The Indians spent their time "drinking only water and throwing up without effort." They advised Belle-Isle that he should do the same, that it was good for him. Still naked, Belle-Isle was made to fetch wood or water, and was knocked around cruelly by his captors. They took him hunting with them, but he was not permitted to ride a horse. They made him understand that it was not fitting for a man of a different color to ride a horse. He had to keep up with his mounted captors or be flogged. On the third day of the hunt the Indians killed fifteen or sixteen bison which they ate voraciously, having had no food for two days.

The hunting party encountered another group of Indians which Belle-Isle called "Toyals," an enemy tribe. The Attakapas killed one of the Toyals and brought the body back to their camp site. There Belle-Isle said they cut off the dead enemy's neck and arms and skinned the body. Some

---

18 Fortier: *History of Louisiana*, 139

Shards of Attakapas Indian pottery, excavated by Rev. John Engbers at Shell Island in Vermilion Parish. The designs were made with a finger-nail and a reed.

ate of the raw fat; afterwards they ate everything. Their women danced for joy when they learned that an enemy had been killed; they danced for two days without stopping, while holding in their hands a bone or a nail.[19]

Some historical writers discount the "man-eating" reputation given the Attakapas. In "Louisiana, a Guide to the State," the writer states:

"The Attakapa . . . were regarded as cannibals by early historians. Such a reputation is largely undeserved, though the Attakapa were probably inferior in most respects to their neighbors and apparently did indulge in some ritualistic form of cannibalism."[20]

On the other hand, archaeological evidence from an Attakapas site occupied as late as 1200 showed extensive broken and burned human bones in the midden with other food refuse. This has led some archaeologists to the conclusion that humans must have constituted a source of protein.[21]

The only conclusion to be drawn from the foregoing opinion is: the question of the cannibalistic reputation of the Attakapas is moot, and will no doubt continue to be debated.

Nor can it be determined whether the Attakapas were "wandering Indians" who subsisted on the bounty of nature, or were "a settled, agricultural people."

In the latter part of the 18th century some of the Indians owned cattle; Indian cattle brands are on record.[22] This would seem to indicate that they were settled. On the other hand there is evidence that they did re-establish their villages in new locations from time to time.[23]

Bienville's report of 1733 says "these cannibal Indians" had come to New Orleans to ask that men be sent to their country to trade for their furs, tallow and horses. The Indians promised that if the white men came to trade with them they would "settle in villages like the other nations."[24]

The report contained information that the Attakapas were "rather numerous, but they are nomadic and separate into little bands to live by hunting and fishing." Bienville concluded his report with: "There is...

19 Cassidy and Allain: "Simars de Belle-Isle Among the Attakapas, 1719-1721", *Attakapas Gazette*, Vol. III, No. 3, a summary

20 *Louisiana, a Guide to the State*, 33

21 Jon A. Gibson

22 *Brand Book for the Districts of Opelousas and Attakapas*, University of Southwestern Library

23 *ASP*, Vol. III, 111

24 Dunbar Rowland and A. G. Sanders: *Mississippi Provincial Archives, 1729-1740* 204

no ground to expect that a fur trade could be carried on with these Indians. They are so lazy that they hardly have anything with which to cover themselves. It is true that they have horses, but the difficulty of bringing them would cancel the profit that might be derived from this trade."[25]

A most valuable source of information about the Attakapas Indians is the American State Papers — Public Lands. The descriptions of land sales by the Indians in these records provide documentation on the location of the villages, the number of Attakapas warriors participating in the American Revolution, the names of the chiefs and the decline in Indian population.

Moreover, the Indian land sales recorded in the American State Papers clearly establish Acadia Parish as the center of Attakapas activity and population during the last half of the 18th century.

An examination of these government documents locates the sites of three Attakapas villages within the present confines of Acadia Parish: one on Bayou Plaquemine Brûlée about two miles west of the Branch community (approximately ten miles northeast of Crowley as the crow flies); another on Bayou Queue de Tortue, about three and one half miles south of Morse, and the third on Bayou Wikoff, some four miles northeast of Rayne.

Three other Attakapas villages were situated just outside the parish limits: two on the Mermentau River and one on Bayou Nezpique.

As early as 1760, when Louisiana was subject to France, the Attakapas began selling land in the eastern sector of their territory. The first sale recorded was to Gabriel Fusilier de la Claire, commandant of the settlements at Attakapas (St. Martinville) and Opelousas, 1763-1774. Fusilier bought an entire Attakapas village, located between the Vermilion River and Bayou Teche, from Kinemo, the Attakapas chief. At about this same time several other large land purchases were made from the Indians in the same area.[26]

The Attakapas village on Bayou Plaquemine Brûlée was on land owned by Antoine Blanc. In 1784 Blanc purchased a tract of land, one league front by the depth of 40 arpents (2,820 86/100 acres) from Nementou, chief of the Attakapas. The deed of sale was signed by Nementou and 13 of his warriors who inhabited the village at the

---

25 *Ibid*
26 *ASP*, Vol. III, 94

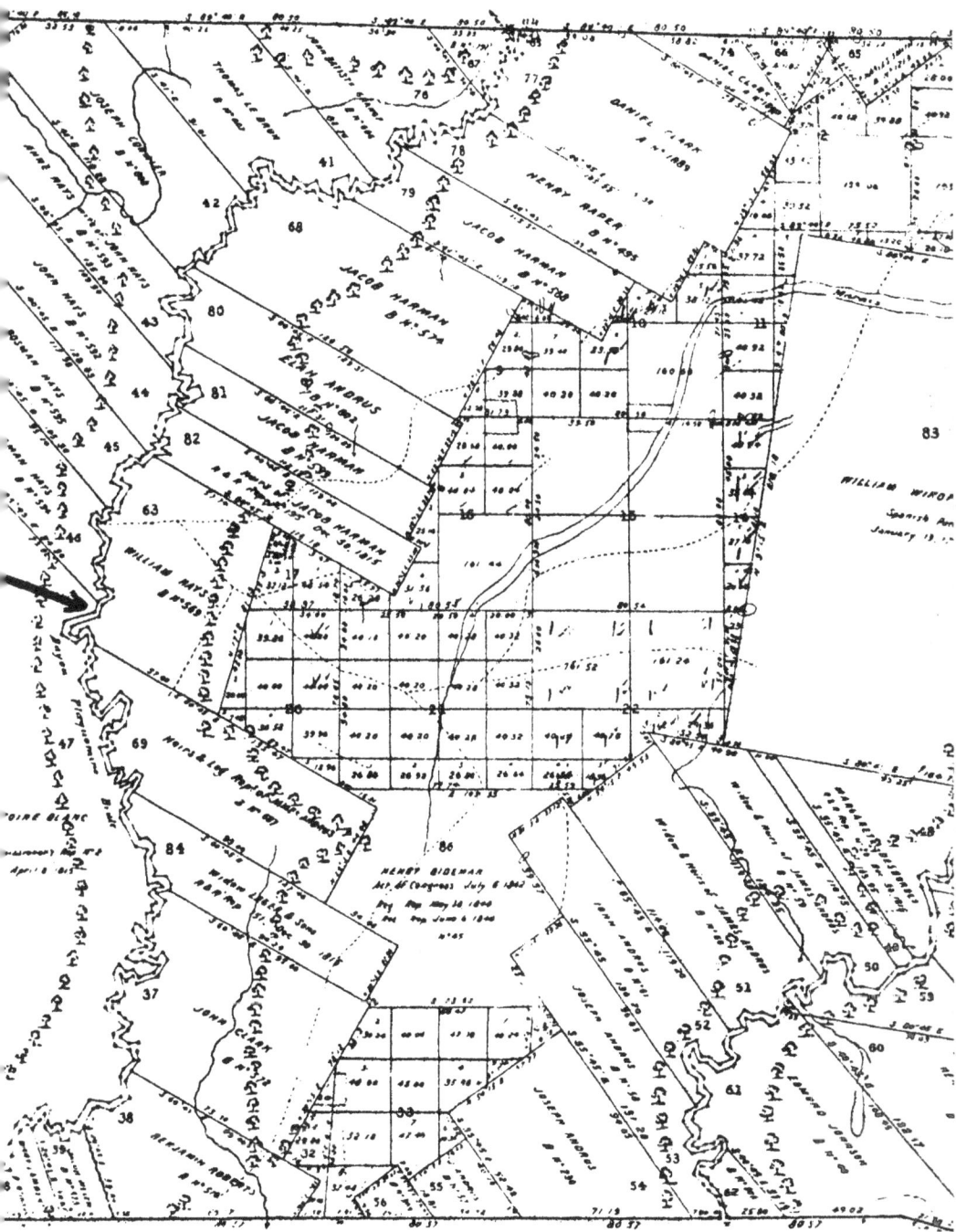

Arrow indicates the approximate site of an Indian village on Bayou Plaquemine Brûlée about two miles west of the present community of Branch. (Official survey plat, T.8SR.2E, Acadia Parish)

time. The deed of sale was passed before Alexander Chevalier De Clouet, then commandant of the districts of Opelousas and Attakapas, and was witnessed by William Hays and Louis Latiolais.[27]

The land was described as "very specially located on the bayou Plaquemine Brule, adjoining the land of Hays, an American. In the concession from the Spanish Government to Bosman Hays . . . it is seen that the said Hay's land is situate on the bayou Plaquemine Brule, and was adjacent to the Indian village at the date of the concession."[28]

The Bayou Queue de Tortue village was on property purchased from the Indians in 1801 by John Lyon, one of Acadia's colonial settlers and the progenitor of the large Lyons family of Louisiana.

John Lyon (Lyons) bought property from the Indians in both the Attakapas and Opelousas districts. His holdings on the south side of Bayou Queue de Tortue, in what is now Vermilion Parish, was described as "fifty arpents front by the ordinary depth" of 40 arpents. The deed of sale was signed by Bernard, the chief Celestin and Little John designated "captain." The price paid was $87.[29]

Lyon's property on the north side of the bayou, in Acadia Parish, was bought from an Indian named Tichot. The land, with a bayou frontage of some 50 arpents, was purchased for "four cows and four four-year-old beeves." The deed of sale was signed by Tichot, "married to the widow Potate, and acting for her and the Attakapas Indians." Paul Boutin, in 1812, testified that he was present when the sale was passed.[30]

John Coleman also testified in the land claim, stating that he knew that John Lyon was then living on the tract on the north side of the bayou; Coleman explained to the Land Office commissioners exactly how the boundaries of the property were established by Lyons and the Indians from whom he bought the land. Coleman added that the property limits thus established on the north side of the bayou embraced "an old village which had been inhabited by the Indians, and that some of the posts of their huts were standing at the time the boundaries were established."[31]

The site of the Attakapas village on Bayou Wikoff was on property owned by William Gilchrist, who held a certified copy of the sale from Jacob, an Indian of the Attakapas tribe. The location of the 2,000 acre

---

27 *ASP*, **Vol. III**, 97
28 *Ibid*
29 *Ibid, 138-139*
30 *Ibid*
31 *Ibid*

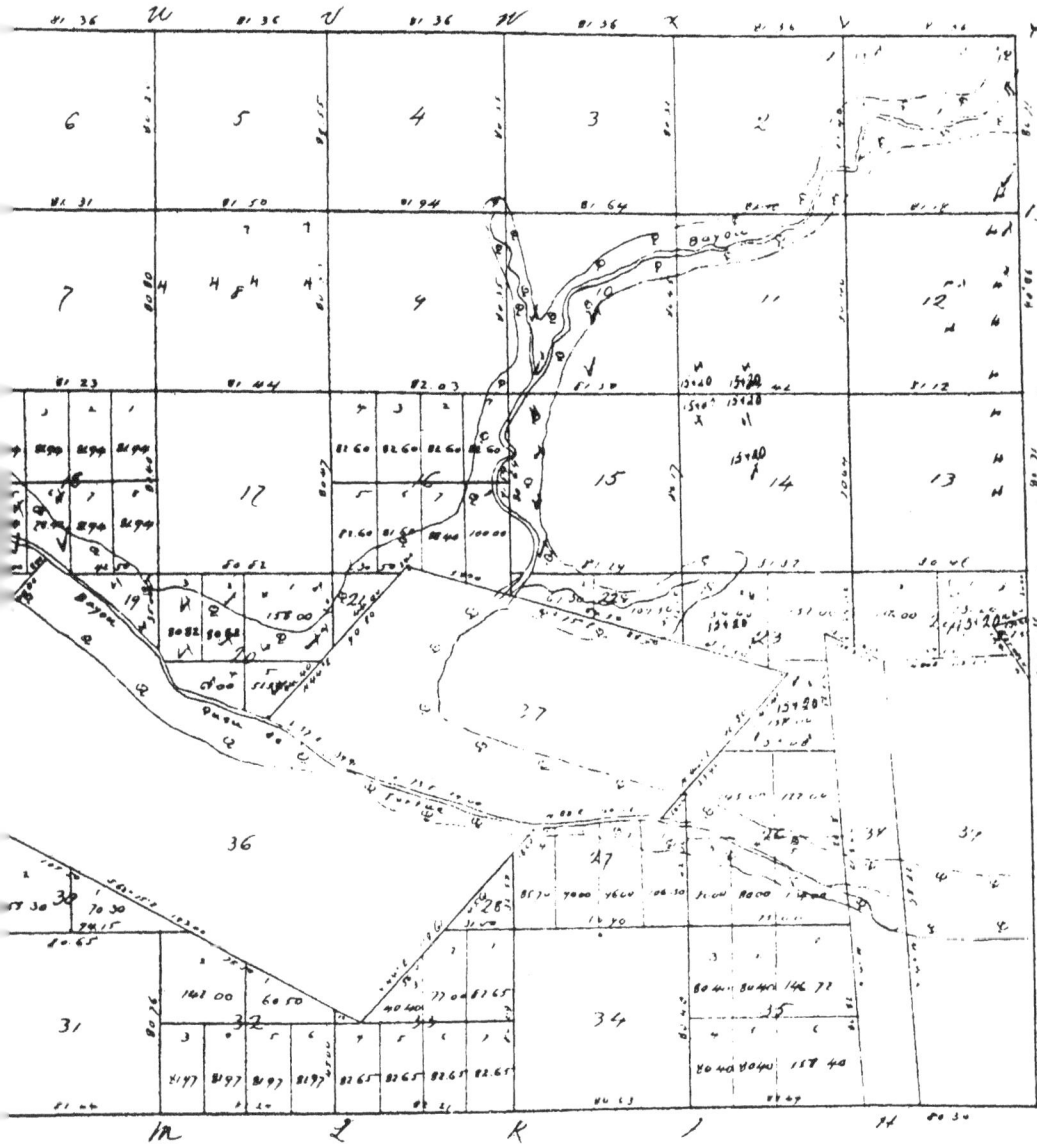

The John Lyons tracts, Sections 36 and 37, on both sides of Bayou Queue de Tortue. An Indian village was located in Section 37, on the north side of the bayou in Acadia Parish. (Official survey plat, T.11S-R.1W, Acadia Parish)

tract was given as "on the bayou Plaquemine Brule, bounded above by land of Duralde."[32] This would seem to contradict the location of the village on Bayou Wikoff; however, there are several factors to be considered. The first is: Bayou Wikoff is frequently identified in the American State Papers — Public Lands as "bayou Plaquemine Brule," also as "a branch of bayou Plaquemine Brule" or "the east branch" of the same bayou. Also, the "Duralde" referred to was most certainly Martin Duralde, commandant of the Opelousas post, who had extensive land holdings by Spanish grant. Only one of Duralde's land tracts was described as being on Plaquemine Brûlée, yet the old plat map and numerous published sources locate the Duralde *vacherie* (cattle ranch) on Bayou Wikoff, just north of the city of Rayne.

The evidence of an Attakapas village on the Gilchrist property was provided by Dotrif Andrus before the board of commissioners in 1814. Andrus said that "fourteen or fifteen years ago, the Indians abandoned this land, where they had their village, since when it has been uninhabited and uncultivated. That the Indian who sold Gilchrist was an Indian of note, but not the chief of the village."[33]

In 1799 the Attakapas sold a village on the west side of the Mermentau River to André Martin for $100. The record of this transaction gives the origin of the name Mermentau, and tells of the Indians who joined the Galvez expedition in 1799.[34]

Martin bought 1,523 acres on the river from Celestin la Tortue, chief of the Attakapas, "adjoining the lower side of the village then occupied by the Indians." Louis de la Houssaye, aged 52 years, told the Land Office commissioners in 1814 that "from his earliest recollections" . . . Nemento, the chief of the village on the river by the same name, with the other Indians of the tribe, "were residing on the land now claimed by André Martin, where they ever since continued to reside, and have never had any other village" to his knowledge.[35]

In his testimony de la Houssaye said that the inhabitants of the Indian village were "very numerous" when he first knew it. He recalled: "about thirty years past, when there was a Spanish expedition against Baton Rouge, then in the hands of the British, there were about four hundred

---

[32] *ASP*, Vol. III, 239
[33] *Ibid*
[34] *Ibid, 111*
[35] *Ibid*

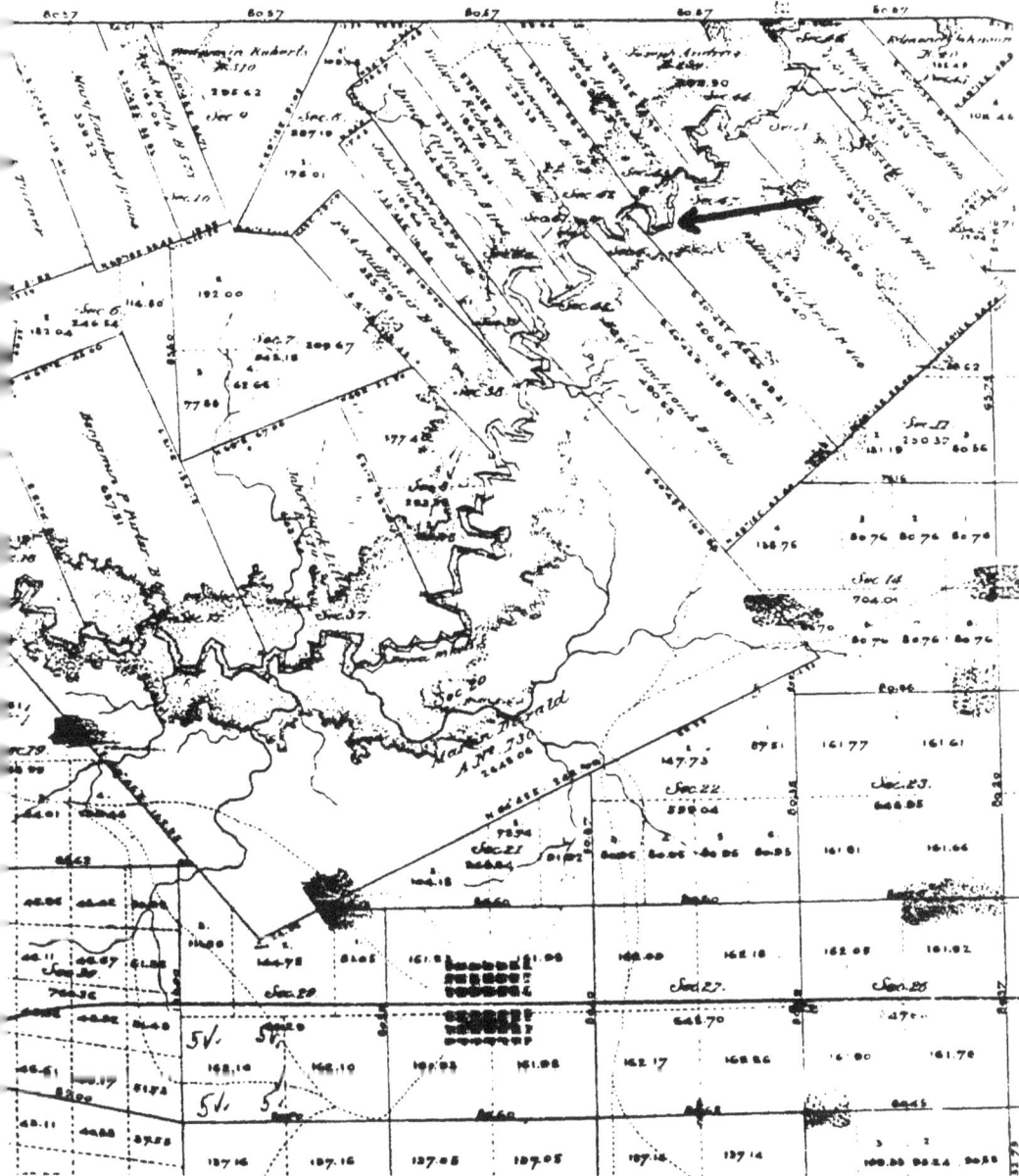

An Attakapas Indian village, indicated by arrow, was located on Bayou Wikoff approximately four and a half miles northeast of Rayne. (Segment, official survey plat, T.9S-R.2E, Acadia Parish)

Indians who joined the Spanish army, of which about one hundred and twenty were from the Nementou village . . . "[36]

The second Attakapas village on the Mermentau was on land claimed by David Guidry and Jean Mouton. The claim was for 2,000 arpents on the west side of the river. The deed of sale was from Celestin La Tortue, chief of the Attakapas, acting for one of his men named Potate, "the old village being in the center of the fifty arpents." Jean Baptiste Chiasson, testifying in 1811, said that he had visited the village in about the year 1775; that he believed they (the Attakapas) had resided there many years.[37]

The Bayou Nezpique village was near property owned by William Wikoff. Wikoff bought 2,733 acres on the west bank of the bayou from "Le Tortue, an Indian, calling himself chief of the village of Nezpique, and his son, Celestine," in 1791. The price paid was ten cows and calves. Thomas Berwick, one of the three men who testified in the Wikoff claim in 1814, said he recollected perfectly "the Indian village was in sight of the (Wikoff) vacherie."[38]

Other landowners who bought Indian property in Acadia Parish were Reuben Barrow, 2,000 arpents on Bayou Queue de Tortue, sold by Celestin, chief of the Attakapas; Bernard, a "medal chief," and Little John, an Oscal captain;[39] Francois Stelly, who bought land on Bayou Queue de Tortue from Tichaw, Attakapas chief;[40] John Coleman, who purchased a league (about three miles) frontage on Bayou Queue de Tortue from Celestin Bernard and other Indians.[41]

One of the villages on the Mermentau was the last settlement of the Attakapas. This was brought out in testimony given in another transaction involving Indian lands. The evidence in this case was given by a man named John Teller who was well acquainted with the Attakapas; he understood their language and had served as translator between the commandant and the Indians. Teller said he had hunted for many years with the Indians; that he knew they had moved their village to the Mermentau River from the "Island of Woods, now known by the Island of Lacasine." He said the chief of the village was named Lacasine. At about the time

36 ASP, Vol. III, 111
37 Ibid, 106
38 Ibid, 118
39 Ibid, 239
40 Ibid, 98
41 Ibid, 99

et Sans aucun trouble de qui que ce Soit.

Fait et passé en notre Domicile de
Commaudement en présence des Sieurs
Jean Gradenigo et antoine Boisdoré
nommé par Nous interprete pour lesdits
Sauvages qui avec Nous Commandant
par leurs marques ordinaires ont Signé
le Séizieme jour du mois d'avril de l'année
mil Sept Cents quatre vingt ouze. In
deux mots rayés nuls. marque ordinaire du
marque ordinaire

       X   Sauvage la tortüe
du Sauvage Celestin

Wm Wikoff

Gradenigo   *A Boisdoré*

N Forstall

The signatures of La Tortue, chief of the Attakapas, and his son
Celestin are shown on this colonial document, executed in 1791 by Nicolas
Forstall, commandant of the Opelousas post. Jean Gradenigo and Antoine
Boisdore acted as interpreters for the Indians and signed as witnesses to
the transfer of land by the Indians to William Wikoff. (Reproduced from the
original in the Southwestern Archives, University of Southwestern
Louisiana).

Chief Lacasine died, circa 1799, Lacasine village, which had been inhabited by the Indians at least fifty years, "was abandoned by the surviving inhabitants, the principal part of whom removed to the now only remaining village, on the river Nementou."[42]

Within the century the Attakapas population had dwindled to less than 100: "Many of the sales from Attakapas Indians were obtained about the time of the change of Government by which Louisiana was transferred to the United States; some of them subsequent to that change, and at a time when it was known, from good information, that those Indians were reduced to one single village, the inhabitants of which were short of one hundred."[43]

Scarcely a trace of the Attakapas remains in Acadia Parish at present. Some Indian artifacts, such as arrowheads, are the only relics of "those who came first."

But Acadia has its Indian heritage preserved in place names, and in the language of the people.

The Indian place names in the parish which have survived are the names of the streams upon which the Attakapas once lived: the Mermentau, modern spelling of the River Nementou; Plaquemine Brûlée, meaning burnt persimmon;[44] Bayou Nezpique, named for an Indian with a scarred nose;[45] Bayou Queue de Tortue, believed to have been named for Chief Celestin la Tortue.

There are also many words in common use which have Indian origins: *ouaouaron*, the Indian word for the bull frog, the amphibian hero of Rayne, "The Frog Capital of the World;" *chaoui*, the raccoon; *choc*, the blackbird or grackle; *choupique*, swamp fish; *patassa*, flat fish; *latanier*, the palmetto shub; *maringouin*, the mosquito; *pacane*, the pecan nut; *soco*, the muscadine; *topinambour*, the edible tuber of the Jerusalem artichoke, and bayou, for stream.[46]

And the name of the parish, Acadia, is itself of Indian origin.[47]

42 *ASP*, Vol. III, 114
43 *Ibid*, 95
44 Read: *Louisiana Place Names of Indian Origin*
45 Deville: *Opelousas*, 21; Read: *Louisiana-French* 177
46 Read: *Louisiana-French*, 82
47 Read: *Louisiana Place Names of Indian Origin*

CHAPTER II

Colonial Landowners

The Louisiana territory, claimed by France in 1682, was held as a French colony until 1763, when the territory was ceded to Spain. In 1800 Napoleon persuaded Spain to return Louisiana to France, then sold it to the United States in 1803.

During the French regime two Indian trading posts were established in the southwest section of the territory: *Poste des Opelousas,* at what is now Opelousas, and *Poste des Attakapas* at St. Martinville. Both trading posts were named for the Indian tribes which inhabited the areas. French and Canadian traders, known as *coureurs de bois,* visited the post to trade with the Indians for furs, tallow, bear grease, indigo, horses and other items of trade value. Settlements grew up around the trading posts; after the Spanish took over, the posts were made centers of government. Commandants of the posts served as military officers, civil judges and were in charge of administering the law.

Acadia Parish was a part of the vast district of *Poste des Opelousas,* which was later to be designated St. Landry Parish. The present parishes of Evangeline, Jefferson Davis, Beauregard, Allen, Calcasieu and Cameron were also included in St. Landry Parish.

In 1777 the entire Opelousas district had a population of 756 persons. There were 100 white men, 139 women, 211 boys and 123 girls; 120 male Negroes and 98 female Negroes. The black population included 11 *gens de couleur libres,* free persons of color.[1]

Original land titles in Acadia Parish were acquired by purchase from the Attakapas Indians, by grant from the Spanish government, by *requête**** and order of survey, and by occupation and settlement. After the Louisiana Purchase all land claims, to be valid, had to be verified and confirmed by the government of the United States.[2]

Like the French, the Spanish used the "riverbank system" for granting of land. Land holdings were long, narrow strips, fronting on a river or bayou. Each grant began at the bank of the stream and extended between parallel lines for an ordinary depth of 40 arpents, an arpent

---

*requête: a request for permission to occupy a certain tract of land

1 *Recensements General des Oppeloussa du 4th Mai, 1777* (Archivo General des Indias, Sevilla, Cuba, 2358) Hereinafter referred to as the 1777 census. This census does not include the Indian population.

2 *American State Papers -- Public Lands,* Vol III, 172

being about 192 feet. The width was also expressed in arpents, so a tract of six arpents by the ordinary depth of 40 arpents measured six by 40 arpents.[3]

A number of advantages accrued from the riverbank system of land ownership. The streams were the highways of commerce and of social life. The banks of the streams were high ground, natural levees that had built up over centuries of overflow; the soil was rich and well drained. Here the settler built his home and planted his field; he had the river or bayou for fishing and other water uses, he had the woodlands along the stream for building, for firewood, and for hunting.

In Acadia Parish these narrow strips of land abutting on streams are most numerous along Bayous Plaquemine Brûlée, Wikoff and Mallet, with a lesser concentration on the Mermentau River, Bayous des Cannes, Nezpique and Queue de Tortue. A few are located on smaller streams.

By contrast is the "checkerboard pattern" of lands in the prairie areas of the parish; this is the Rectangular System of Surveys introduced by the United States Land Office, based upon the use of townships, sections and quarter sections, in which all holdings seem to be squares or combinations of squares. The open prairies, referred to as *au large,* remained unclaimed and unsettled until after 1803, the beginning of the American period.[4]

There are more than 200 "riverbank strips" shown on an Acadia Parish land map. Approximately 160 of these represent land ownership prior to 1803. Individual ownership of these lands is shown on the official survey plats in the Acadia Parish courthouse. Thus it is not difficult to ascertain the names of the landowners and the location of their lands.

Acadia's colonial landowners, given here in alphabetical order and using commonly accepted spellings of surnames, were:

Elah Andrus, James Andrus, John Andrus, Joseph Andrus, Alexandre Arceneaux, Cyprien Arceneaux, François Arceneaux, Louis Arceneaux, Pierre Arceneaux, Joseph Armand;

Isaac Baldwin, Reuben Barrow, Thomas Bledsoe, Guy Hamilton Bell, Donato Bello, Pierre Bernard, Thomas Berwick, Henry Bideman, Jacob Bihm, Antoine Blanc, Antoine Boisdore, George Bollard, Clautilda

---

3 Post: *Cajun Sketches,* 26
4 *Ibid,* 27

20

Bourassas, Valery Bourque, Paul Boutin, Joseph Breaux, Rev. Louis Buhot, William Bundick, Sr.;

Daniel Callaghan, William Callaghan, Francois Carmouche, Michel Carrier, Jean Louis Cart, Louis Chachere, Pierre Chretien, Claude Chabot, Basil Chiasson, Daniel Clark, John Clark (Turner), John Clark (Little), John Clay, James Cole, Solomon Cole, Nathaniel Cochran, Robert Cochran, Anthony Corkran, Joseph Cormier;

Etienne Daigle, Jean Baptiste David, Joseph Alexandre Declouet, Jacques Deshotels, Marguerite Desbordes, Maria Donatto, Victorie Donatto, Martin Donatto, John Dunman, Martin Duralde;

James Foreman, Jean Baptiste Fruge, William Gardner, William Gilchrist, David Guidry, Pierre Guidry, Jean Guilbeau, Le Bray de Gonor, Pierre Gourrinat, Jean Baptiste Granger, Patrick Gurnett;

Henry Hargroder, David Harmon, Jacob Harmon, Bosman Hayes, James Hays, John Hays, William Hays, Francois and Amelia Hoffpauir, Thomas Hoffpauir, Joanesse, Bennett Jopling, Edmund Johnson, William Johnson, George King;

Mary Lambert, Isobel Landry, Antoine Langlois, Celestin Lavergne, Lufroi Latiolais, Louis Latiolais, La Rouillé, Thomas LeBrun, Michel Ledoux, Louis Leger, Michel Leger, Widow Leger, Blaise Lejeune, Joseph Lejeune, Basil Lincecomb, Louis Louallier, John Lyons;

Joseph Giron Mallet, Jean Malveau, Rosalie Malveau, Andre Martin, James Martins, John McDaniel, James McClelland, William McKoy, Frederick Miller, John Miller, Andre Mondon, Jean Mouton, Francois Nerault, Alexandre Nezat, Augustin Nezat, Joseph C. Piernass, Joseph C. Poiret, Benjamin Penrose Porter, Michel Prudhomme, Michel Prudhomme, Jr.;

Henry Raper, John Rhea, Fabian Richard, Louis Richard, Victor Richard, Benjamin Roberts, Francois Rozas, David F. Sackett, Charles Smith, Raphael Smith, Silvain Sonnier, Benajah Spell, Francois Stelly, John Baptiste Stelly, Pierre Trahan, John Baptiste Young, Jacob Welch, Benjamin Winfree, William Wikoff.

Not all of these landowners lived within the present boundaries of Acadia Parish. Many lived at, or nearer to, Opelousas or St. Martinville—the centers of civilization at the time—and maintained their more distant property as *vacheries,* or cattle ranches. Some were land speculators who registered multiple land claims throughout the Louisiana Territory.

Even so, these colonial landowners left their mark on southwest Louisiana, and on Acadia Parish in particular. Many did settle on their land, and have numerous descendants in the parish; some figured prominently in the development of Louisiana as a state; all had a part in extending the frontiers of the United States.

It is not the purpose of this history to delve extensively into the backgrounds of these early landowners. There is, however, certain information readily available from published sources, church, court and private genealogical records, which is of interest and historical value.

Military records of the Opelousas and Attakapas posts show that a number of Acadia's landowners were in the area more than 200 years ago. The Opelousas Militia of 1770 lists nine: Antoine Langlois, Donato Bello, Antoine Boisdore, Joseph Cormier, Andre Mondon, Pierre Mallet, Louis Richard, Victor Richard and Sylvain Sonnier.[5]

Six years later, in 1776, some of these names are repeated, others are added: Antoine Langlois, Donato Bello, major; Blaise Lejeune, Michel Prudhomme, Victor Richard, Fabien Richard, Sylvain Sonnier, Pierre Trahan, Charles Bourassas, Joseph Cormier, Jean Baptiste Stelly. Soldiers exempt from the company review because of age or illness include three, who at that time or subsequently, owned land in what is now Acadia Parish: Paul Boutin, Pierre Guidry and Antoine Boisdore.[6]

These same names, with the exception of Boutin and Guidry, are on the 1777 militia list for Opelousas, with three additions of interest to this history: Joseph Poiret, Michel Carrier and Pierre Richard.[7]

The Attakapas Militia of 1774 has the name of one colonial landowner in Acadia Parish: Jean Guilbeau. Company records of 1777 list two: Jean Guilbeau and Jean Mouton.[8]

Approximately one fifth of the parish's colonial landowners were Acadian exiles. These were French colonists in Acadia (Nova Scotia) who had been deported by the British in 1755. Several thousand of the exiles eventually made their way to south Louisiana where they were given land by the Spanish authorities.

------

5 LeBlanc: *Acadian Miracle,* 409
6 Griffin: *Attakapas Country, A History of Lafayette Parish, Louisiana,* 219-224
7 *Ibid*
8 *Ibid*

22

The 29 Acadian exiles and/or their sons with land claims in what is now Acadia Parish were those bearing the names of Arceneaux, Bourque, Breaux, Bernard, Chiasson, Cormier, Granger, Guilbeau, Guidry, Lambert, LeBrun, Leger, Lejeune, Martin, Mouton, Richard, Sonnier and Trahan.[9] These names may now be found in every community of Acadia Parish, and the parish fittingly bears the name of the homeland of the Acadians.

Other nationalities represented among the colonial landowners were French, German, Irish, Spanish, Italian, Swiss and English. Five landowners were free persons of color.

These land holdings may best be located, and at the same time the owners further identified, by a break-down of land ownership along the seven major waterways of the parish: Bayous Mallet, Plaquemine Brûlée, Wikoff, des Cannes, Nezpique, Queue de Tortue and the River Mermentau.

Bayou Mallet

Beginning at the northeastern corner of Acadia Parish, then following Bayou Mallet until its confluence with Bayou des Cannes, landowners were:

Jacob Bihm (Bohm, Bim), a native of Germany who married Marie Raiternauer (shortened to Raiter), also of Germany.[10] Bihm owned two pieces of property: a Spanish land grant of 1781, a small segment of which extended across the St. Landry Parish line into Acadia, and another tract about four miles down the bayou.[11] Jacob Bihm died in 1804, at age 60.

Joseph C. Poiret, *Chevalier de l'Ordre Royal et Militaire de Saint Louis,* married Marie Francoise LeDoux. Their daughter, Marianna, was baptized at Opelousas in 1785. The Poiret property extended over the present St. Landry line into Acadia. The land, situated in *Bois de Mallet,* was acquired from Catherine Bello, was claimed ownership under a Spanish patent.

Joseph Armand owned a large tract on "Prairie Cottereau" by Spanish patent of 1785. Marie Joseph Armant married Marie Therese LeGros in 1775 at Pointe Coupée. The groom signed the marriage register as "Armant;" the priest recorded his name as Marie Joseph Harman.

---

9 Arsenault: *Histoire et Genealogie des Acadiens* Tomes 1 and 2

10 St. Landry Catholic Church records. All genealogical information which follows will be from this same source, unless otherwise noted.

11 *American State Papers -- Public Lands;* official township survey plats of Acadia Parish. Unless otherwise noted all further information concerning land claims, ownership and locations will be from these same sources.

23

Therese, the wife, is listed in the American State Papers index as "Armond (*dit Sans Façon*) Therese." The nickname, *"Sans Façon,"* meaning "without ceremony" indicates that the bearer was by nature jovial and informal.

Francois Rozas (Roze, Roza, Rozat) was the original owner of land described as "twenty-six arpents and four perches* front, by forty arpents deep, situated on the left bank of bayou Catar, in the county of Opelousas, bounded on one side by land of Michel Prudhomme, and on the other side by Joseph Arman."

Francois was the son of Alexandre Joseph Roza of Canada and Agnes Vidrine (le Viderine). He married Louise Desmaret (Demarais), daughter of George Desmarets of Pointe Coupee and Francoise Fontenot.[12]. He acquired the land on Bayou Mallet about 1795, but "did not inhabit or cultivate it." His succession, filed in the St. Landry Probate Court in 1820, indicates that the family residence was at "Grand Prairie." This may, or may not, have been that area of northwestern St. Landry Parish now known as Grand Prairie, as several prairies in the large parish were once called "Grand Prairie."

The Rozas succession papers tell a poignant story of family tragedy. When the succession was opened, both Francois and Louise (Lise) were deceased, leaving three minor children: Delphine, 7; Caroline, 5; and Pierre, 2½. Uncles and great-uncles of the orphaned children, Michel Galand, Pierre Baptiste Vidrine, Henry B. Fontenot, Toussaint Demarais and Laurent B. Fontenot, petitioned the court to appoint Jean Ponsony as tutor for the children. The same group subsequently returned to the court and asked that a new tutor be named. They said that Ponsony, despite having given bond, had disappeared and "had not been heard of since."

Included in the inventory of family effects was a violin, an unusual possession for the times. The instrument was later sold at auction to Francois Brignac for $10.

Michel Prudhomme and his son, Michel Prudhomme Jr., owned land on both sides of Bayou Mallet. Prudhomme, a native of Strasbourg, also owned land within the present limits of the city of Opelousas. He donated

---

* perch: a French measure, equal to 5½ yards

[12] Ruth Robertson Fontenot genealogy records

the property for the St. Landry Catholic Church, and his body is interred beneath the foundations of that church.[13]

Michel Prudhomme was born circa 1740; the 1777 census gives his age as 37, and his wife Catherine Andeymistre, 28. He was married a second time to Marie Snayler. He died in 1828.

One of the Prudhommes, either the father or the son, resided in Acadia Parish. The following is an excerpt from the Crowley Signal of August 25, 1888:

'On the next page we give a wood cut of the oldest house now standing in the parish of Acadia. It is what has always been known as the 'Prud' homme house' and the beginning of its erection dates back to the

---

[13] "Some History of St. Landry Parish, from the 1690s" published as a special supplement to the *Opelousas, La. Daily World*, Nov. 3, 1955

The Prudhomme house, built in 1796, was the oldest residence in Acadia Parish in 1888. The house was located in the northeastern section of the parish, near Bayou Mallet. (Enlargement of woodcut from Crowley Signal, Aug. 25, 1888).

year 1796. Some few years prior to that date the Spanish government granted to Michel Prudhomme a certain tract of ground fronting on the Bayou Mallet and upon which is now located the post office bearing the old family name. The name however was not spelled as at this date but a short cut spelled Prudhom. But for the fact that the name of the stream upon which Prud'homme located suggested an earlier settler or explorer we should have given to Michel Prud'homme the honor of being the first settler of what is now Acadia Parish."

John Baptiste Young had land on the north side of the bayou, about three miles east of Eunice. The property was originally owned by Francois Marcantel. The name of this landowner is believed to be the Anglicized version of Jean Baptiste Lejeune; documents in the St. Landry Parish courthouse refer to persons named Young as "alias Lejeune." St. Landry Catholic Church records show the baptisms of three Jean Baptiste Lejeunes between 1777 and 1786.

John Fruge (Frugee, Fruger) owned land on the north side of the bayou adjacent to the Young tract. William Hay, witnessing for Fruge at the Land Office in 1813, said: "the land has been inhabited and cultivated for fifteen consecutive years . . . John Frugee was inhabiting said land in 1798 or 1799." John Fruge was the son of Pierre Fruge and Catherine du Moulin; he married Eleanor Olivier.

Frederick Miller's property, located north of the Fruge tract, extended across the parish line into St. Landry. A native of Germany, he was the son of Jacob Miller and Anna Marie Thaim. He married Victoria Meyer of Mississippi, daughter of Andreas Meyer and Marie Anne Stelly. Their son, Jean Frederick, married Louise Fruge in 1814.

John Miller, Frederick's brother, owned a rectangle of land on the prairie just south of Eunice, intersected by two small, unnamed streams. John married Maria Francesca Meyer, Victoria Meyer's sister.

Jean Baptiste Stelly Jr. (Staley, Schetely, Steli, Stely) had land on a small stream west of, and adjoining, the John Miller tract. A native of Germany, born about 1753, he married Madelone Ritter in Opelousas in 1781. His succession, opened in 1814, includes his will, in which he left his estate to "my wife, Madelon, and my six children." The inventory of the estate included 11 slaves, an unknown quantity of horned cattle, and eight horses, one of which was named *"Belle Etoile,"* Beautiful Star.

Across the bayou from the Fruge property was land claimed by Pierre Gourrinat (Gouriner, Gourenot) by "ten years occupancy." The land, located about two miles northwest of the community of Richard, was previously claimed by Francois Nerault (Herault). Gourrinat was said to be "an inhabitant of the village of Baton Rouge."[14]

Michel Carrier (Carriere) owned land on both sides of the bayou; he had 800 arpents extending into "Prairie Facquetike" and 1,000 arpents in "Woods Bayou Mallet," by order of survey and requete. Born about 1755, he was the son of Jacques Carriere and Marie Louise Lavergue (Lavergne). He married Julia Marcantel. He died at age 60, in 1815. The officiating priest noted that he was "a native of St. Charles of the Mississippi delta."

Jean Baptiste David's land was on both sides of Bayou Mallet, the south tract encompassing the present community of Hundley. He was the son of Baptiste David and Marie Riders. In 1798 he married Escolastica Savois, daughter of Pedro Savois and Liseta Bourg.

Margaret Desbordes' property was on both sides of the bayou just below the David tract. In the descriptions of the claim in the American State Papers Margaret Desbordes is designated "the widow of Cloree and formerly wife of Francois Brunet."

In Margaret Desbordes' background will be found a direct connection with the earliest beginnings of the Opelousas post. The 1777 census lists Marguerite Deborde, 15, an orphan. Her father was Claude Desbordes of Auxerre in Bourgoyne; her mother was Marguerite Kinterek (Le Kintrek), daughter of Joseph Le Kintrek, the Frenchman who opened southwest Louisiana to trade, and the first *coureur de bois* at the Opelousas post.

The first recorded church ritual at Opelousas was performed at the home of Jacques Guilliame Courtableau, a leading military figure in the formative years of the Opelousas post. This was the baptism, on May 16, 1756, of Jacques Andres Desbordes and Jean Desbordes, sons of Claude Desbordes and Marguerite Kinterek. The priest noted in the record that the baptisms were done at the home of Sieur Courtableau by special permission of the Bishop of Quebec "because of distance and difficulty of roads."[15]

In 1765 Courtableau married Marguerite Le Kintrek, the widow Desbordes. Therefore Margaret Desbordes was a step-daughter of Courtableau and granddaughter of Le Kinterek.

---

[14] Francois Nerault succession, 1836, No. 708, St. Landry Parish
[15] Deville: *Opelousas*, 69

Margaret Desbordes' first husband, Francois Brunet, had extensive land holdings in the Opelousas district. These lands, acquired during the 1780s, were later claimed by "the widow of Cloree." Margaret was widowed three times; Francois Brunet died in 1792, and in 1810 when she was married to John Joseph Clorec (Cloree) she was listed as the widow of Cornelius Ploy.[16]

Bennett Jopling claimed a large tract "in the bayou of Mallet's woods." The land, on both sides of the bayou, was originally claimed by Joseph Chevalier Poiret. Jopling's succession was filed in 1901 in the Acadia Parish Probate Court by Ferdinand M. Joplin, who stated in his petition that Bennett Jopling had "many years ago died, leaving an old private land claim against the United States government for nearly 1,000 acres."

The land was appraised at $500, the date of the auction was set and duly advertised in the Crowley Signal. Documents in the succession refer to a lawsuit filed against the estate by T. C. Chachere. In the final disposition, the estate was reduced to 48.70 acres. The land was sold at public auction in 1904 to Arthur D. Buskill, the high bidder, for $60.

Adjacent to the Jopling tract was land owned by Thomas Bledsoe (Bedsoe). The property, on the south side of the bayou, was originally claimed by Jean Doucet. The son of John Bledsoe and Mary Frank, Thomas married Susanne Duffin, daughter of Roger Duffin and Margaret Patterson, at Opelousas in 1811. Both Thomas and Susanne were natives of Kentucky.

Rev. Louis Buhot's land on the south side of the bayou was situated approximately half way between Mowata and Eunice. A French priest from Normandy, Father Buhot was curate for the Opelousas church about 12 years, coming there in 1801 and remaining until his death in 1813.[17]

Father Buhot also claimed land in St. Landry Parish and the Avoyelles district "for the use of the church." He claimed the Bayou Mallet property by order of survey and occupancy; it is safe to assume that the "occupancy" of the Acadia Parish property was provided by a tenant, and not by the priest, who was domiciled at Opelousas.

Patrick Gurnett's land was on the south bank of Mallet, just west of the Frey community. The succession of Patrick Gurnett and his wife Ann Tear was filed in 1825; they left seven children, four of whom were minors.

16 Hebert: *Southwest Louisiana Records, Church and Civil Records of Settlers, 1756-1810* 133
17 Baudier: *The Catholic Church in Louisiana,* 244, 252

The inventory of the estate included one female slave, Grace and her four children; two boy slaves, 30 head of horned cattle; 5,000 pounds of cotton in the seed, valued at two and a half cents per pound; 60 hogs, four bee hives, one loom, two spinning wheels. The Gurnetts also owned property on Bayou Boeuf; this property was sold at auction for $1,000. There were no bidders on the Bayou Mallet property.

William Johnson's large rectangle of land was "in the prairie Faquetack," about one mile north of the bayou and the same distance from the northern boundary of Acadia. Johnson (Jeansonne), of Denmark, son of Joseph Johnson (Jonsown) and Christina Janson (or Hansen) of Copenhagen, was married in 1798 to Theresa Rayter (Ritter), daughter of Miguel Rayter and Marie Luisa Stelly, "Germans living in this parish" of Opelousas. The groom signed the marriage register as William Johnson; the bride signed Tereze Ritter.

Johnson's neighbors to the west were two Acadians, Fabien Richard and Louis Richard, each of whom owned a rectangle of land on the prairie between Bayou Mallet and Bayou des Cannes.

Fabien and Louis Richard were probably brothers, or nephew and uncle. The 1777 census lists a Louis Richard, age 16, a bachelor. The same census gives Pierre Richard, 48, and his wife, Marguerite Dugat, 49. Their children were Fabien, 20; Louis, 10; Pierre, 9; Olivier, 5; Philippe, 3; Marguerite, 6. The Richards owned no slaves; their possessions included 100 head of cattle, 12 horses and mules, and 20 hogs.

Fabien Richard's wife was Francoise Thibodeau, daughter of Pierre Thibodeau and Francoise Sonnier of Beau Sejour, Acadia, Nova Scotia.[18]

Along the south bank of Bayou Mallet, north and west of the Frey community, was a colony of free persons of color. These were Maria, Victorie and Martin Donatto (Donato), George Bollard and La Rouille.

Martin Donatto was the son of Don Donato Bello and Maria Juana Taillefer.[19] Donato Bello, the father, was an Italian. He had extensive land holdings in St. Landry and owned a small segment of land (one and one-half acres) in Acadia. This was part of a Spanish grant of 1787. Bello inhabited and cultivated this land for 35 consecutive years, beginning in 1772.

Martin Donatto had large land holdings in the Opelousas district. When he died in 1848 he bequeathed liberty to his slave wife and her

---

18 Hebert: *Southwest Louisiana Records, 1756-1810* 477
19 Ruth Robertson Fontenot genealogy records

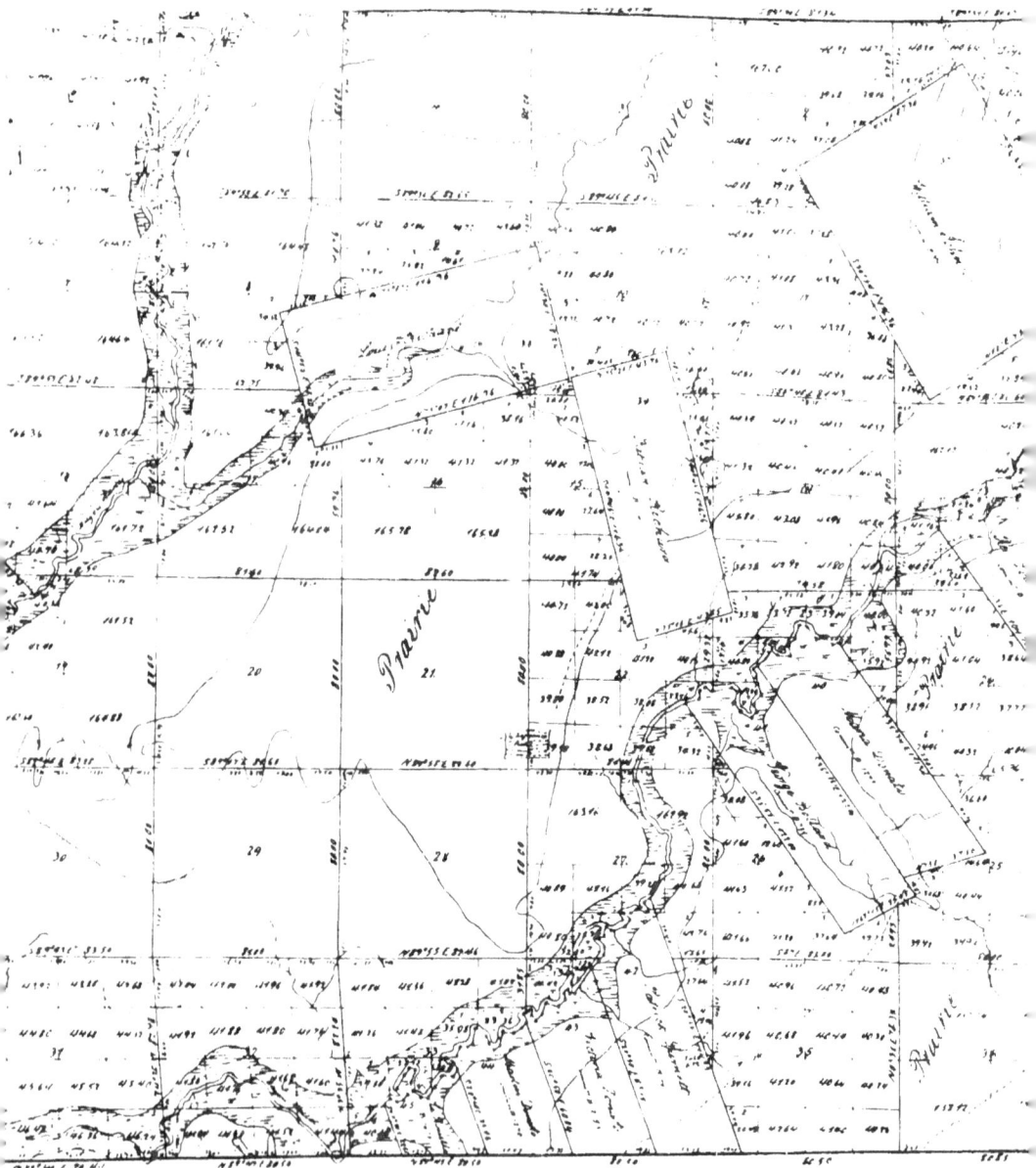

Ten Spanish land grants are shown on the official survey plat of Township 7 South Range 1 West, Acadia Parish. Along Bayou Mallet's south bank were grants claimed by Rev. Louis Buhot, Maria Donato, George Bollard, Patrick Gurnett, Victorie Donato, Martin Donato and La Rouille. The large rectangle at upper right is the William Johnson grant just south of Eunice; Louis and Fabien Richard owned grants on tributaries of Bayou des Cannes.

seven children; he left them 89 slaves and 4,500 arpents of land, as well as notes and mortgages valued at $46,000.[20] Alexandre Barde refers to the "Donats of Opelousas, patriarchal family who have recently carried in we know not what Mexican province, a fortune acquired by the sweat of the brow."[21] Maria Donatto was the daughter of Martin and Marie Anne Duchesne; she was married to Francois Lemelle at St. Martinville.

George Bollard was in the Opelousas district as early as 1780. Luke Collins and his wife Sarah sold a slave to George Bollard, a free mulatto, in Opelousas that year.[22]

La Rouillé, which means "the rusty one," was Nicholas Simon. When his mother died the priest at Opelousas recorded the following information in connection with the last rites:

"Died: Jeane, *dit* Jeaneton, Castillon, aged about 100 years; she was free, died at her son's Nicolas Simon, *dit* La Royé, free *mulatre*, in Grand Prairie. This woman has seen three centuries; the last years of 1600, all of 1700 and this year of 1800."

Two of St. Landry Parish's best known early political figures were Acadia Parish landowners. These were Louis Louallier and George King, whose adjacent tracts of land were located about three miles northeast of Iota.

Louallier, a native of France, was a member of the first police jury of St. Landry, in 1811;[23] he was a member of the Louisiana Legislature under Governor Claiborne and was termed "a most efficient member."[24] After the Battle of New Orleans Louallier published an open letter in *Courier de la Louisiane* objecting to General Andrew Jackson's general orders, which directed all Frenchmen in New Orleans to leave the city within three days. As a consequence Louallier was arrested and jailed as a spy.[25]

George King, born in Virginia in 1769, came to Opelousas district in 1805 as first territorial clerk of court. In 1806 Governor Claiborne appointed him first parish judge, a post he held until 1842. He died at his

20 Stahl. "The Free Negro In Ante-Bellum Louisiana," *Louisiana Historical Quarterly*, Vol. 25, 371
21 Barde: "History of the Vigilance Committees of Attakapas" Translation by Henrietta Guilbeau Rogers, 346
22 Coker: "Luke Collins Senior and Family," *Louisiana History*, Journal of the Louisiana History Association, Vol. xiv, No. 2, 148
23 "Some History of St. Landry Parish from the 1690s," 68
24 Martin: *The History of Louisiana From the Earliest Period*, 390
25 *Ibid*

home in Opelousas. He was a kinsman of William Rufus King, elected vice president of the United States in 1852.[26]

Joseph Giron Mallet, *fils,* owned land "situated at a place called Points of Marrons, a wood of bayou Plaquemine Brulees." Joseph Giron was the only heir of Pierre Mallet, for whom the bayou was named. Pierre Mallet and his brother Antoine were early French settlers of the Opelousas post; they were of minor age in 1768 when Jacques Courtableau acted as their guardian in a transaction involving a French land grant.

The Mallet land was situated about one-half mile west of the Louisiana Meridian just west of the Maxie community, about eight miles north of Crowley. The property was described as "bounded by vacant land" and was claimed by Pierre Mallet in 1803. Bonaventure Martin, 58, gave testimony in the Mallet land claim in 1813, stating that the land was occupied and cultivated for several years previous to the change of government in 1803, "by Bradley Gardiner, who sold to P. Mallet, who inhabited and cultivated the same until about nine years ago: (the time of his death) that Mallet having no title from Gardiner, applied for and obtained the commandant's approval of his settlement."

William McKoy owned property on Coulée Pointe au Loup just south of Iota. McKoy, "of north America," was the son of William McKoy and Margaret Menard. He married Francoise Carriere, daughter of Pierre Carriere and Marie Louise Vivarene of Illinois. Their daughter, Euphrosine, was baptized at Opelousas in 1816.

Bayou Plaquemine Brûlée

Bayou Plaquemine Brûlée enters Acadia Parish about two and one half miles north of Church Point and virtually bisects the parish from northeast to southwest. At a point just north of Crowley is the confluence of Bayou Plaquemine Brûlée and Bayou Wikoff; Plaquemine Brûlée continues on a southwesterly course until it empties into the Mermentau River.

Approximately half of Acadia's early landowners were on Plaquemine Brûlée. Just inside the St. Landry-Acadia line was property owned by Widow Mondon (Mundo). This was Magdalene Blanchard, daughter of Todas las Santon Blanchard and Angelica Bertrand. She was the widow of Andre Mondon, native of France, whom she married in 1790. The 1777 census lists Andre Mondon, a bachelor, aged 36; at that time he

---

[26] Perrin: *Southwest Louisiana Biographical and Historical,* Part I, 53; "Some History of St. Landry Parish from the 1690s," 54

owned 60 head of cattle and eight horses. Mondon was the original claimant of the tract on Plaquemine Brûlée, by Spanish grant.

Across the bayou on the north bank was Pierre Trahan's Spanish land grant. Trahan was 27 at the time of the 1777 census; he was married to Anne Brasseux, 23, and had one daughter, Marie, 2. He owned 26 head of cattle, 3 horses and 12 hogs.

Adjacent to the Trahan property was land owned by Jean Louis Cart. He was the son of James Cart and Susanna Rochat, and in 1806 married Julienne Chiasson, daughter of Jean Baptiste Chiasson, at Opelousas. The succession of Jean Louis Antoine Cart was filed in 1833 by his son, Antoine Cart. The inventory of the estate included one female slave, Celia; 49 volumes of books, valued at $5; a writing desk, $2; two violins, $1 each; a "musical box," $8; medical scales and weights, $1; one case of bottles, $5.37½. His copy of Dr. Cooper's Surgery Book was sold to Dr. George Hill for 36 cents; the same buyer was the high bidder for a copy of "The Life of Henry Clay" at 75 cents.

Across the bayou, on the south bank, was Antoine Langlois' tract of land. A native of the Illinois territory, he was born in 1749, the son of Augustin Langlois and Marie Louise Graveline; he married Francoise Carriere, native of New Orleans, daughter of Joseph Carriere and Marie Louise Lavergne, in 1781.[27]

Jacques Deshotels (Deshautelle) had bayou front land south of, and adjacent to, the Langlois property. He owned 800 arpents by Spanish grant. Jacques Deshotels was born in Montreal, the son of Pierre Deshotels and Angelique Thuillier de Vemar. He married Anne Stephan de Quefray.[28] A granddaughter, Maria Luisa, was baptized at Opelousas in 1782.

A landowner identified only by the name "Joannesse" had a narrow strip of land across from the Deshotels property; the land was "claimed under a requete by Joannesse" in 1788. In William Henry Perrin's "Southwest Louisiana: Historical and Biographical," published in 1891, is an interesting reference to a person by this name: "Joseph Cheasson (Chiasson), alias Joannes, died several years ago in this parish (St. Landry) at the advanced age of nearly one hundred and thirty years. When he was one hundred and fifteen years old he moved to Texas, and after living in that state several years returned to St. Landry."

27 Deville and Vidrine: *Marriage Contracts of the Opelousas Post,* 8
28 C. Kenneth Deshotel genealogy records

Lufroi Latiolais was Joannesse's neighbor on the north bank of Plaquemine Brûlée. His land was situated just north of the town of Church Point. The son of Louis Latiolais and Julienne Bar, Lufroi was of French ancestry. He married Marie Josephine d'Aigle, daughter of Joseph *dit Chevalier* d'Aigle and Lile Dupre.[29]

Etienne Daigle (d'Aigle), the first of this family to settle in southwest Louisiana, owned land adjacent to the Lufroi Latiolais property. The land was claimed by settlement in 1801. The son of Etienne d'Aigle and Angelique LaPrade, he married Marie Anne Taillon of Illinois; Lufroi Latiolais' wife was his granddaughter.[30]

Louis Leger (Legee, Legea) owned land west of the Daigle tract, acquired by requete in 1787. He also owned property across the bayou, adjacent to the Langlois land. The son of Michel Leger and Angelica Pinet, he married Anne Doucet, daughter of Joseph Doucet and Anna Landry, in 1792.[31]

Louis Latiolais, Lufroi's father, had land fronting on the south side of the bayou, situated southeast of the present town of Church Point. The 1777 census designated him "Sieur" Louis Latiolais, age 30; his wife, Julienne Bar (Barre, Barthe), 25. Three of their children are listed: Joseph, Modeste and Constance. They owned eight slaves, 36 cows and three hogs.

The Church Point settlement developed on land originally owned by Sylvain Sonnier (Saunier, Sognyer). His Spanish grant was described as being "in the cove of bayou Plaquemine Brule." Sylvain Sonnier's age is given in the 1777 census as 40; his wife, Magdaleine Bourg, 27. One of their sons, born circa 1768, was also named Sylvain, or Silvain. At the time of the census taking the Sonniers owned 150 head of cattle, 11 horses and mules and 45 hogs. Sonnier probably used his Bayou Plaquemine Brûlée property for a *vacherie*. The American State Papers identifies him as "an inhabitant of Bellevue," a settlement south of Opelousas, where he also owned land.

Jean Baptiste Malveau (Malvot, Malvo) and Roselie Malveau owned adjoining tracts on the north side of the bayou. Jean Baptiste was the original owner of both tracts. He was the son of Jean Malvot, native of the parish of St. Pierre de Lande, Diocese of Xaintes, and Jeanne Bou-

29 Guidry: *La Pointe de l'Eglise* 115
30 *Ibid*
31 Thelma Pierrel genealogy records

Aux Opelousas le vingt unième jour du mois de Juillet
de l'année mil huit cent Sept. Moi Martin Duralde habitant
des Atacapas en ma qualité d'exécuteur testamentaire que
le défunt Jean Baptiste Malveau habitant des dits Opelousas
m'a nommé tant par Son testament clos du vingt huitième
jour du mois d'octobre de l'année mil huit cent trois, que
par Son codicile du Sixième jour du mois d'avril de la
présente année, me Suis transporté au domicile dud. défunt
Sis dans le quartier de Plaquemine brulé accompagné de
Messieurs Pierre Chretien & Benjamin Smith comme
estimateurs et de Messieurs françois Drouet & Jean Louis
Antoine Kart comme témoins, que j'ai nommé à cet effet
pour procéder à l'inventaire de tous les biens quelconques
appartenant à Sa Succession, la difficulté de réunir les
animaux qui en font le principal objet ayant empêché
de l'effectuer plutôt. & y étant après avoir reçu le Serment
de chacun des dits estimateurs & témoins de S'acquitter
leurs fonctions respectives Selon leurs consciences, plus
grande Capacité & fidelité, J'ai requis la nommée Rosalie
mulâtresse libre fille naturelle & l'une des héritiers du dit
défunt également que les negres nommés Laurent & Jean
Baptiste ci devant esclaves de cederniers à la charge de
qui Sont restés Ses biens de me les exhiber, & exécuté le dit
inventaire, Comme il Suit, Savoir,

A document among the succession papers of Jean Baptiste Malveau reveals that Pierre Chretien and Benjamin Smith made the inventory of the estate, and named Francois Drouet and Jean Louis Antoine Kart (Cart) as witnesses. The document, written in 1807 by Martin Duralde, former commandant of the Opelousas post, identifies Rosalie Malveau as a "free woman of color, natural daughter and one of the heirs of the deceased man." (St. Landry Parish courthouse records)

chereau. He married Perrine Tesson, daughter of Jean Tesson and Marie Desmoulins, "natives of Opelousas" in 1783. Their marriage contract showed the groom owned eight slaves, valued at 2,400 *piastres*,* 90 head of cattle, five horses and land valued at 300 *piastres*. The bride's dowry included one slave woman, 30 *bête-a-corne* (horned cattle), two mules and household belongings valued at 300 *piastres*.[32]

Rosalie Malveau was Jean Baptiste Malveau's daughter. A document in Jean Baptiste Malveau's succession papers, written by Martin Duralde, identifies Rosalie as a "free woman of color, natural daughter and one of the heirs of the deceased man . . . " The succession was opened in 1807.[33]

Michel Ledoux's land, adjacent to the Malveau property, was acquired by possession and occupancy. He was the original claimant. The son of Michel Ledoux and Lisette Maux, he was married to Modeste Bellard, daughter of Antoine Bellard and Maria Trahan, at Opelousas in 1789.

Across on the bayou's south side were two tracts of land owned by Charles Smith. The original claimants were Christoval Gomez and Vincent Escovear. Charles was the son of Leonard Smith and Elizabeth Neal of Frederick County, Maryland. He married Mary Sentee at Opelousas in 1792. He also owned land on Bayou Bourbeux in St. Landry Parish, and is credited with making large donations of land in the Grand Coteau area to the Catholic Church. The Academy of the Sacred Heart, constructed in 1831, is on land that was once a part of the Smith plantation.[34]

Adjacent to the Smith property was land owned by Daniel Clark, a wealthy and influential New Orleans merchant, and perhaps Acadia's best known colonial landowner. Clark owned two tracts of bayou front land; the original claimants of the tracts are given as Narcisco Brontin and Francois Brutin.

Born in Ireland in 1766, Clark was well educated in English schools, including Eton. He came to New Orleans when he was 20 years of age and began a colorful and successful career. In association with his uncle of the same name he became a merchant and landholder. Socially and

---

piastre: Spanish piece of eight, the equivalent of an American dollar; the term is still used extensively by French-speaking people of Louisiana.

32 Deville and Vidrine: *Marriage Contracts of the Opelousas Post* 15
33 Jean Baptiste Malveau succession, 1807, No. 2, St. Landry Parish
34 "Some History of St. Landry Parish from the 1690s," 187

politically ambitious, he was considered thoroughly honest and public-spirited.

He served as clerk in the office of the Spanish governor, became an American citizen in 1798 when the Territory of Mississippi was formed. In 1801 he was appointed consul at New Orleans by Thomas Jefferson. During the uncertain period of the transfer of Louisiana to France, and in 1803 to the United States, he played an important role in safeguarding the interests of New Orleans.

In 1806 Clark was elected the first delegate to Congress from the Orleans Territory. He served only one term. He died in New Orleans in 1813, at the age of 47.

Eventful though his career was, Daniel Clark is remembered best as the father of Myra Clark Gaines, his only heir. The settlement of Daniel Clark's estate, which included vast tracts of land in New Orleans, involved treachery and the suppression of his will in which he had acknowledged Myra as his daughter. Determined not to be disfranchised, Myra Clark Gaines fought her legal battle through the courts; it required some 60 years and 17 appeals to the Supreme Court of the United States to achieve recognition of her status and of her rights. The Myra Clark Gaines case is said to be the longest litigation in the history of America.[35]

Across from the Clark property, on the bayou's north bank, were bayou front strips owned by Francois Nerault (Herault, Neraut), Basil Chiasson and Clautilda Bourassas (Bourassa).

Francois Nerault acquired his land from Antoine Langlois, the original claimant. Nerault's succession was filed in Opelousas in 1836. Marie Melazia Breaux is named as his widow; he left three adult children by a former marriage, all residents of Iberville Parish, and seven minor children by his marriage to Marie Melazia.

Basil Chiasson was the original claimant of his land, by requete. A native of Beau Sejour in Acadia, Nova Scotia, he was the son of Pierre Chiasson and Catherine Bourgeois. His first wife was Monique Comeau. He was married a second time to Marie Thibodeaux, a native of Beau Sejour, daughter of Pierre Thibodeaux and Francoise Sonnier and widow of Gang Bourg, at Opelousas in 1789.[36]

---

35 Unpublished summary by Rev. Paul B. Freeland, taken from I. J. Cox's article on Daniel Clark, *Dictionary of American Biography;* Deutschs: "Myra Clark Gaines vs New Orleans," *The Louisiana Bar Journal,* December, 1971; Harmon *The Famous Case of Myra Clark Gaines*
36 Deville and Vidrine:, *Marriage Contracts of the Opelousas Post* 33

Clautilda Bourassas, the widow of Charles Bourassas, was the daughter of Manuel Quinteros and Maria Granger. She married the son of Charles Bourassas and Magdaline Lalonde, Acadians, in 1797 at Opelousas. Charles Bourassas was the original owner of the land, by settlement.

Blaise Lejeune and Joseph Lejeune had rectangles of land on a tributary of Bayou Plaquemine Brûlée north of the Bourassas property. Blaise and Joseph were brothers, sons of Blaise Lejeune and Marie Josephe Breaux.[37] Blaise acquired his land from his father, and both he and his father "inhabited and cultivated the land" beginning in the early 1780s. Witnessing in Joseph Lejeune's land claim in 1812, Louis Richard said that Joseph had been inhabiting and cultivating his land since 1790.

Jean Baptiste Granger (Grangé) was the original owner of his tract on the north side of the bayou, adjacent to the Bourassas property. This landowner was probably the Jean Baptiste Grangé listed in the 1777 census as a 25-year-old bachelor. There were however two other early settlers by this name; a Jean Baptiste Granger was married to Suzanne Cormier at St. Martinville in 1779, and another, of different parentage, was baptized at Opelousas in 1784.

Across the bayou, adjacent to the Daniel Clark holdings, was property owned by Henry Raper (Rapier), claimed by requête. Raper's succession, filed at Opelousas in 1814, identifies his widow as Nancy Ann Rule. Jacob Harmon and Joseph Elah Andrus appraised the estate, which included three slaves, valued at $1,100. The public auction, held at the residence on Plaquemine Brûlée, brought a total of $4,727.50.

Thomas LeBrun (Brun) was the original owner of land on the west side of the bayou, adjacent to the Granger tract. LeBrun married Marguerite Muns in Pointe Coupée.[38]

Joseph Cormier's land was just below, and bounded by, the LeBrun tract. Joseph Cormier was one of the early Acadian arrivals, coming to the Opelousas district in 1766.[39] The 1777 census gives his age as 37; his wife, Anne Michel, 44. Their eight children included twin daughters. The Cormiers owned 150 head of cattle, 15 horses and mules, and 20 hogs in 1777. One of the Cormier sons was named Joseph, born circa 1766. It is not certain whether this Acadia Parish landowner was the

37 1777 census
38 Bodin: *Selected Acadian and Louisiana Church Records* Vol. I, 110B
39 Arsenault: *Histoire et Genealogie des Acadiens* Tome 2,1054

father or the son. Joseph Cormier (probably the father) also had a Spanish land grant at Bellevue which was claimed by his widow. Cormier *père* died in 1795.

The next 11 "riverbank strips" on Plaquemine Brûlée were owned by colonial families that settled on their lands, became prominent in affairs of Imperial St. Landry, and, after 1886, became equally prominent in building the new parish of Acadia.

These were the Andrus, Harmon and Hays families, all of which settled in the Branch area of Acadia Parish. Some had land holdings on Bayou Plaquemine Brûlée, others owned property fronting on nearby Bayou Wikoff, identified in early times as "the eastern branch of Bayou Plaquemine Brûlée."

Jacob Harmon (Harman) had land on the east side of the bayou, beginning at the point where Plaquemine Brûlée curves to a north-south direction. About half a mile down the bayou were two additional tracts owned by Harmon. A native of Strasbourg, he and his wife, Hannah Guice, came to the area about 1780.[40]

Joseph Elah (Hilaire) Andrus owned the strip of land between the Harmon holdings. The son of Joseph Andrus of Virginia and Mary Hays of Pennsylvania, he was twice married: first to Catherine Harmon, daughter of Jacob, and second to Sarah McClelland, daughter of James McClelland and Sarah Celeste Andrus.[41] Elah also owned property farther down the bayou, just north of Crowley. His land was claimed by order of survey and possession and occupancy; original claimants were John Clark and Joseph Villiers.

The William Hays property was located adjacent to the Harmon land, the eastern boundary extending to the present community of Branch. A native of Pennsylvania, William Hays was born circa 1730; he married Sarah Celeste Bozman.[42]

North of William Hays, on the west side of the bayou, were four tracts owned by two of his sons, John Hays and Bosman Hays. John was twice married; first to Anna Clark, then to Fanny McClelland; Bosman's wife was Jane Foreman.[43] The John Hays land was adjacent to the Joseph

---

40 Guidry: *La Pointe de l'Eglise* 74
41 Sybil Parrott Andrus genealogy records
42 Ibid
43 Ibid

39

Signatures of appraisers and witnesses of the Jacob Harman (Harmon) estate. Signing as appraisers were William Wikoff, Sr., Bosman Hayes, George Forman (Foreman), Abraham Harman and W. Cormier. Witnessing the signature, by mark, of the widow, Mary Harman, were Joseph Elah Andrus, Jacob Harman, Jr. and D. S. Sutton. The succession was opened in 1809. (St. Landry Parish courthouse records)

40

Cormier tract; Bosman's property was bounded on the north by John's property line. This family settlement and the general area west of the bayou became known as Prairie Hays.

Antoine Blanc owned two large tracts of land in what is now Acadia Parish: the land on upper Plaquemine Brûlée which he purchased from the Indians in 1784 (previously described in Chapter I) totaled 3,333 and ⅓ arpents; his second tract of 3,200 arpents was on both sides of Bayou Plaquemine Brûlée, northwest and west of Crowley. Bayou Blanc, a tributary of Plaquemine Brûlée, bears his name.

Antoine Blanc's succession was opened in 1868 in Opelousas. Alfred Foy Brown was named administrator of the "vacant estate." A year later, another administrator, Elbert Gantt, was appointed; the document states that Brown, who had not given bond, had "left permanently and had abandoned all claims as administrator." Blanc's property is described as "3,200 superficial arpents on both sides of Bayou Plaquemine Brûlée in Township 9 South, Range 1 West, and Township 10 South, Range 1 West," which locates the tract near Crowley. The land near Branch which he bought from the Indians was not included in the estate.

A new inventory was ordered by the Probate Court in 1869 "of the estate of Antoine Blanc, who came to this state from the Empire of France, whither he returned many years since, and died." The 3,200 arpents, appraised at 25 cents an acre for a total value of $800, was auctioned at the St. Landry courthouse in 1870, after legal notice in the "Opelousas Journal," and sold to James K. Dixon for $600. After the legal fees were paid, this amount was cut to a little more than half.

Antoine Blanc was a great-uncle, or great-great-uncle, of Mrs. Joe Latour of Rayne. The former Ester Blanc, she is the daughter of Antoine Blanc, a nephew, or great-nephew, of the first Antoine Blanc. In a 1974 interview Mrs. Latour said that her father, who came to Rayne from France after the first Antoine Blanc died, told her his uncle had never married; that he (Mrs. Latour's father) came to America too late to claim his uncle's property. This Antoine Blanc died in Rayne in 1922, at age 73.[44]

Across the bayou from the Blanc property were tracts owned by James Andrus, Widow Leger and John Clark (Turner).

The James Andrus land was bounded on the north by William Hays. The original claimant was Benjamin Andrus Jr. The son of Benjamin

---

44 St. Joseph Catholic Church, Rayne, La. records

Andrus Sr. and Mary Hargrove, James was born circa 1760. He married Lucy Hays of Pennsylvania.[45]

The Widow Leger was Angelica Pinet, widow of Michel Leger and mother of Louis and Michel Leger. The land claim was registered in 1787.

John Clark (Turner) had land adjoining the Widow Leger, acquired by settlement and occupancy; he was the original claimant. He was a native of Maryland, the son of Lorenzo Clark and Susan Cowden, and married Maria Estevan (Mary Stephens), daughter of Enrique Estivan and Rosa Anna Poiret.

John Clark was a turner by trade; he used the word after his name for identification purposes. His succession was filed in 1813 in St. Landry under the name John Clark (Turner). The estate was appraised by Jacob Walsh and Solomon Cole, with John Donman acting as umpire. One of the witnesses to the appraisal was identified as John Clark (Cut Lip). It was stated in the succession that his widow, Mary Stevens (Stephens) was his second wife; that he left two children by his first wife, and seven children of minor age by his second wife. The inventory of the estate included five slaves, blacksmith tools, turning tools, three turning lathe benches, a weaving loom, two rifle guns and two *fusils,* musket rifles.

Benjamin Robert, the man who gave his name to Robert's Cove, was the original claimant of a sizable tract of land by possession and occupancy, located on the bayou just below the Clark tract. A native of Wales, Robert married Elizabeth Cole of Virginia.

The Jacob Welch (Walsh, Walch, Welsh) property lay west of the Robert land. Welch was the original claimant. The son of Pierre Welch and Catherine Upuard, he married Susanne Robert, daughter of Benjamin Robert.

Mary Lambert was the original claimant of the tract west of the Welch land, by order of survey and settlement. The daughter of Jean Baptiste Lambert and Catherine Lacrois, she married Marin Mouton, son of Salvador Mouton and Anna Bastarache.[46]

Across on the bayou's north bank was the property of James Foreman, the original owner, claimed by settlement and occupancy. The Foreman land was adjacent to Antoine Blanc's large holdings on upper Plaquemine Brûlée. The son of Edward Foreman, native of Virginia, and

45 Sybil Parrott Andrus genealogy records
46 Bodin: *Selected Acadian and Louisiana Church Records* Vol. I, 308

Marie Burnett (Bonnet, Barnett), he was married in 1805 to Susan Cole, daughter of James Cole, originally of Natchez, and Maime Cotter.[47]

West of James Foreman was another original claimant, LeBray de Gonor (Gonnor). The land was described as located "at a place called Point of Pines," bounded on one side "by the domain of the King," and claimed by order of survey in 1787. Gonor petitioned for the land rights to establish a *vacherie*. Joseph Andrus witnessed in the land claim in 1813. He said he was well acquainted with Gonor during his lifetime; that Gonor had died in 1788, leaving a widow and four minor children, the eldest about seven or eight; that the eldest child was drowned during his minority. Two years after the husband's death the widow moved to New Orleans, Andrus said. LeBray de Gonor registered his cattle brand in the Attakapas district in 1770.[48]

Solomon and James Cole owned rectangles of land next to the Gonor property. Solomon Cole had only a few arpents of frontage on Plaquemine Brûlée, but another stream, a tributary of the larger waterway, ran through both his land and the James Cole property. Solomon acquired his land from Isaac Johnson, the original claimant; James Cole was the original claimant of his land, by settlement and occupancy.

The Coles were brothers. This is established by Solomon Cole's succession, filed at Opelousas in 1825. Solomon's brother-in-law, James Foreman, was named tutor for a minor son, Stephen Cole. This was done at the request of the widow, Elizabeth; Jam s Cole Jr. and James Cole Sr., uncle of Stephen. In one of the succession documents Judge George King wrote that he had gone to the Cole *vacherie* "in Prairie Soileau" to make an inventory of the estate, which included 6 10 acres valued at $320; 191 head of horned cattle and eight horses.

David Harmon owned land situated at the juncture of Bayou Plaquemine Brûlée and Bayou Wikoff, just north of Crowley. The Harmon property was on the north side of the bayou, bounded on three sides by vacant land. Bosman Hays, testifying before the Land Office commissioners in 1807, said that in 1801 Phillip Winfree, about 21 and the head of a family, went with his family to reside on the land to keep stock for David and Jacob Harmon. Hays said that Winfree had cultivated the land for three years, then the Harmons removed their stock, and "Winfree

47 Henry Newton Pharr genealogy records
48 Sanders: *Records of the Attakapas District,* 1739-1811, 11

continued to live on, and cultivate the land for two years, then he removed."

The son of Jacob Harmon and Hannah Guice, David was married in 1804 to Elizabeth Lyons, daughter of John Lyons and Nancy Ahart.[49] David Harmon had a *vacherie* in the Attakapas district, on Vermilion River, in 1797; John Harmon lived on the land and cultivated it, beginning in 1803.

Across the bayou, on Plaquemine Brûlée's south bank, was the second tract owned by Elah Andrus. This land, also bounded on three sides by unclaimed land, extended almost to the present city limits of Crowley.

The remainder of the landowners along Bayou Plaquemine Brûlée were located west of the Antoine Blanc land near Crowley to the point where the bayou flows into Bayou des Cannes and the Mermentau River.

On the bayou's north bank, about two miles west of Crowley, was the Raphael Smith land. The tract was isolated, bounded on three sides by vacant land. Raphael was Charles Smith's brother. In 1826 he married Clemence Guilbeau at St. Jean du Vermilion (Lafayette).[50] Most of the Smiths of the Grand Coteau area are descendants of Raphael Smith.[51] Raphael is identified as a *chirurgien,* surgeon, in the succession of Jean Baptiste Malveau, opened in 1807.

About two miles farther down the bayou was another isolated bayou front strip, owned by Jacob Harmon. Some two miles farther west were three strips, two owned jointly by Jean Mouton and David Guidry, the third by Pierre Guidry. These will be described with the property owners on the south side of the bayou, as all belong to the same group.

The last tract on the north side of Plaquemine Brûlée, situated about half a mile from the juncture of the two bayous, belonged to William Callaghan, who claimed by order of survey. The original claimant was Garret Yarbre. William Callaghan, son of Daniel Callaghan and Catherine Ouest (West) was baptized at Opelousas in 1793.

An Acadia Parish map shows 28 strips of land, most of them quite narrow, on the south bank of Plaquemine Brûlée between Crowley and Mermentau. Only 12 of these strips were claimed, 11 of them by Acadians. The 12th and largest tract, of some 1,200 arpents, belonged to Robert

49 Bodin: *Selected Acadian and Louisiana Church Records* Vol. II, 120, 161
50 Griffin: *Attakapas Country, A History of Lafayette Parish Louisiana,* 231
51 Mrs. Oscar Olivier genealogy records

Cochran and John Rhea, and was acquired from David Lejeune, the original claimant.

Major Robert A. Cochran, native of Maryland, married Elisa Voorhies, daughter of Cornelius Voorhies and Aimee Gradenigo, in 1825. John Rhea was a land speculator; he purchased 18 different claims totaling more than 10,000 acres of land, seven of which were later rejected as fraudulent.[52]

The Acadian landowners were Pierre Arceneaux and his five sons, Alexandre, Louis, Cyprien, Pierre and Francois; his three sons-in-law, Jean Guilbeau, Francois Carmouche and Joseph Breaux; Pierre Guidry and his son David; Jean Mouton and Pierre Bernard.

Pierre Arceneaux (Arsenau, Arsenault), born at Beaubassin, Nova Scotia, in 1731, came to St. James Parish, Louisiana, in 1765, thence to the Attakapas district in 1787. He married Anne Bergeron about 1758 and had five sons and three daughters.[53]

It is generally accepted, on the basis of family tradition, that Pierre Arceneaux was the prototype of Gabriel in Longfellow's poem, "Evangeline." Dr. Thomas J. Arceneaux,[54] a direct descendant of Pierre Arceneaux who has done extensive genealogical research, has established that Pierre Arceneaux also carried the name of Louis, and was also known by the nickname, "Penault." Dr. Arceneaux has further established that Pierre (Louis) Arceneaux was the only Arceneaux listed among the exiled Acadians.

Pierre Arceneaux was one of the eight Acadians who signed a contract with Captain Antoine Bernard d'Hautrive to raise cattle on the Attakapas and Opelousas prairies. This historic agreement, signed in New Orleans in 1765, is considered the beginning of the cattle industry in southwest Louisiana.[55]

Pierre Arceneaux was the original owner of eight tracts of 328 arpents each on Bayou Plaquemine Brûlée between Crowley and Estherwood. These were later claimed by his five sons and three sons-in-law.

Pierre Bernard was one of twin sons born in 1762 to Michel Bernard and Marie Guilbeau of Port Royal, Acadia, Nova Scotia.[56] Pierre Guidry,

---

52 Davis: *Louisiana, A Narrative History* 172
53 Arsenault: *History of the Acadians,* 198
54 Dr. Thomas J. Arceneaux, retired Dean College of Agriculture, University of Southwestern Louisiana.
55 Griffin: *Attakapas Country A History of Lafayette Parish, Louisiana,* 15
56 Arsenault: *Histoire et Genealogie des Acadiens* Tome 2,1047

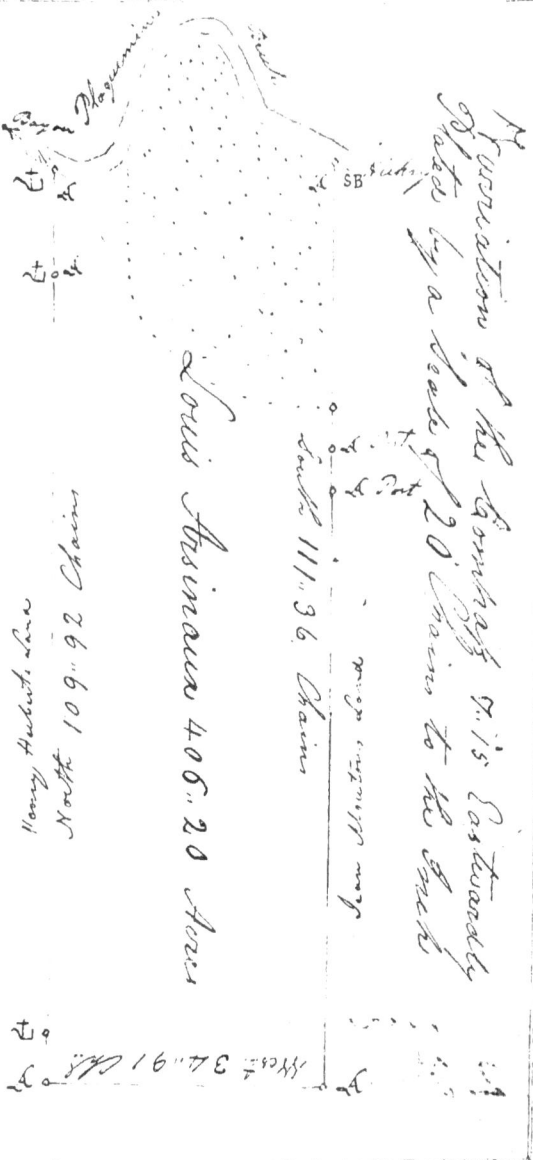

An 1806 survey of the Louis Arceneaux tract on Bayou Plaquemine Brûlée. The property is described as being located on the south bank of the bayou, with the boundaries designated by a hickory tree distinctively marked, and two marked posts. (Copy of document courtesy Claire Gomer Anding)

born circa 1742, was married to Claire Babin, daughter of Antoine Babin and Catherine Landry. David was the son of Pierre and Claire Babin.[57]

Jean Mouton, son of Salvador Mouton and Anne Bastarache, was the founder of Vermilionville, later to become the city of Lafayette. He donated land for the church and courthouse, and was the progenitor of a distinguished line, including a governor of Louisiana.[58]

Jean Mouton and David Guidry married sisters, Marie Marthe and Modeste Bordat. The background history of the Bordat sisters ties in closely with the exile of the Acadians from Nova Scotia in 1755.

Marie Marthe and Modeste were daughters of Dr. Antoine Bordat, ex-surgeon of the French army, and Marguerite Martin, a widow who had been driven from Nova Scotia at the time of the expulsion of the Acadians. With the children of her first marriage she fled from Grand Pré to the forests. After great hardships she finally reached St. Louis, and from there came to New Orleans where she married Dr. Bordat.[59] Her account of the Acadian exile, as she related it to her grandson, Felix Voorhies, is told in "Acadian Reminiscenses, the True Story of the Acadians."[60]

Jean Mouton was a brother of Marin Mouton, husband of Mary Lambert, previously identified as a landowner on upper Plaquemine Brûlée. Jean and Marin had one sister, Celeste Mouton; she was Jean Guilbeau's first wife.[61]

Bayou Wikoff

The next group of landowners to be considered are those who had property fronting on Bayou Wikoff. With Bayou Plaquemine Brûlée, Bayou Wikoff forms a crooked "Y" through the northeastern section of Acadia Parish.

The first landowner was William Wikoff, the man who gave his name to the bayou which bisected his immense square of land between Branch and the Higginbotham community. Wikoff acquired the land in 1798, by Spanish patent. He also owned a large tract on the west bank of Bayou Nezpique, in what is now Jefferson Davis Parish; this tract has been previously described as an Indian purchase, located near the site of an Attakapas village.

57 Virginia Terrell Chrisopher genealogy records
58 Griffin: *Attakapas Country, A History of Lafayette Parish Louisiana*, 186-190
59 *Ibid*
60 Perrin: *Southwest Louisiana, Biographical and Historical* Part I, 81
61 Griffin: *Attakapas Country, A History of Lafayette Parish, Louisiana* 190

Acadian claims to Spanish land grants along the south side of lower Bayou Plaquemine Brûlée. This official plat of Township 10 South Range 2 West, Acadia Parish, last surveyed in 1875, gives the name of the Mermentau River as "Nementou River."

The son of William Wikoff and Inez Wendole, William Wikoff married Susanne Watts, daughter of Estevan Watts and Francesco Astin in 1791.[62] Wikoff was a brother-in-law of Gayoso, Spanish governor of Louisiana, 1797-1799. His wife's sister, Margaret Cyrilla Watts, married Don Manuel Gayoso de Lemos.[63]

William Wikoff died at his home on Bayou Wikoff in 1821. His body, along with those of his wife and children, is interred in the Catholic cemetery at Grand Coteau. His succession, opened at Opelousas in 1821, shows the total value of his estate as $230,732.64. William Wikoff is mentioned in several published works, including Gayarre's History of Louisiana. William Darby termed him " . . . Col. William Wikoff, the most wealthy stock-holder in the United States."

Margaret Desbordes, previously identified as a property owner on Plaquemine Brûlée, owned a second tract of land just south of the Wikoff property.

Across on Bayou Wikoff's south bank were three large tracts belonging to Henry Hargroder (Hargroider, Hergereder). Hargroder also claimed land in the Attakapas district. A document filed at Opelousas in 1796 identifies him as a carpenter and native of Maryland.[64] He married Marie Prudhomme.

Edmund Johnson owned land adjacent to the south boundary of the Hargroder property. His claim to the land, originally owned by Michel Stouts, was based on requete and settlement. Edmund Johnson, witnessing an allegedly fraudulent land claim in the Rapides district in 1815, was termed a person "of unquestionable probity." His succession, filed at Opelousas in 1838, identifies his heirs as Henry B. Milburn, Thomas J. Johnson, Edmund Johnson, D. A. Choate and C. B. Garrand. His property is described as "nine miles from the courthouse, on Bayou Grand Louis, bounded by Pierre Wartelle and Thomas Quirk." This locates his last place of residence in the area between Washington and Grand Prairie in St. Landry Parish.

Along the north bank of Bayou Wikoff, situated southwest of the Desbordes and Wikoff properties, were six tracts of land of varying acreage belonging to James, Joseph and John Andrus. These tracts extended

---

62 Devillier: *The Opelousas Post,* 146
63 Thelma Pierrel genealogy records
64 Henry Newton Pharr records

from the bayou in a northwesterly direction to within a mile or two of the James Andrus property on nearby Bayou Plaquemine Brûlée.

James and Joseph Andrus were brothers, sons of Benjamin Andrus Sr. and Mary Hargrove. Their wives have been previously identified. John Andrus was the son of Joseph; he was thrice married. His first wife was Mary Collins, daughter of Theophilus Collins and Anne Eva Hays; his second wife was Charlotte Hanchette, daughter of Seth Hanchette and Charlotte Leonard of Spain; his third wife is identified only as Sophie Russ, widow of J. Russ.[65]

Joseph Andrus was a hatter by trade. He made hats of the furs of native animals; the fine hats he made of rabbit skins were said to be very durable and "would last a man a lifetime."[66]

On the south (or east) side of the bayou, across from the Andrus holdings, landowners were William Gardiner (Gardner), James Martin (Martins) and William Gilchrist (Gilkris, Kilkris).

Gardner acquired his land from Michel Rayter and claimed under order of survey. Gardner witnessed in a land claim in 1815, along with Edmund Johnson, and like Johnson, was termed a person of "unquestionable probity" by the land office officials. William Gardner is listed as a resident of the Opelousas district in the 1810 census; however, his name does not occur in the genealogy of the Gardiner family which came to Louisiana from Maryland in the 1830s, from which is descended the Gardiners of St. Landry and Acadia Parishes. Records in the Opelousas courthouse show that William Gardner sold several pieces of property circa 1810. Buyers included James Martin, Jean Mouton, David Guidry and Thomas Bledsoe.

James Martin's land was acquired by order of survey. The original claimant was Elizabeth Estouts (Stouts). James Martin is not listed in the early records of Opelousas and St. Martinville churches, nor in the 1810 census of the Opelousas district. In the Gardner land transaction of 1810 he is referred to as James Martin "of Attakapas."

William Gilchrist's land on Bayou Wikoff was purchased from the Indians as described in Chapter I. The son of John Gilchrist, native of Johnson County, North Carolina, and Dame Betchabee, Gilchrist married Susanna Roy, daughter of Joseph Roy and Perrine Lacour, at Pointe

65 Sybil Andrus genealogy records
66 Perrin: *Southwest Louisiana Biographical and Historical* Part I, 34

Coupee in 1772. His succession, filed at Opelousas in 1827, lists the names of seven children: Julian, Davis, John, Charles, Onezime, Louisa (Lovisey) and Mary.

The Basil Lincecomb (Bazile, Bazeel, Linchcomb, Lynchcomb) property is described as located on the "east branch of bayou Plaquemine Brule." He married Mary Gilchrist, daughter of William; Mary is designated "the widow of Basil Lincecomb" in her father's succession. Basil built a lime kiln on the Daniel Callaghan property in 1805.[67]

Across the bayou from Lincecomb, on the north (or west) bank, were tracts owned by John Dunman, Victor Richard and Daniel Callaghan.

John Dunman (Donman) owned two pieces of land on Bayou Wikoff, the tracts separated by the properties of Richard and Callaghan. One tract, originally claimed by Antoine Corkin (Anthony Corkran) was claimed by Robert Collingwood, by order of survey. Both pieces of property were assigned to John Dunman heirs. Dunman also had land in the Attakapas district and registered his cattle brand there in 1790.[68] He was married to Jeanne Kilkris (Gilchrist).

Victor Richard bought his land from Edward Foreman in 1794. Thomas Huffpower (Hoffpauir), age 76, testified in the land claim in 1812. Hoffpauir said the land had been occupied by Foreman "more than thirty years ago, for several years;" that, after the sale to Richard, "one Primo occupied same on Richard's account for two or three years, after which Foreman was employed to tend Richard's cattle, where he resided and cultivated for five successive years."

The 1777 census lists Victor Richard as the husband of Marie Brasseux; the owner of 70 head of cattle, nine horses and 10 hogs. His succession, filed at Opelousas in 1809, names as heirs Pierre Thibodeaux, Jean Baptiste Richard, Joseph Richard, Vidal Estilete and A. W. Cormier. The public auction of the estate was held "at the church door." The inventory included eight slaves, two feather beds, one bolster and 46 "carrots of tobacco."*

Daniel Callaghan purchased his Bayou Wikoff land from Robert Brazil, "who bought from Edward Foreman, who claimed under his brother." Callaghan, an early migrant from the English colonies, was

---

* *carottes de tabac,* rolls of tobacco

[67] *American State Papers -- Public Lands,* Vol. III, 99

[68] Sanders: *Records of the Attakapas District, La., 1739-1811*

manufacturing shoes at the Opelousas post in 1791. In March of that year he ordered 60 calf or deer skins so he would be well supplied with leather.[69]

It is reasonable to assume that Daniel Callaghan did not reside on his Bayou Wikoff property. According to testimony given in another land claim, he lived on Bayou Bellevue in 1794; he stripped the bark off the trees on this property for use in his tanyard, he constructed a road and built a bridge over the bayou.[70] A native of County Cork, Ireland, Daniel was first married to Catherine Ouest (West); his second wife, to whom he was married in 1801, was Maria Mulholland of the Florida post.[71]

West of John Dunman's second tract was property owned by Francois and Amelia Hoffpauir, claimed by order of survey and settlement. Francois and Amelia were children of Thomas Hoffpauir and Marie Charlotte Perillard. Francois married Charlotte Foreman, daughter of Ephraim Foreman and Elizabeth Brown, formerly of North Carolina. Amelia married Peter Stutes (Stouts).

Martin Duralde owned a large tract of land on the south side of Bayou Wikoff, situated just above the present city of Rayne. Duralde, commandant of the Opelousas post, 1795-1803, married Marie Josephe Perrault, native of Quebec, in 1776. One of their daughters, Clarisse Duralde, married Governor William C. C. Claiborne in 1806.[72] Duralde also had close family ties with another family of distinction; his daughter, Julie, married John Clay, brother of the celebrated patriot, Henry Clay;[73] his son, Martin Duralde Jr., married Susan Hart Clay, daughter of Henry Clay.[74] Martin Duralde had a *vacherie* on his Bayou Wikoff property.[75]

At the point where Bayou Wikoff curves westward, on the bayou's north side, was the property of John Clark (Little), claimed originally by Clark by possession and occupancy. The son of Francis Clark of Ireland and Rachel Melon of Maryland, he married Sarah Robert, daughter of Benjamin Robert and Elizabeth Cole. The succession of Sarah Robert

---

69 Deville: *Opelousas,* 97

70 *American State Papers — Public Lands,* Vol. III, 217

71 Ruth Roberston Fontenot genealogy records

72 Arthur: *Old Families of Louisiana,* 147

73 Huey Henry Breaux genealogy records

74 Burns: "Henry Clay Visits New Orleans," *Louisiana Historical Quarterly,* Vol. 27

75 Post: *Cajun Sketches,* 175

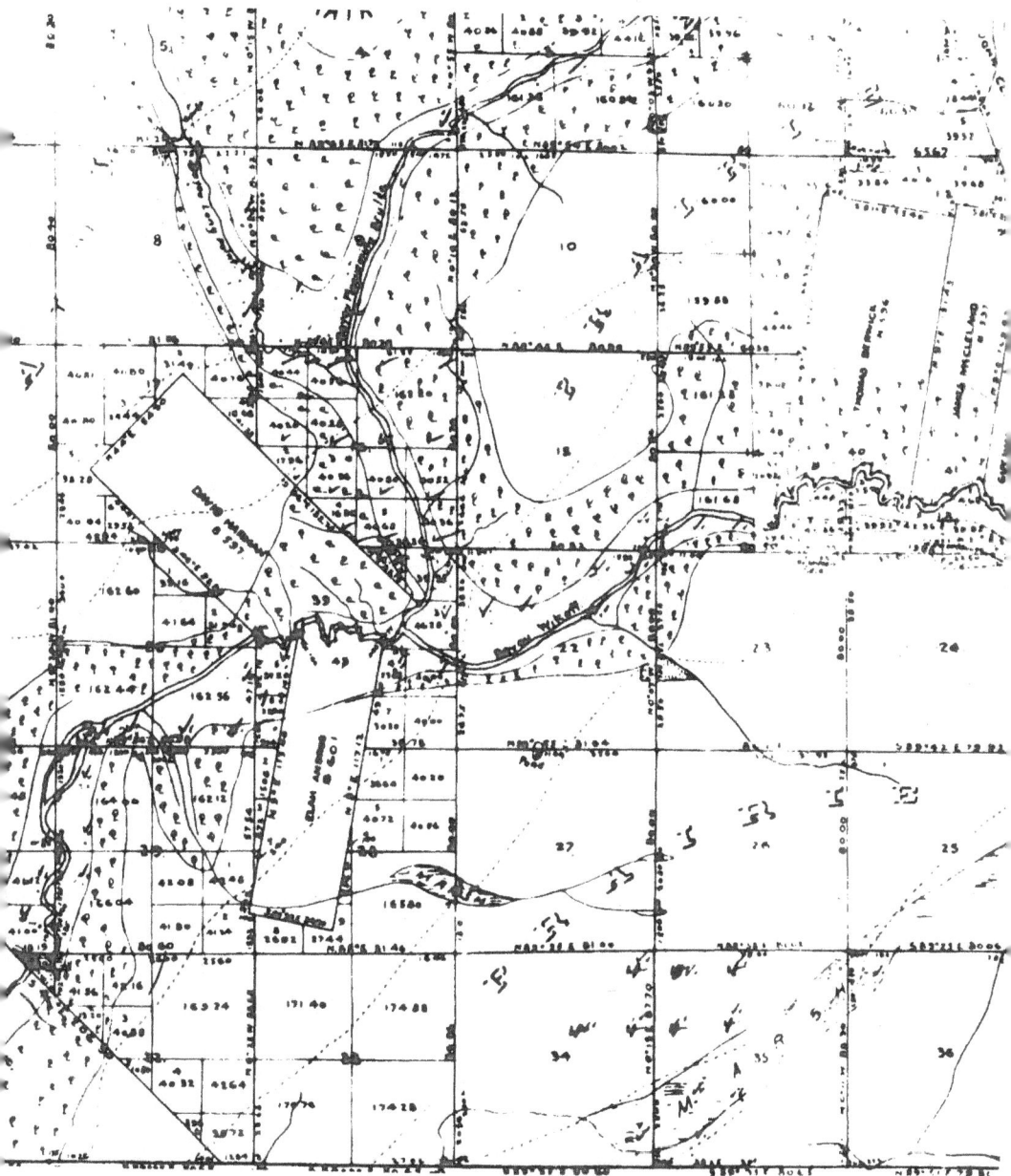

Near the junction of Bayous Plaquemine Brûlée and Wikoff north of Crowley, Spanish land grant claimants were Elah Andrus and David Harmon. At lower left is a portion of the 3,200 arpent tract claimed by Antoine Blanc. At right, fronting on Bayou Plaquemine Brûlée's north side, is land granted to Thomas Berwick. (Official survey plat, T.9S.R.1E, Acadia Parish)

Clark was opened at Opelousas in 1820; the community property was appraised at $500. This John Clark, like his neighbor, John Clark (Turner), evidently used the word "Little" after his name for identification purposes.

The four remaining landowners on the north bank of Bayou Wikoff were Benjamin Penrose Porter, Guy Hamilton Bell, James McClelland and Thomas Berwick.

Benjamin Penrose Porter was attorney for the Opelousas and Attakapas districts, appointed by Governor Claiborne, and was a land agent for the western district of Louisiana.[76] Together with William Darby, an early surveyor for the United States government, he claimed other properties in the district.

Guy Hamilton Bell was clerk and translator at the Opelousas Land Office in 1815. Writing about early leaders of St. Landry Parish, William Henry Perrin relates an anecdote about Guy Hamilton Bell:

"Guy H. Bell was a character, who, perhaps, might also be mentioned with the bar. He came here at a time when he was most needed to hold all the offices. He was justice of the peace, postmaster and a militia officer, and had there been more offices he would probably have had them too. It was in the latter position, perhaps, that he shone most brilliantly. As on training days he got into his gorgeous uniform, with a long red plume in his hat, a sword belted around him like the broadsword of Rhoderick Dhu, and mounted his prancing steed (a broncho pony) that 'snuffed the battle from afar,' then it was he rode in front of his lines with a Napoleonic air, giving his orders in tones that would have put to shame Beauregard or Stonewall Jackson. Ah! these old militia displays had to be seen to be appreciated. But Squire Bell was a fine man. He did a great deal of good and but little harm in the world. He was a Scotchman, warm-hearted, sociable, whole-souled and a very popular man with everybody — could have been elected President of the United States had the vote depended alone on St. Landry Parish."[77]

James McClelland was the original claimant of his land, bounded on the east by the Bell property. He claimed by settlement and 10 years occupancy. McClelland, of Pennsylvania, married Sarah Celeste Andrus.

---

76 Perrin: *Southwest Louisiana, Biographical and Historical,* Part I, 54, 55
77 *Louisiana Territorial Papers, Territorial Papers of the United States,* Vol. IX 662, 741

Thomas Berwick bought his land from James McClelland. The son of Thomas Berwick and Elena Bois, he married Rachel Comstock, daughter of William Comstock and Rachel Edward, at Opelousas in 1795. The officiating priest noted in the marriage record that the Berwicks were Presbyterians, and that the bride's family was "of the United Provinces." Thomas Berwick was an early settler in the Opelousas district where he served as a surveyor for the Spanish government as early as 1784. He later removed to the lower Atchafalaya region and occupied land on the bay that bears his name.[78]

Henry Bideman owned property on the prairie between Bayous Plaquemine Brûlée and Wikoff, about a mile south of Branch. His land claim is not listed in the American State Papers — Public Lands, Volumes II and III along with other early land claims in southwest Louisiana; however, a legend on the official survey plat gives information that his private claim was confirmed by Act of Congress July 6, 1842.

Henry Bideman is listed in the 1810 census of the Opelousas district. His succession was opened in St. Landry in 1851. The property, described as 710 acres situated "in what is called Robert's Cove" together with the buildings and improvements thereon, was auctioned to Gabriel Lyons for $800. The estate included five slaves. Unusual items listed in the inventory were nine gold buttons, which brought $5 at the auction, and 12 silver buttons, which sold for ninety cents. In 1876, 25 years after the succession was opened, Bideman's niece, Elizabeth Spangler Kent of Ohio, through Ferreol Perrodin, attorney for missing heirs, filed a lawsuit to recover $1,116.74 from the State of Louisiana.

Bayou des Cannes

There were only eight colonial landowners along the entire length of Bayou des Cannes, which enters Acadia Parish about four miles west of Eunice and continues in a southerly direction for some 20 miles. Bayou des Cannes merges with Plaquemine Brûlée about a mile and a half north of the town of Mermentau.

Nathaniel Cochran owned two tracts of land on Bayou des Cannes about three miles south of the parish line; the tracts were bounded on three sides by unclaimed land. Original claimants were Thomas Berwick and John Brinton. Nathaniel Cochran married Celeste Prudhomme, daughter of Michel Prudhomme and Marie Snayler at Opelousas in 1804.

---

[78] _____"Southern Louisiana and Southern Alabama in 1819; The Journal of James Leander Cathcart," *Louisiana Historical Quarterly* Vol. 28, 791, 793

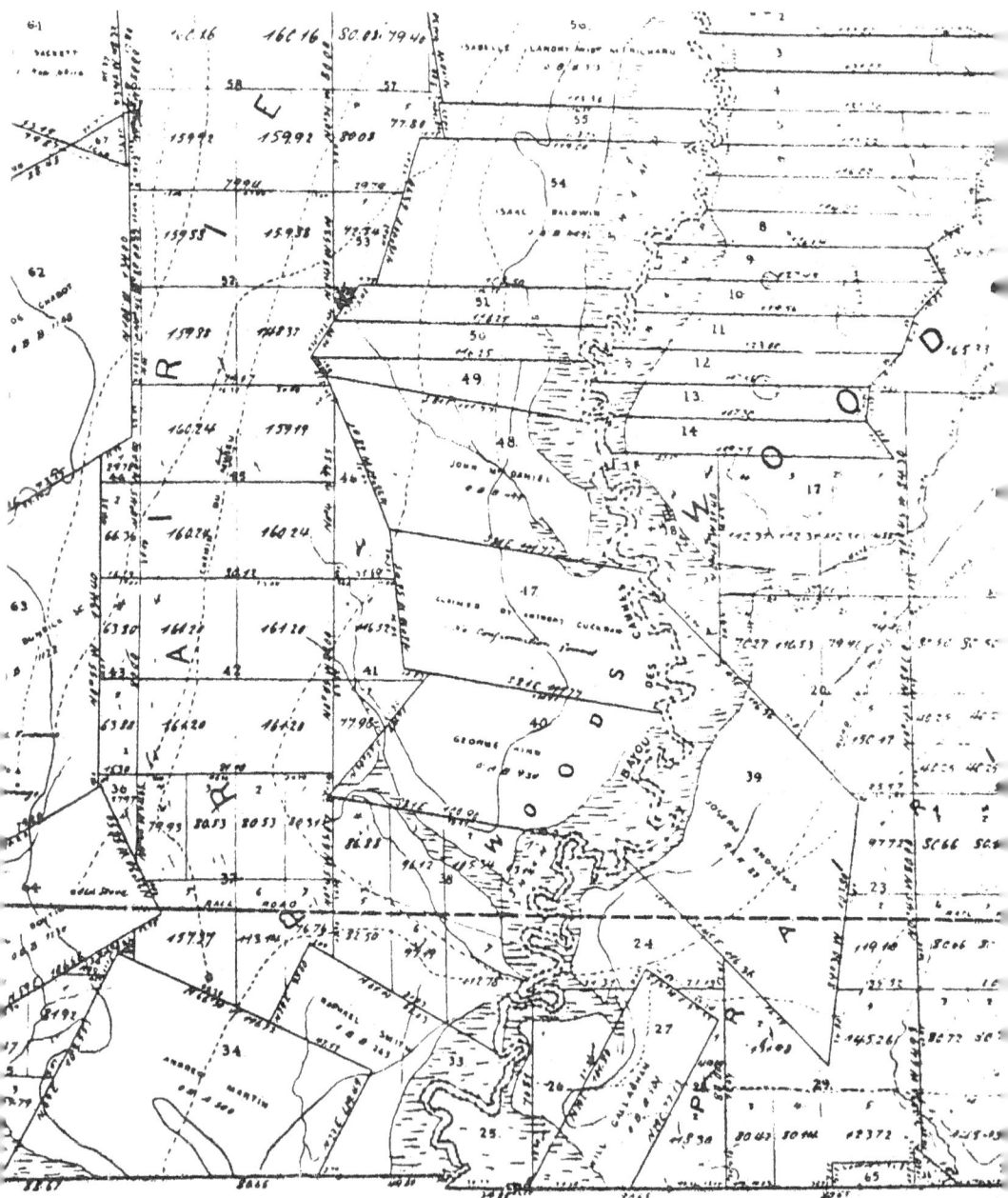

Thirteen persons claimed land under Spanish grant along Bayous des Cannes and Nezpique in Township 9 South Range 2 West. They were Isobel Landry Richard, Isaac Baldwin, John McDaniels, Anthony Cochran, George King. Joseph Andrus, Will Callaghan, Raphael Smith, David Sackett, Claude Chabot, William Bundick, Paul Boutin and Andre Martin.

The officiating priest designated Cochran as "from north of New England, USA."

Nathaniel Martin Cochran, of Scotch-Irish ancestry, was a native of New Boston, N. H. His second wife was Elizabeth Knight, whom he married in 1827 in St. Mary Parish. He died at Franklin in 1838.[79]

Some eight miles south of the Cochran property was land owned by Isobel Landry. Isobel (Spanish for Elizabeth) Landry was the widow of Mathurin Richard. They came to the Opelousas district from St. Gabriel, in Iberville Parish.[80] The 1777 census gives Mathurin's age as 34, his wife's 36. Mathurin was the original owner of the Bayou des Cannes tract.

About a half mile south of the Landry property was a large tract owned by Isaac Baldwin, who acquired the land from Etienne de Lamorandier, the original claimant. Isaac Baldwin is identified as an *avocat*, attorney, in the succession of Jean Baptiste Malveau, opened in 1807. Baldwin married Elizabeth Williams at Opelousas; he died in 1833 at New Orleans.[81] His wife's succession was opened in St. Landry Parish in 1836. The only document in the file is an order from the New Orleans Probate Court for a certified copy of the inventory of the St. Landry property "as her portion of the estate has never been set apart from her husband's and the whole being descended to their only son and heir."

John McDaniel, Anthony Corkran and George King owned adjacent tracts south of the Baldwin property. The McDaniel land was north of the community of Evangeline, the Corkran tract encompassed part of the town and all of the Evangeline Oil Field; George King's land was south of the town.

McDaniel, a native of Ireland, came to Louisiana in 1786. He was first married to Elizabeth Evans; in 1789 he married Catherine Corkran, of Fort Pitt (Pittsburgh), Penn., daughter of Anthony Corkran and Marguerite Watson.[82] Anthony Corkran, witnessing in the McDaniel claim, said that McDaniel kept his stock on the land in 1802 and 1803; that the stock was managed by McDaniel's sons, who lived in the neighborhood. Corkran told the land office commissioners that in 1804 the widow Sloan and her children "went to live on the land for keeping McDaniel's stock."

---

79 Sanders: *Selected Annotated Abstracts of St. Mary Parish, La., Marriage Book I, 1811-1829,* 52
80 Arsenault: *Histoire et Genealogie des Acadiens* Tome 2, 1045
81 Sanders: *St. Mary Parish, La., Successions, 1811-1834*
82 Mrs. A. D. D'Avy genealogy records

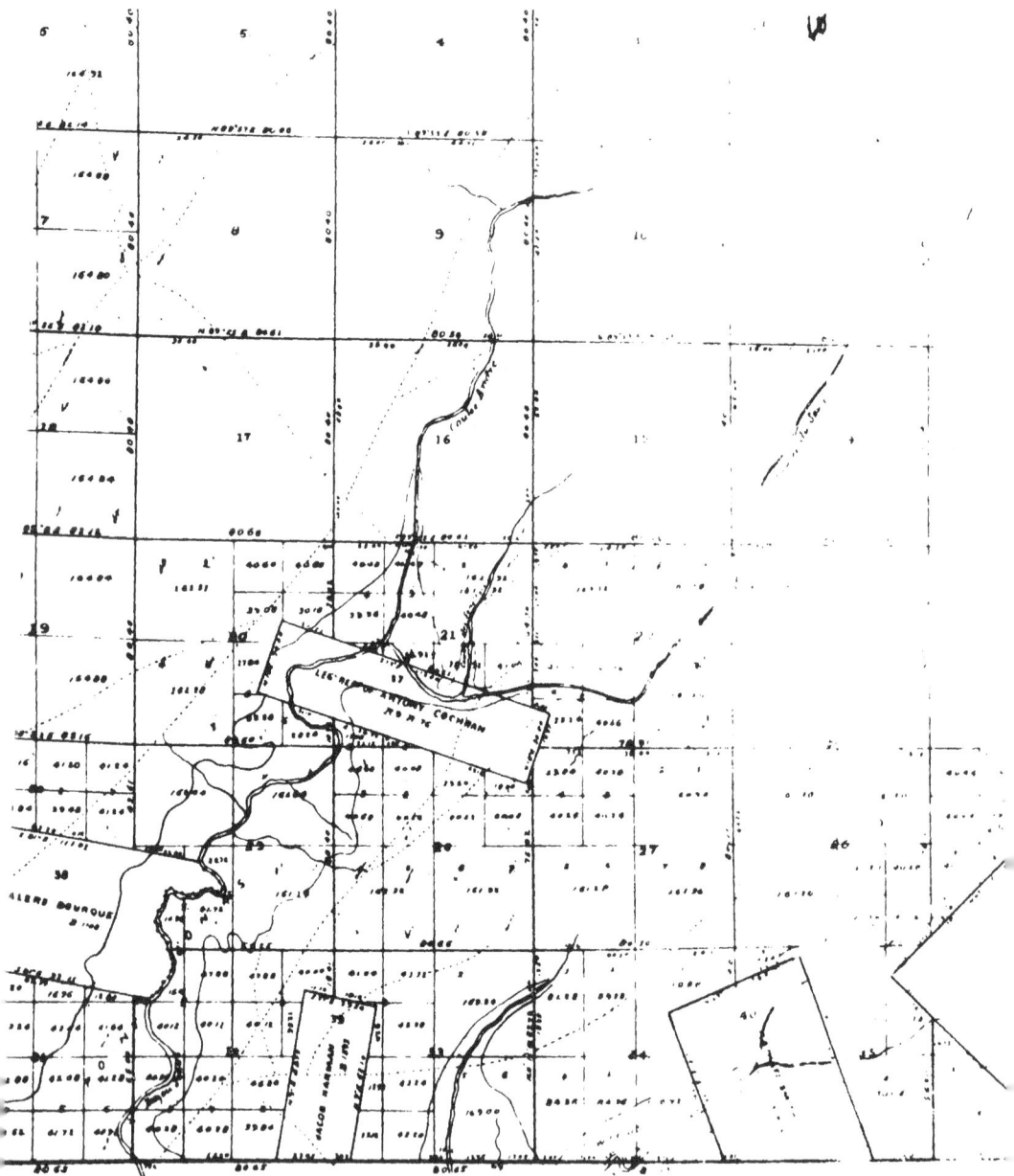

Portion of the rectangle in the right lower corner of this plat of Township 9 South, Range 1 West is part of the Antoine Blanc claim north of Crowley. To the left, fronting on Bayou Jonas near the present community of Egan, are tracts claimed by Valere Bourque and Anthony Cochran. Along the lower line of the plat are portions of tracts owned by Jacob Harmon and Raphael Smith.

Anthony Corkran owned the tract south of the McDaniel land. His land claim on Bayou des Cannes was not confirmed by the United States government until 1897.[83] Corkran was a native of Ireland, the son of John Corkran (Cochran) and Bridget Num; his wife came from Connaught County, Ireland. He was in the Opelousas district as early as 1788, when he occupied land "situated at the cove of the *vacherie* of Sylvain Saunier on the bayou Plaquemine Brule." He sank a well on this property in 1793, and built a house, which later burned.

Anthony Corkran's succession was filed in St. Landry Parish in 1818. The only property listed is a 320-arpent tract located on Bayou Chicot. The heirs named are Catherine, widow of John McDaniel; John McDaniel Jr., John Corkran and Nathaniel West.

Judge George King, previously identified as owning land adjacent to the Louis Louallier tract, had a second piece of property south of the Corkran land. The land was originally claimed by John Lyon, and was described as located "on the branch of Bayou des Cannes." The King property had a wide frontage on Bayou des Cannes, and a small stream flowed through the southwest corner.

Raphael Smith, also previously identified as a Plaquemine Brûlée property owner, owned a tract of 800 arpents with frontage on both Bayous des Cannes and Nezpique. This land, situated above the confluence of the two bayous, was bounded on the north by vacant land.

All of the landowners on Bayou des Cannes except one were situated on the west side of the bayou. The lone landowner on the east bank was Joseph Andrus, whose land was located across the bayou from the Corkran and King holdings, about a half mile north of the William Callaghan tract on Bayou Plaquemine Brûlée. The name of this landowner is given as Andrews on the official township survey plat; it has been established, however, that the name Andrus was often spelled Andrews; that Joseph Andrews is the same person previously identified as a landowner on Bayou Wikoff.[84]

The Andrus land is described as "thirty arpents front by forty arpents deep, on the left bank of bayou Canne, at or near the mouth of bayou Bourbeau." This is obviously an error, either clerical or on the part of

---

83 Official Township Survey Plat, Acadia Parish, TS9R2W
84 Henry Newton Pharr records

the surveyor, as Bayou des Cannes flows nowhere near Bayou Bourbeux,* but rather has its juncture with Bayou Plaquemine Brûlée a little more than a mile before it reaches its confluence with Bayou Nezpique. Joseph Andrus claimed the land in 1791, by requête. John Clarke, testifying at the land office in 1814, said that he had kept a *vacherie* on the land for Andrus for two years, in 1798; after this the stock was removed and the land remained unoccupied.

Two isolated tracts of prairie land, bisected by small streams, were owned by Valere Bourque and Anthony Corkran.

Bourque's land, described as located "on a branch of bayou Plaquemine Brule," fronted on Bayou Jonas and encompassed the present community of Egan. Valere was the son of Joseph Bourque and Suzanne Thibodeaux, exiled Acadians.[85] Anthony Corkran's second tract was about a mile northeast of the Bourque property, on Bayou Jonas.

Bayou Nezpique

Eleven persons owned land along the east bank of Bayou Nezpique, the waterway which divides Acadia and Jefferson Davis Parishes. These tracts were, for the most part, on both sides of the bayou and larger in area than those on other Acadia Parish streams.

Beginning at the St. Landry-Acadia Parish boundary, about three miles down the bayou, was land owned by Antoine Boisdore, one of the early settlers of the Opelousas district. Boisdore, born at Mobile circa 1738, was the son of Joseph Barbo *dit* Boisdore and Marie Louise Brell. He married Francoise Veillon in St. Louis Cathedral in 1762. His father had the title, "Master Tailor for the King."[86]

Information given in this land claim shows that the Boisdore property on Bayou Nezpique was previously owned by Maria de St. Denis, daughter of Louis Antoine Juchereau de St. Denis, founder of Natchitoches, French commandant of the Natchitoches post, 1722-1744, and termed "one of the most romantic figures in Louisiana history."[87] Boisdore bought the land from Maria de St. Denis in 1784. In the deed of sale Maria de St. Denis made "an express reservation . . . of the use of the plantation and houses thereon for one year after the sale."

---

*Bourbeux, sometimes erroneously spelled Bourbeau or Bourbeaux, Bayou Bourbeux means "muddy bayou."

[85] Arsenault: *Histoire et Genealogy des Acadiens,* Tome 2, 1054

[86] Ruth Robertson Fontenot genealogy records

[87] Davis: *Louisiana, A Narrative History,* 41

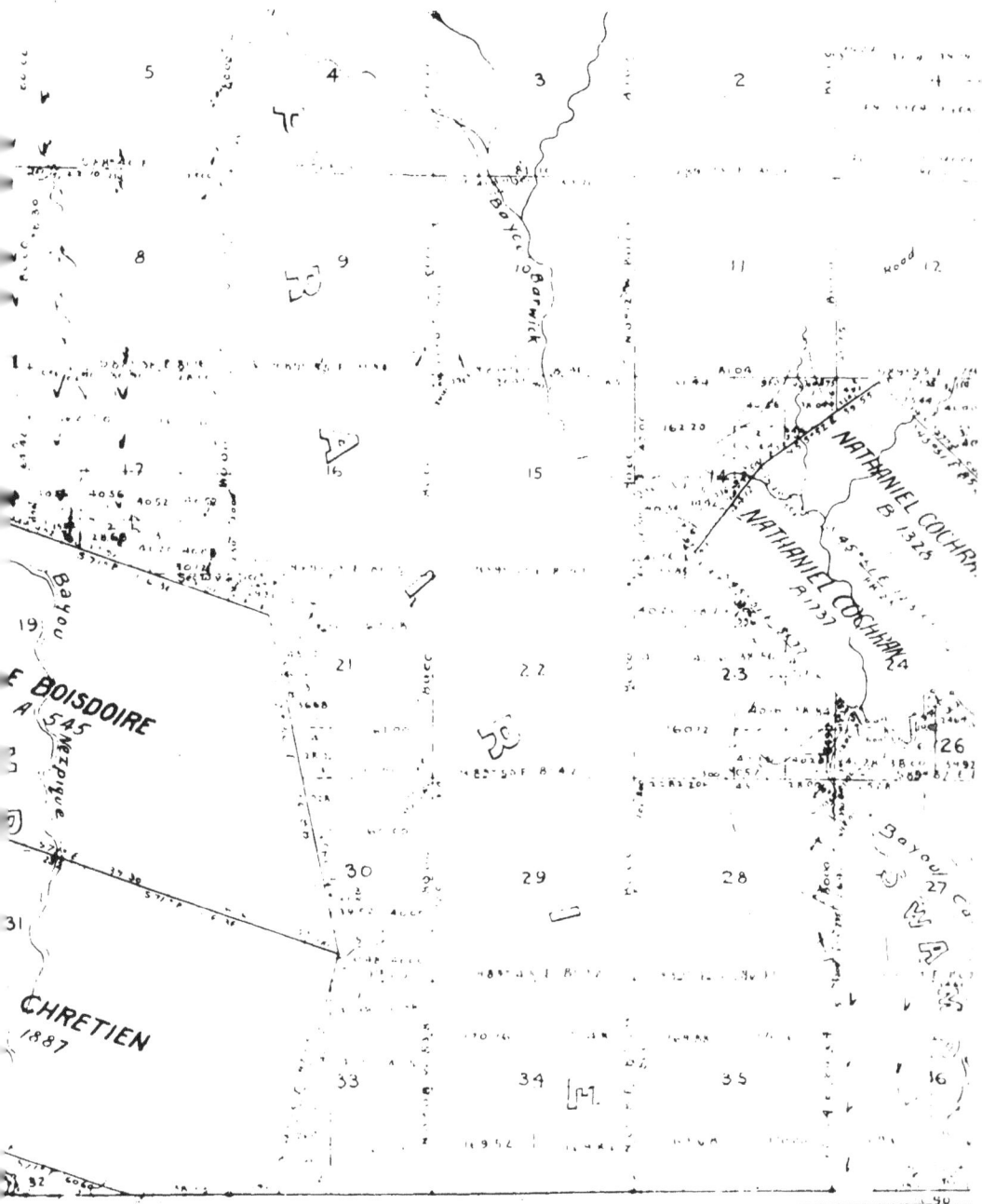

Colonial landowners in the northwest corner of Acadia Parish were Antoine Boisdore and Pierre Chretien, with land on both sides of Bayou Nezpique, and Nathaniel Cochran on Bayou des Cannes. The land area between the two bayous was known as Prairie Mammouth.

South of, and adjacent to, the Boisdore land was a large tract owned by Pierre Chretien. The original claimant was Pierre Lacoste. Pierre Chretien, born circa 1777, was the son of Joseph Chretien, an early settler in the Opelousas district.

John Clay's property, situated south of the Chretien tract, was originally claimed under Spanish patent by Francois Lemelle. John Clay was a brother of Henry Clay; he married Julie Duralde, daughter of Martin Duralde.[88]

The next tract belonged to Joseph Francois Alexandre DeClouet (Declouette). Born in 1716 in the Province of Picardy, France, he entered French military service in 1740. He came to Louisiana in 1758, and 10 years later entered the service of Spain. DeClouet replaced Gabriel Fusilier de la Clair as commandant of the Opelousas district in 1774, a post he held until 1787. He died in 1789, having served Spain and France for almost 50 years in Europe and Louisiana.[89]

Louis Chachere, the progenitor of the large Chachere family, owned a tract south of the DeClouet property. Chachere was the original claimant of the land. Louis Chachere married Catherine Vauchere; they came to the Opelousas post from Natchez prior to 1790. According to family tradition, Chachere was a nobleman of the Bourbon line who came to America to escape the French Revolution.[90]

Celestin Lavergne, also an original claimant on Bayou Nezpique, owned the land south of the Chachere tract. The son of Louis Lavergne and Marie-Anne Lacasse, he married Louise Henry.[91]

Lavergne was evidently a colorful character whose reputation survived him for many years. William Henry Perrin writes: "Celestin La Vergne was a native of France, and was very weathly; he owned a great deal of land, large numbers of slaves, and was an extensive planter. He was eccentric, honest, high toned and popular. He decided, after a residence of many years in St. Landry, to revisit his native France, and spent a week packing and arranging his trunks, which outnumbered those of a modern Saratoga belle. Upon his arrival in the old country, the customs officers in making an examination of his trunks emptied out the contents, and then told him, when satisfied they contained nothing contraband, that

---

88 Huey Henry Breaux genealogy records
89 Deville: *Opelousas*, 77
90 "Some History of St. Landry Parish from the 1690s," 16
91 Hebert: *Southwest Louisiana Records*, 357

he could take them and go on his way. 'No sir,' said he, 'I will not receive them until you replace everything as you found it. You pack them as they were and send them to me _____, Paris,' and he made the customs officers repack them."[92]

Property adjacent to the Lavergne tract was owned by David F. Sackett. Sackett bought the land from Henry Hargroder, the original claimant. Anthony Corkran witnessed in the land claim in 1811; he said that John McDaniel had resided on the land for several years, but had been forced to remove because of "ravages committed by the Indians on the stock and plantation." Corkran added that he himself and several other persons who had settled in the neighborhood "were obliged to remove for the same reason."

Sackett was an associate of George King; the two had a joint land claim at Grand Prairie. Old records at St. Landry Parish courthouse show the sale of this property (originally a Spanish grant to Bartholemy Rozat) by Sackett and King to Ceazer Hanchett. Reuben Sackett of Alexandria was the attorney acting for David Sackett.

Claude Chabot was the original claimant of his land on Bayou Nezpique. Chabot was in the Opelousas district in 1788; that year he was witness to a marriage contract between two Acadians, Claude Aucoin and Marie Brasseux.[93] His succession was filed at Opelousas in 1867. He left a vacant estate; no known heirs. James G. Hays was appointed curator of the estate.

William Bundick Sr. owned land on Nezpique which extended to within a mile of the present community of Evangeline. He was the original claimant. Church records at both Opelousas and St. Martinville show marriages of a William Bundick; it is not certain whether this was the same man, or two different individuals. The earliest record at the Opelousas church is the baptism, in 1780, of Angelique, daughter of William Bundick and Mary Hesse (Hays)

Paul Boutin, the next Nezpique landowner to be considered, was 52 years of age at the time of the 1777 Opelousas census; his wife's name is given as Magdelon Digrist. Of Acadian parentage, Boutin was born at Baltimore. He was the original claimant of the Bayou Nezpique tract, also had a Spanish grant on Bayou Bourbeux.

---

92 Perrin: *Southwest Louisiana, Biographical and Historical*, 34
93 Deville and Vidrine: *Marriage Contracts of the Opelousas Post*, 29

Mermentau River

The land below the Boutin tract was owned by Andre Martin. This property was situated on Bayou Nezpique about a mile north of the town of Mermentau. Martin also owned three riverbank strips about a mile and a half south of Mermentau, on the Mermentau River. His property on the west side of the river, described in Chapter I, was bought from the Attakapas Indians.

The son of Claude Martin and Marie Babin of Attakapas, Andre married Catherine Sonnier, daughter of Silvain Sonnier and Magdalena Bourg at Opelousas in 1795. He also had a Spanish grant on the Vermilion River in the Attakapas district, and held joint ownership with his brother, Marin Martin, to land in the Attakapas.

Andre Martin was one of the first settlers at Vermilionville, later to become the city of Lafayette. Harry Lewis Griffin writes of him: "His pastures were the boundless grass-covered prairies, and he used Indians as herders. Soon his cattle were numbered by the thousands. It was said that he could speak the language of the Indians, was their equal in the chase, and when occasion demanded, dared to slay them. Nor was his good wife less fearless than he in the face of danger from the Indians. On one occasion, it was related her husband lay sick and helpless in bed. An Indian came to their house and demanded taffia (whiskey) which Mrs. Martin refused to give him. Drawing a long knife the savage swore 'by the graves of his fathers' that he would have taffia or kill the sick man who lay there helpless in bed. But the 'pale face squaw' was equal to the occasion, and, grabbing a pestle from a heavy mortar, she struck him such a blow on the head that his skull was crushed and he died instantly."[94]

Besides Andre Martin, there were but five landowners on the Acadia Parish side of the Mermentau River. These were Pierre Bernard and Louis Arceneaux, who owned two tracts jointly; Alexandre and Augustin Nezat, and Joseph C. Piernass.

Bernard and Arceneaux have been previously identified as landowners on lower Bayou Plaquemine Brûlée. The Nezats were brothers, sons of Pierre Nezat and Magdalene Provost (Provot) of Illinois, and were natives of Point Coupee.[95] The father, Pierre, served in the Attakapas

---

[94] Griffin: *Attakapas Country, A History of Lafayette Parish, Louisiana,* 16
[95] Ruth Robertson Fontenot genealogy records

Militia in 1774 and 1777.[96] The Nezat brothers were original claimants of their riverbank strips, by order of survey and settlement.

The 1766 census of Pointe Coupee lists Auguste (Augustin) Nezat as the owner of a *vacherie* at Nementou in 1766. Augustin married Magdalene Barry, daughter of Charles Barry and Magdalene de Cuir, in 1791.[97] Alexandre married Yphamie Roy, daughter of Joseph Roy and Anna Bordelon, in 1803.[98]

The Joseph C. Piernass claim of 6,400 arpents "on each side of the river Nementou" was situated mostly on the west bank; only a small segment, located at a point where Bayou Queue de Tortue empties into the Mermentau, extended into Acadia.

Joseph Chevalier Piernass, a retired lieutenant of infantry for the Spanish government, bought the land from the widow of Louis Pellerin in 1786. Shortly after Piernass obtained the official documents on the land transaction from the commandant of the post, he was involved in a boat accident and lost the valise containing the papers. The Widow Pellerin signed papers which confirmed Piernass' right to the land.

Testimony in the land claim establishes that the Pellerins had a *vacherie* on the land, and that the land was inhabited and cultivated prior to the sale to Piernass. Louis Pellerin was the first commandant of the Opelousas post, appointed in 1763; he was unpopular with the people, and in 1767 the settlers complained to the Spanish governor. He was accused, among other things, of using sacred vessels of the church at his own table.[99]

Chevalier Piernass is best known for his efforts, in 1795, at colonizing the sparsely settled Calcasieu River valley. The project failed, and the area was left vacant for many years.[100]

Bayou Queue de Tortue

Bayou Queue de Tortue forms a natural boundary between Acadia and Vermilion Parish on the south, also marks the dividing line between Acadia and Lafayette Parish on the east.

The Reuben Barrow tract, situated just above the Lafayette-Vermilion Parish line in Acadia Parish, was previously described in Chapter I as property purchased from the Indians. Reuben was the son of Richard

---

[96] Griffin: *Attakapas Country, A History of Lafayette Parish, Louisiana,* 219-224
[97] Ruth Robertson Fontenot genealogy records
[98] Deville and Vidrine, *Marriage Contracts of the Opelousas Post.*
[99] Deville: *Opelousas,* 67-69; Baudier: *The Catholic Church in Louisiana,* 171
[100] Deville: *Opelousas,* 40

Barrow and Maria Godinne. The priest at Opelousas noted in his baptismal record that Reuben's parents were "of North America" and lived " by the bay of Vermilion." Reuben married Maria Johnson, daughter of Daniel Johnson and Susan Daly. His land extended from the bayou front to within a mile of the present community of Ebenezer.

About a mile down the bayou was Benajah Spell's property, which also extended almost to Ebenezer. His land, claimed by settlement, was originally owned by John Dunman. A native of England, Benajah was the son of Sterling Spell; he married Dorethea Foreman of South Carolina. They were parents of eight children. The large Spell family of Louisiana and Texas descended from Benajah.[101]

Benajah Spell's neighbor to the west was Thomas Hoffpauir. Thomas was the original claimant of a tract about a mile southwest of the Spell property, by order of survey and settlement. Peter Stouts, testifying before the board of commissioners in 1813, said that Thomas had begun improving the land about 1800, and had moved his family there. About 1809 he left for four years, but the land remained "occupied for his benefit." Thomas moved back onto the land shortly after the first of the year of 1813.

Southwest of, and adjacent to, the Thomas Hoffpauir land were two tracts belonging jointly to Thomas Hoffpauir Jr. and Francois Hoffpauir, sons of Thomas Hoffpauir and Marie Charlotte Perillard. The Hoffpauir brothers settled on the land in 1786. Thomas Jr. married Julie Foreman.

About four miles farther west was property owned by Benjamin Winfree (Winfrey, Winfrie). He was the original claimant, by settlement. A native of Georgia, Benjamin Winfree was married to Anne Freeland (Freland, Fralon) "of Cumberland in USA" at Opelousas in 1810.

Francois Stelly's land west of the Winfree tract was acquired by purchase from the Indians (Chapter I). Stelly married Marie Louise Berthelot, daughter of Louis Berthelot and Louise Fontenot.

Adjacent to the Stelly tract was the John Coleman property, which Coleman bought from the Indians (Chapter I). The son of Santiago Coleman and Marie Boyard, Coleman married Rebecca Holstem, daughter of Esteban Holstem, in 1787.

The John Lyon property, also bought from the Indians and previously described in Chapter I, was situated about three miles southeast

---

101 Judge Carrol L. Spell genealogy records

of the present community of Morse. The son of Samuel Lyon of Germany, he married Nancy Ahart about 1760.[102] An Acadia Parish settlement, Lyon's Point, and a stream, Lyon's Point Gully, bear the name of this family.

Leufroy Latiolais, previously identified as a landowner on upper Bayou Plaquemine Brûlée, had a tract of land on Bayou Queue de Tortue about four miles west of the Lyon property. He was the original claimant, by order of survey.

The final land claim on Bayou Queue de Tortue, adjacent to the Latiolais land, belonged to Michel Leger. The original claimants were Louis and Joseph Latiolais. Michel was the son of Michel Leger and Angelica Pinet, and brother of Louis Leger. He married Marguerite Louise Boutin, daughter of Paul Boutin and Ursula Guidry, in 1787.[103] Michel Leger settled "in the Prairie Grand Coteau" in 1796, on land he bought from Paul Boutin.

From the foregoing it will be seen that Acadia's landowners during the Spanish colonial period included many persons of note: three commandants of the Opelousas post, land office officials, widely known public figures and politicians, heroes of poetry and prose.

More importantly, many of the landowners were also settlers who lived on their lands in the wilderness. These were the real pioneers of Acadia Parish; despite the hazards and hardships of frontier life they endured; they lived and loved, increased and multiplied. They bred a new generation — a first generation of American citizens.

---

102 Sybil Parrott Andrus genealogy records
103 Thelma Pierrel genealogy records

67

CHAPTER III

Some Place Names, Frontier Life

The official township plats and the American State Papers — Public Lands are sources of information on old (and in many cases, long-forgotten) names of streams and land areas of Acadia Parish.

An area in the northeast corner of the parish (west of the Pitreville community) was at one time known as "Prairie Cottereau" or "Point Cataro." These place names occur in the description of Joseph Armand's land claim.[1] Bayou Mallet, which flows through this area, was once called Bayou Catar. The Francois Rozas land claim is described as being situated on the left bank of Bayou Catar; the description further states that the Rozas property was bounded by land of Michel Prudhomme and Joseph Armand,[2] which establishes the waterway as Bayou Mallet. The name of this bayou is spelled three ways in the American State Papers: Mallet, Malette and Maltete, this last possibly a contraction of the French *mal de tête,* or headache. The bayou name appears on the official survey plats as Mallet.

There are several references to "the prairie Faquetaique" in descriptions of land claims in the Acadia Parish area. William Johnson's land claim, just south of Eunice, and the Michel Carrier properties on Bayou Mallet's north side were described as situated in Prairie Faquetaique.[3] This land area lies between Bayous Mallet and des Cannes in the northern section of Acadia Parish and extends across the boundary into St. Landry. The word Faquetaique is a derivative from the Choctaw *fakit tek,* turkey hen.[4]

Coulée Blaise Lejeune, a tributary of Bayou Plaquemine Brûlée, bears the name of a colonial landowner of Acadia Parish. Another tributary of Plaquemine Brûlée is Bideman Gully, named for Henry Bideman. Just north of Rayne is Coulée Duralde, a tributary of Bayou Wikoff, which bisects the Martin Duralde land grant.

Two tributaries of Bayou des Cannes are named for colonial landowners. Bayou Barwick flows into Bayou des Cannes through land originally owned by Thomas Berwick and was undoubtedly named for

---

1 *ASP* III, 815, 851
2 *Ibid,* 183
3 *ASP* II, 807, 834
4 Read: *Louisiana-French,* 107

Bayou Mallet was once known as Bayou Catar. This 1801 map of the Francois Rozas Spanish land grant identifies the stream as "Bayou Cataro." The original map and accompanying document is owned by Claire Gomer Anding.

Berwick. Coulée Richard, unnamed on the official survey plat but identified on modern maps as Richard Gully, flows through the Louis and Fabien Richard land grants.[5]

A small stream, a tributary of Bayou Mallet, appears on the official survey plat as *Coulée de la Pointe* à *Marcelle.* This stream flowed through the tract of land owned by La Rouille. Two other small streams, located between Mowata and Maxie, fed into Long Point Gully, which in turn empties into Bayou Plaquemine Brûlée north of Crowley. These streams appear on the official plats as *Coulée de la Pointe de Lynch* and *Coulée de la Pointe des Marrons.* The origin of these names, which no longer appear on maps,[6] is obscure. The names Marcelle and Lynch could have been derived from names of persons; the word *marron* has several meanings in French, one of which is "fugitive slave." *Coulée de la Pointe des Marrons* flowed through the land claimed by Joseph Giron Mallet, *fils.*

South and east of Iota is *Coulée Pointe aux Loups,* a tributary of Bayou des Cannes. West of Iota another stream is identified on the official survey plat as "Branch of Coulée Pointe au Loup." The word *loup* means wolf in French.

Nezpique, the name of the bayou which forms the western boundary of Acadia Parish, is a combination of two French words, *nez,* for nose, and *piqué,* meaning pricked, or scarred.

Jonas Bayou, a tributary of lower Plaquemine Brûlée, is identified in the American State Papers as "a branch of bayou Plaquemine Brule."[7] Bayou Jonas has three small tributaries with interesting old names: *Coulée André, Coulée de Senelier* and *Coulée de Saule.*[8] André is French for the name Andrew; "Senelier" is believed to be a corruption of *cenellier,* French for haw tree; and *saule* means willow. *Coulée André* and *Coulée de Saule* are identified on modern maps; *Coulée de Senelier* no longer appears.[9]

Names of Bayous des Cannes and Plaquemine Brûlée are descriptive of flora native to the region. The first is French for "bayou of canes," and the second means "burnt persimmon." William Read says the word *plaquemine,* meaning the fruit of the persimmon tree, came into Louisiana-

---

5 T7SR1W, U. S. Geological Survey, Basile Quadrangle
6 U. S. Geological Survey, Eunice Quadrangle
7 *ASP* III, 179
8 T9SR1W, Official Survey Plat, Acadia Parish
9 U. S. Geological Survey, Eunice Quadrangle

French through the Mobilian dialect from Illinois *piakimin*.[10] The word *brulé* (feminine *brulée*) was used by French settlers to describe an area which had been burnt over for clearing.[11]

A tributary of Bayou Plaquemine Brûlée was called Cole's Bayou. This stream entered the larger waterway through the James Cole land claim; the land area was known in early days as Cole's Cove.[12] The area was also called Prairie Soileau. In 1825, when the succession of Solomon Cole was opened, Judge George King stated that he had gone to the *vacherie* of Solomon Cole "in Prairie Soileau" to make an inventory of the estate.

Bayou Wikoff was known by other names prior to 1798, the year that William Wikoff received his Spanish land patent. Descriptions of land claims along this waterway identify it as "a branch of Plaquemine Brule" and "Buller's Bayou."[13] It is understandable that this watercourse would, in time, come to be known as Bayou Wikoff. About three miles of the bayou bisected Wikoff's immense square of land east of Branch; this landowner was both wealthy and influential. William Darby called him Col. William Wikoff, and labeled him "the most wealthy stock-holder in the United States."[14] Wikoff had connections with high ranking Spanish officials; after the change of government he was named to several important posts: Dr. John Watkins, acting for Governor Claiborne in 1804, appointed Wikoff commandant of the district "opposite Baton Rouge, from Plaquemine to Fausse Riviere." Dr. Watkins described Wikoff as "a gentleman well known to Your Excellency, a native of the United States, and remarkable for his attachment to its government."[15] Wikoff was appointed St. Landry treasurer and auctioneer in 1805, and was a member of the Legislative Council.[16]

Bayou Blanc, a tributary of Bayou Plaquemine Brûlée south of Crowley, was at one time known as Bayou Miers. This is shown on an early survey plat of the township in the St. Landry Parish courthouse.[17]

---

[10] Read: *Louisiana-French*, 103

[11] Guidry: *La Pointe de l'Eglise*, 8

[12] *ASP* III, 106

[13] *Ibid*, 186

[14] Darby: *A Geographical Description of the State of Louisiana and the Southern Part of Mississippi and the Territory of Alabama*, 147

[15] Robinson: *Louisiana Under the Rule of Spain, France and the United States, 1785-1807*, Vol. 2, 346

[16] *Louisiana Territorial Papers*, Vol. IX, 291, 601

[17] T9SR3E, old survey plat book, St. Landry Parish

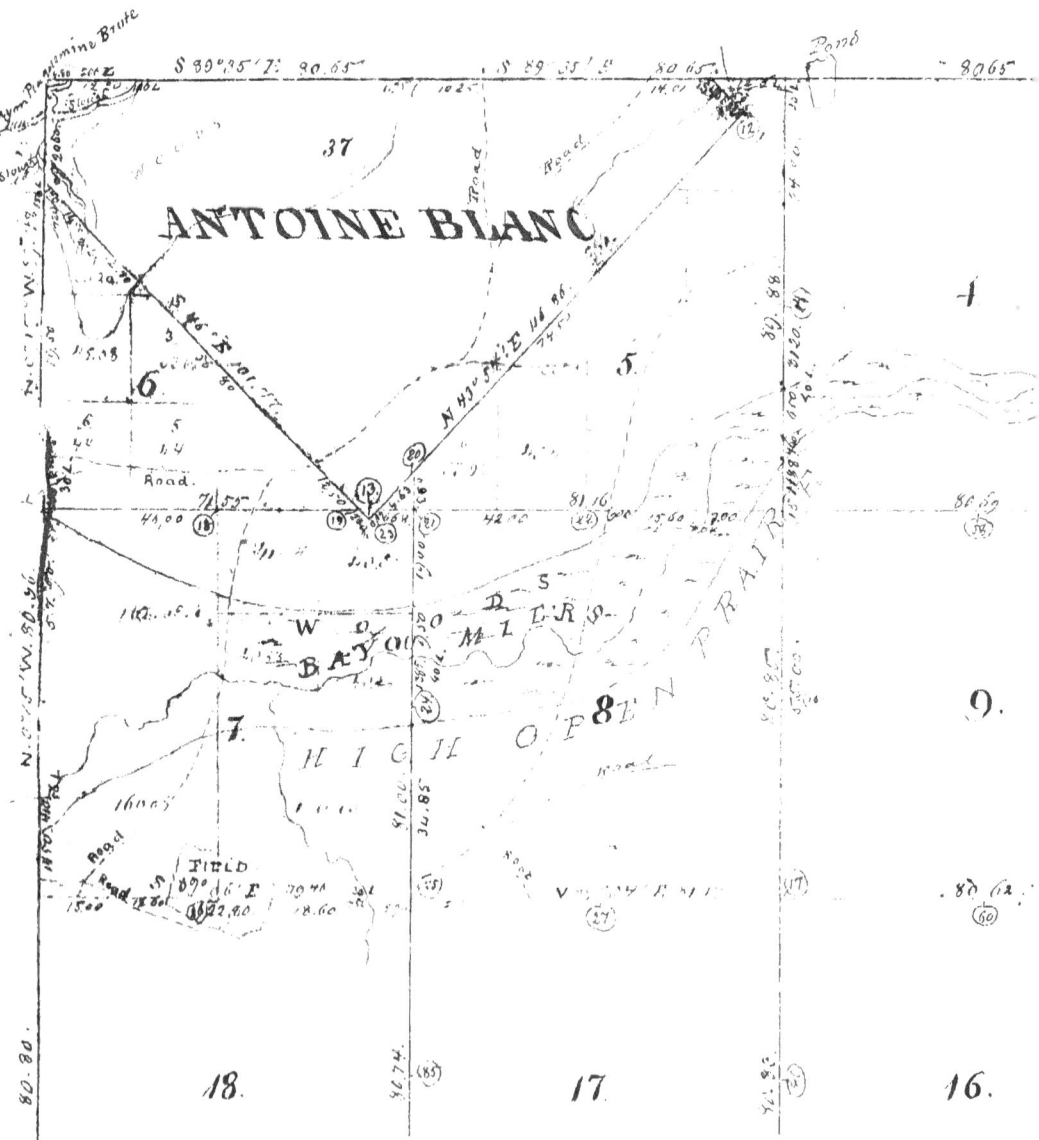

Bayou Blanc, a tributary of Bayou Plaquemine Brûlée which runs south and west of Crowley, was once known as Bayou Miers. James Miers, who came to the area about 1820, is believed to have been the first settler on the stream. (Old survey plat, St. Landry Parish).

72

The newer name may have stemmed from the large Antoine Blanc land tract just north of the stream.

Another old survey plat in the St. Landry courthouse labels the area east of Rayne as "very level open prairie." Samuel Johnson, deputy surveyor, surveyed the township in May, 1807. This plat, and others of the prairie regions, shows dozens of marshy areas and ponds, characteristic features of the southwest Louisiana prairies which led to the cultivation of rice.

It is generally accepted that the name of the Mermentau River is derived from Nementou, a chief of the Attakapas Indians. The American State Papers identify the river as the Nementou or Nementau; these spellings also appear on plats of townships surveyed as late as 1885, and in legal documents. The present spelling is attributed to clerical error in transscribing handwritten reports.

Meander lines on the official survey plats show that all except one of the main waterways of Acadia Parish were navigable, or navigable in part, at least in the legal sense. (Robin described southwest Louisiana streams as being clogged and obstructed with tree trunks and debris; he says that such had to be navigated like a canal, by poling, and that navigation was "subject to expensive portages at certain times of the year.")[18] Bayou Queue de Tortue, named for Celestin la Tortue, an Attakapas chief,[19] is the only one of the parish's seven major streams which shows no meander lines. Why this should be is a matter for speculation, as it is reasonable to assume that this waterway was at least navigable in part during high water. Also, there is reason to believe that the bayou was navigable in the early days, at least for some 10 miles from its confluence with the Mermentau River. This belief comes from a documented incident that happened in 1819, involving John Lyon, a colonial landowner on Bayou Queue de Tortue, and the notorious pirate, Jean Lafitte:

On the night of September 27, 1819, a band of armed men, with their faces blackened, forcibly entered the plantation home of John Lyon, tied up Lyon, his wife and children and threatened to take their lives if they resisted. The men spoke English, and pretended to be officers of the government.

---

[18] Robin: *Voyage to Louisiana, 1803-1805* (Landry trans.) 191
[19] Read: *Louisiana-French,* 179

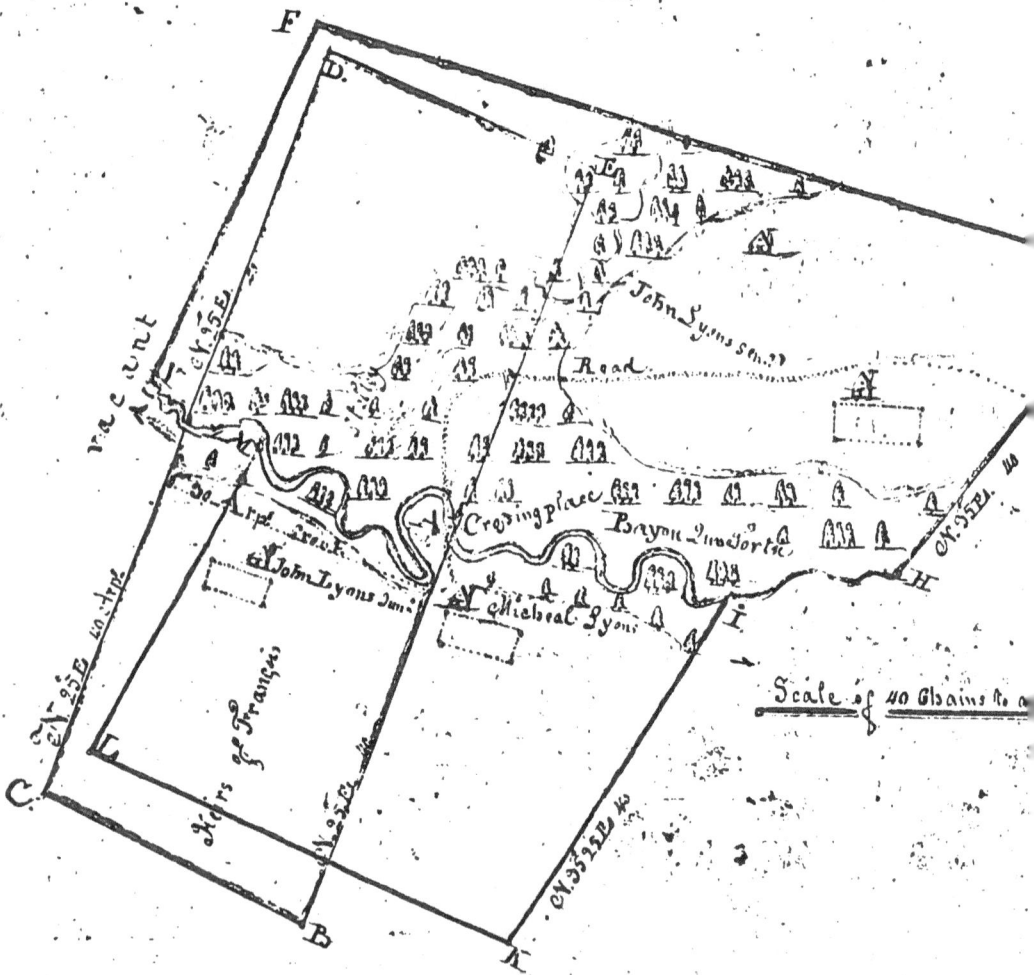

Western District   State of Louisiana

The location of the John Lyons, Sr. residence in 1819 is shown on this survey plat by William Johnson, deputy surveyor. This reproduction, from the original in the Louisiana State Archives, is by courtesy of Margery Johnson Lyons, a descendant of both John Lyons and William Johnson.

The intruders ransacked the house and carried off the linen and wearing apparel of the family, together with the slaves, some of whom were raped on the spot while the rest of the bandits were pillaging the house.

Ten slaves were taken. These included a 25-year-old woman named Flora, said to be "near the time of.lying in;" Jack, about 50; two 12-year-old boys, and six girls, of ages ranging from 4 to 11.

Lyon's son, John Lyon Jr., offered a $500 reward for the recovery of the slaves and also a reward for the detention and conviction of the robbers.

News of the crime reached Captain J. H. Madison, commander of a United States schooner, the Lynx, patrolling Gulf waters for pirate vessels. At this time Jean Lafitte and his band of pirates were headquartered at Galveston. The Navy vessel pursued the robbers to Galveston, and Lt. James M. McIntosh was sent ashore to demand that the criminals be turned over to the United States for punishment.

The officer was received courteously by Lafitte, who said that the robbers had acted under no authority from him. Lafitte promised to deliver the culprits to the authorities, which he did — with the exception of the leader, a man named George Brown.

"Tell your commander," said Lafitte, "I found the principal of this gang so old an offender, and so very bad a man, that I have saved the trouble of taking him to the United States. I hung him myself."

As the Lynx sailed away, the officers saw Brown's body swinging from a gallows.[20]

One account of this incident relates that "Brown led his band of men on a slave-stealing foray into the interior of Louisiana, going up Bayou Queue de Tortue until they reached the plantation home of John Lyon."[21] The assumption therefore is that the pirates came up the bayou in a boat (or boats) large enough to accommodate the pirate crew plus the stolen booty and the 10 slaves.

Specific information about that part of old St. Landry that was later to become Acadia Parish is virtually non-existent. Published material about southwest Louisiana during the first half of the 19th century deals with the region in general, and is of little practical use in this work.

---

[20] Summary, from Arthur: *Jean Laffite, Gentlemen Rover*, 189; Saxon: *Lafitte the Pirate*, 233-236
[21] Arthur: *Jean Laffite, Gentlemen Rover*, 189

Columns of early newspapers were given mostly to advertisements and news of faraway places, with scant attention to items of local interest.

One source of information is the minutes of the early meetings of the St. Landry Police Jury, the governing body of the parish. The development of this unique form of local government began in 1804, when Louisiana was divided into 12 counties, one of which was the County of Opelousas. The counties proved too large for satisfactory administration, and in 1806 the state was divided into 19 parishes which were based for the most part on the boundaries of 21 Roman Catholic ecclesiastical parishes established in 1762. Thus the parish became the local government district.

Government of the 19 parishes was at first along lines established for the counties wherein county judges served as chief governing officers. A revised form of government for the parishes was established in 1807. This act provided for a 12-member jury to serve with the parish judge and the justice of the peace, both the latter being appointive officials. The body was charged with the responsibility for "execution of whatever concerns the interior and local police and administration of the parish."

Three years later, in 1810, legislation was adopted creating the office of sheriff for each parish and providing that he should be paid from the "police assembly of the parish." On April 30, 1811, the state adopted an act making members of the police assembly elective and designating this body officially as a "police jury." Powers of the judges were reduced and justices of the peace made ex officio members. Later legislation provided for wards within parishes and for election of members from wards to serve on the police juries.

Records of the St. Landry Police Jury begin July 16, 1811. Minutes, written in both English and French, disclose that the first order of business was to order the immediate construction of a jail, to be built adjoining the "old prison." The old prison, where debtors were to be confined, was ordered repaired. The new jail was to be used for the incarceration of criminals.

Another important matter of business was the building of roads and bridges. A tax on property, slaves, cattle and horses was levied for financing road and bridge construction; job contracts were to be given to the lowest bidders after the bids were advertised, this to be accomplished by the town crier making the announcement at the church door on three consecutive Sundays.

Minutes of subsequent meetings show the police jurors continuing to give attention to the construction of roads and bridges, pointing up the need for providing better routes for overland travel.

Colonial landowners and/or settlers of Acadia Parish who served on the police jury during the period 1811-1818 were Joseph Andrus, Louis Louallier, Pierre Chretien, Jacob Harman, James McClelland, Michel Carrier, Celestin Lavergne, Raphael Smith, John Clark (Little), Bosman Hayes, Solomon Cole and Elah Andrus.

In April of 1812 the police jury named 13 parish directors, whose main duties involved the policing of cattle and horses and the curbing of livestock thefts. Among the appointees were Elah Andrus, Michel Prudhomme and Michel Carrier.

In 1813 the police jury encouraged the destruction of wolves; persons offering proof of having killed a wolf could collect a bounty of $2.

On July 26, 1813, the police jury convened "for the purpose of laying out and dividing said parish into suitable wards and districts for the election of police jurors." The parish was divided into six districts, each to be represented by two police jurors; the boundaries of the districts were determined by the boundaries of "the six militia companies."

At the August, 1813 meeting Joseph Elah Andrus was named director of a project to build two bridges "on the main branch of Plaquemine Brulee." Two other bridges, "over the eastern branch of said bayou" were to be supervised by John McClelland. The directors were instructed "like wise to make the necessary roads to said bridges." All male residents of the parish, white and black, between 16 and 50, were obliged to work on the roads and keep the parish roads in repair, or find substitutes to do the work. The police jury specified that each man was to work not more than six days per year.

The jury also adopted a resolution that the inhabitants "of the bayou Mallet" be authorized and required to make a bridge over the bayou, and to cut a road to the bridge "at the most convenient place between Coulon Villier's and Michel Prudhomme." All persons residing within one league (three miles) of the bridge on both sides of the bayou were obliged to work on the bridge. The work was directed by Michel Carrier.

Centers of population of the large parish are indicated by the election procedures of 1814. In June of that year the police jury divided the parish into three districts, "in each of which the Judge of Elections shall attend one day to take the votes; that is to say, the election shall be held the first day at Andrew Weaver's in the Grand Prairie; the second day at John Clark's (Little) at Plaquemine, and the third day at the courthouse."

The police jury undertook the responsibility of caring for insane persons and indigents. At the July 11, 1814 meeting John Bihm presented an account against the parish for $28.50 for services rendered an insane person, and a committee was named to make arrangements for the support, on behalf of the parish, "for an old man, an invalid." The jury, however, did not accept all claims concerning paupers. In May, 1818, Edmund Johnson presented a bill for $20 incurred in burying an insolvent citizen, George Tanner. The jurors recommended that Johnson's bill be rejected, as Tanner had for a number of years been in Johnson's employ, and there was no proof of pauperism.

At the July meeting in 1814 the police jury ordered that "all taxes due on billiard tables and taverns shall be recovered in a summary manner by the treasurer." Also adopted was a resolution regulating the sale of cattle for slaughter, requiring that "every person who keeps a public butchering shall take from those persons he purchased cattle of a bill of sale in writing." The butcher was obliged to keep the bill of sale for at least three months after the cattle were killed, and the hides were to be "always subject and liable to be viewed and inspected by any Director of Police or public officer at the house of the butcher and also at the tánners or wherever."

The first sheriff of St. Landry Parish, Cornelius Voorhies, was taken to task by the police jury in 1814 for failure to provide bond. The minutes of the November meeting record that Sheriff Voorhies had had two delays granted him; that he had not appeared to offer security and had failed to comply with the requirements of the law in the matter. Therefore the jury ordered that the governor be informed of the situation. The assessor presented the tax list for the year, explaining that the list had been ready, but "there was no collector to deliver it to."

During these early years it appeared to be difficult to get a quorum for police jury meetings. No meetings were held from Nov. 7, 1814, to May, 1815. Again the jury was unable to get a quorum from September, 1815 to June, 1816, when the members were summoned by Judge George King. According to law members absent without cause were fined $2.

The bilingual treatment of police jury minutes was discontinued after 1816. After this year minutes were recorded in English only. However, alternate pages in the minute book were left blank, leading to the assumption that the intention was to continue the record in the two languages. A note in the minutes of August 4, 1818 states that the resolutions of the meeting, presented by Guy H. Bell, were "read and explained to the French members."

Police jury members incurred strongly worded censure from the parish grand jury in 1816. The grand jury, composed of John D. Schmith, Dennis McDaniel, Joel West, Green Hudspeth, Joseph Elah Andrus, Pierre Courville, Leufroy Latiolais, Jean Baptiste Stelly, Joseph Savoy, Simon Marks, Andre Neraut, Francois Richard, Etienne Daigle, Jean Baptiste Castille and Daniel Zeringue, ordered the police jury to write the charge into the minutes of the September meeting.

Terming themselves "good and lawful men, sworn and empanelled" the grand jurors stated that "the present situation of the bridges and roads present a great grievance to the public" and that the situation was fraught with "evils which loudly call for redress . . . discouraging of every improvement in the parish calculated to increase the convenience of the inhabitants."

The grand jurors held that "nothing is better calculated . . . (than) good roads, bridges over watercourses, so as to render them passable at all times;" that repairing of old bridges and building new ones would be "productive of greatest benefit." These public works, added to a strict attention of the situation of the roads, "must enhance the value of property, render easy the land carriage of the planter for the product of his plantation."

The grand jury charge spurred the police jury into action; members assembled five times during a two-month period that fall. Three of the many road and bridge-building projects initiated concerned areas within the future parish of Acadia. Francois Coulon de Villier, Michel Prudhomme *fils,* and Baptiste Lejeune were appointed to choose a suitable place, between the land of Michel Prudhomme and Jacob Bihm, to build a bridge over Bayou Mallet and "to call out the inhabitants of the quarter to build said bridge." A two-member committee, consisting of Jacob Harman and Joseph Elah Andrus, was named to oversee the building of a bridge over Bayou Plaquemine Brûlée, and a bridge to be built farther up the same bayou was the responsibility of Lufroy Latiolais, Jean Blaise Lejeune and Bonaventure Martin.

The year 1819 found the police jury again having difficulty in getting a meeting quorum. There are no minutes from January 4, 1819 to Oc-

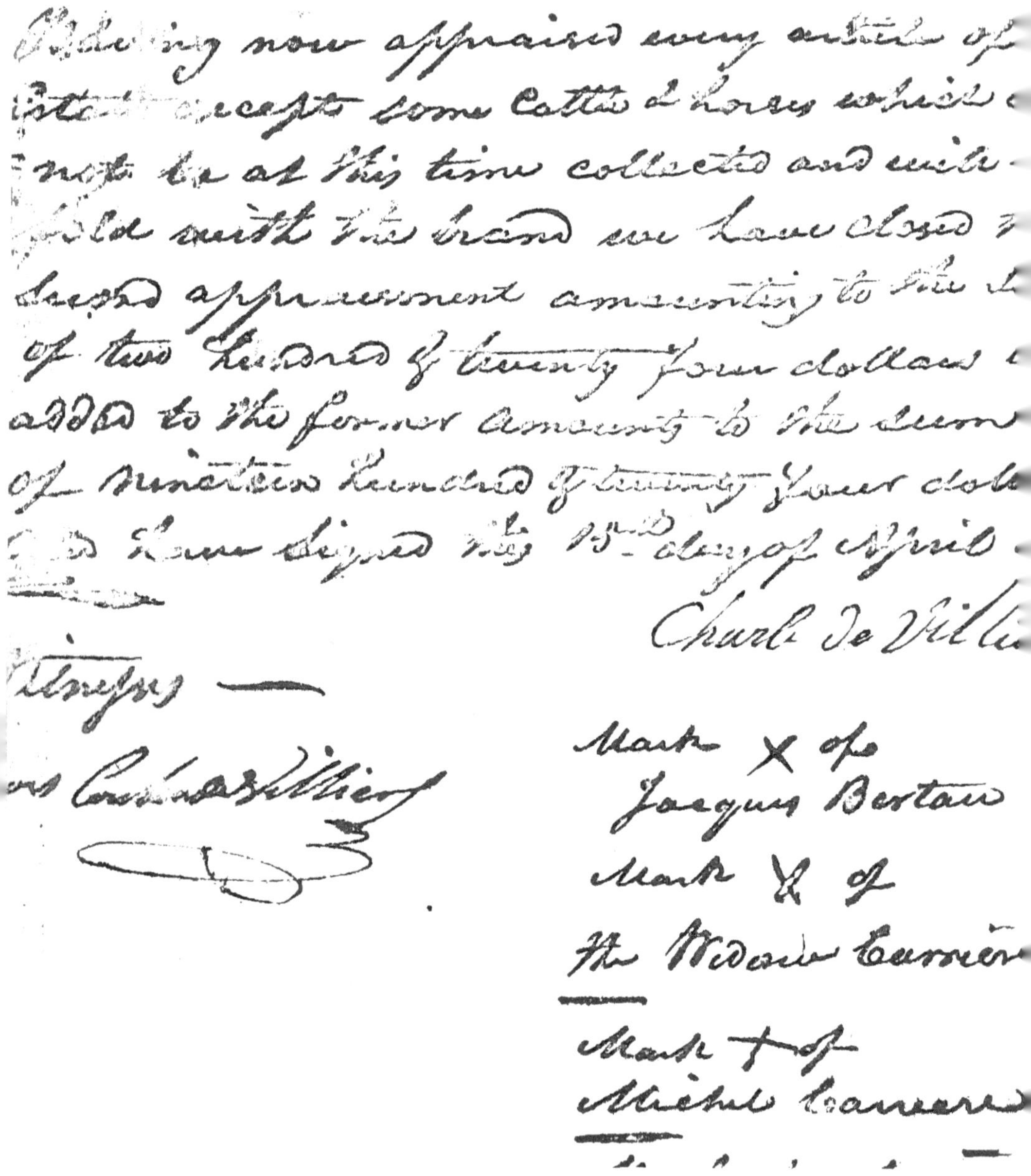

...now appraised every article of...except some cattle & horses which...not be at this time collected and will...sold with the brand we have closed the...appraisement amounting to the sum of two hundred & twenty four dollars... added to the former amounts to the sum of nineteen hundred & twenty four doll... have signed this 15th day of April...

Charls De Villi...

Witnesses —

...Charles De Villiers

Mark X of
Jacques Bertau

Mark X of
The Widow Carrier

Mark + of
Michel Carriere

The appraisers of the estate of Michel Carriere in 1816 noted that they had appraisd every article of the estate "except some cattle and horses which cannot be at this time collected. . ." The Carriere property was on Bayou Mallet about three miles northwest of the present community of Richard. Excerpt, Michel Carriere succession, No. 76, 1816, St. Landry Parish.

tober 4 of that year, when the clerk, Guy H. Bell, recorded: "This being the day appointed by law for the meeting of the police jury, no person appeared but William Haslett."

There is a gap of more than 42 years, from August 4, 1819, to November 8, 1862, in the police jury minutes. The missing records may have been burnt in a fire which destroyed the St. Landry Parish court-house in 1886, when many valuable documents and records were lost.

Cattle raising was the principal agricultural activity of Acadia's early settlers. This is shown by the numerous references to *vacheries* in the American State Papers, also in succession records.

Farmers with sizable herds seldom knew how many cattle they owned; many estate inventories list "an unknown quantity of horned cattle." Animals, except those kept for domestic use, were branded and allowed to roam at large on the prairies.[22] The inventory of the Michel Carrier estate, opened in 1816, lists "horses and horned cattle of unknown quantity and quality, being in their winter range."

Farm implements and agricultural tools appear in practically all of the early estate inventories. These included plows, harrows, hoes, spades, scythes; crosscut saws, whip saws, hand saws, augers, tongue-and-groove, pincers, grindstones and griding mills, wheelbarrows, axes and adzes, and hammers.

One type of plow, called a "fluke," appears in many inventories. The word is sometimes spelled "flouque" or "flouke." This name for a handmade sodbuster type farm implement is still in use among south Louisiana's farm people.[23] Michel Carrier owned a "fluke;" Cyprien Arceneaux's succession lists two "flouques."

Large quantities of cotton and corn, sometimes entire crops, appear in estate inventories of the period 1807-1840. The Joseph Andrus (Mary Hays succession) cotton crop was valued at $1,974 and the corn crop at $630 when the estate was inventoried in 1817.

For fencing, the early farmer used *pieux,* split cypress rails pointed at each end. The rails were held by vertical cypress posts; pointed ends of the rails were fitted into properly spaced holes cut into the posts.[24] The

---

22 Post: *Cajun Sketches,* 42
23 Oral History Harry Frame, Ourelie Landry, Dr. Thomas J. Arceneaux, 1974
24 Post: *Cajun Sketches,* 82; Robin: *Voyage to Louisiana,* 1803-1805, 124

First. A negro woman named Celia aged about ... y

+ two hundred dollars ... 11

2nd. A grey horse appraised at twelve dollars.

3rd. Forty nine volumes of books appraised at five dollars

4th. A lot of ... and hair ... appraised at two
dollars —

5th. A writing desk appraised at two dollars —

6th. A case of bottles appraised at six dollars —

7th. Six pair of pantaloons appraised at four dollars

8th. Four shirts appraised at one dollar —

9th. One pen knife appraised at fifty cents —

10th. One small trunk appraised at two dollars —

11th. Two violins appraised at one dollar each —

12th. Six cloth coats appraised together at twelve
dollars —

13th. One overcoat appraised at six dollars —

14th. Three vests appraised at one dollar —

15th. One pair scissors appraised at two dollars

A case of bottles was appraised at $6, three times as much as two violins, in the inventory of the estate of Jean Louis Antoine Cart. The Cart succession, opened in St. Landry Parish in 1833, shows that Cart owned one slave, whose value was appraised at $200.

John Lyon Sr. succession, opened in 1834, lists "old pieux appraised at two dollars per hundred," and 215 cypress *pieux* appraised at $4 per hundred.

Estate inventories also reflect the life styles of the settlers. These frontier farmers, even the wealthier ones, owned few luxury items. Musical instruments, clocks, jewelry and such appear in few of the inventories; Francois Rozas had a violin, Jean Louis Cart owned two violins, plus a "musical box." Henry Bideman's estate included gold and silver buttons. Cart's 49 books were indeed unusual items; few persons of that time owned books because only a handful could read and write. This is shown in old court and church records, where most signatures were executed with an "x."

Mirrors, called "looking glasses" in the succession records, were also rare items. Bottles and demijohns were hard to come by, therefore were prized possessions. Only one of the many successions examined lists alcoholic beverages: Father Louis Buhot's estate included two barrels of porter (a weak, sweet stout containing about four percent alcohol), a barrel of whiskey and a demijohn of claret.

Most households had at least one spinning wheel. The Patrick Gurnetts owned two spinning wheels, the Joseph Andrus inventory shows "spinning wheel, cards and loom," valued at $25. Other common household items were feather mattresses, pillows, *paillasse,* a pallet bed or straw mattress*; *armoires,* chairs, tables, bedsteads, crockery, pots and pans, bed linens, churns, salting tubs, candle molds, soap pots and irons.

Conspicuous by their absence from the estate inventories of Acadia's early settlers are boats and watercraft. Only one of the more than 50 successions examined lists a skiff, pirogue, or any other kind of boat. It is strange that these bayou-front landowners had no boats; or, if they had (and it seems reasonable to suppose that they did), why such items were not listed in estate inventories, some of which were itemized in great detail. Even if overland travel was more in use than water transportation, it would seem that ownership of some type of boat would be a practical necessity, certainly for those who owned property on both sides of a bayou.

Oxcarts were common items; few persons owned horse-drawn vehicles. A few inventories list a *caleche,* a two-wheeled vehicle drawn by one

---

* This definition of *paillasse* is from Cassell's *New French Dictionary.* The Acadian definition of *paillasse* is a mattress tick stuffed with dried corn shucks; a broomstick or wooden paddle was inserted through slits in the sides of the mattress to fluff up the shucks.

30th A table appraised at one dollar — — — — 1

31st A looking glass appraised at fifty cents — — ,,

32d Two spinning wheels appraised at four
dollars each — — — — — — — — 8

33d A lot of Coopers ware appraised at five
dollars — — — — — — — — — 5

34th A lot of Pots appraised at five dollars — — 5

35th A Loom appraised at four dollars — — 4

$ 1031

There being no other property belonging to the
Estate we have closed this Inventory amounting to
the sum of one thousand and thirty one dollars a
cents and have hereunto signed with the appraisers
in presence of the undersigned Witness the day &
year above written — — — — — — — —

                                        Asa Foreman

Witness —   Isaac Foreman

Geo. R. King   Joseph Foreman

                                        Thomas Hoff

Valentine King   Ephraim Hoff

The Francois Hoffpauir succession, opened in St. Landry Parish in 1831,
is one of the few from that period where all persons connected with the
inventory of the estate signed their names instead of marking with an
"X". Appraisers who signed this document were Asa Foreman, Isaac
Foreman, Joseph Foreman, Thomas Hoffpauir and Ephraim Hoffpauir.

horse, or a carriage. The Giles Higginbotham estate, opened in 1858, shows a four-wheel carriage; Joseph Andrus had a four-wheel carriage valued at $100; the John Lyon Sr. estate inventory shows "an old caleche."

Virtually all estate inventories show ownership of firearms, usually shotguns or *fusils,* a type of musket. Guns were a necessity, for security and an adequate food supply.

There were some advantages to prairie settling. The land needed no clearing. As Robin wrote: "The prairie land . . . awaits only the plow and the spade. The landowner may easily house himself. It takes only a few days to build a cabin. It takes only a few morning's work to place this prodigious land into production sufficiently to support a family."[25]

Wild game was abundant on the prairies. Robin reported the prairies well stocked with game, "and especially during the winter they are covered with ducks and geese, so the inhabitant has his choice of birds as if they were in his own poultry yard."[26] More than three quarters of a century after Robin's visit the editor of the Courier offered editorial comment on game: "Wild geese, sandhill cranes and robins are flying over . . . [27] jacksnipe are worth 75¢ a dozen, large ducks, 12½ to 15¢ each[28] ducks are so abundant in the market that mallards sold at 10 cents and teals at 4 cents. This is cheaper and better than buying beef or pork."[29] Quail and *papabottes** were also plentiful. In the Courier of August 20, 1887 the editor wrote: "Papabottes are very fat now. The birds are wild, however, and not so abundant as in former years. This is owing to the prairies being nearly all wired in for pasture and the grass being too high for the birds to feed on. The papabotte wants short grass to ramble in."

The soft feathers plucked from the wild game and domestic fowl made warm mattresses and soft pillows for the settler and his family. Another native product was put to good use: Spanish moss, used from earliest colonial times for pillows and mattresses and woven into braids for bridles, saddles, blankets and horse collars.[30] The moss, which drapes and beautifies several species of Louisiana trees, was available to all for the picking. The moss was picked from the trees, stacked in piles and

---

* *papabotte:* the papabot, Louisiana upland plover

25 Robin: *Voyage to Louisiana,* 186

26 *Ibid*

27 *Opelousas Courier,* Nov. 6, 1886

28 *Ibid* Dec. 4, 1886

29 *Ibid* Dec. 11, 1886

30 *Louisiana, a Guide to the State,* 621

soaked in water until the gray outer coating rotted away, exposing the fine black fiber in the center. It was then hung out on fences or clothes lines to dry.[31]

The prairirie dweller needed shade. For this he planted several varieties of common trees: oak, catalpa and chinaberry[32] The chinaberry was the most popular shade tree because of its rapid growth. Introduced from Asia by way of Haiti[33] the chinaberry formed an umbrella of shade for both people and animals during the summer months. In spring the chinaberry puts out clusters of lilac colored flowers, and was called *lilas parasol,* lilac parasol, by the Acadians. After the blooms fall the seeds form perfectly round green berries somewhat smaller than marbles. These made fine ammunition for small boys to use in their popguns made of elderberry or *roseau** canes. The chinaberry seed were also used for beads and bracelets. The fleshy part of the seed could be boiled off, or allowed to rot away, exposing the attractively shaped hard centers, which could then be dyed and strung into necklaces and bracelets.

Some of the medical and home supplies available to the pioneers were advertised in the Opelousas Courier several times during 1858. Listed for sale was one lot of Hungarian leeches; quinine, brandy, London porter, syrup of iodide of iron, hair dye, patent lye of saponifier; manaju, claimed to be "first rate as a preventative against lockjaw;" hydroclise and bed pans.

Market reports, giving prices for products in demand, began to be a regular feature of the Courier in the 1880s. The issue of March 10, 1883 lists the following: cotton seed, $7 per ton; gray moss, 1¢ per pound; mixed moss, 1½¢; black moss, 2¢. Green hides brought 5 to 5½ ¢ per pound; green salted, 6 to 6½; dry salted, 9½ to 10; grubby or damaged green hides, 2¢ less per pound; damaged dry hides, ½ off. Dry hides had to be perfectly dry, and the green salted hides well drained. Clean, clear wool brought 18 to 19¢ per pound; burry wool, 10¢. Beeswax brought 18 to 19½¢ per pound, tallow, 5 to 5½, and bones, $6 a ton.

Whatever the advantages, these were far outweighed by the disadvantages, especially for the Acadia Parish settler. Frontier life was rugged

---

* *roseau:* common reed-grass

31 *Ibid*
32 Post: *Cajun Sketches,* 180
33 *Ibid,* 181

and hazardous; as was noted in Chapter II, John McDaniel and others were forced to leave land on Bayou Nezpique "because of ravages committed by the Indians on the stock and the plantation." The John Lyon family was victimized by bandits; wolves and other wild beasts preyed on farm animals. Travel, by oxcart over rough and rutted trails, was slow and difficult and was undertaken only at times of dire necessity or emergency. The Acadia Parish settler lived virtually in isolation, depending almost entirely on his own resources.

CHAPTER IV

Early Post Offices 1832 - 1900

The records of the appointments of postmasters in the National Archives show that five post offices were established in the Acadia Parish area prior to the Civil War, the earliest dating back to 1832.*

The official record gives the names of the post offices, the postmasters and the dates of their appointments; the dates of discontinuance and re-establishment, if such were done; also the new name and date when the name of a post office was changed. The locations of post offices are not given, except by county and state. In cases where place names have changed or no longer exist additional research is necessary in order to determine the approximate locations of early post offices.

The first post office to be established in what is now Acadia Parish was at Cole's Settlement. Joseph T. Calligan (or Colligan) was appointed postmaster on December 6, 1832. Colligan served until October 3, 1833, when Solomon Bonds was appointed postmaster. The post office was discontinued March 1, 1836, then re-established January 24, 1838 with Abraham Cole as postmaster. The Cole's Settlement post office was terminated November 18, 1840.

The conjecture is that the Cole's Settlement post office was located on the Spanish land grant claimed by Solomon Cole, some five miles north northeast of Crowley. There is strong evidence to support this: Abraham Cole was the son of Solomon Cole.[1] In addition, the official record gives the names of the persons who gave bond for the Cole's Settlement post office; these were Samuel E. Bell, John T. Heath, William Foreman and J. Simmons. Both Foreman and Simmons were married to daughters of Solomon Cole.[2]

A post office was established at Plaquemine Brûlée May 11, 1838, with John Cook as postmaster. The post office was discontinued March 1, 1842, then re-established September 23 of that year with Joseph Clark as postmaster. The name of the post office was changed to Branch November 12, 1890. Early postmasters (1844-1900) included Jesse B.

---

* All information in this chapter pertaining to post offices, unless otherwise noted, is from records of the Post Office Department, National Archives and Record Service.

1 Hebert: *Southwest Louisiana Records,* Vol. II, 204
2 *Ibid*

Clark, Orasamus Hayes, Joseph E. Andrus, Dallas B. Hayes, George J. Rose, Colbert W. Foreman, Edmund L. Harmon and Edgar Barousse.

The Mermentau post office was established September 2, 1857. Early postmasters were William Cottrell, John O. Wright, Jules Castel, William Wallis, Hilaire Desessarts, John A. Rowell, Jules Castel, Jean Castex and Victorin Maignaud.

The Coulee Blanc post office was established September 17, 1857, with James Miers as postmaster. The post office was discontinued February 28, 1859. The location of this post office is believed to have been approximately two miles southwest of Crowley, on or near Bayou Blanc, where James Miers settled during the 1820s.[3]

A post office was established at Poupeville August 5, 1858, with Octave P. Bonin the first postmaster. D. Bernard, John H. Huffpower and Mrs. Scholastie Sittig served as postmasters. The post office was discontinued January 24, 1870 then re-established October 24, 1878 with Joseph D. Bernard as postmaster. The name of the post office was changed to Rayne May 21, 1881. Other early postmasters (1883-1905) were Nicholas Young, Alphonse Duclos, C. Poulet, Michael D. Coleman, Blaise A. Chappuis, Romanta T. Hart, Charles W. Lyman.

The Prudhomme City post office was established April 15, 1873. Postmasters, in the order of their appointments, were Spotswood H. Sanders, Theodore C. Chachere, Etienne Stagg, Raymond Chachere. The post office was discontinued July 6, 1894.

The settlement of Faquetaique had a post office for six months in 1873. Joseph Chenier was appointed postmaster May 5, 1873; Joseph Fabacher was postmaster June 18, 1873, the post office was discontinued December 15, 1873. The record shows Faquetaigue with a post office established February 17, 1880, Edward Dardeau postmaster, discontinued November 18, 1880. The first Faquetaique post office is believed to have been in the Acadian Parish area since Joseph Fabacher purchased land in lower Faquetaique prairie in 1871. The second post office at Faquetaique is in a separate entry in the record; the location could have been anywhere within the large land area known as Prairie Faquetaique.

The Fabacher post office was established June 11, 1873, with Joseph Fabacher postmaster. Other postmasters were Zenon Huber, Joseph Kopps and Calvin Heath. The last date on this entry is April 16, 1891, when Zenon Huber was appointed postmaster a second time. The record does not give a date for discontinuance or change of name.

---

[3]*Crowley Signal,* Aug. 25, 1888

89

The Cartville post office, established February 6, 1884 with the appointment of Samuel Cart, postmaster, was changed to Iota May 1, 1900. Other early postmasters were Savinien Cart, Louis Cart and Adolph Baumann.

The post office at Church Point was established September 29, 1873 with Jules David as postmaster. Other postmasters (to 1900) were Charles A. Perrodin, P. L. Guidry, Laurent Barousse and Emile Daigle.

A post office was established at Crowleyville on February 26, 1887 with J. Frankel postmaster. The name of the post office was changed to Crowley on May 14, 1887. Other postmasters (to 1900) were J. A. Williams, Dallas B. Hayes, Frank C. Labit.

Joseph Roy was first postmaster at Estherwood, appointed May 3, 1881. Other postmasters who served prior to 1900 were Eugene D. Roy, Sam H. Goldberg, Dupre LeBlanc, Mary A. Coles, Thomas E. Lewis, J. J. Aulds.

Evangeline's first postmaster, appointed April 21, 1887, was Andrew D. Tomlinson. Other early postmasters were Miles T. Tomlinson, Mrs. Susan G. Hines, Arthur Latrielle, Elizabeth E. Trubshaw.

Between 1887 and 1900 a total of 13 new post offices were established in Acadia Parish. Most of these were discontinued prior to 1900.

Millerville, on Bayou Nezpique about six miles west of Iota, had a post office for eight years. Dennis Miller was appointed first postmaster on May 18, 1887. Other postmasters were Leon Viterbo, Mrs. Hannah O. Beals, Walter S. Cocke, John D. David, Mary P. Figueron. The name of the post office was changed to Lodi November 5, 1890, then discontinued December 14, 1895. Another post office, called Miller, was established February 16, 1892 with Isaac G. Jarvis postmaster, the name was changed to Millerville August 26, 1892.

The Schamber post office, established April 4, 1888 with Louis F. Schamber postmaster, had its name changed to Basile January 16, 1889. Frank E. Garrould was second postmaster. This post office, in the northwest part of Acadia Parish, was later moved to what is now Evangeline Parish.

Another post office established in the same general area was named Genois, for Rene Genois the postmaster, appointed May 20, 1896. William S. Case was the second postmaster. Julia Redlich was appointed postmistress August 27, 1897, and the name of the post office was changed to Redlich January 20, 1903.

The appointments of 11 early postmasters of Acadia Parish are shown on this segment of a page reproduced from records in the National Archives.

The Egan area had three post offices between 1888 and 1900. The first was called Regan, for the first postmaster John Regan, appointed June 15, 1888. Thomas D. Schrock served as postmaster from June 1890 to February 10, 1891 when the post office was discontinued. A post office named Canal was established August 30, 1890 with Joseph H. Fabacher as postmaster; the post office was discontinued July 19, 1892 and the mail sent to Crowley. The third post office, named Abbott, was established December 3, 1900 with Joseph Rose postmaster. The name was changed to Egan August 11, 1903.

A post office by the name of Redtop was in operation for approximately three years. James R. McMillan was appointed postmaster August 25, 1891. Louis McMillan was postmaster when the post office was discontinued June 8, 1894 and the mail sent to Crowley.

The post office at Ebenezer, established September 11, 1891, was in operation almost 29 years. The post office was discontinued January 31, 1920. Only two postmasters served: Charles W. Faulk and Haughton Faulk.

Whitehouse was the name of a post office established January 11, 1893 with Anna B. Jarvis as postmistress. The post office was discontinued July 21, 1904 and the mail sent to Evangeline. Whitehouse was located in Mamou Prairie, on Bayou des Cannes near the Acadia-St. Landry boundary.[4]

The Thrailkill post office, established July 13, 1888, was given the name of the first postmaster, William F. Thrailkill. David B. Dobbs succeeded Thrailkill as postmaster, then on August 2, 1895 the name of the post office was changed to Coe. Louis F. Tully and Frank E. Robinson served as postmaster at Coe. The post office was discontinued April 30, 1914. The Thrailkill — Coe post offices were located in Prairie Hayes, at or near what is now known as the Richard community.

The Echo post office, established August 20, 1890, had Henry A. Abney as first postmaster. Other postmasters were Avery Tobey and James E. Andrus. The Echo post office was discontinued February 29, 1892 and the mail sent to Crowley.

John Frey was postmaster when the Santo post office was established August 16, 1895. He was succeeded, in 1896, by Frank H. Klein. The name of the post office was later changed to Gassler, then to Frey.

[4]*Crowley Signal,* February 23, 1895

The Lorna post office was established April 30, 1898, with M. Belle Gault as postmistress. The name of the post office was changed to Morse March 24, 1900.

The Star post office, with Lyman L. Clark as postmaster, was established May 10, 1899. Rupert V. Sloane was second postmaster. The name was changed to Maxie March 4, 1908.

CHAPTER V

Plaquemine Brûlée

The first settlement of any consequence in the Acadia Parish area was Plaquemine Brûlée. It was at Plaquemine Brûlée that the first seeds of the new parish were sown; here also was the first manifestation of Acadia's dual heritage of Anglo-Acadian culture which distinguishes the parish to this day.

As was brought out in previous chapters, land holdings were once identified in legal records by the name of the nearest waterway. Therefore all lands located along the length of Bayou Plaquemine Brûlée were described as "situated on Bayou Plaquemine Brulee." By the same token, all settlers along the length of the bayou were said to be "of Plaquemine Brulee." These generalities, expedient to the times, have led to confusion and misconceptions concerning the specific location of this settlement and other early communities.

After another area on the bayou became sufficiently populated to warrant a voting precinct, the first Plaquemine Brûlée settlement was designated Lower Plaquemine Brûlée, to distinguish it from the newer settlement some seven miles to the northeast. This new settlement (Church Point) was called Upper Plaquemine Brûlée.[1] After Church Point became established as a place name the first settlement was known simply as Plaquemine Brûlée.

Earliest reference to the settlement is in the St. Landry Parish Police Jury minutes of August 4, 1818, when Jacob Harmon was named overseer for constructing a road "from the village (Opelousas) to Plaquemine Brulee." Jacob Harmon was the son of Jacob Harmon Sr. and Hannah Guice, who had settled in the area in the 1780s;[2] his neighbors were the families of Andrus, Hayes, Clark and Lyons, all of Anglo-Saxon ancestry, and a sprinkling of Acadians.

Many of the early settlers of Plaquemine Brûlée were Protestant. This is shown in the marriage records of St. Landry Catholic Church of Opelousas, the only religious institution in the district at the time. Despite the fact that many of the settlers were married and had their children bap-

---

1 *Opelousas Courier*, Dec. 11, 1852
2 Guidry: *La Pointe de l'Eglise*, 74

tized in the Roman Catholic rite, from its earliest days Plaquemine Brûlée was considered a predominantly Protestant community.

The settlement was probably visited by a Methodist missionary as early as 1805. Rev. Elisha Bowman was assigned to the district that year. Reporting on his first visit, Rev. Bowman said that when he reached the Catholic church in the Opelousas district he was "surprised to see a pair of race paths at the church door." He found a few Americans, "swearing with every breath." When he reproved them, they said the priest swore as hard as they did, and that he (the priest) played cards and danced with them every Sunday after Mass.[3]

About 20 miles from the village of Opelousas Rev. Bowman found a settlement of Americans who "didn't know more about salvation than untaught Indians."[4] This place was probably Plaquemine Brûlée, said to be the oldest American settlement in south Louisiana.[5]

Rev. Daniel Devinne, another early Methodist circuit rider, came to the district in 1820. "We built a church in Plaquemine Brulee," Devinne wrote in his autobiography, "the first Protestant edifice in the beautiful country of the Opelousas."[6] This was also the first church established in what is now Acadia Parish, pre-dating the missionary ministrations of the Jesuit priests, who began work in the area in 1837.

In his autobiography Devinne described the church at Plaquemine Brûlée:

"It was about twenty-four by thirty-six feet, and on the Spanish model, roof largely projecting, and walls of wattle plaster, white-washed on both sides; the outer walls of which gave the church, at a distance, a very fine appearance."[7] The "wattle plaster" was no doubt *bousillage,* or mud-and-moss construction, in common use at the time.

The church building may have been under construction even before Devinne arrived. The deed to the church property is recorded in the St. Landry Parish courthouse, dated November 18, 1819.[8] The indenture was made between Joseph Elah Andrus and trustees of the church, wherein Andrus agreed to sell them a square acre of land for $50.

---

3 Jones: *A Complete History of Methodism in the Mississippi Conference,* 150-151

4 *Ibid*

5 *Crowley Signal,* Aug. 25, 1888

6 *Crowley Daily Signal,* 50th Anniv. Ed., 1899-1949, 24-25

7 *Ibid,* 25

8 Conveyance Book E-I, p.175-176, St. Landry Parish

...ame ℒamorandier fils (Seal) — Witnesses — James Ray — *...eng...*
...aw — Geo. King Judge.

...s Indenture made this eighteenth day of November in the Year of *o...*
...usand eight hundred and nineteen between Joseph Elah Andru*s*
... Saint Landry in the State of Louisiana of the one part, and *be...*
...min Palmer, Nehemiah Parrish, Joseph Forman, Thomas Owen*s...*
...rish of Saint Landry, John Dunwoody of the Parish of Rapide*s...*
...son of the Parish of Saint Mary, all the said parties being of *t...*
...na of the other part Witnesseth, that the said Joseph Elah Andru*s...*
...sideration of the sum of fifty dollars to him in hand paid, at *the...*
...ling and delivery of these presents, the receipt whereof is hereby *...*
...th given, granted, bargained, sold, released, Confirmed, and Co*n...*
...se presents doth give, grant, bargain, sell, release, confirm ana *...*
...m the said (Seth Lewis, Benjamin Palmer, Nehemiah Parrish, *...*
...an Thomas Owens, John Dunwoody Rufus Nicholson and their *...*
...trust for the uses and purposes herein after mentioned and decla*red...*
...te, right, title, interest, property, Claim and demand whatsoeve*r...*
...quity, which he the said Joseph Elah Andrus hath in, to, or *...*
...gular a certain Lot or piece of Land, situate, lying and being *...*
...Saint Landry and State aforesaid, bounded and butted as foll*ows...*
...re to be laid off in a Square on the lower line of the tract wh*ich...*
...ndrus purchased of Robert C. Fryer, and to be laid off adjoinin*g...*
...ther with all and singular the houses, woods, waters, ways, privileg*es...*
...rances thereto belonging or in anywise appertaining — To have an*d...*
...d singular the above mentioned and described lot or piece of l*and...*
...d being as aforesaid together with all and singular the houses, *...*
...y and privileges thereto belonging or in anywise appertaining *...*
...d Seth Lewis, Benjamin Palmer, Nehemiah Parrish, Joseph *...*
...ens, John Dunwoody, Rufus Nicholson and their successors in *...*
...trust, that they shall erect and build or cause to be erected an*d...*

The deed to the land on which was erected the first church in the
Acadia Parish area was recorded November 18, 1819. Joseph Elah Andrus
sold the acre of land to the trustees of the church for $50.

The land was described as "situate, lying and being in the Parish of St. Landry and State aforesaid, bounded and butted as follows to wit; one acre to be laid off in a square on the lower line of the tract which he, the said Andrus, purchased of Robert C. Fryer, and to be laid off adjoining the woods, together with all and singular the houses, woods, waters, ways privileges, and appurtenances thereto belonging or in anywise pertaining."

Trustees of the church named in the historic document are Seth Lewis, Benjamin Palmer, Nehemiah Parrish, Joseph Forman and Thomas Owens of St. Landry Parish; John Dunwoody of Rapides and Rufus Nicholson of St. Mary. The deed specified that the trustees "shall erect and build or cause to be erected and built thereon a house or place of worship, for the use of the members of the Methodist Episcopal Church in the United States of America, according to the rules and discipline which from time to time may be agreed upon and adopted by the ministers and preachers of the said Church, at their general conferences in the United States of America . . . that they shall, at all times forever thereafter, permit such ministers and preachers, belonging to the said church as shall from time to time be duly authorized by the general conference . . . to preach and expound God's holy word . . . . "

The Plaquemine Brûlée church became known as "the cradle of Methodism in southwest Louisiana for some 40 years before the Civil War."[9] In 1895 the building was moved about a mile northeast of the original location, onto land donated by W. W. Duson.[10] The building that was moved was evidently not the original building; an item in the Crowley Signal of November 9, 1895 stated that the Plaquemine Brûlée church had been built "nearly 40 years ago," which would indicate that a new building had been erected about 1855.

The present (1975) church was erected in 1947. According to the annals of the church, the old structure was carefully taken down and much of the material, such as heart-of-cypress timbers, was incorporated into the new building. Hand-hewn cypress pews, believed to have been made by slaves for the first or second church, are stored in the building.

The exact spot on which the historic first church stood was almost obliterated from human memory during the passing of the years and transfers of property. Largely through the efforts of Clyde L. Bibb, a

---

9 *Crowley Daily Signal*, 50th Anniv. Ed., 1899-1949, 24
10 *Ibid*

The Plaquemine Brûlée Methodist Church, reproduced from the Crowley Signal of May 10, 1898. This is the building believed to have been moved in 1895.

member of the present church, the original site was determined in 1975. The one remaining landmark is a large pecan tree standing in a rice field on property now owned by Rufus Fruge. Long time residents say there was once a grove of pecan trees at the spot; the last but one to go was destroyed by Hurricane Carmen in 1974.[11]

The first church was a place of worship for both whites and blacks. Daniel Devinne wrote that the church had in it "a few of the Lord's precious ones — some carved in white wood and some in ebony."[12]

---

[11] Oral history, Charles Rosinski, 1975
[12] *Crowley Daily Signal*, 50th Anniv. Ed., 1899-1949, 24

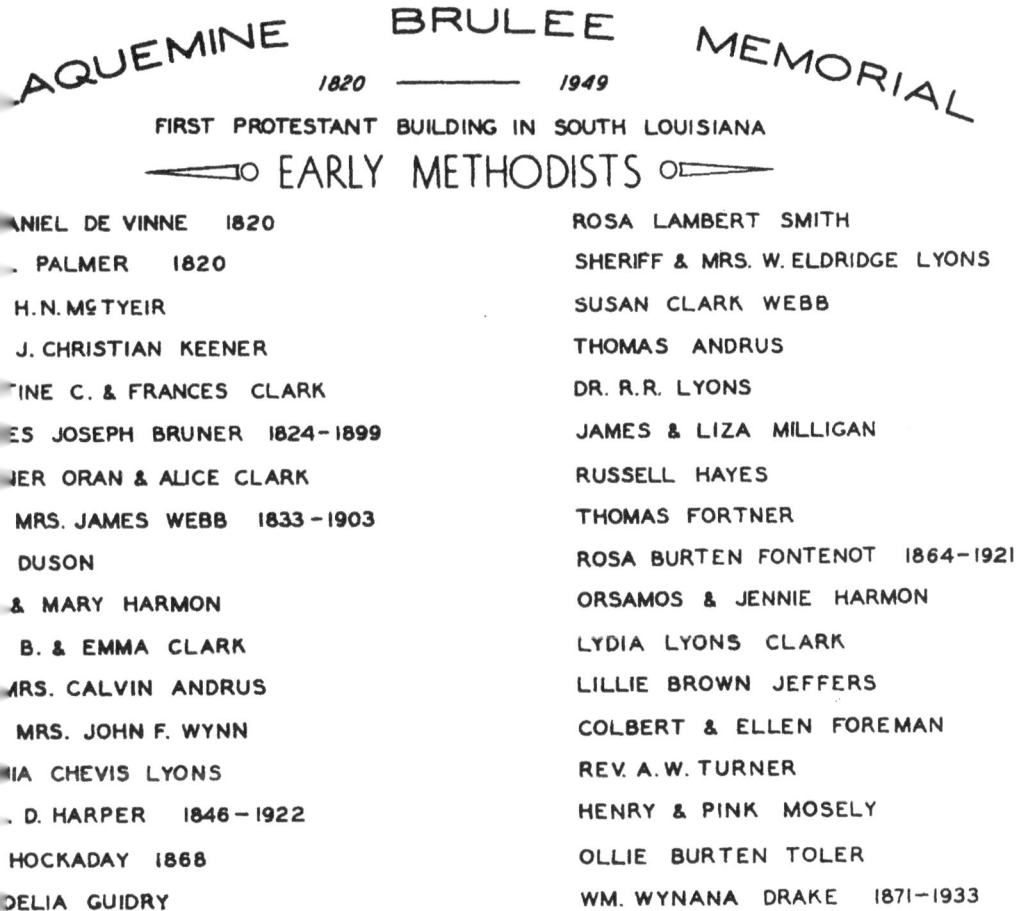

PLAQUEMINE BRULEE MEMORIAL

1820 ———— 1949

FIRST PROTESTANT BUILDING IN SOUTH LOUISIANA

EARLY METHODISTS

DANIEL DE VINNE 1820	ROSA LAMBERT SMITH
. PALMER 1820	SHERIFF & MRS. W. ELDRIDGE LYONS
H.N. McTYEIR	SUSAN CLARK WEBB
J. CHRISTIAN KEENER	THOMAS ANDRUS
INE C. & FRANCES CLARK	DR. R.R. LYONS
ES JOSEPH BRUNER 1824-1899	JAMES & LIZA MILLIGAN
ER ORAN & ALICE CLARK	RUSSELL HAYES
MRS. JAMES WEBB 1833-1903	THOMAS FORTNER
DUSON	ROSA BURTEN FONTENOT 1864-1921
& MARY HARMON	ORSAMOS & JENNIE HARMON
B. & EMMA CLARK	LYDIA LYONS CLARK
MRS. CALVIN ANDRUS	LILLIE BROWN JEFFERS
MRS. JOHN F. WYNN	COLBERT & ELLEN FOREMAN
IA CHEVIS LYONS	REV. A.W. TURNER
. D. HARPER 1846-1922	HENRY & PINK MOSELY
HOCKADAY 1868	OLLIE BURTEN TOLER
DELIA GUIDRY	WM. WYNANA DRAKE 1871-1933

Reproduction of a framed placard presently (1975) displayed in the Plaquemine Brûlée Memorial Church at Branch. Names of early church members are listed.

Social activities of the community centered around the church for many years. A letter to the editor of the Opelousas Courier, published July 12, 1879, reported on a July 4th celebration held at Plaquemine Brûlée. The writer, who signed his letter "Vox," said that it had been a grand celebration, held on the grounds of the church located in a beautiful grove near the bayou. A large crowd was entertained by declamations, recitations and songs by pupils of the Sunday School. Addresses were by B. F. Jones and Dr. Rafe Lyons, superintendent of the Sunday School. "A delicious feast was spread on tables under the trees," Vox wrote. The food, he said had been prepared by the ladies. After the picnic meal the older ones talked while the young people played croquet, and the children were swinging and "in joyful romps."

The July 4th celebration at Plaquemine Brûlée was an annual affair, according to the Crowley Signal of July 7, 1888. At this time the observance of the nation's birthday had been continued "without a skip" for 15 years; the 1888 celebration, the only one held in Acadia Parish that year, was under the auspices of the Sabbath School of Plaquemine Brûlée; music was provided by the young people of the church, and Dr. R. R. Lyons presided. The picnic dinner, prepared by the ladies, "was served in the grove."

Legal notices and advertisements in early newspapers indicate that there were several businesses operating at Plaquemine Brûlée prior to the Civil War. The Opelousas Gazette of April 9, 1842 carried notice that a tanyard would be sold at public auction at Plaquemine Brûlée. The tanyard was said to be "in complete order, having 30 vats, with limes, pools and bates,* with 60 cords of bark, with all necessary buildings. Yard to be sold with from 10 to 1,000 acres of land, to suit purchaser." The advertisement was inserted by A. Clark.

Plaquemine Brûlée residents voted in 1842 "at the place where Benjamin McClelland resided in 1834."[13] In 1846 the polling place was "at the house-store of Benjamin McClelland."[14] Other notices show the firms of Joseph Clark, Carroll & Keough, J. B. Clark & Co., Clark, Hayes & Co., Foreman and Webb Store, at various times during the period from 1844 to 1856.

---

* bate: a bath, originally of a fermented infusion of dung, used by tanners after liming to remove the lime and soften the hides.

13 *Opelousas Gazette,* May 28, 1842
14 *St. Landry Whig,* July 18, 1846

Newspaper columns of the times give little information as to the type of wares available at these early stores. However, a front page advertisement in the Courier announced that 40,000 *pieux* would be offered for sale at Carroll & Keough's on December 20, 1856. The *pieux* were to be sold in lots to suit the purchasers. A similar advertisement, by Clark, Hayes & Co., in the Courier of January 16, 1858 offered *pieux*, shingles and boards, to be sold for cash or terms. The stock included 40,000 8-foot *pieux;* 10,000 covering boards; 59,000 good cypress shingles, and 3,000 3-foot boards.

Listings of election officials and delegates to political conventions published during the 40-year period prior to the establishment of the

This house, built circa 1813, is believed to be the oldest building in Acadia Parish. It is presently located on the Walter Bruner farm near Branch. (Fontenot photo, 1975)

parish identify some of the leading citizens of Plaquemine Brûlée: Gabriel Lyons, Valentine Clark, Joseph Harman, Joseph H. Andrus, C. W. Foreman, F. J. Bruner, J. C. Lyons, J. M. Lyons, A. V. Lyons, W. W. Duson, R. T. Clark, J. J. Lyons, Jim B. Clark.

At a state election in 1855, 86 persons voted at the Lower Plaquemine Brûlée poll.[15] Compared with voting totals of other St. Landry Parish precincts, this was a large turnout. Some 20 years later newspaper columns show that Plaquemine Brûlée voters were continuing to take an active part in politics: In the May 23, 1874 issue of the Courier a group of citizens endorsed the candidacy of Dr. William Kirkman of Calcasieu for the state senate. The following week the newspaper carried a letter to the editor asking that the endorsement be withdrawn. The letter, dated May 24, 1874, read as follows: "You will please withdraw the names of the undersigned from the endorsement, published in your last issue, recommending a candidate for the Senate from this District. Upon reflection, we have determined to vote independently for the candidate we think can accomplish the most for this and our Sister Parishes, irrespective of party. Respectfully, Daniel Lyons, Richard Hightower, Ozeme Trahan, C. W. Foreman, Jos. E. Andrus, Gabriel Lyons, J. H. Andrus, Offutt Lyons, I. E. Clark, J. G. Lyons, J. B. Clark, R. R. Lyons, M.D., William Lyons."

A church for black people was established at Plaquemine Brûlée in 1870.[16] This was the Maryland Chapel, Christian Episcopal Church, built on one acre of land given by Mrs. Jesse Clark. This church building, the first church for blacks to be erected in the Acadia Parish area, also served as the first public school for blacks; it was used as a school three months a year after the crops were laid by. Maryland Chapel is the mother institution for churches built in Crowley and Rayne. The church was re-built in the same location, off Louisiana Highway 35 about five miles north of Rayne, in 1944.[17] The church is located about a half mile from the original site of the church dedicated by Daniel Devinne in 1820.

The post office established at Plaquemine Brûlée in 1838 had its name changed 52 years later. On November 12, 1890 the name of the post office was changed to Branch, so named for Branch Hayes, a grandson of Bosman Hayes, the first merchant of Plaquemine Brûlée.[18]

---

15 *Opelousas Courier*, Nov. 10, 1855
16. Records, Maryland Chapel C.M.E., Rayne, La.
17 Ibid
18 Guidry: *La Pointe de l'Eglise*, 74

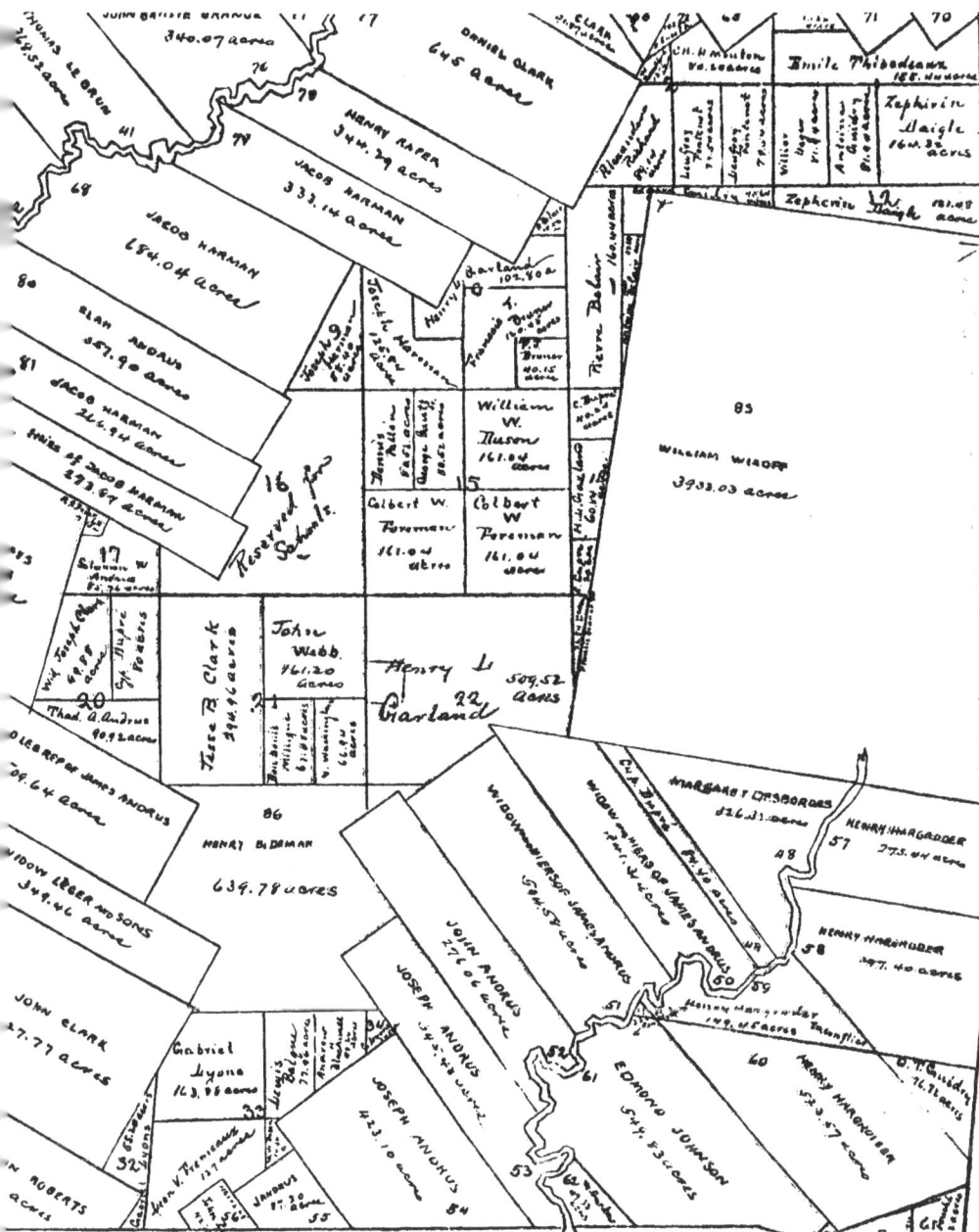

1881 survey of Township 8 South Range 2 East by John P. Parsons shows the colonial landowners along Bayous Plaquemine Brûlée and Wikoff in the Plaquemine Brûlée area. Names of the prairie landowners were inscribed by an unknown person at an undetermined time, probably in the early 1890s. (Map courtesy Rev. Donald J. Hebert)

In 1874 residents of Plaquemine Brûlée were receiving mail once a week. The Opelousas Courier of March 28, 1874 carried notice of a change in United States mail routes; the schedule called for the mail to leave Opelousas every Saturday at 6 a.m., and arrive at Plaquemine Brûlée on Sunday by 12 noon; leave Plaquemine Brûlée on Sunday at 1 p.m. and arrive at Opelousas by 6 p.m. the same day.

The published schedule for this specific route made no mention of mail stops between Opelousas and Plaquemine Brûlée, but the timing (18 hours from Opelousas to Plaquemine Brûlée) leads to the conclusion

Maryland C.M.E. Church was founded in 1870. Inset at upper right shows detail from a plaque on the outside of the present building. (Fontenot photo, 1975)

Commercial buildings at Plaquemine Brûlée, from a photograph made in 1888. Fencing around the buildings is made of cypress pieux. The original photograph, in the Freeland Archives at Crowley, is one of three oldest known pictures of Acadia Parish.

that the mail carrier made deliveries at intermediate points before reaching the end of the route.

Plaquemine Brûlée had a public school in 1877. The Courier of April 20, 1878 published a report on the schools in St. Landry Parish which had been in operation for the 1877-1878 school year. The Plaquemine Brûlée school had an enrollment of 282, and an average attendance of 234; the school was operated for four and a half months, from October until March, and the one teacher (unidentified) was paid a salary of $225.46.

At the beginning of the following school year, two schools were listed for Plaquemine Brûlée: a school for colored near Colbert Foreman's, and a school for whites near Keough's.[19]

A new Plaquemine Brûlée firm began an advertising campaign in the St. Landry Democrat in 1880. In the October 2 issue of the Opelousas newspaper a display ad for the Foreman and Duson store named C. W. Foreman and W. W. Duson as partners in the business. The firm dealt in "dry goods, clothing, boots and shoes, hardware, tinware, crockery, notions, groceries, provisions, &c., &c., &c." The advertisement also invited readers to market their produce with the firm: "All country produce, such as cotton, sugar, molasses, rice, wool, hides, chickens, eggs, etc. bought at the highest market prices; also, split lumber, such as pieux and shingles. Be certain to give them a call before buying or selling elsewhere."

The colonial settlement of Plaquemine Brûlée has faded into history. Its successor, the village of Branch, is today (1975) a post office, an elementary school, two churches and several small businesses, all situated at a crossroad of Acadia Parish in the center of a rich agricultural region. The Opelousas, Gulf and Northern railroad came through Branch in 1907 and apparently spurred hopes for civic development. A map, made in 1907, shows a survey of the town; 12 town lots were laid out with the streets named as follows: Plaquemine, Western, Eastern, Haralson, Barousse, Lyons, Hudson, Andrus, Hayes and Commercial.

Long-time residents of Branch contend that the community lost its chance for development when a number of the more aggressive and influential residents moved to Rayne and Crowley. This is borne out by published sources. Those who are known to have moved from Branch (at that time Plaquemine Brûlée) to either (or both) Rayne or Crowley

---

19 *Opelousas Courier*, Sept. 28, 1878

include E. O. Bruner, Raymond T. Clark, W. W. Duson, D. B. Hayes, J. C. Lyons, R. R. Lyons, James Webb, Colbert W. Foreman.[20]

William H. Perrin, in his "Southwest Louisiana Biographical and Historical" gives some interesting sidelights on several of the early families of Plaquemine Brûlée. He relates that Bosman Hayes Jr. was shot and killed by Jayhawkers in 1864 while attempting to defend his own property.[21] This substantiates a tradition in the Hayes family, told as follows: Bosman Hayes Jr. owned a white mare which he kept strictly for his own use, refusing to let anyone else ride. One night he heard a disturbance in the direction of the stable where the mare was kept; he got his

---

[20] Perrin: *Southwest Louisiana*, etc. Part II 252, 258, 261, 262, 267, 268, 274; *Crowley Signal*, Oct. 27, 1894; *Crowley Daily Signal*, Oct. 4, 1937, Crowley sec., 4

[21] Perrin: *Southwest Louisiana*, Part II, 263

RESIDENCE OF J. M. LYONS, PLAQUEMINE BRULEE, LA.

RESIDENCE OF JOHN E. PELTON, PLAQUEMINE BRULEE, LA.

Residences of Plaquemine Brûlée, reproduced from wood cuts in the Crowley Signal of August 25, 1888. The Pelton place was known as Linden Grove.

shotgun and went to investigate. The night was clear and moonlit, after a rainy day; clothes had been left on the line to dry. He saw two men leading his white horse away; he called out, but the men didn't stop. Hayes shot one of the mes; the other hidden by a bedsheet on the line, shot and killed Hayes on his own back porch.[22]

Hayes was a wealthy man and owned all the slaves he could use on his plantation.[23] Another legendary story concerning him tells of the time, about 1840, when he and his wife went to New Orleans on a pleasure trip. While there Hayes bought a young slave boy — for no other reason except that the boy was a gifted dancer.[24]

Another Plaquemine Brûlée planter first tried his luck in the California gold fields. This was Francis T. Bruner, native of Ohio, who came in the early 1850s and used gold nuggets to buy land — land which later produced the golden grain which became a mainstay of the economy of the parish.[25]

The immense (5,000 acres) William Wikoff *vacherie* tract just east of Branch was one of the few Spanish land grants maintained intact until 1875.[26] It was then bought by a man named John E. Pelton, who built a mansion on the property in 1882.[27] The Pelton house was the show place of the area; pictures of it appear in two early issues of the Crowley Signal.[28]

Some of the colonial period settlers of Acadia Parish may be interred in a forgotten cemetery of Plaquemine Brûlée. The Opelousas Courier of March 14, 1874 carried an article written by an anonymous person who signed himself J.M.T. The article, titled "The Little Rustic Grave Yard," told how the writer, "wandering along the banks of the Plaquemine, with rod and line to catch the delicious perch of its quiet waters, paused at the neglected, but sacred and beautiful spot which forms the last resting place of a few unknown fellow mortals." The cemetery, the writer stated, was situated on a gently sloping ridge "which rises to the dignity of a bluff against the bayou." The cemetery was devoid of any enclosure and the graves were unmarked. The place was in "utter seclusion, surrounded by large magnolias, oaks and hickories."

---

22 Oral history, Sybil Parrott Andrus, 1975
23 Perrin: *Southwest Louisiana,* etc., Part II, p. 263
24 Oral History, Sybil Andrus
25 Perrin: *Southwest Louisiana,* etc. Part II, 253; *Crowley Daily Signal,* Anniv. Ed. 1899-1949, 117
26 Post: Dr. Lauren C., unpublished material.
27 *Crowley Signal,* Aug. 25, 1888
28 *Crowley Signal,* Aug. 25, 1888; Oct. 27, 1894

The James Webb place at Plaquemine Brûlée, from an 1888 photograph. The original photograph, used in the Crowley Signal of August 25, 1888, is in the Freeland Archives at Crowley.

110

CHAPTER VI

Rayne

Before Rayne was Rayne it was Poupeville, and before it was Poupeville it was Queue Tortue, a settlement which developed near the waterway Bayou Queue de Tortue.

Queue Tortue was a voting precinct of St. Landry Parish in 1852. Because of gaps in the police jury records and the scarcity of early publications it is not possible to determine precisely when the voting poll was established. The first mention of voting at Queue Tortue appeared in the first issue of the Opelousas Courier* when the newspaper gave notice of the forthcoming election. The two polling places in the sixth ward of St. Landry Parish were Plaquemine Brûlée and Queue Tortue; the voting at Queue Tortue was to take place "at the house of Eugene Valette."

Queue Tortue has a unique place in the history of southwest Louisiana. The settlement — specifically, the house of Eugene Valette — was the site, on September 3, 1859, of the historic confrontation between the Vigilantes and the anti-Vigilantes, an event which terminated a troubled period of strong feeling and controversy that threatened to plunge the state into its own civil war.

The Vigilantes, or Committees of Vigilance, were organized in January of 1859. Members were citizens of southwest Louisiana who decided to take the law into their own hands. For some time law-breaking activities had been rampant in the sparsely settled region; the seats of justice were remote, known criminals went unpunished. As time went by the crime rate increased and the outlaws became bolder; there were numerous cases of cattle thefts, plundering, arson and murder.

The Vigilantes recruited a small force of armed men; members, sworn to secrecy, met regularly to drill. Committees were organized in five southwest Louisiana parishes: St. Martin, Lafayette, Vermilion, St. Landry and Calcasieu. Many prominent citizens of the area were active in the Vigilantes; Major Aurelien St. Julien was commander-in-chief of all forces; General Alfred Mouton, a West Point graduate later to become the hero of the Battle of Mansfield, was drillmaster; a former Louisiana governor, Alexander Mouton, and another highly respected citizen, Alcee Judice, were among those who took active part.

* December 11, 1852

111

Punishment administered by the Vigilantes was swift and severe, especially for those suspected of having been acquitted because of perjured witnesses or a packed jury. Punishment consisted of banishment, the lash, or the rope.

The unorthodox tactics used by the Vigilantes in dispensing justice attracted attention throughout the state. Their actions were defended by some newspapers, castigated by others. Governor Robert C. Wickliffe denounced them as rebels against the law and order of the state, and ordered the committees to disband, an edict that went unheeded by the Vigilantes.

This led to the organization of a strong anti-Vigilante movement. Encouraged by the attitude of the governor and public officials of the district, the anti-Vigilantes began to recruit their own forces and gather arms. Believing that the governor would send the militia to their aid, the anti-Vigilantes made plans for an open military campaign against all those identified with the Vigilantes.

The Vigilantes learned, through spies, of an alleged plot: a large number of anti-Vigilantes were to assemble at a fortified house at Queue Tortue on September 3, there to complete plans to attack, pillage and burn the village of Vermilionville (Lafayette) and wipe out the Vigilantes. Part of the alleged plot was to murder Emile Mouton, brother of the ex-governor, and François d'Aigle.

The Vigilantes immediately mounted a counter-attack. On the morning of September 3 some 600 armed and mounted men converged on the anti-Vigilante stronghold at Queue Tortue. They had with them a brass cannon.

As the Vigilante forces neared the scene of the encounter they were joined by other Vigilante groups from Prairie Robert (Robert's Cove) and Faquetaique, and several sympathizers from Calcasieu Parish. They surrounded the place; the six-inch field gun was mounted and pointed at the house.

At the sight of the cannon many of the anti-Vigilantes fled into the thickets along the nearby bayou. The remaining anti-Vigilantes then acceded to the demands of the Vigilantes and surrendered their arms. Inside the house the Vigilantes found large amounts of ammunition and weapons of every kind.

Of the 200 prisoners taken by the Vigilantes, all but 80 were released on their solemn promise to never again disrupt the peace of the region. The rest were bound and lashed until they swore to leave the state forever.[1]

Alexandre Barde, native of France and itinerant newspaperman, wrote a history of the Committees of Vigilance. His book provides an eye-witness account of the encounter, termed "the battle of the spurs" by one historian.[2] In his recital of the events at Queue Tortue, Barde writes that the farmhouse selected for the assembly of anti-Vigilantes belonged to "a man of very bad reputation answering to the name of Emilien Lagrange," and adds that "the widow of a Frenchman named Valette, mother of a tall and beautiful girl, had become the concubine of this man . . ."[3] The Lagrange house "was a vast house with walls made of tree trunks, crenalated on all four sides. It contained a store constructed in the fashion of a log cabin . . . "[4]

The Lagrange house, according to Barde's description, "faced the Coulee of Queue Tortue which was at a few meters' distance and its battlements could plainly be seen from the ground floor to the attic . . . in the yard a few chinaberry trees spread out the green canopy of their branches . . . "[5]

Eugene Valette's succession shows that he died in 1851.[6] His widow was Marguerite Quebedeaux, and he left two daughters of minor age. The inventory of the estate lists in detail the drygoods, groceries and other items of merchandise in the Valette store.

One of the two persons appointed by the court to inventory the Valette estate was Maximilien* Lagrange. The inventory was taken "at the last residence of the deceased on Queue Tortue, about 30 miles from the (St. Landry Parish) courthouse." The estate included 156 acres of land,

---

* Maximilien, or 'Emilien, a contraction or "petit nom" (nickname) for Maximilien.

1 Summary: Barde: *Histoire de Comites de Vigilance aux Attakapas*, Guilbeau trans.; Perrin: *Southwest Louisiana Biographical and Historical*, Part I, 71-79; Dismukes: *The Center: A History of the Development of Lafayette, La.*, 14-16; *Louisiana, a Guide to the State*, 273; Griffin: *The Attakapas Country*, 130-136; unpublished memoirs of Alexandre Mouton.

2 Perrin: *Southwest Louisiana*, Part I, 79

3 Barde: *Histoire*, etc., 289

4 *Ibid*

5 *Ibid*, 401

6 Eugene Valette succession, No. 145, Acadia Parish transferred from St. Landry.

bounded north by vacant land, west by Joachim Provost, south by Coulée Tortue, and east by vacant land.

The succession of Widow Valette, Marguerite Quebedeaux, identifies her as the legal wife of Maximilien Lagrange. Her heirs were eight children, two daughters by the name of Valette, and six children bearing the name of Lagrange.[7]

The description given of the Valette property does not define its location — the land could have been almost anywhere along the length of Bayou Queue de Tortue — except for the Joachim Provost land on the west. Provost owned 68.59 acres in the southwest quarter of the northwest quarter of section 34 and the southeast quarter of the northeast quarter of Section 33, in Township 9 South Range 2 East.[8] These two sections lie in the southeast portion of the present city of Rayne, placing Eugene Valette's property approximately two miles southeast of the present Rayne post office. Maximilien Lagrange and his wife, Marguerite Quebedeaux, sold 98 acres of this land to Portalis Doucet in 1870.[9] Thus it can be determined that the erstwhile voting precinct of old St. Landry, the house and store of Eugene Valette on Bayou Queue de Tortue, was the site of the Vigilante battle.

This detailed documentation is presented here to clarify some misconceptions concerning the site of the affray. Bayou Queue de Tortue, which divides Acadia and Vermilion Parishes, also forms part of the boundary line between Acadia and Lafayette Parishes, becoming little more than a coulee, or drain ditch, between Rayne and Duson in Lafayette Parish. Another watercourse, Bayou Tortue, is the boundary between Lafayette and St. Martin Parishes. The similarity of names of the two bayous is believed to have led some historical writers to the erroneous conclusion that the dubious honor of the battle site belongs to Lafayette Parish.

Barde names other leaders of the anti-Vigilante forces at Queue Tortue as Jean Baptiste Chiasson, alias John Jones, who owned a plantation neighboring that of Lagrange;[10] James Jenkins, a Kentuckian who managed a sawmill on the Mermentau River; Joseph Dédé Istre and Balthazard Plaisance, ex-convicts; Eugene Aloué (probably Halloway), an

---

7 Marguerite Quebedeaux succession, No. 146, Acadia, trans. St. Landry
8 Joachim Provost succession No. 4719, St. Landry
9 Conveyance Book Y-I, No. 9884, St. Landry
10 Barde: *Histoire*, 391

outlaw; a justice of the peace named Dr. Wagner; Geneus Guidry, *dit* Canada; the Widow Valette and her 16-year-old daughter, who together had made and embroidered the anti-Vigilante flag which was found with the stores of ammunition in the fortified house.[11]

Barde's account of the Vigilante activities is of course biased, since he himself was a member of one of the committees. All members of the anti-Vigilantes were not outlaws; many were law abiding citizens who believed that the controversy was a class struggle between the rich and the poor. These were men who were also interested in preserving law and order, but were opposed to those who took the law into their own hands.

Barde's history says that there was only one death at Queue Tortue, that of Geneus Guidry, *dit* Canada, who took his own life rather than surrender.

The affair at Queue Tortue marked the end of Vigilante activity. One other incident, attributed to the Vigilantes, was reported in 1873. The editor of the Vermilionville Cotton Boll wrote that he was under the impression that the Vigilance Committees had finished their work, but such was not the case. They had, he said, hung one Severin Boudreau, who lived at Long Point (in Acadia Parish). Boudreau's crime, the editor wrote, was "too dark . . . to pollute the columns of this paper."[12]

There are numerous other references to Queue Tortue as a place name of old St. Landry. In 1855 Elbert Gantt, tax collector, announced tax collection points for the parish. One of the two such points in the sixth ward was at the house of Hypolite C. Guidry, Queue Tortue.[13] Guidry owned land in Section 27, Township 9 South Range 2 East.[14] In 1868 Sheriff James G. Hays announced tax collections points; one of the two for the sixth ward was at the J. D. Bernard store at Queue Tortue.[15] Ten years later, in 1878, the Courier carried notice of an election of delegates to the Democratic convention. Voters at the Bernard store at Queue Tortue were to elect nine delegates; election commissioners were J. D. Bernard and Benjamin Avant.[16]

---

11 Barde: *Histoire,* 394-405
12 *Opelousas Courier,* Oct. 25, 1873
13 *Ibid,* April 14, 1855
14 Marguerite Quebedeaux suc. Acadia Parish.
15 *Opelousas Courier,* May 7, 1868.
16 *Ibid,* June 8, 1878

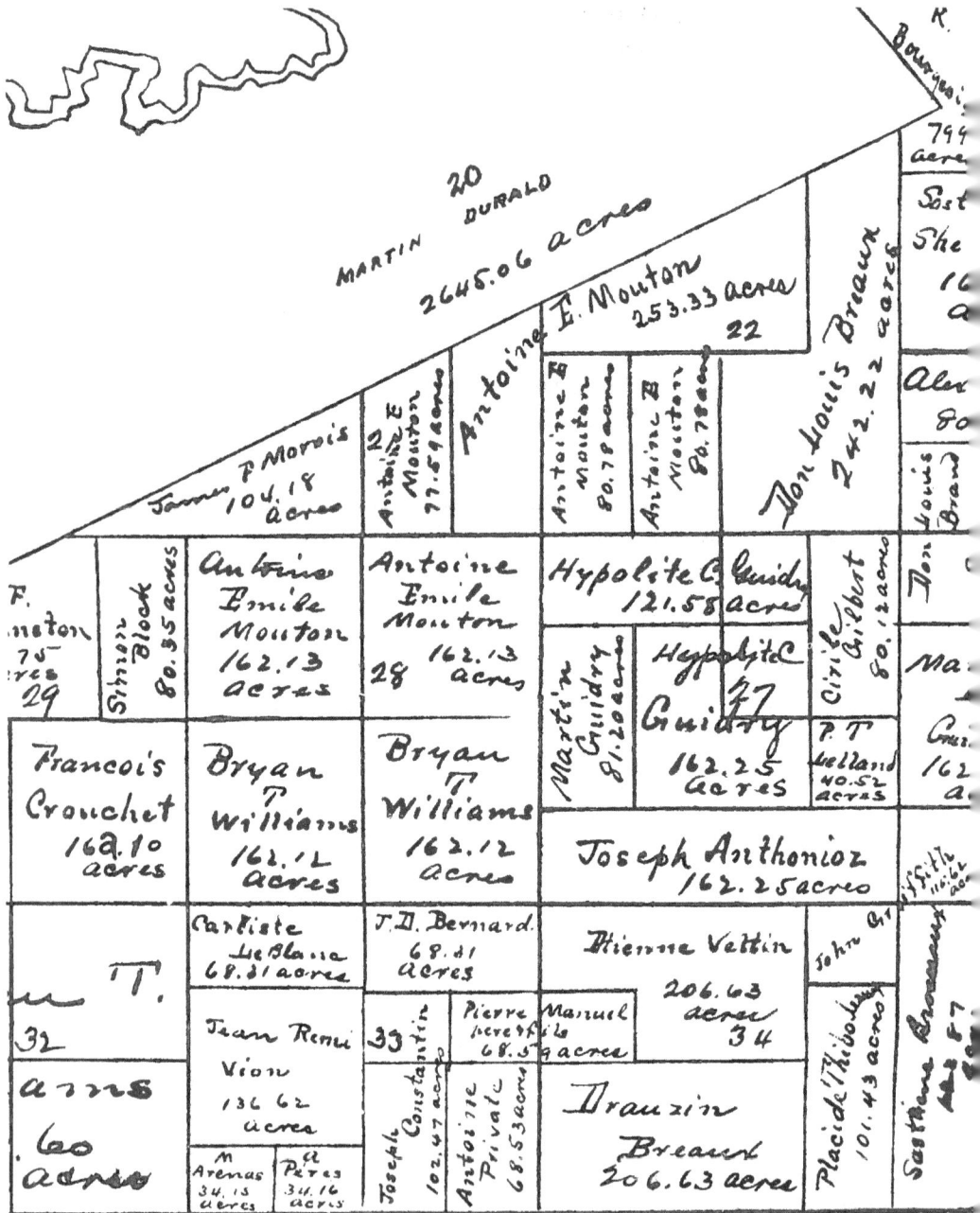

Land ownership in the Rayne area is shown in this segment of a survey of Township 9 South Range 2 East. The survey was done by John P. Parsons in 1881; names of landowners were written in by an unknown person at an undetermined time.

Results of an election held May 22, 1853 give only a vague idea of the population of the settlement at that time, as the Courier reported that balloting was unusually light; only 18 ballots were cast at the Queue Tortue poll.[17] A better population picture emerges from results of the state election of November, 1855, when 72 persons voted at the Queue Tortue poll.[18]

The voting precinct list for 1863 shows two polls for Queue Tortue: one at Onezime Trahan, *fils,* with Onezime P. Guidry, Joseph T. Guidry and William Johnson as commissioners; the other at the store of Damonville Bernard, with Etienne Veltin, Ozeme LeBlanc and Joseph Constantin as commissioners.

The settlement was identified as Queue Tortue as late as 1882. The editor of the Courier reported in the January 7 issue that he had met "Mr. Numa Chachere of Rayne station, Queue Tortue."

While the name of the settlement remained Queue Tortue in legal records for many years, inhabitants of the area called it Poupeville, a name it was to carry until the railroad came and the village became Rayne Station. But before Queue Tortue became Poupeville its name was perpetuated in a folk song:

> *Allons à la Queue Tortue*
> *C'est pour vivre sur le pain perdu*[19]

The name Poupeville probably came into usage through colloquial expressions, such as "je vais au magazin de Poupeville" (I am going to Poupeville's store). A merchant named Jules Poupeville, believed to have been a native of France, came to the area at an undetermined time. He set up his residence and a store on public land. In 1854 he sold the movables on the property to Jean Remy Vion. The movables included two houses, one occupied as a store, the other maintained as a residence; a corncrib, fencing and other improvements; a horse cart and four horses. The movables were described as being "on a piece of public land lying on Bayou Queue de Tortue said to be occupied by the present vendor."[20] Vion bought 136.62 acres of land in Section 33, Township 9 South Range 2 East from the United States government,[21] which is undoubtedly the "piece of public land" where Poupeville had set up his home and business.

---

17 "Some History", *Daily World,* 200
18 *Opelousas Courier,* Nov. 10, 1855
19 Whitfield: *French Songs of South Louisiana,* 89-90
20 Conveyance Book P-1, No. 509, Vol. I, 473 St. Landry Parish.
21 Abstracts, U.S. Land Entries, No. 1, Acadia Parish

In 1871 the editor of the Courier, accustomed to identifying the village as Queue Tortue, seemed uncertain of the location of Poupeville. In the issue of December 30 he reported: "We learn that a man by the name of Louis Anding was shot and killed at a ball near Poupeville, in the western part of this parish, on the night of the 23rd inst. There is no clue as to who perpertrated the deed, nor were we able to learn the particulars of the affair."

Rev. Joseph Anthonioz, a Jesuit priest stationed at St. Charles College, Grand Coteau, began missionary work in the Acadia Parish area in 1855. He covered a wide field in his ministrations, visiting families on the prairies and traveling as far west as the Mermentau River. Jesuit records show that he taught mathematics in St. Charles College in addition to his missionary work. Like the other early Jesuits he would ride over the prairies on horseback, visiting the scattered settlements, then hasten back to the college to fulfill teaching assignments.[22]

Father Anthonioz had charge, at different times, of the settlements at Upper Plaquemine Brûlée, Queue Tortue, Pointe-aux-Loups, Coulée Trive, Lyon's Point and Mermentau. He and other Jesuit priests alternated in their work at these mission points. He was put in charge of the Queue Tortue settlement in 1872, and is best known for his work there.[23] His records, kept at St. Joseph Catholic Church of Rayne, begin in 1872. Written in French in his own handwriting, the records show that the first baptism and the first marriage took place on the same date, January 18, 1872. The child baptized was Valerien Dupuis, son of Alexandre Dupuis and Ordalise Blanchard; godparents were Dupre Dugas and Philomene Dupuis. The marriage was between Louis Theogene Richard, son of Jean Richard and Zelonise Plaisance, and Celeste Trahant, daughter of Onezime Trahant and Celeste Curather. Witnesses to the marriage were Jean Broussard, Onezime Melancon and Ambroise Offpower.*

In 1875 Father Anthonioz bought 162.25 acres of land from the United States government, the tract located in the southwest quarter of Section 27, Township 9 South Range 2 East.[24] A church building, erected by the Jesuits, was completed early in 1877.[25]

---

* Offpower: Father Anthonioz' spelling of the name Hoffpauir.
22 Baudier: "History Our Lady of the Sacred Heart Catholic Church," booklet, 47
23 Ibid
24 Abstracts US Land Entries No. 1, Acadia Parish
25 Baudier: OLHS booklet, 59

When Poupeville post office was re-established on October 23, 1878, its location was described as "in the northeast section of Section 33, Township 9 South Range 2 East, two miles north of Bayou Queue de Tortue." The official name of the post office was spelled "Pouppeville," and the population was given as 150.[26]

The Courier of September 28, 1878 listed the 44 schools of St. Landry Parish — 25 for white students and 19 for colored. Among these was a school for whites located "in Poupeville near the Bernard store."

The coming of the railroad changed the geographical location as well as the name of the village. In 1880, when the main line of the Louisiana

---

[26] US Post Office records

South Western Dist La

No. 4222   Receiver's Office at *New Orleans La nov 15 1876*

RECEIVED from *Joseph Anthonioz*

of *St Landry Parish* County *Louisiana* — the sum of *Two* hundred (200) — dollars and —————— cents; being in full for the *South half of South West quarter and South half of South East* —————— quarter of Section No. *Twenty seven* — in Township No. *Nine (9) South* — of Range No. *Two (2) East* —— containing *One hundred + sixty two* — acres and *Twenty five (25)* — hundredths, at

$ 1 25/100 per acre.

$ 200 00/100 .

Julian Neville Receiver.

Receipt from the New Orleans Land Office, dated November 15, 1876, showing Rev. Joseph Anthonioz's purchase of 162.25 acres of land in Section 27, Township 9 South Range 2 East. The above is a reproduction of the original document in the National Archives.

119

First installed in 1880 in St. Joseph's Church of Poupeville, this bell continues to summon the faithful to worship in St. Joseph's Catholic Church of Rayne. The late Rev. Hubert Lerschen had this photograph made before the bell was placed in the belfry of the present church. (Photo courtesy St. Joseph's Church Rayne)

Diagram showing the site of the *Poupeville* Post Office in Township *nine* Range *two* of _____ Principal Meridian, County of *Saint Landry* _____, State of *Louisiana* , with the adjacent Townships and Post Offices.

It is requested that the exact site of the proposed, or existing Post Office, as also the roads to the adjoining offices, and the larger streams or rivers, be marked on this diagram, to be returned as soon as possible to the Post Office Department.

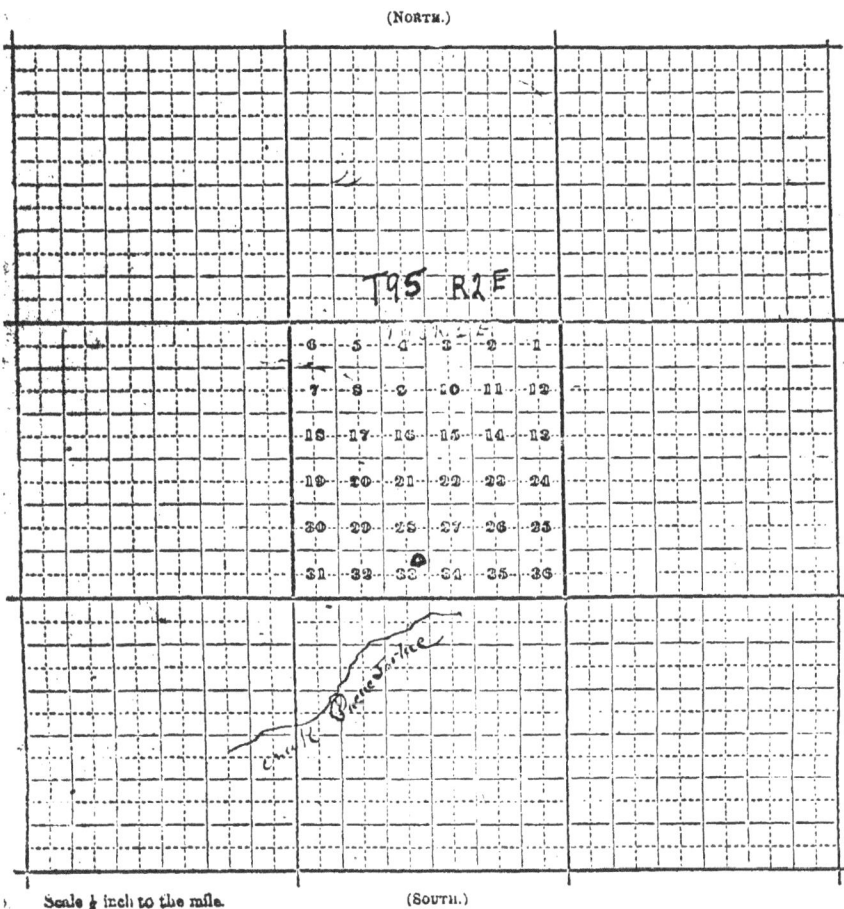

(NORTH.)

T 9 S   R 2 E

```
 6   5   4   3   2   1
 7   8   9  10  11  12
18  17  16  15  14  13
19  20  21  22  23  24
30  29  28  27  26  25
31  32  33  34  35  36
```

Queue Tortue
Creek

Scale ⅛ inch to the mile.   (SOUTH.)

The location of the Poupeville post office, re-established in 1878, is pin-pointed in Section 33, Township 9 South Range 2 East on this official diagram. Bayou Queue de Tortue is identified on the diagram as "Creek Queue Tortue." (Document reproduction courtesy Myrta Fair Craig)

121

The depot at Rayne, from an 1888 photograph. This railroad station was the magnet which caused the merchants of Poupeville to move their businesses to Rayne Station. The original photograph is preserved in the Freeland Archives at Crowley.

122

Western Railroad was nearing completion, Poupeville was by-passed and the new town of Rayne was born.

Dr. William H. Cunningham, at the time in the employ of the railroad company, was the founder of the town. B. W. L. Rayne, also connected with the railroad, was the godfather — the new railroad station was named Rayne.[27]

In July of 1880 Dr. Cunningham bought considerable acreage in the Rayne area from the heirs of Antoine Mouton. He had his holdings in Section 28 surveyed and laid out in town lots by Romain Francis. In November of 1880 he sold lots on Texas Street to J. F. Morris and Numa Chachere for $62.50 per lot. An 80-foot-front lot on Texas Street was

[27] *Crowley Signal*, Aug. 25, 1888

Rayne's first church, moved from the Poupeville settlement in 1882, served the Catholics of the community until 1899, when a second church building was erected. The first church building, now 100 years old, is presently (1976) being used as a parish hall for the Church of the Assumption at Mier. (Photo courtesy St. Joseph's Church, Rayne, from memorabilia kept by Rev. Hubert Lerschen)

sold jointly to Morris and Chachere for $75; W. S. McBride signed as witness to the land sales.[28]

The three merchants of Poupeville, J. D. Bernard, M. Arenas and Francois Crouchet, moved their businesses about a mile north to the railroad and Rayne Station.[29] Father Anthonioz, in 1882, had the church raised and placed on large wooden wheels; teams of oxen hauled the edifice to the new village site,[30] onto a tract of land donated to the church by M. Arenas.[31] The 160-plus acres of land bought by Father Anthonioz in 1875 were sold to three persons, all of whom already owned land adjoining the property. Armand Breaux bought 80 acres; 40 acres were sold to Aladin LeBlanc and the remaining 40 acres to Joseph C. Guidry.[32]

By 1883 the town was incorporated, with J. D. Bernard serving as first mayor. Councilmen were B. H. Harmon, A. S. Chappuis, L. R. Deputy, M. Arenas and J. F. Morris. First town clerk was E. C. Fremaux and J. O. Bull was town marshal.

Dr. Cunningham did not live to see the realization of his dream of building a new town. He died in 1881. His land holdings, consisting of town lots and acreage north of the town site, were sold at public auction on October 7, 1884. His widow, Mrs. Mary Cunningham, bought 23 of the lots. The remaining lots went to the following buyers: W. W. Duson, 13 lots; Joseph Trahan, 8; Edwin O. Bruner, 3; E. C. Legnion, 2; Widow Josette Trahan, 3; D. Casaux, 4; J. F. Morris and Sydney Arceneaux, 4; Ernest Chappuis, 1; A. S. Chappuis, 7; A. C. Poulet, 4; R. J. C. Bull, 5; M. Arenas, 4; Ernest Capel, 1; Walter Foreman, 2; Louis R. Deputy and Brother, 6; J. F. Morris, 2; Sidney Arceneaux, 5.[33]

Social activities of the bustling new town were reported in the Opelousas press. On May 5, 1883, the Courier listed the names of committees organized in St. Landry Parish to give charity balls and fairs to benefit the charity hospital in New Orleans. The Rayne committee consisted of E. C. Fremaux and lady; Dr. J. F. Morris and lady; D. M. Bull and lady; C. A. Perrodin and lady; L. R. Deputy and lady; H. W. Anding and lady; A. S. Chappuis and lady; Mrs. J. A. Smith, Miss Anna Bernard, Miss Maggie Anding, Paul J. Manouvrier.

28 Conveyance Books G-2, 364-366, 626-629; 1-2, 23, St. Landry Parish
29 Crowley Signal, Aug. 25, 1888
30 Baudier: OLHS booklet, 60
31 Donation Book 3, No. 19791, 506-507, St. Landry Parish.
32 Conveyance Book L-2, 132-133, St. Landry.
33 Conveyance Book R-2, 244-247, St. Landry

This two-story frame building housed the first Mervine Kahn store of Rayne. The smaller structure at left was the first Rayne State Bank building. (Photo courtesy Leo H. Kahn)

125

Mervine Kahn,

Carries a Full Line of

GENERAL MERCHANDISE,

And is Prepared to Sell You Anything From a

Paper of Pins up to a Threshing Machine.

He Will Also Pay You The

HIGHEST MARKET PRICE FOR ALL FARM PRODUCE.

My Line of Dry Goods

Is Complete and Entirely New

Our Groceries are fresh and

OF THE BEST GRADES AND BRANDS

This advertisement, shown in part, appeared in the Crowley Signal of August 25, 1888. The oldest business firm in continuous operation in Acadia Parish, the Kahn store marked its 90th anniversary in 1974.

Two years later the Courier editor visited "the thriving little city of Rayne." He reported in the March 21, 1885 issue that he had heard of the rapid growth and development of the place, but "was not prepared for the wonderful development" which he had witnessed. Four or five years before, the editor wrote, when the place was known as Poupeville, there were "only two stores, a blacksmith and a wagon shop to dignify it with the name of a hamlet. Now it is an incorporated town whose limits cover a mile and a half square, with commodious business houses fronting on each side of the Louisiana Western Railroad and neat residences spreading in every direction, facing well-graded streets and forming the pleasant home of about 600 as hospitable, energetic and thrifty inhabitants as occupy any country."

DR. J. F. MORRIS' DRUG STORE, RAYNE, LA.

Rayne's first business building, reproduced from a wood cut in the Crowley Signal of August 25, 1888. Dr. J. F. Morris was the first druggist in Acadia Parish; he was also a practicing physician.

Rayne was, the editor write, "the youngest town in St. Landry." While there he met people from Michigan, Iowa, Illinois, Kansas, Minnesota, Connecticut and Mississippi. There were four hotels, eight houses doing general merchandise and grocery trade; a large establishment for sashes and blinds; two drug stores, a lumber yard, two saloons; two physicians, two real estate dealers, three notaries; an auctioneer and a justice of the peace; two painters, a baker and a shoemaker, a butcher and a barber; two blacksmiths, several carpenters and a brick-mason.

The editor continued his progress report on Rayne, reporting on town facilities which included a large town hall and dramatic hall "for home talent and other theatrical troups;" Catholic and Methodist churches; two schools, one public, one private; six trains daily, and the Rayne Brass Band, led by Prof. Chappuis.

The same issue of the paper, in a separate story, gave the names of the members of the band and the instruments each played. Band members were P. J. Chappuis, A. L. Chappuis, M. Brien, L. Ohlmeyer, A. J. Guidry, L. R. Deputy, E. W. Roy, Arthur Bonnet, Eugene Chappuis and Abraham Christman.

This was followed, in the September 5 issue, by a letter to the editor from O'neal East, which reported further progress: Sydney Arceneaux had received a large quantity of wire for fencing farm land; a cotton gin, equipped with a 20-horse power engine, had been moved into town. Mention was made of business locations: the J. D. Bernard store and the Thomas P. Bowden store on Texas Avenue; a grocery on Adams Street operated by Columbus Hoffpauir; the B. H. Harmon lumber yard and the L. A. Duclos drug store. The letter writer reported that George H. Tolson, a druggist, had purchased half interest in the M. P. Young and Co. drug store on Adams.

Some six months later Rayne had its own newspaper, the first to be published in the Acadia Parish area. The Rayne Signal began publication on March 13, 1886. The proprietors were C. W. Felter and George Addison, grandson of George Washington Addison, the first printer and newspaper publisher in St. Landry Parish.[34] The newspaper was purchased by W. W. Duson September 1, 1886.[35] A second newspaper, the

---

[34] *Opelousas Gazette.* Nov. 21, 1841
[35] *Crowley Daily Signal,* Oct. 4, 1937, Signal Sec., 5

Rayne

VOL. 1.   RAYNE, ST. LANDRY

THE RAYNE SIGNAL.

. W. FELTER, - - - - Editor.

. C. ADDISON, - - - Publisher,

Terms of Subscription.

INVARIABLY IN ADV NCE,

1 copy, one year.................................$2 00

1 copy, six months.............................1 25

Town Council Officials.

B. H. HARMAN Mayor.

hos. P. BOWDEN,   H. W. ASDING

RAYMOND T. CLARK,

onstable,   J. E. WIMBERLY.

ecy and Tax-Coll.   P. J. MANOUVRIER

reasurer,   A. S. CHAPPUIS

ustice of Peace,   R. T. CLARK

on. Queue Torine Ward,   A. V. LYONS.

eputy Sheriff,   DAVID M. BULL.

Laws of Newspapers.

1. Subscribes who do not give express notice, to e contrary, are considered as wishing to continue eir subscription

2. If subscribers order the discontinuance of ir paper the publisher may continue to send

GEO. K. BRADFORD,

Real Estate Agent,

Surveyor and Land Attorney,

Rayne, St. Landry Parish, La.

Has for sale improved and unimproved land in tracts from 40 acres, to 40 thousand acres.

HOMESTEAD.

TIMBER CULTURE

and other entries. Perfect titles to unconfirmed Spanish, French and other land claims.

PAYS SPECIAL ATTENTION

to contested land other land cases before all land offices in Louisiana and before the Interior Department at Washington. Will practice all land cases with Messrs. Drummond & Bradford, Attorneys at Law, of Washington, D. C.

COLLECTIONS PROMPTLY ATTEND-
ED TO.

While

Whom

But th

O, my

That t

Each 8

To leav

And wl

Stood

And ne

Only to

Morg

of the

Rayne,

Addiso

able.

thes

Alex

ceip of

a neat

Messrs.

Landry

will be

with p

Robe

of the

a most

publis

places

list wil

for i s

The Rayne Signal, first newspaper in Acadia Parish, began publication March 13, 1886. The segment shown was reproduced from an original copy preserved by the Addison family of Rayne.

129

Acadia Sentinel, began publication September 14, 1886, with George K. Bradford as editor and publisher.[36]

At this time Rayne had five registered physicians and surgeons: Dr. G. C. Mouton, Dr. J. F. Morris, Dr. F. L. Licht, Dr. A. W. Harrington and Dr. Rufus C. Webb.[37] Another Rayne physician, Dr. A. J. Hooker, had been fatally shot three years earlier.[38]

Dr. Morris, later to be named coroner of Acadia Parish, was involved in a shooting in the fall of 1886. He shot and killed Dave Bull, a Rayne constable, on September 26, 1886. The shooting was said to have been the result of an old feud "with an unfortunate woman at the bottom of it." The men involved had had more than one encounter, and each went armed; the community, it was reported, expected a tragedy and was little surprised. Bull was said to have made open threats to kill the doctor; Morris got his shotgun and opened fire before Bull could draw his pistol, then fired several more shots into Bull's body. Dr. Morris surrendered himself immediately, and was admitted to bail in the sum of $2,000 on a charge of manslaughter.[39]

In July of 1886 the Courier reported that Rayne had a flourishing Literary Club and had recently organized a Hook and Ladder Company. The place was, the editor said, "a wide-awake, progressive town, full of push and energy, and deserves to be the parish seat of the new parish of Acadia, which will doubtless be established in the near future."

One last echo of Queue Tortue appeared in the Rayne Signal. The paper listed the town officials as follows: B. H. Harmon, mayor; J. D. Bernard, M. Arenas, Thomas P. Bowden, H. W. Anding and Raymond T. Clark, councilmen; J. E. Wimberley, constable; P. J. Manouvrier, secretary and tax collector; A. S. Chappuis, treasurer; R. T. Clark, justice of the peace; D. M. Bull, deputy, and A. V. Lyons, constable at Queue Tortue.[40]

Perrin's biographical sketches contain relevant material concerning some of Rayne's pioneer residents. Father Anthonioz, the first priest, was a native of Savoy, France.[41] One published source says that Father

---

36 *Acadia Sentinel*, Oct. 23, 1886, Vol. I, No. 7
37 *Rayne Signal*, April 3, 1886
38 *Opelousas Courier*, Oct. 30, 1883
39 *Ibid*, Oct. 30, 1886; *Acadia Sentinel*, Oct. 30, 1886
40 *Rayne Signal*, April 3, 1886
41 Perrin: *SW La.*, Part II, 251

The residence of Mr. and Mrs. Anselm C. Chappuis, Rayne, 1884. Chinaberry trees, with white-washed trunks, shaded the front yard and wide front porch. The home was located behind the Mervine Kahn store. (Freeland Archives photo)

131

Anthonioz died of yellow fever after nine years service in Acadia Parish;[42] this is incorrect. The priest was alive when interviewed by Perrin about 1890; records of St. Joseph's Church show that Father Anthonioz died August 22, 1891, some three weeks after the last dated record of his work in Rayne — the baptism on August 4, 1891 of Marie Edna Wilson.

Two other prominent Rayne citizens were foreign-born: Louis Alphonse Duclos, druggist and early postmaster, was born in France;[43] Mathias Arenas, one of the first merchants, was a native of Havana,[44] Cuba. The parents of Anselm S. Chappuis were both natives of Lorraine, France; in 1890 when Perrin visited the area Anselm Chappuis was considered the wealthiest businessman in Acadia Parish.[45]

James Webb's father, John Webb, was a British sailor and was on board the ship of which Nelson was in command at the Battle of Trafalgar during the Napoleonic Wars. He came to the Acadia Parish area in the early 1820s, learned the tanner and saddler trade, at which he worked most of his life.[46]

Henry W. Anding's father, W. H. Anding, fought in the Black Hawk and Seminole wars in 1836 under General Winfield Scott.[47] The father of Joseph D. Bernard, first mayor of Rayne, participated in the Battle of New Orleans in 1812.[48] The father of Dr. James F. Morris, M. D., was a Methodist minister of the West Tennessee Conference.[49]

Records of the Rayne Town Council begin in July, 1886. A brief entry explains the three-year lapse: "The minutes of the last meeting having been destroyed by fire on June 30th, it was impossible to read them."

A copy of the town charter, secured after the fire from St. Landry Parish records, shows Rayne as having been chartered March 20, 1883. The charter empowered the town officials to enact such laws and regulations as necessary, and to make such arrests as necessary for violations of ordinances. Upon conviction the violator was to be put to work on the streets instead of being put in jail.

---

42 Baudier: *Catholic Church in La.* 448
43 Perrin: *SW. La.,* Part II, 261
44 *Ibid,* 251
45 *Ibid,* 258
46 *Ibid,* 274
47 *Ibid,* 251
48 *Ibid,* 253
49 *Ibid,* 269

Town officials in 1886 were B. H. Harmon, mayor; Thomas P. Bowden, M. Arenas, R. T. Clark, H. W. Anding and J. D. Bernard, trustees. This slate of officers went in in 1885; the charter provided that the first officials hold office until July 1, 1885.

One of the ordinances enacted by Mayor Harmon and his council made it unlawful "to holler, swear or disturb the peace in any manner within the corporation limits by getting drunk and disorderly or by racing or exposing his person in said town." Another prohibited the discharging of firearms wtihin the corporate limits and made it unlawful to carry concealed weapons, such as pistols, dirks, bowie knives, razors or sling shots.

"Rayne Station," from a tintype made in 1881. Buildings are (from left) the Crouchet hotel, Numa Chachere's cafe and bar, the J. D. Bernard store, Dr. J. F. Morris' drug store, R. J. C. Bull's office and the Bourdier home, which was Rayne's first hotel, known as "Strangers Home." (Freeland Archives photo)

St. Joseph's Church, Rayne, La.

The parish of Rayne was founded by the Jesuits of Grand Coteau and the first church was built at the ancient village of Poupeville in the year 1876. In the year 1882 the church building was rolled on wheels drawn by four pairs of oxen, to Rayne, one mile distant. In 1891 the Jesuit Fathers turned over the parish to the archdiocese, and Most Reverend Francis Janssens, who was then Archbishop, appointed Rev. Father Branche rector of the church at Rayne. Father Branche was in charge of the parish

ST. JOSEPH'S CHURCH, RAYNE, LA.

or eight years during which he worked with success. During his pastorate he erected a fine two-story presbytery in 1894, and a large church in 1899. The old church was rolled for a second time to a point near the Mount Carmel convent, where it is now used as a parochial school for the boys.

Rev. Father Branche was replaced by Father A. S. Doutre on May 1, 1899. Father Doutre had the church finished, painted inside and outside, and last year in order to accommodate the growing number of Catholics he built two side chapels to the church.

The early history of the Rayne Catholic church was published in a 1911 issue of the Morning Star, official organ of the Catholic Church in Louisiana 1868-1926. The photo shows the second church built in 1899, and one of the two side chapels built in 1910. (Reproduction courtesy Rev. Donald J. Hebert)

Rayne had sidewalks in 1886. One of the town ordinances prohibited the hitching, driving or leading of any animal or team on the sidewalks. The morality of the community was taken into consideration; persons keeping disorderly houses were fined not less than $20 or more than $50, and no dice or card playing was allowed on the streets or sidewalks.

The town constable could make extra money by picking up unpenned hogs. The constable received 25 cents for catching the animal and putting it in the pound, and an additional 15 cents for feeding the hog. Owners could redeem the hogs for 50 cents each, but if unredeemed the animals were sold to the highest bidder.

The health, sanitation and neatness of the community were given attention. Residents were ordered to keep yards and water closets on their premises "in a clear condition" or have same done at the property owner's expense.

Minutes of the February, 1887 meeting show that the council considered bids for public printing. The Rayne Signal bid $50 for the job; the Acadia Sentinel offered it gratis. The free printing was accepted.

A new set of officers went in in 1887. R. J. C. Bull was mayor, and the aldermen were R. C. Webb, G. C. Mouton, M. Kahn, A. S. Chappuis and L. H. Keller.

In January of 1888 Aldermen Kahn and Chappuis were authorized to buy four street lamps; at this meeting the council accepted the resignation of Dr. Mouton, who had moved to Lafayette. H. W. Anding was named to replace Dr. Mouton.

In May of 1888 the council received a communication from W. C. Chevis, editor of the Acadia Sentinel. Editor Chevis informed the council that he could not publish the proceedings of the town council unless he was paid $100 a year, or $1 per square, for same. The council decided to invite bids "from other papers published in this parish." Later, Chevis agreed to take the job for $30 per year.

There was also a hassle between Mayor Bull and Editor Chevis. The editor charged the mayor with public bribery in a matter involving a railroad crossing, but the charges were refuted and peace was restored.

A new mayor and council went into office in 1889. Thomas P. Bowden was the mayor and council members were Armas Gillard, G. J. Malone, E. O. Bruner, J. F. Morris and W. C. Chevis. The town attorney, F. F. Perrodin, who had been appointed in 1888, was retained.

Some new problems faced the council in the fall of 1889. One, evidently precipitated by the more daring youth of the town, resulted in an ordinance providing for fining "persons jumping on and off trains for sport while the trains are in motion." Offenders were subject to a $1 fine for the first offense, $2.50 for the second, $5 for the third, and after that the matter was left to the mayor's discretion.

The most important matter to be taken up by the council in 1889 was building a new school house, a two-story building to be erected on donated land.

Englargement of a portion of a quaint old photograph, owned by Winston Barousse of Rayne. The picture is believed to have been taken in the early 1900s in front of a school building in Rayne. Faint pencil markings on the back identify the three gentlemen in right foreground as R. J. C. Bull, A. Broussard and George K. Bradford.

One final abstract from the town council records shows a problem resulting from the mushrooming rice industry: On January 6, 1890, Dr. J. F. Morris, chairman of the committee on sanitation, reported that he had examined the rice chaff thrown out by the rice mill; he said that the health of the community "would be seriously jeopardized by allowing same to decompose within the corporate limits." The council ordered same to be destroyed or removed from the town limits.

The first rice mill in Acadia Parish was built in Rayne in 1887. First name for the business was the Rayne Rice Mill and Manufacturing Company, and the first officers were A. S. Chappuis, president; M. Arenas, treasurer and August L. Chappuis, secretary. The building was described as "a very substantial one" in the Crowley Signal of August 25, 1888. The dimensions were given as being 40 by 90, and 34 feet high, and the top of the cupola 50 feet from the ground; an adjoining warehouse was 40 by 60 by 14. "The machinery is all first class and is driven by an engine of one hundred horse power. The capacity of the mill is calculated to be one hundred barrels per day of clean rice."

In 1890 Emile Daboval bought an interest in the rice mill, the name of which was changed to Acadia Rice Milling Company. Daboval, the eldest son of Emile Daboval and Angela de Lesseps, had been in the rice milling business with his father in New Orleans. He married Lydia Deynoodt, daughter of a former Belgian consul. In a biographical sketch published in the Crowley Signal, October 27, 1894, Daboval is described as "a typical gentleman of the old school. His suavity of manners, his integrity have won him a host of friends."

Background information on other early businessmen of Rayne is contained in the following abstracts from the Crowley Signal of August 25, 1888:

Mervine Kahn came to Rayne in 1884, and in 1888 was considered the leading man in the merchandising business.

J. D. Bernard, Rayne's first mayor and first general merchant, was elected to the Louisiana House of Representatives in 1888.

Moise Dupuis came to Rayne from Breaux Bridge in 1882 and started a general merchandising business; M. L. Melancon, another general merchant, came in 1886 from Port Barre, then called Barry's Landing.

Thomas P. Bowden went into the grocery business in Rayne in 1883; his cousin, G. J. Malone, became the junior member of the firm in 1888.

RICE MILL, RAYNE, LA.

First rice mill in Acadia Parish, from a wood cut in the Crowley Signal
of August 25, 1888. The mill began operations in the fall of 1888.

138

Other grocers were George Lagroue, M. Brien, L. A. Keller and Paul Caillouet.

A. S. Chappuis came to Rayne in 1882 and opened a general merchandising business which he sold to Mervine Kahn in 1884. He opened a lumber business in 1886; the junior partner in the firm was his nephew, A. L. Chappuis. Others in the lumber line were W. C. Dunshie and L. R. Deputy.

Rayne's first hotel was The Stranger's Home, operated by Mrs. George Bourdier; in 1888 the hotel had been taken over by Mrs. Numa Chachere. Francois Crouchet was operating the Rayne Hotel in 1888, and a new hotel, the Iowa House, had as its proprietor S. M. Woolsey, native of Iowa.

R. J. C. Bull was in the real estate business and also had a livery stable; a second livery stable was operated by E. O. Bruner.

W. F. Johnson, native of Scotland, came to Rayne in 1880. He was a painter by trade. E. Capel, the proprietor of the Rayne Tin Shop, came in 1883 from Thibodaux; he also had a shop at Crowley.

There were two Bradfords in Rayne: Welman Bradford, a surveyor and civil engineer, and George K. Bradford, publisher of the Acadia Sentinel, real estate agent, land attorney and surveyor. George K. Bradford came to Rayne in 1885, and started the newspaper in 1886. W. C. Chevis joined the staff of the Acadia Sentinel in 1887.

The first Rayne newspaper, the Rayne Signal, was published at Rayne from March 13, 1886, until January 1, 1888, when it was moved to Crowley.

Abstracts from advertisements in the Rayne Signal of 1886 and 1887 show additional business people of Rayne:

Charles A. Perrodin was a notary public and auctioneer; Edgar W. Roy was a house and sign painter, and W. C. Dunshie a contractor and builder.

There were three saloons in Rayne: The Rayne Drop Saloon, Donat Pucheu, proprietor, and the Bon Ton Saloon, owned by L. Deputy. The McBride and Stephens barroom was also an oyster bar.

The Acadia Bakery and Cake Shop was operated by L. A. Keller; Dr. A. W. Harrington sold drugs and "fancy articles." J. N. Laney was the first dentist.

The Methodist congregation of Rayne built this first church in 1884
on land donated by Mrs. Mary Cunningham, widow of Dr. William
Cunningham, the town's founder. This building served the community
until 1967, when it was replaced by the present (1976) edifice. (Freeland
Archives photo)

William M. Carlin was a partner in the Capel tin shop business; A. C. Poulet was an agent for a lumber firm; H. Picard sold wholesale and retail merchandising; R. T. Clark and E. O. Bruner had a livery stable. F. M. Levy owned a cash bargain store; P. J. Manouvrier was manager for Isaac A. Smith grocery; J. S. Stephens was the proprietor of the Stephens' House hotel; Mervine Kahn advertised wagons, buggies, hacks, agricultural implements, clothing, hats, shoes, boots, hardware, furniture, paints and oils.

CHAPTER VII

Church Point

The present corporation lines of the town of Church Point take in portions of seven Spanish land grants: those claimed by Etienne Daigle, Lufroy Latiolais, Jacques Deshotels, Louis Leger,* Louis Latiolais and Sylvain Sonnier.

The settlement at Church Point, like others along the length of the bayou, was once known as Plaquemine Brûlée. Notice of the public sale of the estate of Marie Josephine Daigle, widow of Lufroy Latiolais, published in the Opelousas Courier of September 4, 1858, situated the Latiolais plantation "in the quarter commonly called Plaquemine Brulee." The place was also known as Plaquemine Point. The voting place for Plaquemine Point in 1842 was "at the house of the widow Latiolais on Upper Plaquemine Brulee."[1] The Louis Leger property was described as located "at Plaquemine Point."[2]

The earliest known settler in the Church Point area was Louis Latiolais, who came in the 1770s.[3] His son, Lufroy Latiolais, married Marie Josephine Daigle, daughter of Etienne Daigle III, in 1811.[4] Both Lufroy and his brother-in-law, Etienne Daigle IV, were prominent in affairs of St. Landry Parish; both served on the grand jury in 1816. Latiolais, with Jean Blaise Lejeune and Bonaventure Martin, was named to a committee to build a bridge over the bayou in his neighborhood, and was authorized to call out the inhabitants of the area to help with the bridge-building.[5]

The nucleus of the settlement began in the 1840s, when two grandsons of Etienne Daigle III, Joseph E. and Theodule Daigle, built homes in what is now the town proper.[6] Other early settlers were the families of Barousse, Bergeron, Breaux, David, Guidry, LeBleu, Leger, McBride, Thibodeaux and Wimberley.[7]

---

* Louis Leger owned two of the seven tracts.

1 *Opelousas Gazette*, May 28, 1842
2 *Ibid,* Nov. 18, 1843
3 Guidry: *La Pointe de l'Eglise*, 73
4 Hebert: *SW. La. Records*, Vol. II, 563
5 St. Landry Parish Police Jury minutes, Sept 4, 1816
6 Guidry: *La Pointe de l'Eglise*, 4
7 *Ibid*, 8

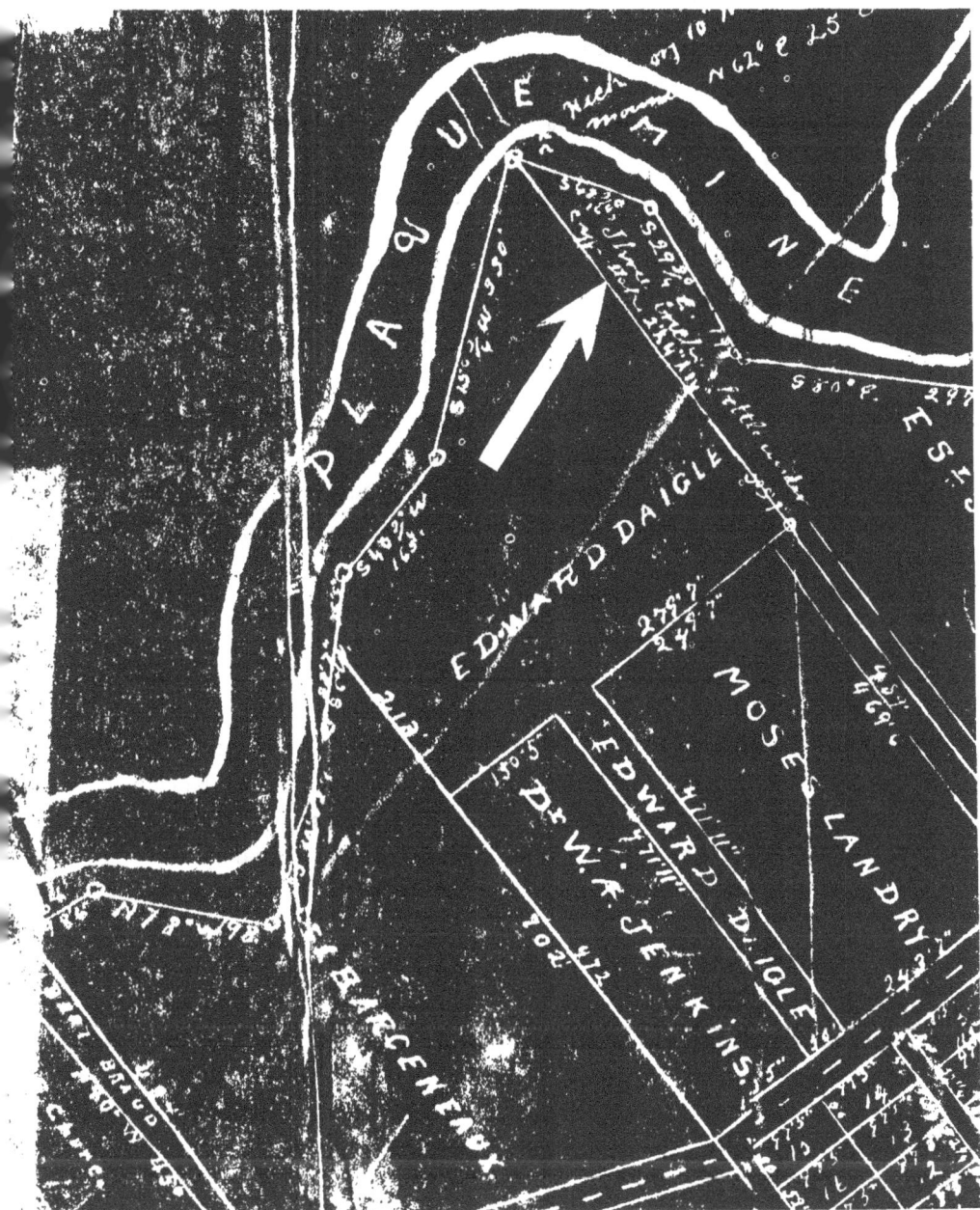

Detail of a map of Church Point made in 1897 by Welman Bradford, parish surveyor. The survey line at the bridge was marked by "three bricks and a bottle under a cypress stake." Arrow points to this quaint legend on the old map. The original map, drawn on linen fabric, is in the Acadia Parish courthouse. (Reproduction courtesy Marie Cook)

143

Returns of an 1842 election show that 95 persons voted at the Plaquemine Point poll.[8] Ten years later, the Joseph Daigle place was the voting poll and tax collection point;[9] even after Daigle's death in 1854 his house remained the polling place for many years. Commissioners who served at the poll in 1863 were Valentin D. Breaux, Theodule Daigle and Louis M. Leger.[10] From 1852 until 1873, when the place name of Church Point came into use, the voting precinct was listed Upper Plaquemine Brûlée.

In 1848 the Jesuits of Grand Coteau were asked to establish a church in the settlement. The Jesuits bought land, and a church building was secured by the Daigle brothers. The small chapel, measuring 20 by 30 feet,[11] was the first Catholic church established in the Acadia Parish area. Preceded only by the churches of Opelousas and Grand Coteau, it was the third Catholic church to be established in St. Landry Parish, which at that time took in the three present parishes of St. Landry, Acadia and Evangeline.

A larger church building replaced the first chapel in 1851. Three years later the Daigles donated five arpents of land to the church, adding to the original tract bought by the Jesuits in 1848.[12] Records of the mission chapel begin March 25, 1851, when four baptisms were recorded by Rev. Aloysius L. Roccofort, S. J. The first was Octave, son of Jean Baptiste David and Marguerite Elmire Breaux; the second was Emilie, daughter of Theodule Daigle and Evelina Fux. The third baptism was the son of a slave: Cesair, son of Sylvestre and Julienne, slaves of Madame Antoine Guidry; the fourth, Cecile, daughter of Henri Johnson and Evelina Quarentin.[13]

A school was in operation at Church Point 30 years before Acadia Parish was established. This was in 1856, when a small room adjoining the Catholic chapel was used as a schoolroom. The school system was semi-public; teachers were paid by the parish for two months work, there-after by tuition paid by parents of the pupils.[14] Thus Church Point can claim another "first" for Acadia Parish — the first school.

---

8 *Opelousas Gazette*, July 9, 1842
9 *Opelousas Courier*, Dec. 11, 1852
10 *Ibid*, Nov. 8, 1863
11 Guidry: *La Pointe de l'Eglise*, 9
12 *Ibid*
13 Our Lady of the Sacred Heart Catholic Church records
14 Guidry: *La Pointe de l'Eglise*, 15

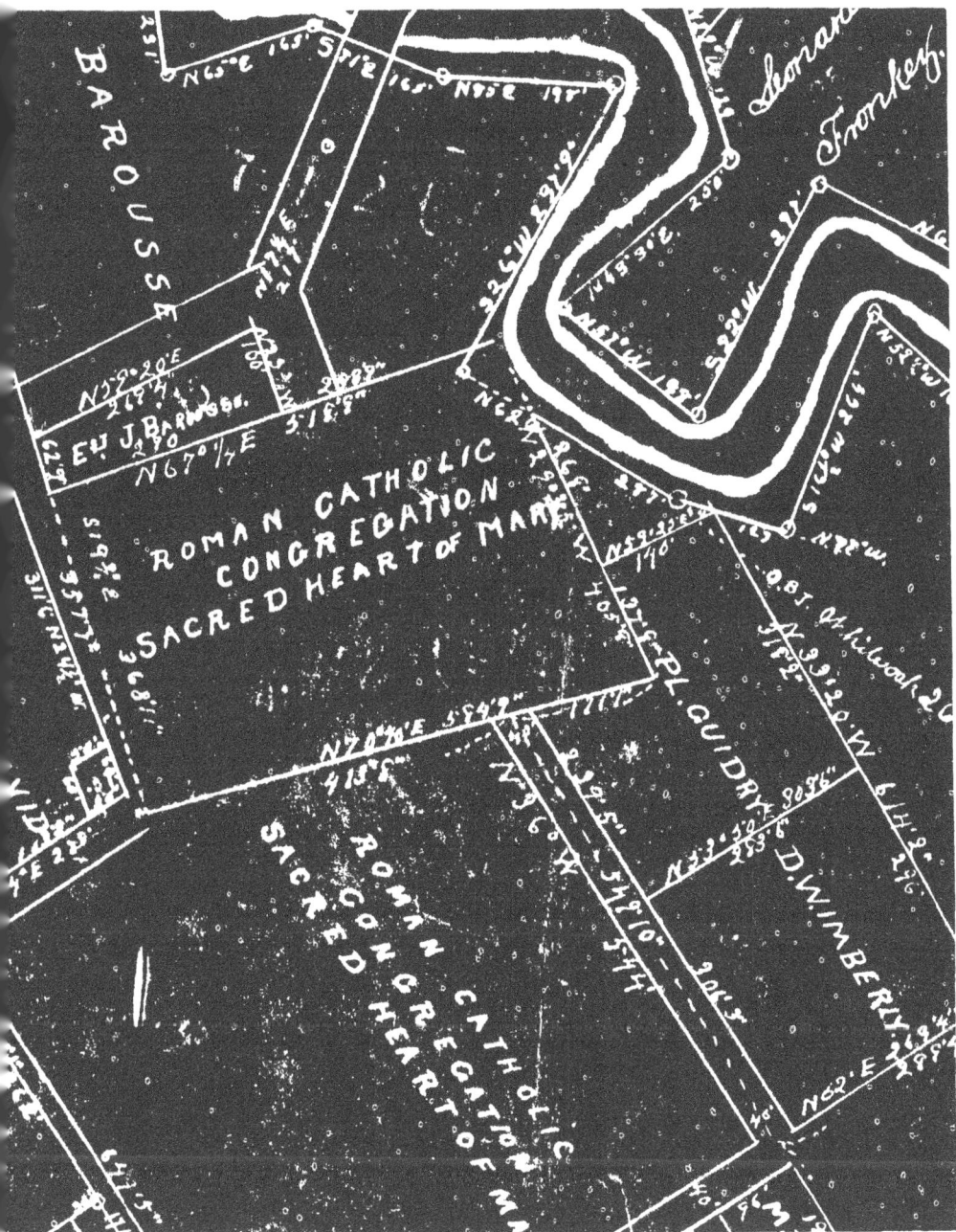

The town of Church Point grew up around its first church. The church property is shown on this segment of a map drawn in 1897. The name of the church was later changed to Our Lady of the Sacred Heart Catholic Church.

Pierre Louis Guidry was the settlement's first merchant.[15] It is not known when Guidry began his business, but it is believed that he operated a store for some years prior to the establishment of the chapel; his home, adjacent to his small store building, was the place where Jesuit missionaries came to say Mass and administer the sacraments before the chapel was secured.[16]

Jean Barousse, native of France and progenitor of a distinguished family, was also a pioneer merchant.[17] He came to the area in the 1840s and married Caroline Fontenot, a descendant of Etienne Daigle. Barousse was assessor for the southern part of St. Landry Parish during the Civil War.[18]

Other early businessmen were Leonard Franques, Jules David and Ernest Daigle, all of whom were in business in the 1870s.[19]

The prairie lands in the Church Point area, despite relative proximity to the parish seat of Opelousas, were virtually unpopulated until after the Civil War. This is shown by legal notices inserted in the Opelousas Courier, for example: The public sale of the estate of Aminthe Fontenot was set for February 1, 1858; the estate included a tract of land, three by 40 arpents, on upper Plaquemine Brûlé bounded on the north by public land, east by Martin d'Aigle, south by the bayou, west by Lufroy Fontenot. Anothes tract in the estate, six by 40 arpents, was bounded north and west by public lands, south by the bayou and east by Don Louis Carrier. Joseph E. Daigle was administrator of the estate. It is interesting to note here that land ownership at this time, more than half a century after the Louisiana Purchase, was continuing to follow the riverbank strip system— both tracts of land in the Fontenot estate abutted on the bayou, and the lands opposite and to the west of the bayou frontage—the prairie lands— were as yet unclaimed.

In April of 1866 the St. Landry Parish Police Jury named a committee of three to repair "the bridge near the Catholic chapel of Plaquemine;" $250 was appropriated for the job, to be let to the lowest bidder. Named to the bridge-repair committee were Valentin D. Breaux, Theodule Daigle and Jean Barousse. The same bridge was ordered repaired again

15 Guidry: *La Pointe de l'Eglise*, 11
16 *Ibid*
17 Perrin: *SW La.*, Part II, 242-253
18 *Ibid*
19 Guidry: *La Pointe de l'Eglise*, 22

in 1869; Theodule Daigle, William Elkins, Jean Barousse and V. D. Breaux were authorized to sell the work to the lowest bidder.[20]

The Opelousas Courier was behind the times in the fall of 1873. An item in the issue of November 15 reported: "A new post office will soon be established at the chapel at Plaquemine Brulee, in this parish, about 13

20 St. Landry Par. Police Jury minutes, Oct. 20, 1869

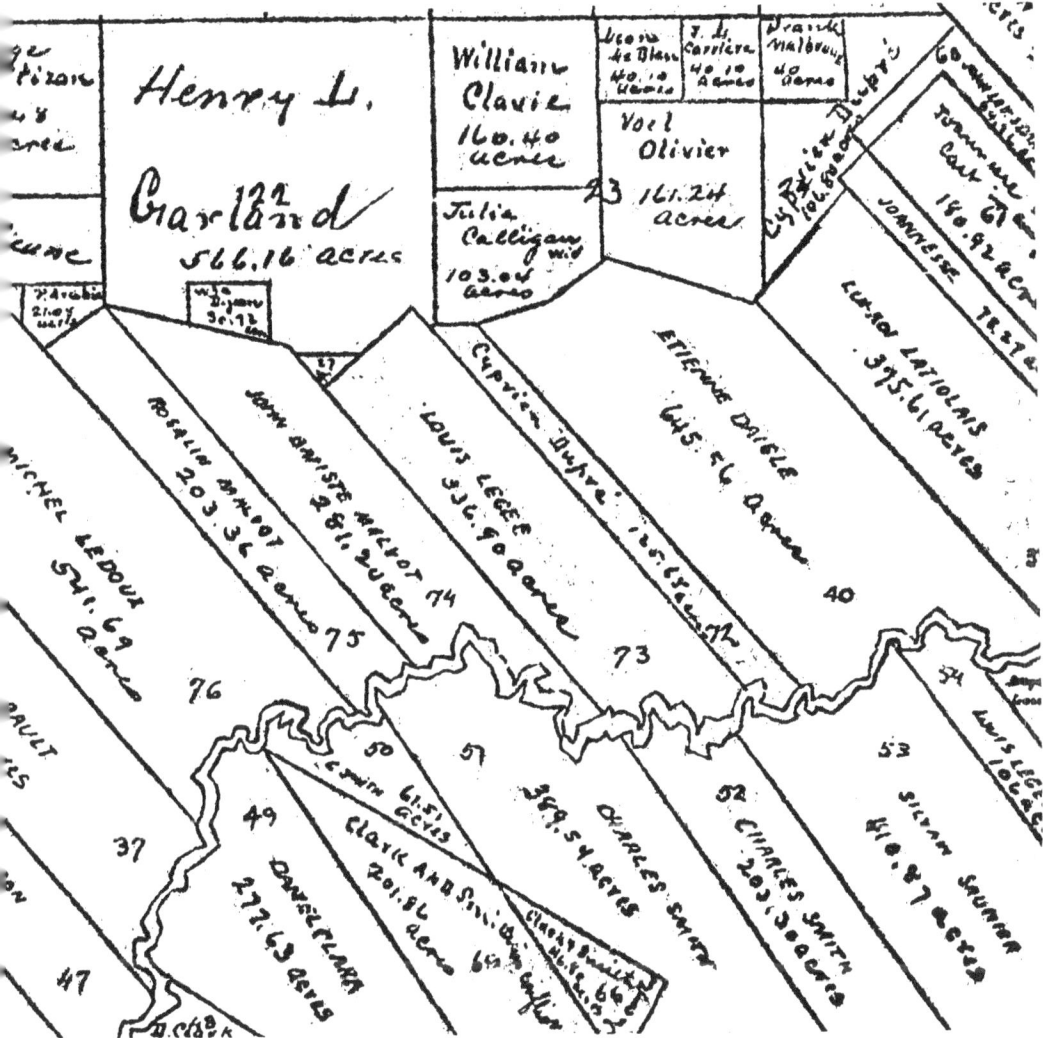

Southeast quarter of Township 7 South Range 2 East, the Church Point area, from Parsons' survey of 1881. Landowners' names, other than those on the riverbank strips which were Spanish land grants, were written in by an unknown person.

miles southwest of Opelousas. Mr. Jules David will be the postmaster and is to have mail once a week." Actually, the post office was established September 29, 1873;[21] after this date the settlement was known officially as Church Point.

A new school building was erected in 1875. Of rough-hewn lumber, the school was built by Homer Barousse and Ernest Daigle, on property owned by Valentin Breaux. The school house, 16 by 30 feet, accommodated about 35 pupils who attended classes three to four months out of the year.[22]

During these early years births, marriages and deaths rated an occasional one or two-line notice in the Opelousas Courier. A wedding in Church Point in 1877 evoked a quaintly worded congratulatory message, published in the June 16 issue: "MARRIED — at the Catholic Church, Church Point, on June 4 by Rev. Father Vialton, Mr. Thelismar Guidry and Miss Armina,* daughter of Mr. Theodule Daigle. Auspicious event! The witness of the most important step taken by two loving hearts in the pilgrimage of life. Mutually pledged in happiness and sorrow, their vows are registered in heaven as the sharers of a single destiny on earth. Hope now holds out her 'bright rainbow of promise' to these our young friends; they are both most estimable and worthy, and the writer sincerely trusts that they may realize the full fruition of a long, a happy, and a prosperous life." The newspaper piece was signed "A Friend."

The attractions and merits of the town were detailed in an Opelousas Courier article of May 15, 1880: "Church Point is the name of a pretty little hamlet situated on Bayou Plaquemine, about 15 miles from Opelousas. It is one of the healthiest locations in St. Landry Parish, and is thickly settled with industrious and neighborly citizens, mostly Creoles yet with quite a sprinkling of the American population." The lands were fertile, the writer continued, and the grasses afforded good grazing throughout the year; many new places had been fenced in, and an increase was noted in corn, sugar and cotton acreage. Advantages to be found in the town were two stores, a blacksmith and wagon shop, a boot and shoe shop; a sugar mill, a school house, a Catholic church and a resident physician. The citizens, the writer stated, were "good, happy and contented;" lands were cheap, with "plenty of room for enterprising immigrants."

---

* Hermina, daughter of Theodule Daigle and Evelina Fux

21 U.S. Post Office records

22 Guidry: *La Pointe de l'Eglise*, 15-16

December 5, 1854.

Portion of document from the St. Landry Parish courthouse, Donations Book 2, pages 176, showing the donation of 4.61 acres of land to the Catholic church by Theodule and Joseph Daigle. The donors stipulated that a 50-foot square in the graveyard be reserved for themselves and their families; they also reserved free use of a pew in the church, and the rights to the wood and trees on the property. (Reproduction courtesy Rev. Donald Hebert)

The resident physician mentioned was either Dr. James Donovan, who was in the area in 1870,[23] or Dr. J. A. McMillan, who practiced there from 1870 until after 1886.[24] Dr. W. Childs was a Church Point physician in 1886;[25] Dr. W. A. Jenkins began practice in 1887.[26]

In 1883 two election precincts served the Church Point area. The polling place for Church Point proper was at McBride's store; Jules David, Homer Barousse and H. D. McBride were election commissioners. A nearby rural area, called Pointe Noire, had its own precinct, with the polling place at Joseph Daigle's. Commissioners were Arthur Daigle, Francois Savoie and Joseph Latiolais.[27]

An election to name delegates to the parish Democratic convention took place in 1883, with P. L. Guidry, Dr. J. A. McMillan and V. D. Breaux as poll officials.[28] Elected to represent Church Point were Homer Barousse, Theogene Daigle, Pierre Richard, Adrien Sonnier, Theodule Thibodeaux, Francois Ledoux, Pierre Bellard, H. J. Daigle and Dallas B. Hayes.[29]

Jesuit priests from Grand Coteau served the Catholic church until 1883, when Rev. Auguste Vincent Eby, of the secular clergy, was assigned pastor. The editor of the Courier, reporting on Father Eby's appointment, noted that $3,000 had been turned over to the new pastor for a new church, and added: "next to Opelousas, we believe that Church Point has a larger congregation of worshippers than any other church in the parish."[30]

A three-day fair for the benefit of the church was given advance publicity in the Opelousas Courier of December 18, 1886. The fair, scheduled to begin on Christmas Day, would include many attractions, such as horse racing. The main event was to be a race between two young horses, "born on the same day and raised with great care." The horses were "Rapp," owned and raised by Father Eby, and "Mixon," raised "by the popular old merchant, Jean Barousse."

The Catholic church remained the only church until 1889, when a Methodist church was organized. First services were held in a brush

23 *Opelousas Courier*, Sept. 17, 1870
24 Perrin: *SW La.*, 268-269; *Rayne Signal*, Apr. 3, 1886
25 *Ibid*
26 Guidry: *La Pointe de l'Eglise*, 43
27 *Opelousas Courier*, Feb. 10, 1883
28 *Ibid*, Nov. 10, 1883
29 *Ibid*, Dec. 8, 1883
30 July 21, 1883

CHURCH AND PARSONAGE AT CHURCH POINT, LA.

The Crowley Signal of August 25, 1888 used this wood cut of the Catholic church and rectory at Church Point. Rev. Auguste Eby was the first resident pastor, assigned to the church parish in 1883.

The Catholic church of Church Point, reproduced from the Crowley Signal of May 10, 1898. This picture shows a clock in the steeple. The steeple was evidently added to the church after 1888, as the wood cut shown previously shows a belfry but no steeple.

arbor, a shelter consisting of rough posts with a skeleton roof onto which leafy branches were piled for protection against the weather.[31]

The "Prosperity Number" of the Crowley Signal, published May 10, 1898, devoted a full page to Church Point. The population of the town, "according to local estimates," was 500; the countryside was described as "very thickly settled, compared to some other portions of the parish." The people, the writer stated, "are almost entirely Creole, but a person of English descent is occasionally met with." The writer found the people hospitable and friendly; French was the language of ordinary conversation, "but most of the people can speak English also." In religious belief, "they are, of course, almost all Catholic."

A picture of the Catholic church accompanied the article. The church had an estimated seating capacity of six or seven hundred persons. The church, despite its size, was "frequently crowded, and many cannot gain entrance." The church stood in the midst of a grove of young trees between the Catholic graveyard and the parsonage, "and lifts its red-painted steeple, surmounted with a gilt cross, far up into the sky, a beacon that can be seen for miles around." The Methodist church was described as a comparatively new church of a recent style of architecture, which stood "in the southern edge of town among the oaks." The Rev. Porter, who lived at Prudhomme City, preached twice a month at the Methodist Church.

The Church Point school had an enrollment of about 100. School funds were supplemented by private means; parents of each child paid an additional fifty cents a month which enabled the school to run 12 months in the year, instead of the usual four to seven months. Prof. F. R. Bartlett was principal of the school and Miss Corinne Guidry was his assistant.

An article about Church Point, published in the Louisiana Review, was reprinted in the Crowley Signal of September 21, 1889. Information given included the following: Jean Barousse had been in business in Church Point some 40 years; Martin Carron had just completed construction of the Barousse cotton gin, and the firm of L. Schmeib and Bro. had been established for two years. Merchants and grocers listed were Leonard Franques, P. L. Guidry and J. B. David; Thelismar Guidry had a saddlery and harness shop, shoe shop and barber shop. Etienne Latiolais made and repaired wagons, H. D. McBride and Moses Landry had blacksmith shops.

---

31 Guidry: *La Pointe de l'Eglise,* 28

Dr. J. A. McMillan and Dr. W. A. Jenkins were the town physicians, Valentin Breaux operated a cotton gin, W. S. Evins owned a sawmill and Jules David was the inkeeper. Mail was being delivered three times a week, on Mondays, Wednesdays and Fridays.[32]

Church Point's first mayor was Homer Barousse, who served from February 11, 1893 to February 1, 1895. The son of the pioneer merchant, Jean Barousse, Homer Barousse married Emily Daigle, daughter of Theodule Daigle, one of the town's founders. Barousse became one of the most influential political figures in Acadia Parish; he was a member of the first police jury and first chairman of the parish Democratic Executive Committee. In 1894 he was elected to the Louisiana Senate, a post he held for 38 years, until he retired in 1932.[33]

The town was incorporated in 1899. Other early mayors were Dr. L. B. Arceneaux, 1895; H. J. David, 1897; H. D. McBride, 1900.[34]

---

[32] *Crowley Signal*, Oct. 5, 1889
[33] Guidry: *La Pointe de l'Eglise*, 24
[34] *Ibid*

Church Point merchants inserted the advertisements shown above in the Crowley Signal "Prosperity Number" of May 10, 1898. Constant Bries was the town's first druggist.

CHAPTER VIII

Pointe-aux-Loups

Pointe-aux-Loups, or Wolf Point, is one of the oldest place names of the Acadia Parish area. First mention of the place in government papers is in records of 1811, when William McKoy purchased 640 acres of land at "Wolf Point."[1] Like other early settlements, the name Pointe-aux-Loups stems from the name of a waterway, Coulée Pointe-aux-Loups, a tributary of Bayou des Cannes. The name is said to have originated because of the presence of large numbers of wolves in the wooded areas adjacent to the stream. One recorded item substantiates this: In December, 1868, the St. Landry Police Jury paid Sifroy Hebert $10 bounty for five wolf scalps; Hebert owned land situated between Bayous des Cannes and Nezpique, in the general vicinity of Pointe-aux-Loups.[2]

First known settlers of the area were the Doucets, the Heberts and the Semars (Simar, Semer). In 1835 Archille and Marcellon Doucet bought 161.26 acres of land in Section 6, Township 9 South, Range 1 West; the same amount of land was purchased the same year, in the same township and section, by Antoine Hebert and Louis Semar. These land sales are the earliest entries in the Abstracts of U. S. Land Entries, No. 1, in the Acadia Parish courthouse.

Citizens of the area voted at the house of Alexandre Daigle, *pere,* in 1852;[3] 24 ballots were counted at the poll at an election in 1853.[4] The Daigle place remained a voting precinct until 1863, when the precinct location was changed to the house of Antoine Cart;[5] election commissioners were Sifroy Hebert, Jean Jacques Bertrand and Alexandre Daigle.[6] That same year the police jury authorized Charles Trahan to keep a public ferry on Bayou des Cannes at what was described as "Daigle's Olde Crossing;" ferriage rates were set at $1 for wagon or ox cart teams; 50 cents for a carriage; 25 cents for a man on horseback and 15 cents for footmen.[7]

---

1 Sheriff's Deeds Book A, St. Landry Parish
2 Abstracts U.S. Land Entries, No. 1, Acadia Parish
3 "Some History of St. Landry Parish," *Daily World,* 201
4 *Ibid,* 200
5 St. Landry Par. Police Jury minutes, Mar. 18, 1863
6 *Opelousas Courier,* Nov. 28, 1863
7 St. Landry Par. Police Jury minutes, Aug. 21, 1863

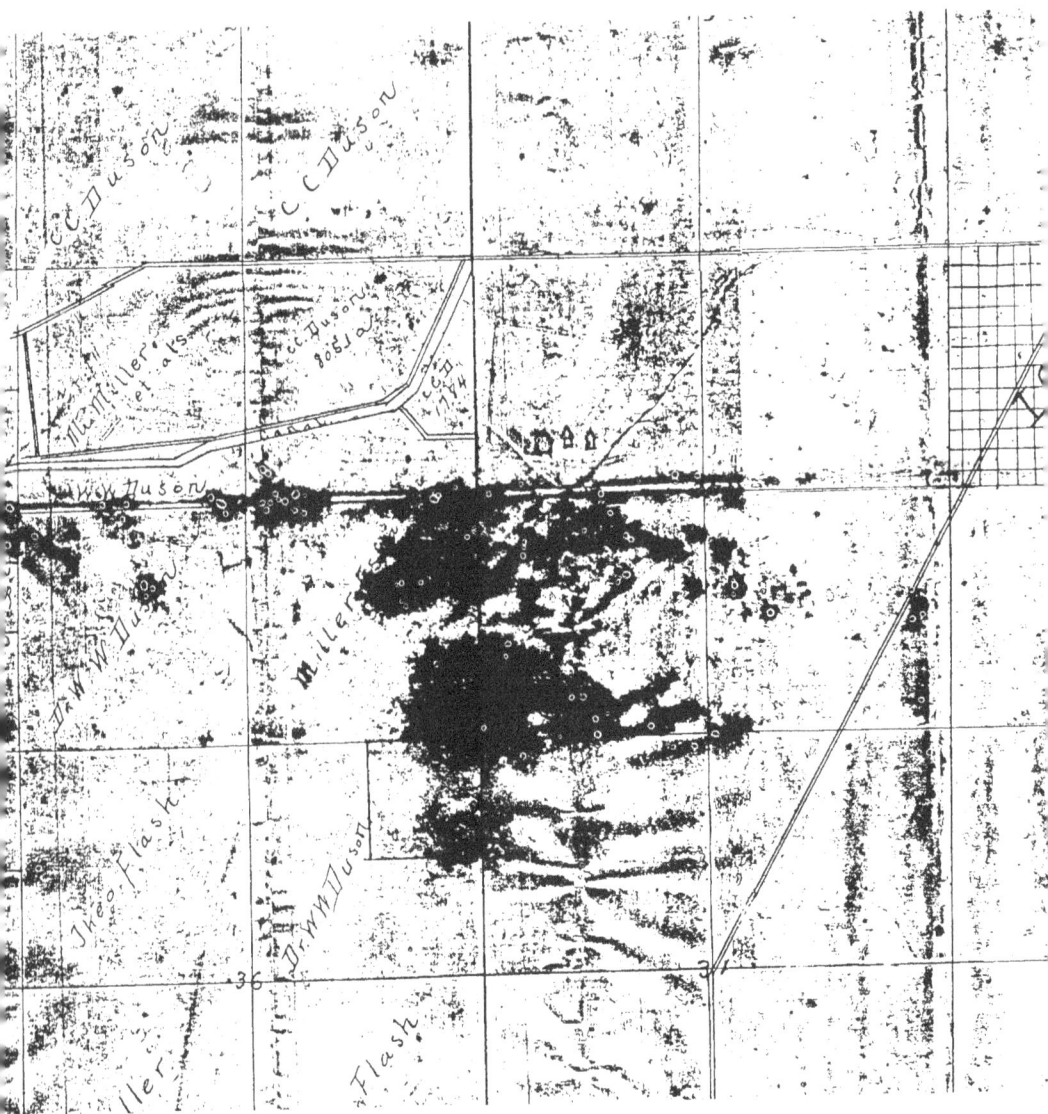

Portion of an old map which shows the location (indicated by arrow at left) of the resort buildings at Pointe-aux-Loups Springs. Double lines at right show the Southern Pacific branch railroad from Midland to Eunice which created the new place name of Iota. Center arrow points out the Cartville settlement. (Reproduced from the original in the Freeland Archives)

Pointe-aux Loups became a well known summer ressort prior to the Civil War. The Opelousas Courier of June 5, 1858 carried the following eloquently phrased advertisement under a boldface headline:

The undersigned takes this mode of notifying the public he is now in readiness to receive all those whose pleasure it be to seek the above as a place of pleasure and recreation as well as those who may be impelled from indisposition to have recourse to them for the remedial agency of the waters. These Springs are situated on the Bayou des Cannes distant about 34 miles southwest of the town of Opelousas. The numerous springs there to be found may be as such as are found abounding with sulphur and preparations of iron. The springs are very abundant and in one instance three of the streams form a large basin which affords a magnificent bathing place, the waters of the said basin can be entirely renewed every hour the circumstance which is certainly calculated to add much to its purity. At the distance of some 500 yards from the principal bathing place areas beside this another is furnished with an abundant stream of water the coldness of which can almost be compared to that of ice.

In announcing the opening of this establishment the undersigned does not pretend to offer to the public as in a fashionable watering place where fine dressing may be exhibited with the other general accompaniments. His object on the contrary, is to offer to the afflicted a means through which a shocked constitution may be restored to health. The remedial agency of these waters in the relief of dyspepsia and in the permanent cure of cutaneous eruptions from past experience now stands uncontradicted. The establishment consists of comfortable dwellings with all the necessary furniture which may be required of such a place, and the table will be always simply furnished with whatever edibles may seem best to suit the taste of visitors. An excellent pasture in which horses may be kept with safety will be at the disposition of such as may desire it, as well as corn, fodder, etc. The charges of the undersigned will be moderate and he feels satisfied that his visitors will not only be satisfied with the accommodations which they may receive but that they will be also equally contented with the degree of health which they may obtain from the healthful use of the waters of the different springs. Antoine Cart.

The advertising evidently paid off, as the advertisements continued to appear in the Opelousas newspaper until the Civil War years, when publication of the paper was suspended. After the war the advertising appeared again; by 1873 the place was attracting visitors not only from Opelousas, but from outside the area. The Opelousas Courier noted the names of some of the visitors to the springs: the editor himself, Joel H. Sandoz; Judge A. Garrigues, A. Levy, Joseph Bloch, his wife, family and servants;

also guests from New Iberia and New Orleans.[8] Testimonials to the curative powers of the waters were also given, and were published "without the knowledge of the proprietor" of the springs, the editor stated. Antoine Labbe said his daughter had been cured of dyspepsia; Charles A. Perrodin's testimonial said that his daughter, 12, had fever and chills and a deranged stomach; the girl couldn't eat or drink for 18 months, but was now in good health. Another of the Perrodin children who had *des dartes* (ringworm) over almost all of its head had been cured; there was mention of others who had been cured of "maladies of the skin."[9]

8 July 12. 1873
9 July 5. 1873

POINT-AUX-LOUPS SPRINGS, LA.

One of the resort buildings at Pointe-aux-Loups Springs, shown in a reproduction of a wood cut used in the Crowley Signal of August 25, 1888. The last of the buildings was destroyed by fire in the 1950s.

Special rates were offered for those who wished to bring their own provisions to the Springs. Accommodations could be had by the day, week or month "at a modest price."[10]

The proprietor of this popular resort, Antoine Belisair Cart, was the son of Jean Louis Antoine Cart,[11] whose Spanish land grant was on upper Plaquemine Brûlée. Also known as Xavier Cart, Antoine Belisair was said to have been in poor health and was advised by physicians to move to Texas. Enroute there he was detained at Pointe-aux-Loups by high water and decided to remain. After several years his health was restored, a benefit which he attributed to the healing properties of the springs. He lived there until his death at age 82.[12]

An interesting sidelight on the early history of the springs at Pointe-aux-Loups comes from the Crowley Signal of August 15, 1888: "The curative powers of these famous waters was first discovered in 1814 by one Placede Richard. He was a refugee from the War of 1812. A son was suffering from scrofula and it was found that by bathing in the water of the spring near their camp a marked relief was effected."

Placede (Placide) Richard, born 1782, was the son of Fabien Richard,[13] whose Spanish land grant was located some seven miles northeast of Pointe-aux-Loups Springs. The information quoted above, presented as fact, can only be interpreted to mean that Richard, with his family, camped out in the wilderness to escape possible conscription for military service. He could have been one of the many Louisianians not in sympathy with the conflict which came so soon after statehood; it is possible that the camp mentioned, located in the then remote area, was a refuge for others who wanted no part of the war.

Pointe-aux-Loups Springs was bought in June, 1877 by G. Miller. The change in management was noted by the Opelousas Courier of June 2, 1877: "The popular Pointe-aux-Loups springs, recently purchased by Mr. Miller and thoroughly repaired and much improved by him, will now be open to the public as in former years." This indicates that the resort may have been shut down for a time. Among the improvements was the erection of a hotel, 60 feet in length.

---

10 *Opelousas Courier,* July 25, 1874
11 Hebert: *SW La. Records,* Vol. 1, 118
12 Cart family history
13 Hebert: *SW La. Records,* Vol. 1, 481

The new proprietor continued the newspaper advertising begun by Cart. Items in the news columns told of Saturday night balls being given at the Springs; these social activities continued on into the fall, and admittance was free.[14] There was even a New Years Eve dance. The advertisement for the *Grand Bal,* inserted in the Christmas, 1878 issue of the Courier, was illustrated with a drawing of a dancing couple.

The resort was opened for the season each June. On May 31, 1879 the Courier reported that Mr. and Mrs. Miller had arrived at the Springs, "that celebrated watering place for health and pleasure," for the season. Noted among the improved facilities were the buildings, four mineral springs and five new bath houses. The main department of the hotel had 12 sleeping apartments; there were three new buildings with two rooms each, and 10 other rooms to rent. The meals were classed as excellent. Rates were $1.50 per day or $40 a month.[15]

Priests from St. Landry Catholic Church of Opelousas began visiting the Pointe-aux-Loups area about 1863, saying Mass and administering the sacraments in the homes of Antoine Cart and Hippolite Andrepont.[16] The first St. Joseph's church, dedicated in 1879, was administered by Jesuit priests from Grand Coteau, who served the spiritual needs of the people from 1867 to 1883.[17] The wooden structure was described as rectangular in shape with a platform similar to a theatre stage, on which the altar was set up. The building was erected during the administration of Rev. C. F. Vialleton, S. J. Father Anthonioz, first pastor at Rayne, was among the Jesuits who came on horseback from Grand Coteau to minister to the people of Pointe-aux-Loups. The Jesuit missionaries made their headquarters at the home of Mathieu Pousson.[18]

The present St. Joseph Church property, acquired in 1893, was a gift from W. W. Duson. On October 28, 1893 Duson donated 40.35 acres of land to Rev. Auguste Thebault of Pointe-aux-Loups, acting as agent for Archbishop Francis Janssens of New Orleans. The consideration was $1, and "the further consideration of furthering and fostering the cause of religion, good morals and education in that neighborhood." The property is described as the northwest one quarter of Section 44, Township

---

14 *Opelousas Courier,* Sept. 7, 1878
15 *Opelousas Courier,* Aug. 7, 1880
16 Baudier: *The Catholic Church in La.,* 451
17 *Ibid*
18 *Ibid*

sh Sale of Property.

— BY —

— TO —

STATE OF LOUISIANA,
PARISH OF ACADIA.

6168

Be it Known, That on this _Twenty Eighth_
day of the month of _October_ in the year of
our Lord one thousand eight hundred and ninety _Three_

Before me. **GUSTAVE E. FONTENOT,** a NOTARY PUBLIC, duly
~~appointed~~ and sworn for the Parish of ACADIA, State of Louisiana, and in the presence of the
~~witnesses~~ hereinafter named and undersigned, **Personally Appeared**

William W. Duson
resident of Crowley Acadia Parish La

declared, that for the consideration, and on the terms and conditions hereinafter set forth,
_he do by_ these presents, grant, bargain, sell, assign, convey, set over and deliver with
legal warranties, unto

Reverend Father Auguste Thibault
resident of Pointe aux Loups Acadia Parish
of Louisiana, acting herein as the agent and
attorney in fact for Reverend Father Francis Janssens
bishop of New Orleans La as per power of attorney here-
to and referred to the present, purchasing and accepting for ~~said parties~~ heirs and assigns, and acknowledging
~~delivery~~ and possession thereof, the following described property, to-wit:

certain tract or parcel of land situated in Acadia
~~parish~~ State of Louisiana with all the improvements and

The deed to the St. Joseph Church property of Pointe-aux-Loups
(Iota) was recorded October 28, 1893 in the Acadia Parish courthouse. W.
W. Duson "sold" the church 40.35 acres of land for one dollar.

161

Within the map:

MAP OF
THE N.W. ¼ OF SEC. 44
T. 8 S. R. 7 W.
SHOWING THE PROPERTY OF THE
CATHOLIC CHURCH
CONTAINING 40.36 ACRES

Reproduction of a map filed with the deed of the St. Joseph Church property. The original map is drawn on linen-like cloth with a silky finish.

8, South, Range 1 West. Witnessing the transaction were P. L. Lawrence and B. M. Lambert, with Gus E. Fontenot as notary public.[19] Father Thebault was assigned pastor of the church at Pointe-aux-Loups in December, 1892 by Archbishop Janssens.[20]

Pointe-aux-Loups had a school in 1881. The July 9 issue of the Courier reported that the closing exercises at the public school were well attended; Miss Maurine Cart, daughter of S. Cart, Esq., sang "Shells of the Ocean," a rendition "full of pathos and well received." John H. Rogers was one of the early teachers; he was assigned to the school in 1884.[21]

An organization known as the Pointe-aux-Loups R.A.R. Club was formed in 1881. G. Miller was president and Savinien Cart vice president. Other officers were Mathieu Pousson, secretary; Cleophas Comeaux, treasurer; Leon Berbail, commissary; Onezime Joubert, conductor; F. F. Perrodin, attorney; M. O. Wilkins, sergeant-at-arms; Antoine B. Cart, Philomine Miller and D. Durio, membership; Neuville Cart, Theodule Deville and Lucien Joubert, ways and means.[22] The club, with 387 members, was cryptically described as being "closely allied and bound with ties of consanguinity to the famous Pot Luck Club of Leonville."[23] No explanawas given of the meaning of the initials "R.A.R." in the name of the club.

The club membership probably included visitors to the Springs, as the large number of members claimed could scarcely be justified by the population at the time. An article in the Opelousas Courier of October 21, 1882 gives some idea of the population of the area: " . . . only a few miles to the south is the beautiful Mermentau, with its lakes and orange groves, and in the vicinity is the famous Pointe-aux-Loups Springs . . . the settlement has made rapid strides in the last 20 years; in this time it has increased from 14 to 50 families; at the present writing this is the bulk of the settlement, in a small district of not more than six miles by three. The number of young people, unmarried, including children of all ages, is 115 souls. The place has a church and a school house; the church is a fine building, but the school house, alas! is a very homely affair indeed."

The newspaper article writer noted that efforts had been made during the previous four years to educate the youth of the settlement; about 25 or 30 of the young people could read and write, he stated, adding, "as they

---

19 Conveyance Book J, 751, 752, Acadia Parish
20 Baudier: *The Catholic Church in La.,* 486
21 *Opelousas Courier,* Jan. 12, 1884
22 *Opelousas Courier,* Oct. 8, 1881
23 *Ibid*

advance in knowledge of English they seem to like that language very much."

Notices advertising Pointe-aux-Loups Springs continued to appear in newspapers until the turn of the century. By 1883 the list of promised cures had grown to include such maladies as rheumatism, kidney and liver disease, paralysis and diseases of the blood. A resident physician was always in attendance in case of need, and hacks could be had at "Mermento Station" for those coming by railroad.[24]

Another medicinal springs in the vicinity was advertised in 1880. This was Nezpique Springs, operated by Francois A. Daigle. The place was described as "set on Dr. Austin's old place some three miles from the

---

[24] *Opelousas Courier,* June 2, 1883

Two-wheeled oxcart driven by Sylvan Simar in front of store buildings in Iota. The business buildings are shaded by chinaberry trees, called "lilas parasol" by the Acadians. (Freeland Archives photo)

mouth of the Nez-Pique," and had been previously known as Trahan's. The place was said to have good bath houses, boarding and lodging, rooms to let, a ball every two weeks, fine fishing and boating.[25]

The mineral springs at both Pointe-aux-Loups and Nezpique gave out sometime after 1900. Several possible reasons have been given for the final failure of the springs: general lowering of the water level; the establishment of rice irrigation canals in the 1890s; the discovery of oil in 1901 and subsequent drilling operations in the area.[26]

The first post office in the Pointe-aux-Loups area, established in 1884, was known as Cartville, in honor of the first postmaster, Samuel Cart. The Southern Pacific railroad branch from Midland to Eunice, completed in 1894, by-passed Cartville by a mile; the railroad station was named Iota. The name of the Cartville post office was changed to Iota in 1900.

---

25 *Opelousas Courier,* June 12, 1880
26 Oral history, 1975, Hugh "Buck" McNeil, Henry T. Duson

CHAPTER IX

Mermentau

Little is known of the early history of Mermentau. The general area at one time was said to be a place of refuge for smugglers, outlaws, slave runners and pirates.[1] Early in the 19th century the river area was described as "a lawless region" by James Leander Cathcart, a government agent who traveled in southwest Louisiana in search of suitable lumber for the construction of navy vessels.[2]

The settlement developed at an undetermined time on the east side of the river at a point where travelers crossed the stream. One of the earliest known settlers was John Webb, native of England, who came in 1827.[3] In 1828 John Webb married Nancy Mayer (Mier), widow of Samuel Rippy (Riper).[4] John Webb lived in an area which came to be known as Webb's Cove, located near the juncture of the river and Bayou Queue de Tortue. Cornelius Duson McNaughton, a political refugee from Canada, joined Webb there about 1837.[5] McNaughton, who dropped his family name and was known as Cornelius Duson, was an expert diver. He and John Webb located the sunken hull of an old pirate schooner in Bayou Queue de Tortue, a few miles from the bayou's confluence with the Mermentau River.[6]

After the Calcasieu district was separated from St. Landry in 1840, Mermentau became the western outpost of St. Landry Parish. Information on early population of the area is virtually non-existent.

Sometime between 1842 and 1852 a voting precinct was established at Mermentau. A listing of St. Landry Parish precincts published in the Opelousas Gazette of May 28, 1842 does not show Mermentau; some 10 years later the first issue of the Opelousas Courier, published December 11, 1852, lists the house of John Wright at Mermentau as a polling place. At an election held in 1855, 101 voters cast ballots at the Mermentau poll.[7] The precinct, however, is believed to have taken in a large part of what is

---

1 *Crowley Signal,* Aug. 25, 1888
2 "Journal of James Leander Cathcart," *Louisiana Historical Quarterly,* Vol. 28, 826-827
3 *Crowley Signal,* Aug. 25, 1888; Perrin: *SW La.,* Part II, 274
4 Hebert: *SW La. Records,* Vol. II, 636, 902
5 Perrin: *SW La.,* Part II, 23
6 *Crowley Signal,* Aug. 25, 1888
7 *Opelousas Courier,* Nov. 10, 1855.

now the southwestern portion of Acadia Parish. Other than Pointe-aux-Loups, the nearest voting precinct was located at Queue Tortue (Rayne).[8]

Jean Castex, a native of France, came to Mermentau about 1856; in 1859 he opened a mercantile business, later became one of Acadia Parish's leading merchants.[9] He was also a cotton and rice farmer, and was probably the first Acadia Parish farmer to own his own cotton gin, which was erected in 1860.[10]

An early resident of the Mermentau area found, for a reason not given, that he couldn't make it alone. The Opelousas Courier of August 21, 1858 carried the following advertisement:

> FOR SALE, or a partner is wanted. A fine plantation, situated in the center of the prairie Mermento, in the parish of St. Landry, measuring about 100 arpents of high land upon which there is a small dwelling house, a quantity of orange trees and a fine canal. This property is the only one in Mermento which is suitable for a sawmill, being situated at the junction of bayous Nezpique and des Cannes; also a cypress swamp of 150 arpents situated on Nezpique, one of the best and richest swamps on that stream. For further information apply to F. Richard in Bellevue or to the undersigned on the premises. L. S. Cousin, Mermentau River.

One source places a sawmill at Mermentau in 1859. A man named James Jenkins, a Kentuckian, was manager of the sawmill.[11]

In 1866 another native of France came to Mermentau. This was Victorin Maignaud, who came to the area as a drygoods and notion peddler. For many years he operated a mercantile business; he also ran a sawmill, farmed rice[12] and ran a ferry boat.

The John Wright place at Mermentau continued to be a polling place and tax collection point for many years. In 1863 election commissioners at the Wright poll were Treville Landry, Hilaire Desessarts and Chancey Seymour.[13] The St. Landry Police Jury, at its meeting of September 18, 1865, named election commissioners to serve at the polling place at "Jack Wright's house;" they were V. T. Landry, George Arrington (Harrington) and H. Dessartes.

Police jury minutes reveal that both Harrington and Dessartes were Mermentau River ferrymen. At the meeting of October 1, 1877 the jury

---

8 *Ibid*

9 Perrin: *SW La.*, Part II, 260

10 *Ibid*

11 Barde: *Histoire, etc.*, Rogers trans., 365

12 Perrin: *SW La.*, Part II, 269

13 *Opelousas Courier*, Nov. 28, 1863

granted to Hilaire Desesoarts (the name appears in several spellings in newspaper and legal records) the privilege of keeping a toll ferry across the Mermentau "at the place formerly occupied by Joseph LeBlanc," and the same to George Harrington "in the place occupied by G. Higginbotham."

Timber from the Mermentau area provided much of the building material and fencing used by the prairie settlers; the lumber was hauled by oxcart to points as far away as Opelousas. On May 18, 1872 the Opelousas Courier reported: "For the last two weeks the streets of our town have been almost daily crowded with carts and wagons loaded with *pieux,* boards and shingles, coming from Pointe-aux-Loups and Mermento. Never has there been such a crowd at one time, and so successively we counted eleven ox-wagons in one expedition in one day this week. Eight feet *pieux* are worth $12 per 100; six feet *pieux,* $6, and shingles $6 per 1,000."

Many of the houses used by prairie dwellers were completely built at the sawmills of Mermentau, then hauled by wagons and teams of oxen across the prairie, sometimes for many miles. These ready-built homes were certainly the first prefabricated houses to be used in southwest Louisiana. When such a house was bought, the owner called his neighbors together and organized a hauling bee, or *halerie.* With a dozen yoke of oxen and three wagons and willing hands, the structure was soon on its way. The loading was accomplished by taking the beds off two of the wagons; in place of the regular coupling poles, long logs, perhaps 30 feet long, were used. The house was jacked up, then the poles run under it The log poles were then chained up to the two front pair of wheels, thus supporting the house. Across the open prairie the haulers could make 12 to 15 miles per day.[14]

Election records of the Mermentau precinct provide names of several more early settlers. The polling place in 1873 was the James Myers (Miers, Mires) house; commissioners were W. W. Burton, John Dunks and Andrew Henry.[15] Notice of an election to name delegates to the Democratic convention of 1878 shows Maignaud's store and Mire's store as polling places; three delegates were to be elected at the Maignaud poll, and one at Mire's. Commissioners at Maignaud's were H. Sellers

---

14 Post: *Cajun Sketches,* 90
15 *Opelousas Courier,* Dec. 27, 1873

and Joseph Roy; at Mire's, Jim and Emile Mire.[16] In 1883 voting was at Maignaud's place; commissioners were Joseph R. Roy, Aurelien Duhon and Dr. Louis Espargelier.[17]

16 *Ibid,* June 8, 1878
17 *Opelousas Courier,* Feb. 10, 1883

The Maignaud family cemetery on Highway 90 in Mermentau. The first Catholic church of Mermentau was located adjacent to this cemetery. (1975 photo by Fontenot)

An illegal hanging took place at Mermentau in 1873. The Courier of November 8, 1873 carried the following news item: "Four individuals residing on or near the Mermento River, in this parish, were arrested and conducted to jail here on Monday last, accused of murder, that is of having hanged two men, Francois Benoit and _____ Thibodeaux, near Maignaud's Ferry, about the 7st inst. The accused are Philosie Broussard, Onezime Cormier, Jean Roger and Dupre Plaisance. After a preliminary hearing before Justice Veazie, in our town, their case was sent up to the District Court which has been in session since Monday."

The newspaper did not follow up with the disposition of the case, nor is there a record of it in the St. Landry Parish courthouse.

There may have been a school at Mermentau in 1878. The Opelousas Courier of September 28, 1878 published a report on the schools of the parish; the report included the information that "if patrons of the school will pay half the tuition, one half a white school will be established at Maignaud's Ferry."

Jesuit priests from Grand Coteau began to visit Mermentau in the 1860s; one of the first baptisms was that of Jean Castex Jr.[18] Rev. Joseph Anthonioz, first pastor at Rayne, was one of the Jesuits who ministered to the people at Mermentau.[19] In 1871, Father Anthonioz, working with the people, had begun to gather lumber to erect a chapel, but the work was not completed.[20] The first church was built under the administration of the Rev. J. Chasles, of the secular clergy, about 1882. The first church, located adjacent to the Maignaud Cemetery on Highway 90 in Mermentau, was destroyed by fire in 1886 and all early records were lost.[21]

A temporary chapel was built at another location some years after the first church building burned. The chapel was very small, about 25 feet in length and 12 feet wide, with a front door, a small door in the rear, and two side windows. The chapel could accommodate only the women and children and the officiating priest; the men were obliged to stand outside. Property for the church in its present location was donated in 1889 by Jean Castex and Mrs. Marie U. Duhon, widow of Aurelien Duhon.[22]

---

18 Baudier: *The Catholic Church in Louisiana*, 451
19 *Ibid*, 452
20 Baudier: "Dedication, New Church Our Lady of the Sacred Heart, Church Point," booklet, 58
21 Baudier: *The Catholic Church in Louisiana*, 452
22 Conveyance Book C, 399, Acadia Parish

To have and to hold the said piece of land full property, unto the said Louisiana Western ilroad Company, with full warranty of title general subrogation of my rights

In evidence whereof these my signature, that of James .... General Agent of said Louisiana ...... Railroad, signed at Mermentau Parish Acadia State of Louisiana, on this second ... of June Eighteen hundred & Eighty ..., in presence of the subscribing ...tnesses

Land for a section house lot was given the Southern Pacific Railroad Company by Jean Castex in 1888. Earlier, in 1879, railroad rights-of-way were given by Victorin Maignaud, Aurelien Duhon, Arthur Gascon, John Arnaux, A. J. Vincent and John P. Parsons. (Photostat from Acadia Parish records)

The Louisiana Western railroad reached Mermentau in 1880. In February of that year only four miles of roadbed remained to be graded between Lafayette and Mermentau; 150 convicts were at work on the stretch near Bayou Blanc.[23] By the end of July, the road was completed from Mermentau westward to the Texas line; the Opelousas Courier of July 31, 1880 reported: "East of Mermentau the track is laid for a distance of 22 miles westward from Vermilionville (Lafayette), leaving a gap of some 14 miles, which is now being tired and ironed as fast as a force of about 70 hands will permit. The bridge over the Mermentau is nearing completion . . ." The delay in finishing the railroad span over the river was due to a scarcity of hands, the newspaper stated.

By the end of August, 1880, the railroad line from New Orleans to Houston was open for freight business. By the beginning of September passenger trains with sleepers attached were running on regular schedule from New Orleans to Houston.[24]

The trains, however, did not solve all transportation problems for the area. Produce, lumber and cattle had to be transported to the railroad shipping point. On January 22, 1887 the Acadia Sentinel noted that Vic Maignaud of Mermentau had purchased "a fine little steam tug called the Harry Bishop" at Morgan City, for use in the Mermentau River and its tributaries. Maignaud planned to use the tug to "tow logs, freight, rice and other produce, and will soon start weekly trips from Mermentau Station to Grand Cheniere."

An unsuccessful attempt to develop the settlement was made in 1889. A sale of town lots in March of that year attracted few buyers; eight lots were sold at prices ranging from $10 to $57. The sale included the Kellogg Hotel, sold to A. D. McFarlain of Jennings and Jean Pierre Fruge for $1,375. Total sales, including the hotel and the three lots that went with it, brought $1,499.50. Fruge, proprietor of a boarding house and saloon at Mermentau, was to run the hotel.[25]

Mermentau achieved legal village status November 11, 1899 when it was incorporated by proclamation of Governor Murphy J. Foster. The proclamation states, in part, that the petition to incorporate "has been conspicuously posted in three different places within the limits of the said proposed village in default of publication in a newspaper, (having

---

23 *Opelousas Courier,* Feb. 21, 1880
24 *Ibid,* Aug. 28, 1880
25 *Crowley Signal,* Mar. 23, 1889

Site of the Edna Rice Mill of Mermentau. The Maignaud sawmill was converted to a rice mill in 1890. (Photostat, Acadia Parish records)

none) for more than three weeks successively, as required by law, and that said village contains at least two hundred and fifty inhabitants."[26]

The sawmill at Mermentau owned by Victorin Maignaud was converted into a rice mill in 1890. Maignaud entered into an agreement with two men from New Orleans, Joseph Menge and William Reese, whereby Maignaud would have a third interest in the rice mill in exchange for his sawmill, a two-flued boiler and Atlas engine. Maignaud further agreed to allow the use of a building, previously used as a stable, for storage of rice; the building was to be enlarged to accommodate 2,000 sacks of rice. Maignaud was also to supply lumber, with the exception of flooring, with which to finish the mill building, and to remove unneeded sawmill machinery, the slab trash and sawdust on the premises. Maignaud's one third interest was valued at $3,500; Menge put up $6,900 and Reese $100 for a capital stock of $10,500.[27] The charter of the Edna Rice Mill Company (Limited) was filed November 14, 1890.[28] It is not known whether the rice mill was ever put into operation; the company went into litigation in May, 1891; the suit was compromised and settled by mutual agreement.[29]

A colorful phase of Mermentau's past was the era of the cattle drives, when large numbers of wild cattle were driven across the prairie for shipment to market. The cattle were herded across the river, then penned in corrals, called cattle guards, until time for shipment by rail. The people of the village would gather on the river bank to watch the drovers expertly herd the cattle into the river and across to the opposite bank.[30]

During the Civil War and the year immediately thereafter there were widespread reports of bushwhackers, robbers and other fugitives hiding out in the Mermentau woods, and tales of hidden treasure in the area. Some of the legends have survived; one story relates that a man named Frank Quebedeaux once found an iron pot filled with coins. The cache had been hidden between four copal* trees which had grown close together.[31]

One of the early business enterprises at Mermentau was the Edward C. Fremaux store. Fremaux came to the Acadia Parish area from New

---

* copal: Acadian name for the sweet gum tree.

26 Conveyance Book R-18, 441, Acadia Parish
27 Miscellaneous Book 1, 151, Acadia Parish
28 Ibid, 158
29 Conveyance Book F, 285, Acadia Parish
30 Mrs. Edna B. Duhon, 1975 oral history
31 Leonie Maignaud, 1975 oral history

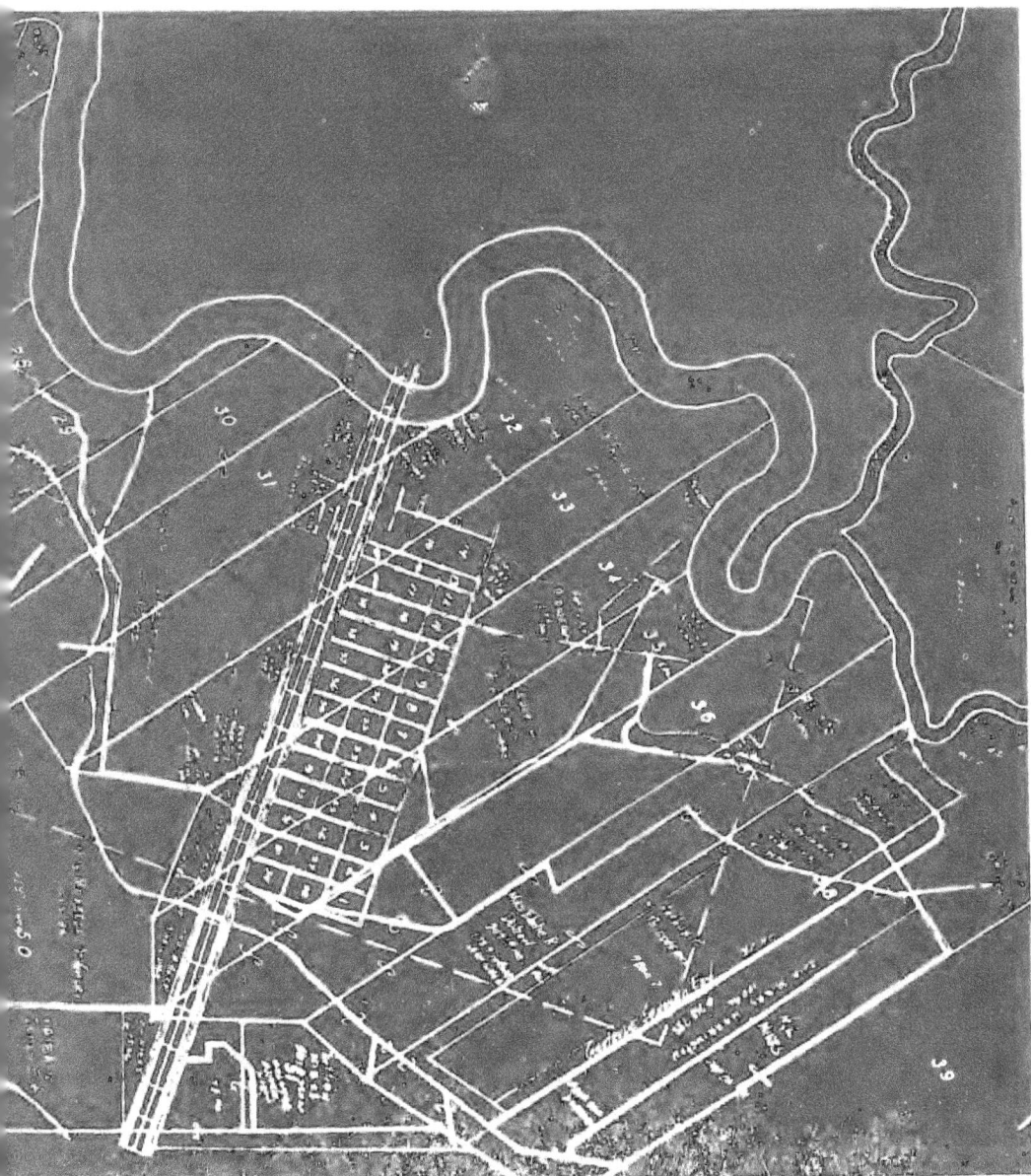

Map of the Village of Mermentau. Some of the early landowners (1871-1885) were V. Maignaud, Jean Castex, Aurelien Duhon, Arcade Dugas, Placide LeBlanc, Cleomile Simon, Emile Guidry, Albert S. Johnson, Celest Navare, Elsina LeBlanc, Francois Sellers Beard, August Dupuis, Jean Pierre Fruge, Gustave Ravet, Marc Pene (or Pine), A. J. Vincent and John Arnaux. (Photostat from Acadia Parish records)

Orleans about 1878 and opened a general merchandise store at Mermentau in 1886.[32]

During the 1890s the *Olive* was a popular pleasure boat on the Mermentau River. Parties of people from Crowley and other points would take the train to Mermentau, then board the *Olive* for a weekend trip to Lake Arthur. The Louisiana Press Association members and their wives, meeting at Crowley in 1894, were entertained on such an excursion.[33]

Mermentau is the one early settlement of Acadia Parish which has retained the same name throughout the years, except for changes in spelling. The settlement took its name from the river; as has been previously brought out, the river was named for Nementou, the Attakapas chieftain. Many variations of the name appear in legal and church records, such as Nementou, Nementau, Nemento, Mermento, Mermenton and Mentau.

---

[32] *Crowley Signal*, Aug. 25, 1888
[33] *Ibid*, May 12, 1894

CHAPTER X

Fabacher and Robert's Cove

Two apparently unrelated events took place during the decade preceding the one which witnessed the formation of Acadia Parish. These events, which were to result in dramatic and far-reaching changes in the agricultural picture and the economy of southwest Louisiana, took place in 1871 and 1881, when two separate colonies of German immigrants settled within the confines of the future parish.

The first German settlement was begun by Joseph Fabacher and Zeno (Zenon) Huber, on Prairie Faquetaique between Bayous des Cannes and Mallet. Joseph Fabacher, born 1830 in Bavaria, emigrated alone to America when he was a small boy. By the time the Civil War started he had amassed a fortune in operating a distillery in New Orleans, later founded the Jackson Brewing Company. The war interrupted his distillery business; afterwards he went into real estate and persuaded a friend, Zeno Huber, to assist him in founding a German colony in southwest Louisiana.

Huber, also a native of Germany, had come with his family to New Orleans in 1850; he was the only member of the family to survive the yellow fever epidemic of 1853. He and Fabacher came to Prairie Faquetaique in 1870 and by January of 1871 the first group of colonists from Germany had arrived. A few months later there were about 60 persons in the colony.[1]

Huber sent a report on the colony to W. H. Harris, commissioner of agriculture for Louisiana, in 1881. In his letter Huber said that each immigrant had planted about 40 acres of rice, in addition to corn, Irish and sweet potatoes, sugar cane and oats. He stated that the Germans bought nothing on credit, but paid cash for all their needs. Improvements in the colony included a church, school, sawmill, grist mill and two rice threshers.[2]

The new settlers on Prairie Faquetaique included Peter Klein, Christian Ruppert, John Linden, Fred Zenter, Vettus Wilfert, Theo Flesh (Flash), John Meyers, John Frey, Frank Krayter, Louis F. Schamber and

---

1 Summary, unpublished material researched by Rev. Charles Zaunbrecher; McCord: "A Historical and Linguistic Study of the German Settlement at Robert's Cove," LSU dissertation, 1969

2 "Louisiana Products, Resources and Attractions," booklet, 43

177

Names of German settlers of the Fabacher colony are shown on this section of a plat of Township 7 South, Range 1 West, Acadia Parish. The area shown is part of Prairie Faquetaique southwest of Eunice.

Louis Schamber. The settlement, first known as Fabacher or Trilby, is now called Ritchie. The area where John Frey settled was known as Frey; after a Catholic mission chapel was established in the vicinity the place was named Gassler, for Rev. F. L. Gassler, the first priest.[3]

Ten years after Fabacher and Huber began their colony, 15 German families settled in *l'Anse Robert,* or Robert's Cove, near the juncture of Bayous Plaquemine Brûlée and Wikoff northwest of Rayne. Rev. Peter Leonhard Thevis, a Catholic priest of New Orleans, was the founder of this second colony. Father Thevis was a friend of the Joseph Fabacher

---

[3] Baudier: *The Catholic Church in Louisiana,* 486-487

Advertisement from the Crowley Signal of October 27, 1894. Joseph H. Fabacher, the general merchandise dealer, was one of the 11 children of Joseph Fabacher, co-founder of the first German settlement in Acadia Parish, and Magdalene Frey.

family; it is believed that this connection led to the selection of the settlement site at Robert's Cove. Father Thevis made two trips to Germany to recruit immigrants; a total of 79 persons settled in the area in 1881 and 1882.[4]

The Opelousas newspaper took note of the arrival of the new settlers. On January 7, 1882 the Courier reported: " . . . about 70 Germans, men, women, and children, stopped at Rayne Station about six weeks ago looking for homes. Mr. J. D. Bernard, than whom a more hospitable man does not live in Louisiana, the leading merchant of Rayne, and Mr. Numa Chachere, also a whole-souled young gentleman, took the immigrants in charge and provided for their immediate needs. They soon found land for them, about four miles from Rayne at Robert's Cove, adjacent to Hoffman's Bridge on Bayou Plaquemine. They purchased 600 acres of land, including a large portion of woodland. Chachere reports them as industrious and thrifty farmers with money enough to make themselves comfortable homes after paying for land. They are setting up a sawmill and will saw all lumber needed for houses and barns. They are pious Catholics and have a German priest to visit the Rayne church every two weeks for their spiritual benefit." The Courier editor predicted that the new settlement would be "a large and flourishing colony in the future and will add materially to the growth of Rayne Station."

These first comers were the families of Thevis, Grein, Vondenstein, Leonards, Achten, Wirtz, Schlicher, Hensgens, Gossen, Reiners, Zaunbrecher, Gielen. Those joining the colony later included the families of Theunissen, Scheufens, Spaetgens, Jacob, Heinen, Dischler, Schaffhausen, Ohlenforst, Habetz, Dorr, Kloor, Dommert, Stamm, **Klumpp,** Olinger, Cramer, Bollich, Ronkartz, Schneider, Neu, Schatzle and Bischoff.[5]

The German immigrants were the first farmers in southwest Louisiana to raise rice for market and to grow rice on high land.

The history of rice cultivation in south Louisiana goes back to the days of the first settlers, who planted the grain for their own use. This was the so-called "providence rice," planted in the shallow ponds which once dotted the prairies. In times of drought the ponds dried up; the result was crop failure. Given sufficient rainfall, the planter had an ample supply of

---

4 Zaunbrecher research
5 *Ibid*

Providence rice was hulled in this primitive fashion, by pounding it with a pestle in a wooden mortar. Once the hulls were separated from the grain, the rice was put into the Indian basket for winnowing. (Reproduced from the Crowley Signal "Rice Number," Jan. 30, 1904)

rice to last his family until the following season. Hence the name, "providence rice." The crop depended entirely on the weather.

When the rice ripened, it was harvested by hand with sickles, brought together into small stacks and thoroughly dried, then threshed with flails. After flailing, a winnowing process separated the grain from the chaff. This was done by turning the product from one vessel to another and allowing the wind to blow the chaff away.[6] Another way of hulling the grain was by the use of wooden mortars and pestles, a method borrowed from the Indians.[7]

The German farmers soon learned how to aid providence. They constructed levees around their rice fields to hold the rain water. When the grain began ripening, the levee was cut and the water allowed to drain off.[8]

The year 1879 was disastrous for providence rice. The Opelousas Courier reported serious crop damage from long continued drought. Water was scarce for stock, wells and cisterns were going dry; all crops were damaged, and the rice crop was "a dead failure."[9] The drought and crop failure evidently did not discourage rice planters. On September 25, 1880 the St. Landry Democrat reported "an enormous rice crop." The editor said there were few threshing machines; that he had seen a man threshing rice "by whacking the bundles over the sharp edge of a log."

Later that year the Democrat commented on the increased production of rice, "destined to become one of the greatest industries of southwest Louisiana." Rice as a crop was certain, the editor predicted, and called attention to the prairies covered with marshes and traversed by navigable streams; he suggested that rice farmers put windmill-powered water wells in their fields.[10]

The year 1880 proved to be the upturning point for rice production. The crop yield was described as "abundant" by the Opelousas Courier; there were at least three threshers in the parish: Two Opelousas residents, Joseph Bloch and Henry Lastrapes, had invested in rice threshers "and

---

6 *Crowley Signal*, Prosperity Number, May 10, 1898
7 Post: "The Rice Country of Southwestern Louisiana," *The Geographical Review*, Vol XXX, No. 4, Oct., 1940, 578
8 *Crowley Signal*, May 10, 1898; Oct. 6, 1900
9 July 19, 1879
10 *St. Landry Democrat*, Dec. 1, 1880

will send them around to clean the grain for the planters. There is a thresher also in the German settlement."[11]

The fine crop produced by the German farmers at Fabacher brought an enthusiastic report in the St. Landry Democrat of September 18, 1880: "At the lower end of Faquetaique Prairie, at what is usually called 'German Settlement,' the land has always been considered completely worthless. But this year about 4,600 barrels of rice will be produced in that neighborhood and within a very small compass, not extending up the prairie, which is quite narrow there — not more than three or four miles. This rice in the 'rough' will net about four dollars per barrel. So we have here a small neighborhood where they used to produce absolutely nothing for sale, a revenue of $16,000. The rice lands in this neighborhood, the marshes, which were once considered not only worthless but a nuisance, are now the most valuable; and it will not be long before they cannot be bought for any reasonable price."

---

11 Sept. 4, 1880

Typical of the style of architecture used for homes built by the German settlers at Robert's Cove was the Joseph Heinen residence. The Heinens were among the second group of German immigrants to come to Robert's Cove. (Reproduced from the Crowley Daily Signal, Golden Anniversary Edition, 77)

Upland, or high land rice, was successfully grown as early as 1882. The St. Landry Democrat of September 2, 1882 stated: "The rice crop of the parish is very fine. This is a most profitable crop — especially as a great many are commencing to successfully grow high land rice." A few years later, in 1887, the Courier reported: "We have been reliably informed that one of our German planters . . . drilled and cultivated rice on lands high enough for cotton last year, and harvested therefrom 22 barrels of choice rice per acre."[12]

Rice from the Nicholas Zaunbrecher farm at Robert's Cove was the first to be shipped by rail to New Orleans. The rice was brought to Bayou Plaquemine Brûlée by wagon, loaded on a boat, then reloaded on wagons for the remainder of the trip to the railroad.[13] Nicholas Zaunbrecher is also credited with being the first rice farmer to effect an improvement in growing providence rice. He constructed a pond to hold the rain for watering the rice land.[14]

The German farmers demonstrated that commercial rice farming could be profitable; their example was soon followed by numerous other planters.[15] Improvements in irrigation, cultivation, harvesting and milling were to follow.

The descendants of the German settlers, have, for the most part, remained with the land. A few are in business, most are farmers. The original immigrants were all Roman Catholic. The majority of the German residents of Robert's Cove remain Catholic; they have had their own church, St. Leo's, since 1893. Prior to that year they attended St. Joseph's Church in Rayne, where their spiritual needs were administered by a German priest, Rev. Aegidius Hennemann of the Benedictine order. One of the oldest traditions in the Cove is that the German farmers provided the teams of oxen with which Father Anthonioz moved the church from Poupeville to Rayne Station.[16]

The Robert's Cove community has a singular place in the history of southwest Louisiana. The German people have maintained, for almost one hundred years, the language, customs and traditions of the old country. One of the more colorful customs which has been continued in the settlement is the observation of the feast day of St. Nicholas, bishop of Myra,

---

12 *Opelousas Courier*, Apr. 9, 1887
13 McCord: "A Historical and Linguistic Study, etc." 90
14 *Crowley Daily Signal*, 50th Anniv. Ed., III
15 *Crowley Signal*, May 10, 1898
16 Zaunbrecher research

This chalice belonged to Rev. Peter Leonhard Thevis, founder of the German colony at Robert's Cove. The hand-crafted chalice, studded with gems and ornamented with delicately wrought figures of the saints, is a cherished family heirloom; it is now being used by Father Thevis' great-great nephew, Rev. William Ohlenforst, pastor of Immaculate Conception Church of Morse. (1976 photo by Fontenot)

Awed children greet St. Nicholas on his annual visit to the descendants of German settlers at Robert's Cove. The saint is represented by a member of the church choir wearing the accoutrements of a bishop and disguised by a flowing white beard. (Morning Star photo by Mike Comeaux, 1975)

in Asia Minor, on December 6. The celebration takes place on the eve of the feast day, December 5. A member of the church choir, chosen to represent St. Nicholas, the patron saint of children, dresses in liturgical robes; he wears the cope and mitre and carries a crosier. Other choir members are costumed in red sweaters and black trousers, or sweaters and skirts. The identity of the principals is kept secret.

At the appointed time during the early evening hours, the group, accompanied by the pastor, sets out for a round of visiting the children in the community. At one time every home was visited; with the increase in population the children are now assembled in a few homes and St. Nicholas visits only those homes. Another member of the entourage is Black Peter, a small boy made up to resemble a native child of Asia Minor.

At each place visited Christmas carols are sung in both German and English and refreshments are served. The bishop questions each child about his behavior; if a good report is given, the child gets sweets; if the report is bad, he gets a switch from Black Peter. The observance is the same as that practiced by the Germans' ancestors in the old country, except for the carols sung in English and the presence of another important member of the choir group — an American Santa Claus.[17]

---

[17] Boudreaux: "German Customs Still Retained in Robert's Cove," *Attakapas Gazette*, Vol. III, No. 2, 16-17

CHAPTER XI

Other Settlements

The names of a number of communities and settlements of Acadia Parish have undergone changes, as has been shown in previous chapters. Some settlements which once had names no longer exist as settlements, some new place names have come into use. This chapter will attempt to trace the history of those settlements which existed prior to 1900 through the limited information available in legal records, newspapers, published works and oral histories.

Two of the long established voting precincts of St. Landry Parish are Mallet and Faquetaique, presently (1976) situated within a few miles of each other north of the Acadia-St. Landry boundary line. It is not possible to pinpoint the exact locations of the early polling places for these precincts because of the indefinite and vague descriptions of land holdings used in the old records. However, the boundaries of these old precincts, prior to parish division, certainly took in areas of what is now Acadia.

Bois Mallet

Bois Mallet, or Mallet Woods, was a voting precinct of St. Landry Parish in 1842; the polling place was at Dominic Richard's.[1] Pierre V. Savoie, Etienne Lejeune and William Prud'homme were the election superintendents,[2] and 13 persons voted in an election held in 1842.[3] Dominic Richard's was still the polling place in 1845; election officials were John M. McGee, Etienne Lejeune and Michel Prudhomme.[4] Fifty two votes were tabulated at the poll in 1855.[5]

A Catholic chapel for free mulattoes was established at Bois Mallet prior to 1856.[6] The settlement had two stores in the 1850s: David Guillory had a store there in 1856,[7] and in 1858 the Courier advertised an auction sale to be held at the store of Verret and Feray; items to be sold included a family of slaves; the stock of drygoods, ready made clothes,

---

1 *Opelousas Gazette,* May 28, 1842
2 *Ibid,* June 25, 1842
3 *Ibid,* July 9, 1842
4 *St. Landry Whig,* July 24, 1845
5 *Opelousas Courier,* Nov. 10, 1855
6 Baudier: *The Catholic Church in Louisiana,* 421
7 *Opelousas Courier,* Feb. 18, 1856

boots, hardware, earthenware of every description, cypress *pieux*, two horse-wagons and "Creole horses gentle enough for a lady to ride."[8] Voting in 1863 took place at the L. D. Verret store,[9] and in 1868 Sheriff James G. Hayes collected taxes at the Charles Francois store.[10]

Faquetaique

Faquetaique is not listed as an election precinct in available issues of early newspapers prior to 1855. It does appear in the Nov. 10, 1855 issue of the Opelousas Courier; election results show 34 persons voted at the Faquetaique poll. In 1878 the polling place of Faquetaique was at Zeno Huber's place;[11] Huber owned land in Prairie Faquetaique in Acadia Parish southwest of Eunice.

Martin Carron had a store at Faquetaique in 1881. Carron owned land in the Acadia Parish area in 1871, just southeast of Eunice; his store is believed to have been located here.[12] Martin Carron's 350-acre plantation was located in both St. Landry and Acadia Parishes.[13] The Courier of April 2, 1881 reported that on March 26 there had been "a fatal affray at Faquetaique, at the store of Martin Carron; Portalla Sonnier was fatally stabbed by Octave Fuselier. The killing was said to have been the result of "drinking too much whiskey," and Carron "announced his intention not to sell whiskey in the future."

The location of the Huber land and the probable location of the Carron store would indicate that a wide area was known as Faquetaique prior to the establishment of Acadia Parish. Since the entire land area between Bayous Mallet and des Cannes was called Prairie Faquetaique, only exhaustive research and abstracts of land could define the location of specific settlements.

Prudhomme City

A specific area near Bayou Mallet in northern Acadia Parish began to be known as Prudhomme City in the 1860s. T. C. Chachere had a store there in 1868.[14] The polling place for the Prudhomme City precinct

---

8 *Ibid*, March 20, 1858
9 *Ibid*, Nov. 28, 1863
10 *Ibid*, May 9, 1868
11 *Ibid*, June 8, 1878
12 Conveyance Book Y-1, 421, St. Landry Parish
13 Perrin: *SW La.*, etc. Part II, 20
14 *Crowley Signal*, Aug. 25, 1888

in 1878 was at Chachere's store;[15] in 1883 the election officials were Raymond Chachere, Etienne Stagg and J. B. McCoy.[16]

There was a sawmill at Prudhomme City in 1881. The St. Landry Democrat of December 31, 1881 reported: "Mr. Louis Savoy had his foot sawed off at Mr. R. C. Sittig's sawmill near Prud'homme City a few days ago." Another reference to the place appeared in the Democrat of December 15, 1883; among visitors to Opelousas during the week were "Rep. Martin Carron of Prudhomme City and Zenon (Zeno) Huber of Faquetaique."

Prudhomme City was a school district in 1878, with six schools located in the district. The schools were listed as follows: one colored in lower

---

15 *Opelousas Courier,* June 8, 1878
16 *Ibid,* Feb. 10, 1883

Relic of Prudhomme City's past, this building was once used as an office by a pioneer Acadia Parish physician, Dr. T. C. Chachere. (1975 photo by Fontenot)

Mallet, near Evariste Guillory's; one white in Church Point, one white in Prudhomme City, one half a white near D. P. Lafleur's, one white in Light and Tie neighborhood, one colored near Francois Simien's place.[17] In 1884 the newspaper announced that schools would be opened January 14 for five months. At this time there were four and a half schools in the Prudhomme City district: one school for colored at Mallet, with B. A. Guidry as teacher; one white at Church Point, teacher not assigned; one white at Light and Tie, with J. W. Young the teacher; one white at

17 *Opelousas Courier*, Sept., 28, 1878

This old Acadian-style house is one of the few of its kind remaining in Acadia Parish. The house, virtually in ruins, is owned by T. Carey Brinkman and is located north of Bayou Mallet just inside the Acadia-St. Landry boundary line. (1975 photo by Fontenot)

Prudhomme City, with J. O. Brunson assigned as teacher; one half at Faquetaique, teacher not assigned.[18]

Prudhomme City was the site of the Chachere family reunion for many years. The Courier of August 28, 1886 carried this brief item: "The annual reunion of the Chachere family was held last Wednesday at Prud'homme City."

There was a resident physician at Prudhomme City as early as 1871. This was Dr. W. T. Jenkins, son of a Mississippi Baptist minister. Dr. Jenkins was also a planter and rice grower. His son, Dr. Walter A. Jenkins, began his practice at Prudhomme City in 1887, then moved to Church Point.[19]

Prairie Hayes

Prairie Hayes was so named for Bosman Hayes (Hays), the colonial land owner and settler. This land area extended roughly from the Bosman Hayes Spanish land grant on Bayou Plaquemine Brûlée for an undetermined number of miles to the west, north and south. The prairie remained virtually unpopulated until after the Civil War.

Prior to the Civil War a man named Thomas Coopwood acquired title to many thousands of acres of land in St. Landry Parish. Approximately 27,000 acres of the Coopwood land lay within the present boundaries of Acadia Parish, with about 10,000 of the acres situated in the north half of Township 8, South Range 1 East, which takes in the Prairie Hayes area. Coopwood acquired the land by buying land warrants which had been issued by the United States government to war veterans as military bounties, or bonuses. These warrants were bought by Coopwood from the owners, who were veterans of the War of 1812 and the Indian Wars, or their heirs. Coopwood acted as agent for a partnership of four men, John A. Winston, William T. Moore, Joel W. Jones and H. A. Ellison, all of Mobile, Alabama.[20]

Coulee Croche

Coulée Croche, meaning "crooked coulee," takes its name from a stream in the southern section of St. Landry Parish. Part of the land area once known as Coulée Croche extended across the parish line into Acadia. The general area northeast of Rayne, from the Mier community to the parish line at Bosco, was once called Coulée Croche. The house of

---

18 *Ibid,* Jan. 12, 1884
19 Perrin: *SW La.,* etc. Part II, 266
20 Conveyance Book U-1, 245, St. Landry Parish

Thomas
4
Coopwood
644.04
acres

E. Hockaday
40.45 acres

Thomas
3
Coopwood
603.89
acres

Thomas
2
Coopwood
644.24 acres

Sylvan Thibodeaux 125.75 acres
Octave Belard 125.75 acres
Celestin Doucet 125.75 acres
Willie J. Hazel 167. ac
Joseph Thibo 167.5 aa

Thomas 3
Applicd for School 40.24 acres
Coopwood
603.64 acres

Thomas 9
E. Hockaday 40.77 acres
10
Coopwood
604.13 acres

Thomas
11
Coopwood
644.24

Thomas
12
Coopwood
629.92 acres

Reserved
16 for
Schools

Thomas
15
Coopwood
603.56
acres
Chas. N. Ealer 40.24 acres

Thomas
14
Coopwood
643.56

Thomas
13
Coopwood
643.56 acres

Charles W. Newton 161.14 acres

Edwin C. Pitcher 161.14 acres

Roger J. Marshall 160.61 acres

Hugh Fitzpatrick 160.61 acres

Vial Thibodeaux 161.46 acres

Theodula Thibodeaux 23 161.46

Thomas Coopwood 320 acres 24

Abram Richard 165.32

Charles W. Davison 160.88 acres

Celestin Matte 161.14 acres

Joseph Bussenberg 160.88 acres

Joseph Andrus 160 acres

Alteon Daigle 161.46 acres

Gustave Thibodeaux 161.46 acres

Uriah Taylor 161.25 acres

Fdk. Emile Kitziger 161.25 acres

Patrick Leaugh 15.72 acres

Joseph Raynd 160.30

Zehine Thibodeaux 161.90 acres

Emile Doucet 80.91 acres 26

Andrew M. Williams

Kosky

Antoine Blanc 664.05

Lyons

Frank Scullin 161.25

Isaac C. Levy

27

46
James Cole
400.96 acres

John Rykoski 112 acres

Rykoski 160.30

Some of the Coopwood lands northwest of Plaquemine Brulee (Branch) are shown on this segment of a survey plat of Township 8 South Range 1 East. Note small rectangles in Sections 3 and 10, labeled "E. Hockaday." The Hockaday land figured prominently in the selection of a parish seat for Acadia.

Heavy lines on this segment of a plat of Township 8 South Range 3 East show part of the eastern boundary of Acadia Parish. The lower right portion (Section 34) took in part of the Coulee Croche area of St. Landry Parish.

Symphorien Meche was the polling place for Coulée Croche in 1852;[21] 17 persons voted at the poll in 1853.[22]

Light and Tie

Most unusual old place name of Acadia Parish — sandwiched between places with names of Indian and Acadian-French origin — was that of Light and Tie. The colloquial name for this settlement, in the northeastern section of the parish, elicited editorial comment in 1882: "Among the most novel of names which has come under our observation is that of 'Light and Tie' a name given to a school or church house near, or probably in, Prairie Hayes. We take it from the assessment roll. The name is said to have originated in this way: While the house was being built some man rode up and was asked to light and tie, since then it has been called by the above name."[23]

This old name for the Richard, or Baptist Academy community, not generally known today, was recalled by one of the parish's oldest residents, Hugh "Buck" McNeil of Iota, who was 97 years old when interviewed in 1975. "There were few trees and no hitching racks on the prairie in the old days," McNeil said. "'Light and tie' meant to dismount and hobble your horse by tying the bridle around the horse's front leg so that the animal wouldn't wander away."

Pilgrim's Rest Baptist Church was organized in the Light and Tie settlement in 1870.[24] After 1917, when the Acadia Baptist Academy was opened, the area was referred to as "Baptist Academy." The school was closed in May, 1973. Another name for the community is Richard, pronounced "Ree-shar," for Theogene Richard, who donated land for the Richard Consolidated School.[25]

Long Point

In the approximate center of Acadia Parish is an area once known as Long Point, located some six miles north of Crowley on Long Point Gully. The Long Point settlement figured in the news in 1886. Both the Opelousas Courier and the Rayne Signal, in the October 23, 1886 issues, reported that a large bear had been killed near the Willie Higginbotham place. The animal was found in the Allen Laughlin corn field, eating corn. Laughlin and his brother, Tom Laughlin, chased the bear with a pack of

---

21 *Opelousas Courier,* Dec. 11, 1852
22 "Some History," etc., *Daily World,* 200
23 *St. Landry Democrat,* Aug. 12, 1882
24 *Crowley Daily Signal,* 50th Anniv. Ed., 21
25 Oral history, 1975, Bessie Richard Courville

dogs and killed it with buckshot. The bear measured five feet, three inches from tip of nose to tail and weighed 230 pounds.

About a year after the bear killing was reported, on January 31, 1887, Tom Laughlin was murdered while crossing Long Point bridge.[26] He was the first person to be buried in the Methodist Church cemetery at Maxie.[27]

After Acadia Parish was created two separate settlements in the Long Point area were named Maxie and Ellis, for Maxwell Duson, son of W. W. Duson, and W. E. Ellis, a pioneer Crowley banker.[28]

Long Point was the location of one of the early schools of the Acadia Parish area. In a listing of schools to be opened, published in the Opelousas Courier of September 28, 1878, one item read: "one half school at Long Point near Robert Sloan's if patrons of the school will pay half the tuition."

Estherwood

The Estherwood area had two earlier names, Tortue, after the Indian chief,[29] and Coulee Trief or Trive.[30] The "Coulee Trief" name origin involves a mysterious person believed to have been one of Lafitte's pirates. About 1816 a man named Jean Baptiste Trief built a cabin on a coulee about six miles west of the present city of Crowley; he was described as "tall, dark and sinister-looking; he mingled little with the Acadian settlers. He wore large earrings of the kind that were worn by buccaneers of the Spanish Main.[31]

Millerville

Millerville, located on Bayou Nezpique 12 miles north of Mermentau, was named for Dennis Miller, native of the area, who owned a general merchandising business and a sawmill.[32] The son of Leufroy Miller,[33] he was a grandson of Frederick Miller, colonial landowner of Acadia Parish.[34]

Dennis Miller was a large shipper of produce; in 1887 he shipped 4,459 sacks or rice, 18,000 eggs, 8,000 chickens, and 16,301 pounds of wool. Miller shipped by boat on the Nezpique to Mermentau, thence by

26 *Opelousas Courier*, Feb. 5, 1887
27 Oral history, 1975, Hugh McNeil
28 *Crowley Daily Signal*, 50th Anniv. Ed., 77; *Crowley Daily Signal*, Oct. 4, 1937, Par. sec. 7
29 Read: *Louisiana French*, 179
30 *Crowley Daily Signal*, 50th Anniv. Ed., 64
31 *Ibid*
32 *Crowley Signal*, Aug. 25, 1888
33 Perrin: *SW La.*, etc., Part II, 270
34 Hebert: *SW La. Records*, Vol. 1, 654

rail. He was also said to have butchered 8,000 pounds of pork in 1887, the hogs raised and fattened exclusively on mast*.[35]

In 1888 there were two general stores, a saloon, a hotel, a blacksmith shop and a "good school house" at Millerville.[36]

Evangeline

The town of Evangeline has an unusual background of religious history. The first Lutheran congregation in southwest Louisiana was established there in 1873, and what is believed to have been the only organized group of Quakers in Louisiana flourished there for a time.

A Lutheran missionary, Rev. H. Gellert, came to the Evangeline vicinity in 1872, along with several other Germans. He acquired land in 1873 and started a congregation of the German Evangelical Lutheran Church. Rev. Gellert returned to the north to resume ministerial labors, then came back to Acadia Parish in 1886. In 1888 he was holding regular services at the school house in Evangeline and at other points in the parish, including Crowley.[37]

Dr. Andrew D. Tomlinson was the minister for the Society of Friends (Quakers). The Tomlinson home was used for church services and also for a school; Mrs. Tomlinson, an experienced teacher, taught classes one half of each day. Some 40 members attended the Quaker Sunday School. Dr. Tomlinson practiced medicine in the area and was also Evangeline's first postmaster.[38]

The Quakers hoped to have a church house, but whether this was ever achieved is not known. An article in the Crowley Signal of April 21, 1888 states: "An effort is being put forth for the establishment of a monthly meeting of Friends (Quakers) at Evangeline. They are a quiet, peaceful religious people desirous of living under the influence of the church, and feeling the need of a church house, they have taken this step, hoping also to furnish a house for all those who may become isolated from the church by coming South on the hunt for a more genial climate. Possibly there is not an organized branch of the Christian Church in the state, and why should not Evangeline be the first?" Nathan Hunt was superintendent of

---

* mast: nuts collectively, especially as food for hogs.

[35] *Crowley Signal,* Aug. 25, 1888
[36] *Ibid*
[37] *Crowley Signal,* Aug. 25, 1888; *Crowley Daily Signal,* Apr. 29, 1957, "Sidewalk Talk," by L. A. Williams
[38] *Crowley Signal,* Aug. 25, 1888; *Rayne Signal,* Feb. 26, 1887

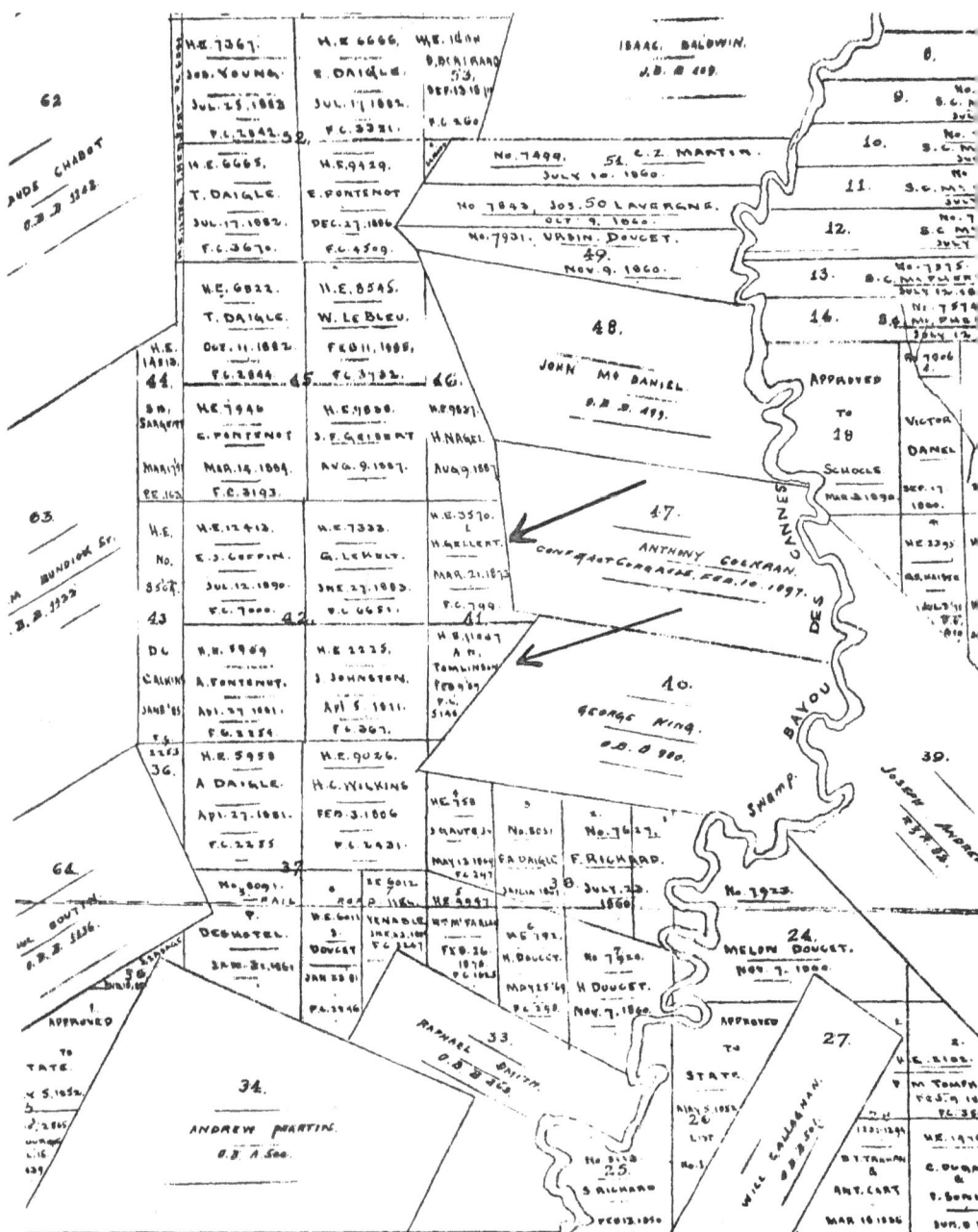

Arrows point out lands owned by Rev. H. Gellert and Dr. A. D. Tomlinson, early religious leaders of Evangeline. Area shown is the southwest portion of Township 9 South Range 2 West, the lower end of Prairie Mamou between Bayous des Cannes and Nezpique.

the Sabbath School for the Quakers and U. G. Wilkins the secretary.[39] Once when Dr. Tomlinson was called to a patient, W. B. Humphreys took over the meeting.[40] These are the only names mentioned in connection with the Quakers.

Egan

The Egan community was named for William M. Egan, a pioneer businessman of Crowley. The place was at various times known as Jonas Point and Canal Switch, later as the Abbott post office.[41] The roadbed for the Louisiana Western railroad was constructed westward from Lafayette as far as Egan in the early 1870s; later, it was decided to re-route the line south of Egan to eliminate bridging Bayous Plaquemine Brûlée and des Cannes.[42] The old roadbed, built by convict labor, remained there for many years. Dirt from it was used to build Acadia Parish roads.[43] Interstate 10 highway was constructed on, or very nearly on, the old roadbed.[44] Among early settlers of the Egan area were the families of Regan, Trumps, Sensat, Leger and Clements.[45]

Midland

Midland, on the main line of the Louisiana Western (Southern Pacific) railroad about nine miles west of Crowley, was the point of intersection for the branch line of the Southern Pacific railroad completed in 1894. C. C. Duson was responsible for getting the branch line from Midland to Eunice, the town he founded in St. Landry Parish and named for his wife, Eunice Pharr Duson.[46]

A ferry over Bayou Plaquemine Brûlée near Midland was operated in 1870 by Frank Quebedeaux. The ferry, built of cypress logs, was poled or hauled across the bayou by ropes, and accommodated horse-and-buggy and foot traffic.[47]

Another old landmark of the Midland area is the Quebedeaux Cemetery, located on the south side of Bayou Plaquemine Brûlée near the ferry landing. Many of the older graves bear no inscriptions or dates. Some of the inscribed tombstones on older graves bear the names of Quebedeaux,

---

39 *Crowley Signal,* April 7, 1888
40 *Crowley Signal,* March 17, 1888
41 *Crowley Daily Signal,* 50th Anniv. Ed, 65
42 *Crowley Daily Signal,* Oct. 4, 1937, Crowley sec., 3; Par. sec., 8
43 Oral history, 1975, Sweeney Stutes
44 *Ibid*
45 *Crowley Signal,* June 30, 1888
46 *Crowley Daily Signal,* Oct. 4, 1937, Par. sec. 14
47 *Crowley Post-Signal,* Aug. 10, 1975, 8

Pierre Herbert 161.26 acres

A and M Doucet 161.26 acres

Clement Doucet 163. acres

Joseph L Semava 162.03 acres

Placide Hamar Jr. 80.77 acre

Cyrus A Johnson 161.93 acres

Charles Hebert 160.90 acres

Louis Simar 80.40 acres

Placide Simar 163.22 acres

Pierre Hebert 162.07 acres

Alfred Hebert 162.07 acres

William H Stockwell 161.94 acres

Calvin White 161.94 acres

Napoleon Breaux

Joseph Simar 80.40 acres

Gilbert Young 80.40 acres

Joseph Trahan 81.40 acres

Marie Bellard 162.07 acres

Thomas D. Doucet 162.07

Owen Duffy 162.49 acres

Jesse A Mitch 161.49 acres

Stephen O McBride 164.50 acres

Onezime Doucet 122.56 acres

John W. Smith 81.03 acres

Joseph H Schrock 162.07 Doucet 162.07 acres

Reserved 16 for

Stephen O McBride 164.50

Columbus Hertes 123.13 acres

Lacombe 163.44 acres

Adam Lacombe 162.20 acres

Adrien

Jefferson Sordo 162.07 acres

Schools.

Vidian Sensat 162.10 acres

Julian Tromps 164.84 acres

George H. Shore 81.16 acres

Mary a Caldwell 150.44 acres

Charles E. Clover 80.44 acres

Ames Ellen

Wm J. Moffat 80.96 acres

Lawrence Kenny

Marcelite Reagan 164.70 acres

Louis Leger 164.70 acres

Louis J. Meyer 162.28 acres

Alexander Hertes

Leo Rep of Anthony Cochran 339 acres

37

Kenny 100

Joseph Reagan

Joseph N Tromps

Jean and Gerard Chaisson

Wilhelm Hommert 161.68 acres

Truman

Land holdings in the southwest quarter of Township 9 South Range 1 West, the Egan area of Acadia Parish. The official survey of the township was made by John P. Parsons in 1881; names of landowners were written in by an unknown person.

200

Gastelin, Daigle, Carpenter, Fremaux, Breau, Lacomb, Romero, Fontenot and Fruge. One inscription reads: "Dr. Louis Isidore Espargeliers died April 5, 1917 at 93 years, native of France. In a strange land away from his loved country he fought his way, made friends by his charitable work, honest and kind dealings; left memories and a name which will always be an honor to his descendants; the next life was always his guiding star and he died with the name of God on his lips." Nearby are the graves of his wife, Josephine, who died in 1901, and a daughter, Julie, age 15, no date of birth or death. The earliest inscription is on the grave of John Fruge, son of J. P. and L. Fruge, 1878 - 1900.

The Southern Pacific branch line from Midland to Eunice created some new place names in Acadia Parish. North of Midland the railroad went through the Pointe-aux-Loups area. The branch line was laid through the Archile Doucet property, homesteaded in 1835. At a point about two miles east of Pointe-aux-Loups Springs the railroad angled off in a northeasterly direction toward Eunice, and a new railroad station was christened Iota. Until that time the post office had been named Cartville and was located in the S. Cart store. After the railroad came through the post office was moved about a half mile to the general merchandise store operated by George Wright and Joe Sabatier.[48]

Morse

South of Midland the railroad was extended into Vermilion Parish. Four miles south of Midland, in Acadia Parish, a railroad station was established to serve settlers who had bought land from W. W. Duson. This became the town of Morse,[49] so named for a Southern Pacific railroad official.

An early settler in the Morse area was involved in a strange incident reported in the press in 1880. The newspaper story related that a New Orleans resident, an Italian physician named Francois Toro, had a son born in 1862. The child's mother died. A relative by the name of Alexandre Borne abducted the child, allegedly to get Dr. Toro's money. The boy was brought to the home of Evariste Navarre "at Queue Tortue." Navarre was told the boy was an orphan and was asked to keep him for a couple of months. Years went by; although a poor man, Navarre was said to have treated the boy well. In October of 1879, when the youth was 17, a Mr. Lebesque of New Orleans came to southwest Louisiana on

---

48 *Crowley Daily Signal*, Oct. 4, 1937, Par. sec., 24
49 *Crowley Daily Signal* 50th Anniv. Ed., 57

201

a business trip and heard the story. This led to a reunion of father and, son, which was effected December 24, 1879. The newspaper article, widely re-printed in south Louisiana, was titled "A Bizarre Christmas Story."[50] Evariste Navarre owned land about four miles west of the present community of Morse, near the western end of Bayou Queue de Tortue.

The Mauboules brothers, A. J. and J. S., settled at Morse in 1892. They homesteaded lands secured through the W. W. Duson Real Estate Company of Crowley.[51]

An unusual burial custom exists in the Morse-Mermentau-Midland area of Acadia Parish. In the Istre Cemetery, located west of Morse and

---

50 *Opelousas Courier*, Jan. 3, 1880
51 *Crowley Daily Signal* 50th Anniv. Ed., 57

Shelters built like miniature houses cover many of the graves in the Istre Cemetery. A few such shelters are also to be found in other cemeteries of the Mermentau-Midland area. (1976 photo by Doug Dardeau)

PUBLIC SALE

Estate of Mrs. Sarah McManus, dec'd.

THE public are hereby informed that there will be sold at public sale, to the last and highest bidder, by a competent officer, on the plantation hereinafter described, in Plaquemine Brulée.

Saturday, 30th day of July, 1853,

the following described property, belonging to the Estate of the late Sarah McManus, dec'd, widow of Malachi Stanton, also deceased, both late of the Parish of St. Landry, to-wit:

A CERTAIN TRACT OR

PARCEL OF LAND,

part of which is well timbered, situated on Plaquemine Brulée, in the Parish of St. Landry, measuring three thousand eight hundred and forty acres, (more or less) bounded on the North by public lands, on the South by lands claimed by Simon Gonor, on the East by Bayou Plaquemine, and on the West by public lands, together with all and singular

The Buildings

And improvements thereon erected and thereto belonging, being the last residence of said deceased.

ANOTHER

Tract of Land,

called "The Cole tract", situated in the same Quarter, measuring six hundred and forty superficial acres (more or less.)

THREE SLAVES,

of both sexes and different ages.

One lot of gentle horned cattle, work Oxen, 1 cart, 1 gig, 1 gun, plantation implements, household furniture and there are many other articles too tedious to enumerate.

The conditions which will be favorable to purchasers, will be made known on the day of sale.

OSCAR F. STANTON.

PUBLIC SALE.

Estate of John Lyons, Senior

THE public are hereby informed, there will be sold, at public sale, to last and highest bidder, by Auguste De a public auctioneer in and for the Parish St. Landry, on the plantation, herein described, late residence of the deceased Robert's Cove, in this Parish, on

Tuesday, 26th day of July 185 and the following days,

the following described property, belong to the Estate of the late John Lyons, Ser of the Parish of St. Landry, to wit:

A CERTAIN TRACT OF

LAND,

situated in Robert's Cove, in this Parish proved as a plantation, where the dece last resided, containing about one thous acres, bounded above by land of Egbert ans and below by land of Jacob Lyons being the same acquired of Joseph I. drus Senior, with all the

BUILDINGS

AND IMPROVEMENTS thereon erected.

ANOTHER TRACT OF

LAND,

situated and lying on the Bayou Queue tue, in the Parish of St. Landry, having arpents front by forty in depth, bounded one side by lands claimed by Michael L and on the other by vacant land, the sam quired by deceased at a Sheriff's sale, on the 6th of June 1840, in the case enti Heirs of Louis Richard and Maria V. D for the use of Joseph L. Richard, in the trict Court of St. Landry;

55 SLAVES.

Notice of the public sale of the John Lyons Sr. estate, in right column, as published in the Opelousas Courier. The sale was scheduled for July 26, 1852 "at the late residence of the deceased, in Robert's Cove . . . " The estate included additional land on Bayou Queue de Tortue, 55 slaves, many animals, farm implements and household articles.

south of Mermentau, a number of the graves have wooden shelters built over them. The structures have gabled roofs and resemble small houses, with doors and windows. The doors, about four feet in height, permit entry, and once inside a person of average height can stand erect under the ridge of the roof. Most of the windows are paned with glass. Wooden crosses ornament most of the grave houses.

No one knows why or when the custom originated. One explanation is that long ago, when other materials were unavailable in the then remote region, the wooden houses were put up in imitation of the above-ground vaults in old cemeteries of New Orleans. Another reason given is that the houses may be a more elaborate modification of the fencing around individual graves used in many family cemeteries in rural areas, the purpose of which was to prevent animals, both wild and domestic, from treading on the graves.

The older grave houses are unpainted and unmarked. Many of the newer ones are freshly painted and well kept. Some of the earlier inscriptions show dates of the late 19th century.[52]

Lyon's Point

Lyon's Point was so named for John Lyon, the colonial landowner and settler. John Lyon did not remain on the bayou tract he bought from the Indians. According to family tradition, after being so badly treated by the pirates in 1819, Lyons bought land in the Robert's Cove area and moved away from Bayou Queue de Tortue. This is substantiated in legal records. The public sale of his estate was held July 26, 1853 "at the residence of the deceased, in Robert's Cove." His possessions included about 1,000 acres at Robert's Cove, improved as a plantation; 55 slaves, also 400 arpents of land on Bayou Queue de Tortue which he had bought at a sheriff's sale in 1840. His original land holdings on Bayou Queue de Tortue were said to have been divided among his children when he moved to Robert's Cove.

There was no voting precinct listed for Lyon's Point in 1852[53]. In 1855, 39 voters cast ballots at the Lyons Point poll.[54] In 1863 the polling place was at Placide LeBlanc's; commissioners were Emile Sellers, Camille Sellers and Placide LeBlanc.[55] In 1865 the St. Landry Parish Police Jury

---

[52] Fontenot: "Houses Over Graves Unique Burial Custom," *Lafayette Advertiser,* May 25, 1975
[53] "Some History," etc., *Daily World,* 199
[54] *Opelousas Courier,* Nov. 10, 1855
[55] *Ibid,* Nov. 28, 1863

appointed election commissioners to serve at a precinct labeled "Queue at Lyon's Point." Commissioners named were John H. Hoffpauir, H. Stutes and William Sarver.[56] Later listings of election precincts and returns do not show Lyon's Point as a precinct.

Jesuit missionaries visited the settlement at Lyon's Point in the 1850s,[57] but there are no available sources which give the names of the settlers they visited.

Some of the pioneer settlers in the southern part of Acadia Parish can be identified by legal notices in early newspapers. The Opelousas Courier of September 12, 1857 carried notice of a public sale "at the last residence of Joseph Gilbert on Queue Tortue." The estate included 120 horned cattle in *vacherie,* 120 gentle horned cattle, two branding irons, 24 horse creatures, one riding horse, six *vacherie* horses, pickets, fencing, etc. Another such notice, published in the same newspaper on June 26, 1858, told of the public sale "on the premises at Queue Tortue in this parish, of the property belonging to the estate in community between the late Firmin Breaux, his surviving children and widow, Clearance Richard." The estate inventory listed 240 acres of land "situated on Tortue," together with the growing crop; a slave woman named Azeline, about 25; one lot horned cattle, one lot gentle cattle, one lot horse creatures, about 500 pannels of *pieux,* sheep, five pair work hoses, Creole ponies, *vacherie* horses and cattle, hogs, one ox cart, one double barrelled shotgun, household furniture, kitchen utensils, etc. Don Louis Breaux was administrator of the estate.

These estates could have been located anywhere along the length of Bayou Queue de Tortue, from Rayne to Mermentau. The only definite information to be extracted from the published notices is that Joseph Gilbert resided on his land, and that the nearest waterway to the two estates was Bayou Queue de Tortue.

The sale of the estate of Julien Leger, published in the Opelousas Courier of October 18, 1858, gives more specific information. The inventory included property described as "that portion of land belonging to heirs of Michel Leger, deceased, 400 acres on Tortue," bounded by lands of the deceased, by Henry Roach and by public land; four slaves, a dwelling house, outhouses, one corn mill, 1700 pannels cypress fencing, 11 pairs gentle work oxen, five cows and calves, 10 head three-year-old

---

56 Minutes of Sept. 18, 1865
57 Baudier: OLHS booklet, 47

cattle, five head gentle horses, 100 head sheep, 6,000 shingles, 600 *pieux,* three pirogues,* three pair iron-tired wheels, three pair wooden wheels with cart bodies thereto, plows, hoes and axes. Theogene E. Leger was administrator of the estate.

Julien Leger, son of Michel Leger and Louise Boutin, was born circa 1794.[58] Michel Leger's land, purchased from Louis and Joseph Latiolais, fronted on Bayou Queue de Tortue about three miles from the bayou's juncture with the Mermentau River.

Ebenezer

First settlers in the southeast section of Acadia Parish were the colonial families of Barrow, Hoffpauir and Spell, who acquired land from the Indians or by Spanish grant on Bayou Queue de Tortue. Settlers who came later included the George Morgan and Edward Faulk families; both Morgan and Faulk bought land in the area from the United States government in 1855 and 1860 respectively.[59]

exan

These people were all Anglo-Saxon and Protestant by ancestry. Although some of their early marriages and baptisms are recorded in the Catholic churches of Opelousas and St. Martinville, the second generation members, for the most part, were married in civil ceremonies, usually at the Opelousas courthouse.[60]

The Ebenezer Methodist Church was organized near the settlement on September 1, 1889.[61] Ebenezer, the name of the church and community, is taken from the Bible* and means "a commemoration of divine assistance."

---

*three pirogues: the only water craft of any kind found in the numerous successions examined.
*One Samuel vii, 12

[58] Hebert: *SW La. Records,* Vol. I, 370
[59] Abstracts U. S. Land Entries, No. 1, Acadia Parish
[60] Hebert: *SW La. Records,* Vol. I, 25, 30, 289; Vol. II, 40, 451, 832
[61] *Crowley Daily Signal* 50th Anniv. Ed., 12

CHAPTER XII

Civil War, Yellow Fever

War and pestilence scourged St. Landry Parish during the third quarter of the 19th century. Particular effects of these disasters on the Acadia Parish area cannot be determined. There are no statistics on deaths from yellow fever, or even any indications that the disease, in epidemic form, ever reached the outlying areas of the mother parish. Nor is it possible to provide a roster of Civil War veterans from the Acadia area; home addresses of soldiers, when given, were usually said to be "St. Landry Parish."[1]

Records of the St. Landry Parish Police Jury provide some information on the participation of individuals, other than the military, in the war effort. Records covering the Civil War period began in November 1862 (there is a gap of 43 years in the police jury entries, from October 4, 1819, to November 8, 1862). Minutes of meetings held during November and December of 1862 show the parish making preparations for defense: a cannon was repaired at a cost of $40; D. C. Sittig was paid $5 for making an assessment of hands in the parish to work on fortifications; a resolution was adopted "that a committee consisting of W. Burton, John Lyon and M. L. Melancon be appointed and requested to proceed at once to Atchafalaya Grand River and Plaquemine (Iberville Parish) and ascertain where and how obstruction can be made to prevent the ingress of the enemy and to defend the country and report to the Military Board of St. Landry so that they can communicate with General Taylor immediately so that the hands can be usefully employed." The four names mentioned above are all associated with that part of St. Landry which became Acadia Parish.

In January of 1863 the police jury paid Louis Lejeune $26.80 for beef furnished the soldiers, also detailed 341 hands from St. Landry to work on fortifications at Butte la Rose.

The devastations of war on the parish in general are shown in the police jury minutes of April 13, 1863: "Resolved: That the collector of the parish taxes be and he is hereby authorized to collect the taxes of such persons as are willing to pay the same."

---

1 Booth: *Louisiana Confederate Soldiers and Their Commands*

The widow of a resident of the **Acadia Parish** area, in the course of opening her husband's succession in 1863, was required to take an oath of non-allegiance to the United States. Luce Lebleu, widow of Hypolite C. Guidry, was administered the following oath: "I do solemnly swear that I have not at any time since the 26th of January 1861 taken

Oath of loyalty to the Confederate States administered to Luce Lebleu, widow of Hypolite C. Guidry Jr. The original document is in the St. Landry Parish courthouse.

an oath to support the Constitution or Government of the United States, nor in any manner made a declaration of allegiance to the United States nor given any information or support, aid or comfort to the United States, or to the soldiers, officers or armies thereof, nor been engaged either directly or indirectly as an agent for others or on my own account in carrying on any trade or traffic for purposes of gain with the citizens, soldiers or Government of the United States, or with any other person, so that the United States has been benefitted thereby during the war waged against the Confederate States by the United States, and that I am not a citizen or resident of the United States."[2]

Two men known to have been residents of the Acadia Parish area were members of the St. Landry Police Jury during the Civil War. They were Drauzin Breaux, who lived near the present city of Rayne, and William Elkins, who lived in the Church Point area.

The police jury minutes also reflect the economic condition of St. Landry Parish during the early years of Reconstruction. On March 6, 1865 the police jurors adopted a resolution "that Elbert Gantt, John C. Barry and Christoval Dupre . . . are hereby recommended to his excellency, Henry W. Allen, governor of Louisiana, as proper and suitable persons to be approved as syndics to take charge of and superintend plantations which have been abandoned by their owners . . . " James G. Hayes, tax collector, appeared before the jury December 28, 1866 and presented a list of names of persons on the tax roll for 1865 who had "become insolvent, left the parish or died, without leaving sufficient property to pay their taxes." Two years later the situation had worsened; the police jury instructed the tax collector to accept certificates for wolf and tiger scalps in payment of parish taxes.[3] The minutes show the following persons were paid for wolf scalps from December, 1868 to October, 1869: Sifroy Hebert, $10 for five wolf scalps; an Indian named John, $2 for one wolf scalp; Lewis Young, $6 for three; Hypolite Young, $2 for one; Andre Miller, fils, $6 for three; Uriah Green, $4 for two.

Main events of the war in St. Landry Parish centered around Opelousas. The Louisiana state capital was located in Opelousas from June, 1862, to January, 1863; one of several military training camps was established at Opelousas. Federal troops occupied Opelousas and Wash-

---

[2] Succession Hypolite C. Guidry, 1863, No. 2614, St. Landry Parish
[3] St. Landry Parish Police Jury minutes, Dec. 13, 1868

ington in April of 1863; the one battle fought on St. Landry Parish soil took place November 3, 1863, on Bayou Bourbeux near Grand Coteau.[4]

Federal troops are known to have come into the Acadia Parish area on foraging expeditions. A Union officer and his platoon, bivouacked in Vermilion Parish, crossed Bayou Queue de Tortue in search of provisions. The officer commandeered 400 beeves and a horse from the Bosman Lyons *vacherie* near the bayou, over the objections of Mrs. Lyons, whose

---

[4] Edmonds: David, Ph. d., assoc. prof. economics, USL

A | 16 | La.
(Thompson's.) | Militia

Joseph Elah Andrus

Priv., { Captain Baptiste Jeansonne's Co. 16 Reg't Louisiana Militia.

(War of 1812.)

Appears on

Company Muster Roll

for *Jan 3 to Mar 12*, 1815

Roll dated *Opelousas Co La*

Mar 13, 1815

Date of appointment, en- } *Jan 3*, 1815
listment or engagement, }

To what time engaged or } *Mar 13*, 1815
enlisted, }

Present or absent, *Present*

Remarks and alterations since last muster :

Joseph Elah Andrus was a veteran of the War of 1812. He served in the Louisiana Militia under Captain Jeansonne. (Document copy courtesy Sybil Parrott Andrus)

husband was away, serving with the Confederate forces. The officer promised payment for the animals, and gave Mrs. Lyons a receipt for $3,400 — $8 a head for the cattle and $200 for the horse. Mrs. Lyons put the receipt away in a box with other papers. It was found there almost 100 years later by her descendants, who entered a claim. The United States government found the claim to be valid; the debt was settled, at compound interest, for $32,000.[5]

The yellow fever epidemic of 1888 caused concern to the residents of Rayne. An item in the Crowley Signal of September 29, 1888 reported that Rayne had quarantined against all points infected with yellow fever; the town marshal had been instructed to meet all trains and inspect all passengers coming into town. Subsequent issues of the newspaper made no mention of the disease or the quarantine, therefore it is presumed that the fever scare was of short duration.

Nine years later, in 1897, the entire parish quarantined against the disease. No one without a health certificate was allowed to enter Acadia Parish, no freight could be delivered, guards stood duty at all railroad stations and at all roads leading into the parish. For the six weeks that the quarantine was in effect, all business and commerce, except what could be transacted within the parish limits, was at a standstill.[6]

---

5 Wall: "Louisiana Family Claims Old Debt," *Beaumont Enterprise,* Aug. 22, 1975
6 *Crowley Signal,* Sept. 18, 1897

CHAPTER XIII

The Dusons

A momentous era in the history of southwest Louisiana begins with the saga of the Duson brothers — Cornelius C. Duson, whose influence and efforts were largely responsible for the creation of Acadia Parish, and William W. Duson, who spent more than 30 years of his life developing that parish.

The Dusons were of Scotch-Irish ancestry. Their father, Cornelius Duson McNaughton, was born June 18, 1819 near Quebec, Canada, son of William McNaughton and Catherine Lambert. A daring and adventurous youth, in 1837, when he was 17, Cornelius joined the French revolutionists against the wishes of his family, who were staunch English loyalists. With a companion, S. Lombert (or Lambert) and eight other rebels, he started up the Ottawa River to recruit more men for the cause. English soldiers captured eight of the group, including Cornelius' close friend, Lombert. Risking capture, Cornelius slugged the jailer and helped his companions to escape.

In an attempt to reach the United States the rebels were pursued by English soldiers; several of the party were killed and Cornelius severely wounded by a musket ball, shot through the thigh. He found sanctuary in a woodman's hut, later went to Boston, where he learned that the English government was offering a reward for his capture. He dropped McNaughton from his name and made his way south, ending up at the Mermentau River. There he met and made friends with John Webb, a former seafaring captain of Essex, England, who had located near the river in the early 1820s, at a place that came to be known as Webb's Cove.[1] Webb had married Nancy Mier (Mayer), widow of Samuel Rippy; he was a tanner and saddler. Cornelius also learned this trade and married the captain's daughter, Sarah Ann Webb, born May 7, 1831. Cornelius and Sarah Ann were married May 6, 1845.[2]

Cornelius and Sarah Ann's first child was a son, Cornelius C., born August 31, 1846, at Webb's Cove. The second child, Mary Ann called "Mollie," was born in 1849; another daughter, Ellen N., was born in 1851.

[1] Perrin: *SW La.*, etc. Part II, 22-25
[2] Rev. Paul B. Freeland genealogy records. All genealogical information on the Duson family which follows is from this same source.

212

The second son, William W., was born October 5, 1853, near Breaux Bridge in St. Martin Parish; the youngest of the family, Laura L., was born November 8, 1856.

The Dusons lived in St. Martin Parish for five years.[3] After Cornelius' death in 1857 his widow and children returned to St. Landry Parish and lived in Plaquemine Brûlée, where Sarah Ann's brother, James Webb, had located.[4]

The widow Duson remarried when her eldest son was almost 16. On July 21, 1862 Sarah Ann married William W. Burton, native of England. They had three daughters: Priscilla, born 1863; Rosa S., born 1866; and Olive Vivian, born 1870.

It is not certain where the Burtons lived. It is believed that the family lived on a tract of land of about 42 acres located about one mile northwest of present Crowley. Sarah Ann Duson bought the land from the United States government in 1860.[5] Later, in 1869, W. W. Burton homesteaded an adjacent tract of about the same acreage.[6] A picture, used in the Crowley Daily Signal's 50th Anniversary Edition of 1949, shows a group of people in front of a structure described as "the ruins of what is believed to be the boyhood home of W. W. Duson." The place was situated about one mile from Crowley. The attire worn by the people in the picture indicates that the picture was taken in the early 1900s.

Mary Ann "Mollie" Duson married David Burns Lyons. Ellen, called "Aunt Diddie," was first married to Colbert Foreman, then to Elisha S. Andrus. Laura L. Duson married Raymond T. Clark.

The half-sisters, daughters of Sarah Ann Webb and W. W. Burton, were married as follows: Priscilla Burton married James Madison Lyons; Rosa S. Burton married Gus Edgar Fontenot; Olive Vivian Burton married Thomas J. Toler. Both Rosa and Olive were married at ceremonies in the Crowley House, Rosa on February 14, 1888, and Olive on October 4, 1888.

Cornelius C. "Curley" was first married to Isora Andrus, daughter of Joseph Elah Andrus, Jr., on November 26, 1867. They had eight children: Morton E., Walter W., Rodney R., Clayton C., Jesse C., Lola, Meta,

---

3 *Opelousas Courier*, Oct. 12, 1872
4 Perrin: *SW La.*, etc., Part II, 274-275
5 Abstracts U.S. Land Entries, No. 1, 119 Acadia Parish
6 Ibid

and George McNaughton. Isora Andrus Duson died July 15, 1892. In June, 1893, C. C. Duson married Eunice Pharr; they had two sons, Curley Pharr and William Herbert.

William W. Duson was married three times. His first marriage was to Anna McClelland, on January 2, 1879. To this marriage were born Mamie Hilliard Lawrence and a son, Robert Rayburn, who died in infancy. Anna McClelland Duson died September 7, 1881. His second marriage, to Julia I. Clark, took place April 7, 1882. Julia died January 20, 1892. There were no children from this marriage. W. W. Duson and Clara May

The log cabin boyhood home of the Duson brothers, one mile northwest of Crowley near Bayou Plaquemine Brulee. The picture was taken about 1904 when a group of young adults on a house party at the nearby home of Dr. J. F. Naftel visited the old Duson place. (Freeland Archives photo)

Thayer were married February 11, 1893. They had five children: Henry Thayer, Maxwell McNaughton, William W. Jr., Marguerite, who died in infancy, and Mildred C. Duson Cossey.

Sarah Ann Webb died December 4, 1901, at the Toler residence in Crowley. She had been a widow for six years, W. W. Burton having died November 18, 1895, while on a trip to England.

Cornelius C. "Curley" Duson died October 19, 1910 in a New Orleans hospital. At present (1975) not any of his 10 children survive.

William W. Duson died in Crowley October 3, 1929. His widow, Clara Thayer Duson, born September 29, 1872, lived to be almost 102. She died in Crowley August 3, 1974.

At present (1975) the three sons of W. W. Duson and Clara Thayer Duson are living. Henry and Maxwell Duson live in Crowley, W. W. Duson Jr. lives in Columbus, N.C.

C. C. "Curley" Duson

Cornelius C. Duson, familiarly called "Curley" began his political career in 1867, when he was 21, as a deputy under James G. Hayes, sheriff of St. Landry Parish.[7] Prior to this he served in the Confederate army, a fact that is not pointed up in early biographical sketches for obvious reasons: some 20 years later, when he and his brother began their advertising campaign to lure northern settlers to Acadia Parish, the country was just beginning to recover from the aftermath of the fratricidal Civil War; wisely, Curley's affiliation with the rebel cause was never mentioned.

There are two published sources which refer to Curley Duson's service with the Confederacy: Judge Gilbert L. Dupre, close friend and associate of the Dusons, wrote in his "Political Reminiscences:" "C. C. Duson . . . had been a Confederate soldier and served a term of imprisonment in the Washington, La., jail with the long haired negro, Edward Babb, as one of his guards." In a statement published in the Opelousas Courier of October 12, 1872, Duson himself said, in referring to his association with Sheriff James G. Hayes, that he and Hayes had "shared the dangers and troubles of the late war, besides the horrors of prison."

Curley was working for his uncle, James Webb, on the farm at Plaquemine Brûlée when Sheriff Hayes offered him a job as deputy. Realizing his need for more education, he attended Rev. C. A. Frazee's

---

7 *Opelousas Courier,* Oct. 12, 1872

school in Opelousas for one session, then began his work in the sheriff's department in August of 1867, the year he was married to Isora Andrus.[8]

Sheriff Hayes was assassinated while campaigning for office, and his brother, Egbert O. Hayes, was elected sheriff. The new sheriff appointed Curley Duson his executive official a post which Duson held until 1872 when he ran for the office against Hayes.[9]

It was during this first campaign that Duson published the statement, referred to previously, in which he addressed himself "To the People of St. Landry." The reason for the statement, he said, was to "contradict certain reports circulated that I was raised by Captain J. G. Hayes, late sheriff of this parish, and that I am now acting with ingratitude in consenting to become a candidate." (The alleged ingratitude, presumably, was based on the fact that Duson was running against the late sheriff's brother) Duson stated that he was indebted to his mother and his uncle, James Webb, for raising; that he had lived with Sheriff Hayes in 1866, when he was 21; this, with the shared war experiences, had resulted in "a warm, personal attachment."[10]

Duson listed as witneses to his public statement the names of Gabriel and Madison Lyons, C. W. Foreman, James Webb, Dallas B. Hayes, Isaac Hayes, H. B. Sloane, Dr. B. E. Clark, Dr. R. R. Lyons, Joseph E. Andrus, Jesse B. Clark, Joseph H. Andrus, Julien Richard, "and many others." He said he had received $100 per month as deputy for Sheriff Egbert O. Hayes, and that the sheriff had fired him for running against him.[11]

Gilbert Dupre summarizes C. C. Duson's political career as follows: "He ran against E. O. Hayes in 1872, but was defeated. He ran against him in 1874 when he was elected. He was thereafter re-elected to succeed himself in 1876, 1878, 1879, 1884, holding the office without break therein for fourteen years, having to run for the same biennially for eight years."[12]

In the 1874 election Duson had two opponents: the incumbent sheriff, Egbert O. Hayes, and J. O. Chachere, both members of large and influential families of St. Landry Parish. Election returns showed Duson

---

8 *Ibid*

9 Dupre: *Political Reminiscences,* 15

10 *Opelousas Courier,* Oct. 12, 1872

11 *Ibid*

12 Dupre: *Political Reminiscences,* 16

Cornelius C. Duson
August 31, 1846 – October 9, 1910
(Freeland Archives photo)

with 2,623 votes; Hayes 1,350 and Chachere, 1,120, giving the 28-year-old deputy a majority of 153 votes.[13]

At that time St. Landry was composed of the three present parishes of St. Landry, Acadia and Evangeline; the Acadia area, the least populated at the time, gave Duson approximately one fifth of his total vote. Of these precincts his largest majorities came from Lower Plaquemine Brûlée, where 105 of the total 116 votes cast were for Duson, and at the two precincts at Mermentau, where he won 72 of the 87 votes cast.[14]

Two years before his election to the sheriff's office, probably after he was defeated by Egbert Hayes, Duson was a mail carrier. The Opelousas Courier of July 6, 1872 published the contracts for carrying mails, one of which reads: "St. Martinville to Opelousas, via Breaux Bridge and Leonville, tri-weekly, to C. C. Duson for three years from July 1, 1872, at $2,300 per annum." In the June 21, 1873 issue of the same newspaper a brief item noted that the postmaster general had completed a contract with C. C. Duson to carry mail to Hickory Flat, Calcasieu, through Prudhomme City and Faquetaique, the German settlement.

The popular sheriff ran into trouble in 1879, when he went down in apparent defeat. Returns of the December 2 election showed C. M. Thompson with 3,005 votes to Duson 2,945, giving Thompson a winning margin of 60 votes.[15] Duson claimed election fraud and contested the election on charges of irregularities at the Leonville poll.[16] The trial ended February 26, 1880, the jury rendering a verdict for Thompson. Henry L. Garland, Duson's attorney, brought the case to the Supreme Court, which ruled in favor of Duson.[17]

Gilbert Dupre, who had been at the polls working for the Duson faction, reported on this contest in his "Political Reminiscenses:" "Here began a fight which involved two principals and their friends in a death struggle. It had to be a fight to the finish . . . Duson got busy. He employed Henry L. Garland, then among the foremost lawyers at the bar, to contest the election . . . The defendant prayed for and obtained a jury trial. The case attracted much attention. It consumed many days. The jury returned a unanimous verdict in favor of the defendant, Thompson.

13 *Opelousas Courier*, Nov. 14, 1874
14 *Ibid*
15 *Opelousas Courier*, Dec. 27, 1879
16 *Ibid*
17 *Ibid*, July 17, 1880

Duson appealed to the supreme court, when Judge Poche, as the organ of the court, set aside the verdict of the jury and announced Duson's election by twenty-five majority . . .

"Thompson's friends always believed he had been counted out. They asserted that the box had been stuffed in the clerk's office. This charge was made but not proven. Be that as it may, Duson got into the saddle once more . . . ."[18]

Curley Duson gained recognition as a law enforcement officer early in his career. In 1871, while a deputy sheriff, his exploits as a lawman were noted in the press; there were repeated references to "C. C. Duson, the indefatigable deputy of Sheriff Hayes" and other such laudatory comments.

When Duson was elected sheriff he had some strong political allies in District Judge George W. Hudspeth and Ferreol F. Perrodin, the district attorney. Gilbert Dupre told how the three worked together:

"With Hudspeth on the bench, Duson to track crime and furnish the evidence, and Perrodin as prosecutor it meant conviction nine times out of ten. Now and then there was an acquittal, but these were at rare intervals. Judge Hudspeth had prosecuted criminals for eight years and he always sided with the prosecution. Duson was zealous in building up his reputation and Perrodin was as anxious to succeed as any or both of them. So that when the poor offender faced the bar of justice he often felt that all hopes were left behind.

"It was Duson's ability to capture criminals and land them behind bars that sustained him. He was his own chief deputy. He paid no attention to the sheriff's office proper. His business was to hunt criminals and send them to the penitentiary or the gallows."[19]

Some of Sheriff Duson's cases attracted widespread attention. One involved two residents of Ville Platte, Louis Rousseau and Cyrius Brignac. Rousseau kept a barroom in Ville Platte; Brignac owed Rousseau some money. Rousseau sent for Brignac and demanded his money; Brignac admitted owing the debt, but said he could not pay. Rousseau killed his customer and fled. Sheriff Duson set out to track Rousseau down; months afterwards he located him in Indian Territory in Oklahoma, captured the fugitive and brought him to Opelousas to face trial.[20]

---

[18] Pages 37 and 38
[19] Pages 29 and 30
[20] Summary, *Opelousas Courier,* June 9, 1877; Perrin: *SW La.,* etc. Part II, 25; Dupre: *Political Reminiscences,* 31

Rousseau was hanged in front of the parish prison on June 8, 1877. It was the first execution of a white man in 30 years in St. Landry Parish.[21]

The two Opelousas newspapers, the Courier and the St. Landry Democrat, kept readers informed of the sheriff's activities. The Democrat, in an 1882 item, reported that Sheriff Duson, who had been absent for some time attending the District Congressional Conference, "and, as some thought, on a pleasure trip, did not return empty handed. He brought Wallace Adkins, accused of horse stealing."[22]

Newspapers outside the parish also sang the sheriff's praises. The Courier reprinted a story which had appeared in the Lake Charles Echo; the newspaper article told how "the efficient and well known sheriff of St. Landry" had apprehended an escaped convict; the man had reached Lake Charles by boarding a train west of the Mermentau River.[23] The Houston Telegram gave an account of another Duson case: In 1871 a man by the name of John Sonnier was indicted for two murders, one in St. Landry and one in Calcasieu Parish. Sonnier disappeared; he returned to St. Landry in 1874 and narrowly escaped capture by Duson. The governor of Louisiana offered a reward of $500 for the arrest of Sonnier, said to be a most dangerous and wily character. Through persistent inquiry, Sheriff Duson learned that Sonnier was in Brazoria County, Texas, working as a guard at a convict camp. In company with two Texas lawmen Duson went to the place. He was astute enough to realize that the fugitive might recognize him and flee; he sent the Texas officers in for Sonnier, then took him into custody. The man was tried and sentenced to life imprisonment.[24]

Another of Sheriff Duson's noted cases was the capture of W. H. Slane, wanted on a rape charge. Duson pursued Slane for 29 days, finally caught the man in west Texas.[25] After Slane was imprisoned in Opelousas the Courier reported that "Sheriff Duson answered charges of mistreating a prisoner, W. H. Slane, arrested in Texas for rape of a 10-year-old child, Maggie Moss, near Big Cane, in May. Slane was captured near San Saba, Texas."[26] The newspaper story did not say in what way the prisoner had been mistreated, or what Duson had said to refute the charges, but the

---

21 *Opelousas Courier,* June 9, 1877
22 *St. Landry Democrat,* Aug. 26, 1882
23 *Opelousas Courier,* Nov. 26, 1881
24 *Opelousas Courier,* April 10, 1880; Perrin: *SW La.,* etc. Part II, 26
25 *Opelousas Courier,* Sept. 6, 1879; Perrin: *SW La.,* etc. Part II, 26
26 Sept. 6, 1879

editorial inference was plain: anyone as low-down as Slane was lucky he hadn't been lynched.

In his relentless pursuit of criminals Sheriff Duson faced death many times, and was wounded at least once. With two fellow deputies he engaged in a gun battle with two wanted men in which both of the fugitives were killed; he tracked two transients, wanted for murder, to the Red River where he killed one of the men in a hand-to-hand fight, wounded the other and brought him back to the Opelousas jail.[27]

Curley Duson was an expert marksman. The late L. A. Williams, a Crowley pioneer and business associate of the Dusons, stated in a 1955 interview: "Curley Duson was a crack shot with the pistol. This section was a hiding-out place for renegades from all over the nation, and our peace officers had to be tough."[28] The St. Landry Democrat of May 6, 1882 noted that Sheriff Duson, shooting from a boat near Morgan City, had killed 96 alligators in 96 shots. A brief item in the same issue revealed that "Duson got his man in Texas, for murder north of Chicot." The placement and wording of the statement would seem to indicate the capture of the criminal was a commonplace event and of secondary interest to the feat of marksmanship.

In the fall of 1883 it was rumored that Duson would not run for sheriff for another term. One of the things which could have triggered the rumor was an advertisement in the Opelousas Courier of July 7, 1883: FOR SALE: My residence in Opelousas, two stories with five rooms and hall, brick kitchen and pantry attached; servants' house, cistern, well, stable, crib, etc., and half square of ground with tenement house, subdivided into yard, garden and lots; buildings all new and of cypress. Price $3,500; $1,500 cash, balance on terms. C. C. Duson

The rumor that Duson would not run led to a flood of protest. Letters to the editor appeared in the newspapers, citing the sheriff as a "Most vigilant, thorough-going officer . . . "he should be drafted again..."[29] and, "let this energetic, temperate, splendid officer remain where he is; Duson's reputation has become almost national; at any rate in the cotton states he is renowned for his wonderfull successes . . . he never fails to get his man."[30]

---

27 Perrin: *SW La.*, etc., Part II, 23-24; *St. Landry Democrat,* Nov. 8, 1883
28 Fontenot: "History of Eunice, Mrs. Duson's Namesake," *Daily World* supplement, Nov. 3, 1955, 116
29 *St. Landry Democrat,* Nov. 8, 1883
30 *Ibid,* Oct. 6, 1883

The Opelousas Courier ran a long feature article about Sheriff Duson under such sub-titles as "The Career of a Noted Capturer of Criminals;" "A Remarkable Record of Detective Skill and Personal Courage," etc., etc.[31] The editor of the Courier wrote: "In view of his (Duson's) long and faithful service and that he is not up for re-election, the parish should offer him a gold medal." The editor announced that the newspaper office was taking subscriptions to buy the medal for the sheriff.[32] However, the presentation of this symbol of long and faithful service to a retiring public servant was not to be — at least, not at that time. The sheriff was persuaded to run again. According to Gilbert Dupre, Duson consented to run again when urged to do so by influential members of his faction. "I was not present at the conference," Dupre wrote, "but I am rather inclined to believe that Duson did not shy at running again . . . His friends insisted he must be nominated again. He mildly demurred, but he was again nominated and again elected."[33]

The election of 1883 was a landslide victory for Duson. He was given 6,200 votes, a majority of 1,843 over a strong opponent, Francois Savoy.[34] Duson's last term as sheriff appears to be rather tame and uneventful, compared with the earlier years. There were few references in the press to activities of the sheriff's department. A few lines in the Opelousas Courier of August 28, 1886 concerned what the editor termed "the Louis Steele - Duson controversy." Auditor Steele, he said, appeared satisfied with Duson's administration of the tax collector's office, and "Mr. Duson does not appear to be much worried over the matter. He is still in Canada visiting relatives."

C. C. Duson served one term as state senator for the district composed of St. Landry and Acadia Parishes. His last job of a political nature was his appointment, by President Theodore Roosevelt, as United States marshal for the western district of Louisiana.[35]

His life-time friend, Gilbert Dupre, wrote of Curley Duson: "Later on in these writings I shall have more to say of this remarkable man . . . I have already written that Duson was ambitious. I might add that he was as ambitious as Lucifer, and he could sense public opinion and take

---

31 Nov. 3, 1883
32 *Opelousas Courier*, Oct. 27, 1883
33 Dupre: *Political Reminiscences*, 40
34 Perrin: *SW La.*, etc., Part II, 25; *Crowley Signal*, Oct. 27, 1894, 5
35 "Some History," etc., *Daily World*, 116

advantage of it . . . Duson knew how to play the game. He did not drink; never smoked; never chewed, never went into a barroom if he could avoid doing so; never played poker. Indeed, he never played cards at all. He knew where to put his money. He had always spent this open-handedly. He would give a friend a dollar or a hundred dollars and never afterwards avert to it. He was courageous, a dead shot, and had absolute confidence in himself."[36]

Dupre classified Curley Duson's education as "very limited." From the standpoint of the scholarly judge, this was true. Be that as it may, his lack of education did not prevent him from reaching goals attained by few of his peers; he achieved a place of distinction not only in the history of Acadia Parish, but in the whole of southwest Louisiana.

W. W. Duson

In 1926, when W. W. Duson was 72 years old, he related the story of his life to a reporter for a Texas newspaper. The reporter, G. V. Burke of the Beaumont Enterprise staff, came to Crowley especially to interview the veteran land developer, who had become a legend in his own time.

Burke's story was published in the Enterprise on February 14, 1926, and reprinted the following day in the Crowley Daily Signal, the newspaper which Duson had founded.

Accompanying the article was a two-column photograph of the subject, identified as Col. W. W. Duson. The "colonel" was an honorary, not a military title; Willie Duson was too young for Civil War service, and was in his 65th year when the United States entered World War I.

The picture used with the article shows a clean shaven, youthful looking man with slightly waving hair and a sensitive face. His expression is semi-serious; his eyes, seen through metal-rimmed spectacles, seem to be looking ahead into the future.

The newspaper article included some family background: Cornelius Duson McNaughton's flight from Canada in 1837, his death, and some sketchy information on Willie's early youth. Part of one paragraph reads: "During the war the family found the business of living difficult, and W. W. recalls selling coffee, rice and other edibles prepared by his mother, among the soldiers. Later he was engaged as a driver, hauling contraband goods from the Teche country to Texas. When he was twelve he engaged in herding cattle in southwestern Louisiana and for this work he received

---

[36] Dupre: *Political Reminiscences,* 16, 35, 66

223

William W. Duson
October 5, 1853 — October 3, 1929
(Freeland Archives photo)

the bountiful salary of $7.50 a month. During 1868-1869 he worked in sawmill camps, during which time he caught another six months of schooling."

As meager as is this information, it is the only published material which deals with the early life of W. W. Duson. The information reproduced above raises some questions that cannot now be answered: Were the soldiers to whom he sold the coffee and food of the Confederate or Union army, and where were they at the time? What type of "contraband goods" did he haul to Texas? Was his herding connected with the historic cattle drives in the days before the railroads came?

Even without the answers, the picture which emerges here is of a youth who very early in life learned to fend for himself.

The newspaper article continues with more of the life of young Willie Duson:

"The following two years he carried the United States mail from Opelousas to Branch (Plaquemine Brûlée) and St. Martinville, a distance of 50 miles, making the trip three times a week. Then at the end of this work he returned home and took up the varied business of herding, sawmill work and trading — most anything to make an honest living. In 1874 he took a contract for transporting logs by water to sawmill camps, following this work about eight months when he entered the employ as clerk of Foreman and Webb, at Branch, La. (Plaquemine Brûlée) At the end of 1875 he had saved $700 from his many labors and giving his mother $300 of this, took the remaining $400 and went to New Orleans where he entered a business school."

These activities cover a five-year period in Willie Duson's life, from about age 17 to 23. The newspaper article continues:

"So apt a student did he make that at the end of seven months he was offered a position in New Orleans paying $125 a month, but declined it to return home where he could take better care of his mother and sisters. He went back into the store where he previously had served as clerk, receiving a salary of $20 a month. The opportunity presenting itself, he bought a half interest in the Foreman and Webb company for $1250 he borrowed from his brother, only to be obliged to close two years later when equinoxial storms wiped out the farming community surrounding Branch (Plaquemine Brûlée). His company was in debt at the time but he gave personal notes for every dollar owed and in two years time had discharged these obligations."

Following through on a chronological schedule, this would place Willie Duson back in his home area in 1877, when he was about 24. His 31-year-old brother was sheriff of St. Landry Parish. He had lost a sister; the oldest of the Duson girls, Mary Ann Duson Lyons, died in 1875. His second sister, Ellen, was married to Colbert Foreman, his partner in the Plaquemine Brûlée firm of Foreman and Duson.

By this time Willie Duson had acquired land at Plaquemine Brûlée. He homesteaded a tract of 161 acres in Section 15, Township 8 South, Range 2 East, in 1876.[37] The Duson tract was adjacent to land homesteaded earlier by Colbert Foreman.[38]

The next several years brought short-lived happiness, then disaster and tragedy. The year following his marriage storms destroyed the crops and forced his business into bankruptcy. Another year went by and he lost his young wife. The Opelousas Courier of September 10, 1881, carried this brief obituary: "DIED — at Plaquemine Brulee, on the 7th September, Anna, wife of W. W. Duson, age 21." He also lost an infant son, Robert Rayburn. Willie was left alone to rear his motherless daughter, Mamie.

Anna died just when the family's financial picture had begun to improve. On October 22, 1881, about six weeks after Anna's death, the Opelousas Courier reported: "Mr. W. W. Duson, who lives in Plaquemine Brûlée, about 18 miles southwest of Opelousas, made 119 barrels of excellent rice from this year's crop, and would have made more were it not for extremely dry weather."

The year 1882 found Willie Duson married a second time and starting a new business. On April 27 he married Julia I. Clark; later that year he began buying and selling land.

Conveyance records in the St. Landry Parish courthouse during the ensuing years show numerous land transactions by W. W. and C. C. Duson. Some of the land bought was in areas of St. Landry and Evangeline Parishes, but the bulk of the real estate handled involved land in the Acadia Parish area.

The largest land transaction was on December 2, 1882. Sheriff C. C. Duson conducted a tax sale at the front door of the Opelousas courthouse; the sale, for taxes due the state for the years 1880 and 1881, had been duly advertised in the St. Landry Democrat of October 18, 1882. The

---

[37] Abstract U. S. Land Entries No. 1, 132, Acadia Parish
[38] Ibid

day of the sale W. W. Duson bought almost 10,000 acres of land, all located in the Acadia Parish area, for $162.78, the amount of taxes owed. Included in the purchase was acreage on the east side of Bayou Nezpique which took in portions of colonial land grants to Antoine Boisdore, Joseph A. Declouet and John Clay. It was stipulated that the lands were redeemable in one year from the date of recordation, which was September 2, 1885. Gilbert L. Dupre was the notary handling the sale.[39]

Sometime during 1884 — probably in the fall, after he bought the 13 lots at the Cunningham Estate sale in Rayne — W. W. Duson left Plaquemine Brûlée and moved to Rayne, the newly incorporated town which had been spawned by the railroad. It is not known whether he moved both his business and his residence to Rayne; he may have continued to live at Plaquemine Brûlée for a while. However, this would have called for daily commuting by horse and buggy over the seven-mile stretch of dirt road.

There are indications that Duson wanted to remove to Rayne earlier, probably about the time the crop failure ruined his business. One source states that he tried to borrow money in Rayne with which to start a store; apparently unable to do this, he returned to Plaquemine Brûlée. Later, he moved to Rayne and came to Dr. J. P. Mauboules and said he needed $2,000 to open his business. Dr. Mauboules took him to his father, Jean Mauboules, who instructed his wife to get the money needed from the *armoire*. Duson offered to sign a note for the money; Mauboules said this was not necessary, that he could repay it whenever he was able. Later, when members of the Mauboules family wanted land in the Morse area, Duson handled the homestead transactions at no cost to the family.[40]

In the spring of 1885, when the editor of the Courier visited "the thriving little city of Rayne" he reported that W. W. Duson, the real estate agent, was "kept busy showing land to newcomers.[41]

Also in the spring of 1885 an auspicious item appeared in the Opelousas Courier: "About six miles west of Rayne our efficient sheriff has a pasture enclosed which contains 3200 acres of the best pasture land; the land has a front of one mile on the Louisiana Western Railroad and running north the same distance is crossed by Bayou Plaquemine for at least another mile along which grows luxuriant switch cane in endless

39 Conveyance Book R-2, 755-762, St. Landry Parish
40 *Crowley Daily Signal*, 50th Anniv. Ed., 110
41 *Opelousas Courier*, Mar. 21, 1885

quantities and affording a rich pasturage during the entire winter season. We were informed that large stock pens would soon be established at this pasture, and before long it would become the rallying point of cattlemen to fatten their beeves before rushing them to market. We consider this a valuable piece of property and believe that ere long it will prove a bonanza for Mr. Duson, either as a pasture for rental to the public, or to be made a stock pen for his own benefit in raising stock for the New Orleans market. He had been offered double for one half of this pasture, of what the whole area originally cost him. It is not for sale."[42]

The newspaper was wrong on one point: this particular tract of land did not have a front of one mile on the railroad. The land, bought September 13, 1884 by C. C. Duson, was the entire Antoine Blanc Spanish land grant.* Situated on both sides of Bayou Plaquemine Brûlée, the tract was 40 arpents front by 80 arpents in depth. Sheriff Duson bought the land in New Orleans from the Louis Blanc Estate for $3,200, or $1 an arpent.[43]

Reference to the Blanc property is made in the Crowley Signal of August 25, 1888: "A Spanish settler bearing the name of LeBlanc was given a grant of 2800 acres** part of which extends within the present town limits. He was a stockman and his residence was not greatly extended. His buildings here were a short distance west of the present home of L. H. Thompson. At so remote a date did he live here that 65 years ago the marks of his habitation were almost obliterated." The Signal writer was wrong only in labeling Blanc a Spaniard instead of a Frenchman, and in the spelling of the name. A considerable portion of the old Blanc vacherie is now within the corporate limits of Crowley.

Another significant land transaction took place in the spring of 1885 when W. W. Duson went to New Orleans and bought, in four separate transactions, more than 500 acres of land within the Acadia Parish area. Two of the tracts purchased lie within the present corporate limits of Crowley. One, a tract of 142.44 acres, bought from Mrs. Bridget Simons, widow of Andrew Dougherty, of New Orleans, is in the northeast quarter of the southeast quarter of Section 32, Township 9 South Range 1 East

---

* not to be confused with the land which Antoine Blanc bought from the Indians, located on the west side of Plaquemine Brûlée adjacent to the Bosman Hayes land grant.
** 2,800 acres, the equivalent of 3,200 arpents.

[42] Ibid
[43] Conveyance Book Q-2, 210-211, St. Landry Parish

(northwest Crowley.). The second tract, purchased from Frederick A. Hottinger of New Orleans and containing 135.93 acres, was the south half of the northeast quarter and the northeast quarter of the northeast quarter of Section 4, Township 10 South Range 1 East, now the main business district of Crowley. This tract had about a half mile frontage on both sides of the Louisiana Western railroad.[44]

These land transactions by the Duson brothers were clearly the preliminaries of a plan to develop a large portion of the southwestern part of St. Landry Parish. The lives of the brothers, which previously have appeared to be going in different directions, come together at this point. The result of that merger of interests was to be of a magnitude that neither could have dreamed of at the time.

------

[44] Conveyance Book R-2, 501-505, St. Landry Parish

CHAPTER XIV

Creation of a Parish

The St. Landry Parish courthouse was destroyed by fire during the early morning hours of March 22, 1886. While Opelousas citizens slept the two-story brick structure was gutted by flames. The court records and some books in Sheriff Duson's office were saved; the tax rolls, all papers in the tax collector's office and some valuable papers in the sheriff's office were destroyed.

The Opelousas Guard had several thousand metallic cartridges stored in the Supreme Court office on the second floor; when these began to explode, the work of saving the records and containing the fire was virtually paralyzed.

There was little money in the building. Several days before Sheriff Duson had made settlement with the state treasurer and had deposited $5,000 in a New Orleans bank. An old safe in the tax collector's office contained a few hundred dollars in silver and gold; the slightly damaged coins were salvaged by firemen.

The fire was believed to have been the work of an incendiary. Since no safes had been tampered with, the suspected motive was destruction of the records. Damage was estimated at between $30,000 and $50,000.[1]

The courthouse fire set off fireworks in opposite directions from Opelousas. Almost before the embers cooled two movements were launched: the people of Rayne began a campaign to divide St. Landry and create a new parish, and the people of Washington initiated action to get the parish seat of St. Landry relocated in their town.

Rayne was the boom town of the parish; the railroad had made it a center of trade and shipping. Washington was seeking an economic boost; for years a thriving port on Bayou Courtableau, the town was beginning to feel the inroads of the Iron Horse.

Some 15 years earlier an abortive attempt had been made to carve another parish out of St. Landry. A bill for the creation of a new parish out of the southern portion of St. Landry was introduced January 20, 1871 by A. L. Durio, state representative of St. Landry. The new parish was to be named St. Joseph. The bill provided for the boundaries of the proposed parish to run within three miles of Opelousas to include Gros Chevreuil, Bellevue, Petit Bois, Prairie des Femmes, Grand Coteau and Plaque-mine Brûlée, also "sparse and detached communities westward to the Mermentaw and Nez-Pique Rivers."[2] The Courier editor editorialized on the proposal; he said this separation would take about one fourth of St. Landry's territory, and stated that a large number of taxpayers in the proposed parish were opposed to the division.[3] At that time the total population of St. Landry was 24,646; 13,135 whites and 11,511 colored.[4]

Subsequent issues of the newspaper made no further reference to the bill, nor is there a record of it in the state archives. The question of division did not again become a public issue until the courthouse fire. In a matter of days after the courthouse burned Opelousas political leaders realized a choice must be made: give in to the demands of Rayne for a new parish, or give up the courthouse to Washington.[5]

One week after the fire, on March 29, Washington sent a committee to Rayne "to get the sentiment of the people on dividing the parish." M. D. Kavanaugh, state senator, headed the committee; others were Thomas D. Cook, Robert Zernott, Laurent Dupre, W. F. Schwing, B. Baillio and O. Fontenot.[6] Rayne's two-weeks old newspaper, the Rayne Signal, provided the answer: "The general sentiment of the people of this section is that a division of the parish would result in great good to all interests. We have no doubt of it. The slight increase in taxes which might result from such a course would be more than offset by the increase in value of all real estate. The sums of money spent by our people at the parish seat during their numerous trips throughout the year amount to quite a tax . . . Ope-lousas is 30 miles from Rayne, 50 miles from Mermentau . . . "[7]

The Signal editor warned that the move for division would encounter opposition from Opelousas, also hinted at overtures from that town: "Any man of common sense can understand that all the interests at Opelousas are opposed to a division of the parish. If they now seem anxious to assist us, it must be because they fear a combination between us and the people of Washington. Why do they fear such a combination? Why is it that these gentlemen so suddenly manifest an interest in our behalf? It is

---

2 *Opelousas Courier,* Jan. 28, 1871
3 *Ibid*
4 *Ibid,* Feb. 18, 1871
5 Dupre: *Political Reminiscences,* 52
6 *Rayne Signal,* Apr. 3, 1886
7 *Ibid*

because we are nearer the accomplishment of our purpose than we ever have been, or are ever likely to be again!"[8]

The final sentence in the editor's statement shows that the blueprint for parish division had not been drafted overnight. In his "Political Reminiscenses" Gilbert Dupre wrote: "They (the people of Rayne) had dreamed that in years to come such a consummation might be wished for, solicited and obtained." However, Dupre believed that without the courthouse fire any attempt at parish division would have been ludicrous. "Poor old Opelousas was between two fires," he wrote. "Rayne, then a little town on the Louisiana Western railroad, took advantage of the situation and demanded a new parish . . . The day preceding the fire such a demand would have been ridiculed out of existence. The day succeeding it, the question had become a grim reality, and, like Banquo's ghost, it would not down. Thus had a stroke from a match changed many things and threatened to engulf Opelousas."[9]

The editor of the Opelousas Courier spelled it out. Washington, he said, had sent a delegation to Rayne with a proposition: if Rayne would support Washington in its bid for the courthouse, Washington would help Rayne to secure a part of the territory of St. Landry to form a new parish. The Courier predicted that Opelousas would fight Washington to keep the courthouse, but would be agreeable to granting land for a new parish.[10] It is clear that the people of Opelousas, faced with the choice of giving up the courthouse or giving up territory for a new parish, considered the latter proposal the lesser of two evils.

Washington lost no time. The town council appropriated $10,000 for the courthouse building and citizens agreed to subscribe the same amount.[11] The editor of the Rayne newspaper favored a coalition with Washington: "If we ignore the assistance of Washington now we may have cause to regret it in the future. Now is the time to act. The legislature meets next month, and will not again for two years."[12]

A mass meeting was called for April 3 at Rayne. The Rayne paper urged attendance: "Let us see how you stand, fellow citizens; for or against the new parish! Recollect the grand mass meeting to be held at the K. of P. hall at 2 p.m. Business of vital importance to Rayne and south-

---

8 *Ibid*
9 Page 52
10 *Opelousas Courier,* April 3, 1886
11 *Rayne Signal,* Mar. 27, 1886
12 *Ibid,* Apr. 3, 1886

western St. Landry requires your personal attention, and each and every one of our citizens who are in favor of a division of the parish should be on hand to give expression to his feelings on the subject . . . Rally 'round the flag, boys, and let everyone, his uncles and all his female cousins be on hand . . . Stand firm to the rack boys, fodder or no fodder, and let us by a unanimous voice proclaim to the public that we want a new parish, and that we will not be content until we get it."[13]

The Signal editor advocated closing all business houses in Rayne during the meeting: "We must strike while the iron is hot," he wrote, "and strike with an eternal vim if we wish to carry our point. Now is the time to assert our rights, and let us not be content until we have them."[14]

The Rayne Signal of April 10, 1886 carried a complete account of the meeting: "The call for a mass-meeting of citizens of southwestern St. Landry, to discuss measures for a division of the parish, was heartily responded to; and on Saturday, April 3, long before the hour fixed for the meeting a large crowd of men, numbering about fifteen hundred, filled the streets of our town. At 2:15 p.m. the doors of the K. of P. Hall were thrown open, and the room filled immediately. Hundreds failed to gain admittance.

"Order being called, Mayor B. H. Harman, was nominated for president of the meeting by Mr. R. J. C. Bull, and duly elected. The Opelousas and Washington delegations were then invited to seats on the stage.

"On motion of Dr. R. C. Webb, duly seconded, Mr. George K. Bradford was elected vice president.

"On motion of Mr. R. T. Clark, duly seconded, Mr. A. S. Chappuis was elected secretary.

"These gentlemen having assumed their stations, Mr. Bradford moved that a committee of five, on resolutions, be appointed and time allowed them to report, seconded and carried. The president appointed G. K. Bradford, chairman, J. L. Lyons, James Webb, M. Arenas and R. T. Clark.

"After a short recess the following resolutions were read.

"Whereas; at a mass-meeting of the people of southwestern St. Landry, held at Rayne, Louisiana, on this third day of April 1886, for the purpose of divising plans for the division of said parish, and formation of a new parish out of the southwestern portion of St. Landry; therefore: Be it

13 *Rayne Signal,* Apr. 3, 1886
14 *Ibid*

"Resolved, That the members of the General Assembly from the parish of St. Landry, at its next regular session in May, 1886, be respectfully urged to introduce as early as possible after the assembly of the next Legislature, and to support to a successful termination, an enabling act, granting to the people of said parish, the right to create a new parish to be taken out of the southwestern portion of said parish, and to be confined strictly within the present existing boundaries of the parish of St. Landry. Be it further

"Resolved, That an executive committee of fifteen, representing the following precincts of said locality, be appointed, whose duty it shall be to conduct to a successful termination, the sentiment of this meeting as expressed in the first resolution. Be it further

"Resolved, That a special committee be appointed to frame a bill in conjunction with the representatives from said parish in the General Assembly; which shall carry out the wishes of this meeting as expressed in the first resolution. Be it further

"Resolved, That the Hon. E. T. Lewis, candidate for the State senate, be invited to address this meeting and to state plainly and simply his position in relation to the foregoing resolution; and whether or not, if elected, he will support the bill to be intorduced in the General Assembly, providing for the formation of a new parish in southwestern St. Landry.

"Moved by Mr. James Webb and duly seconded, that the above resolutions be adopted — carried.

"In accordance with last resolution, the president invited the Hon. E. T. Lewis, democratic candidate for State senate, to address the meeting. In response, Mr. Lewis made a very pretty speech, in which he stated that the question of a new parish was not a new one to him, and that he was much in favor of it as an act of justice to our people. He pledged his hearty support to the measures, and promised that if elected and no one else introduced the bill, he would do so and urge it to passage.

"Mr. Lewis' speech was received with great cheering, and when order was restored, the following resolution was offered by Mr. James Webb.

"That, whereas, at a mass-meeting of the people of southwest St. Landry, held at Rayne this third day of April, 1886: the Hon. E. T. Lewis, candidate for the State senate, having been called upon to express his sentiments, for or against a bill to be introduced in the General Assembly for a division of the parish of St. Landry; and he having pledged himself to support a bill to that effect therefore, be it

"Resolved: That this mass-meeting endorse the nomination of the Hon. E. T. Lewis for the State senate, and pledge him our hearty support in the coming campaign.

"The resolution was adopted with great enthusiasm, the applause seeming to express the relief that our people felt at knowing that they could give their earnest support to the regular nominee, and one whom they greatly admired.

"The vice president then moved that the Opelousas and Washington delegations be invited to address the meeting, and that one hour be allowed each delegation — carried.

"Mr. F. F. Perrodin, of the Opelousas delegation was first speaker, and addressed himself particularly to the French portion of the audience, using their language. He spoke warmly in favor of the new parish and promised his assistance.

"Mr. W. F. Schwing, of the Washington delegation, followed in an eloquent, dignified speech in which he clearly stated the position of the people of Washington with reference to the proposition division, and corrected the erroneous and unjust accusation which Opelousas had made against them, viz: that they had offered their assistance to the people of Rayne in getting a division, providing the latter assisted them in having the courthouse rebuilt at Washington. He said that Washington did not offer such a trade, but simply wanted Rayne to understand that as to a division of the parish, their interests were now the same, and that if the people of southwestern St. Landry wanted a new parish, Washington stood ready with her member of the State senate, Hon. M. D. Kavanaugh, to render every assistance possible. Mr. Schwing was warmly applauded and made a good impression. Messrs. Laurent Dupre, of Opelousas, B. F. Hardesty, of Washington, and E. P. Veazie ot Opelousas, followed in the order named, each promising his assistance and support and endorsing the resolutions.

"After repeated calls Sheriff Duson stepped to the front and spoke quite earnestly and feelingly in favor of division, and said that although he hated to part with his friends in southwestern St. Landry, he was like the girl, who when asked, said 'yes.' He stated that the property owners of Opelousas would soon vote on a proposition to impose a tax of two and a half (2½) per cent on their property for the purpose of raising a fund to assist in rebuilding the courthouse. He concluded by reading a letter from our esteemed and honored d'strict judge, the Hon. G. W. Hudspeth, who offered to pledge himself in writing to support us in our efforts for an early division of the parish.

"Messrs. C. W. Duroy, Gilbert Dupre and F. F. Perrodin, of Opelousas followed, the latter speaking this time in English, and all promising for themselves and the town of Opelousas an earnest support of our demands.

"Mr. Schwing, of Washington, then asked permission to deny a charge made by Mr. Perrodin, to the effect that Washington was not honest in her offer made to the people of St. Landry, to build the courthouse at her own expense providing it was built in the town of Washington. He said that the men pledged to give the various amounts credited to them; were all well able to redeem their pledges and were prepared to do so at the proper time.

"Mr. Schwing's remarks concluded the speaking. The president then appointed Messrs. G. K. Bradford, J. C. Lyons and R. T. Clark as the special committee to frame and care for the bill to be introduced in the Legislature.

"Moved by Mr. James Webb and duly seconded that a copy of the proceedings of this meeting be furnished the RAYNE SIGNAL for publication. Carried.

"At 5:10 p.m. Judge R. T. Clark made a motion to adjourn, subject to the call of executive committee. Carried.

"The following are the names of the gentlemen composing the two delegations: Messrs. Joseph Bloch, Solomon Loeb, E. Latreyte, A. Levy and L. A. Bloch, merchants; Laurent Dupre, G. L. Dupre, E. T. Lewis, F. F. Perrodin, C. W. Duroy and E. P. Veazie, attorneys at law; Judge Hudspeth, represented by letter; also C. C. Duson, sheriff, James O. Chachere, clerk of court; M. G. Wilkins, Dr. Wm. M. Thompson, Thos. Brooks, Claud Mayo and B. F. Maginly.

"Washington sent five delegates. They were Messrs. Wills Prescott, W. F. Schwing, Thos. Cook, B. F. Hardesty and Jacob Ehrhardt.

A. S. Chappuis, Secretary."

(The Rayne Signal editor, so completely dedicated to the serious business of parish division, nonetheless found space in his newspaper for a humorous sidelight on the meeting. Under a heading "$500 Reward" was printed the following: "for party who killed Jacob Ehrhardt at Rayne on April 3, 1886 during the mass meeting held there on that day. This act was committed in open daylight. He was last seen in company of Colonel

Claud Mayo. The weapons used were either the 'Rain Drop'* or the 'Bon Ton'* spirits. The above reward will be paid out of the subscriptions raised for building the courthouse at Washington.")[15]

The editor of the Opelousas Courier felt that Opelousas had won the day: "Opelousas carried the day in debate and convincing arguments . . . the Opelousas committee convinced the people of Rayne that our town was perfectly willing to assist Rayne in forming a new parish and to grant the needed territory . . . We believe that the people of Rayne will be with us on this subject."[16]

Sheriff Duson, the Courier said, had given "a sound and practical speech on the subject, which had a strong weight with the people who had known him from childhood."[17]

At this time the 40-year-old sheriff was at the height of his popularity in St. Landry Parish. He had been sheriff for 12 years, had been virtually drafted for the office two years earlier. He had some strong ties with Rayne; his only brother was in the real estate business in Rayne, his brother-in-law, R. T. Clark, was a member of the Rayne Town Council. The sheriff himself owned land in the proposed new parish.

The pros and cons of parish division were debated through the columns of the four parish newspapers, the Opelousas Courier and the St. Landry Democrat, the Rayne Signal and the Washington Argus.

The Courier, in a lengthy editorial of April 10, said the Rayne Signal was all wrong in its impressions of Opelousas: "Because the people of Opelousas and a majority in the country desire the parish site to remain where it has always been and where it should be, is no argument that they must necessarily be opposed to a division of the parish," the editor wrote. Washington's claims to the parish seat were feeble, he stated, and had nothing at all to do with parish division. "Rayne is not indebted to Washington for a willingness on the part of Opelousas and its friends to grant them territory for a new parish. The sentiment and friendly spirit in its behalf existed before the destruction of our courthouse. Our people always have felt great interest and pride in the marvelous and rapid development of Rayne and its vicinity. We have admired their energy, and now commend their ambition to ask for a more conspicuous promi-

---

* Rain Drop, Bon Ton: early Rayne saloons

[15] *Rayne Signal,* Apr. 10, 1886
[16] *Ibid*
[17] *Opelousas Courier,* Apr. 10, 1886

nence in our judicial and political sisterhood of parishes. With her present population, which is rapidly increasing, Rayne can now justly lay her claims . . . Rayne as a thriving little city, with the phenomenal increase of population in its surrounding neighborhoods, gives it individual and legitimate merits in this question . . . there is no necessity for Rayne or Opelousas either to make any special combinations against each other to secure their just rights in this question . . . Rayne has always been a strong democratic precinct, and has been a strong factor in maintaining democratic majorities in our parish. Hence, in a political point of view we are reluctant to see so strong and valiant ally depart from our support; yet when her citizens ask for a separate parochial government backed by such meritorious claims, as friends and well-wishers, we can but say, 'let them have their just patrimony in our large parochial estate because they are entitled to it and we can spare what they ask for.' But Washington cannot claim to be sole executor in this matter. Opelousas is not dead yet, nor sick, nor does she expect to die soon as the parish site, but what she gives or is willing to give to Rayne will be a donation *inter vivos.*"

The Rayne Signal reprinted the Courier editorial, also a rebuttal editorial which appeared in the Washington Argus.[18] The divisionists were victorious; on May 19, 1886, St. Landry Representative J. C. Lyons of Plaquemine Brûlée introduced a bill in the house entitled "An act to create the parish of Nicholls, and to provide for the organization thereof." Referred to the committee on parochial affairs, the bill came back with the title changed to read: "An act to create the parish of Acadia."[19]

The change of name for the proposed parish was plainly a matter of political expediency. Samuel D. McEnery was governor of Louisiana, his opponent in the forthcoming election was former governor Francis T. Nicholls. Governor McEnery and Sheriff Duson were staunch political allies; in fact, the sheriff was later to be dubbed "McEnery's lieutenant governor in St. Landry and Acadia."[20] Governor McEnery himself may have demanded the change of names for the proposed new parish, or it could have been engineered by the sheriff out of deference to the chief executive.

Be that as it may, the name "Acadia" was substituted for the name "Nicholls" for the new parish. Father Joseph Anthonioz, first pastor of

18 *Rayne Signal,* Apr. 17, 1886
19 *Crowley Daily Signal* 50th Anniv. Ed., 1949
30 Dupre: *Political Reminiscences,* 67-68

238

the Catholic church at Rayne, is credited with suggesting the name, Acadia Parish.[21]

The text of Act No. 39, to create the parish of Acadia and to provide for the organization thereof, is as follows:

SECTION 1. Be it enacted by the General Assembly of the State of Louisiana, That a new parish, in the State of Louisiana, be and the name is hereby created out of the southwestern portion of the parish of St. Landry, to be called and known as the "Parish of Acadia;" that said parish of "Acadia" shall be composed of all that territory of the said parish of St. Landry comprised within the following boundaries, towit: All that portion of territory lying and being south and west of a line beginning on the west boundary of St. Landry parish, at its intersection with the township line between townships six (6) and seven (7) south; thence in an easterly direction on township lines between townships six (6) and seven (7) to the northeast corner of section three (3), in township seven (7) south, range two (2) east; thence in a southerly direction on section lines about three (3) miles to the corner common to sections 14, 15, 22 and 23; thence in an easterly direction about four (4) miles to a point in section seventy-nine (79), in township seven (7) south, range three (3) east, when the section lines if run, would make the corner common to sections 16, 17, 20 and 21, thence in a southerly direction across section seventy-nine (79) and following section lines about six (6) miles to the corner common to sections 16, 17, 20 and 21, in township eight (8) south, range three (3) east; thence in easterly direction between sections 16 and 21, one mile; thence two (2) miles in a southerly direction on section lines between sections 21 and 22, and between sections 27 and 28; thence one mile in an easterly direction to the corner common to sections 26, 27, 34, and 35; thence about two (2) miles in a southerly direction to the division line between the parishes of Lafayette and St. Landry; thence following the division line, as now established between the parishes of St. Landry and Lafayette, and St. Landry and Vermilion, to the existing boundary between the parishes of St. Landry and Calcasieu; thence on existing west boundary of St. Landry parish to the starting point aforesaid.

SEC. 2. Be it further enacted, etc., That the seat of the parish of Acadia, shall be and remain on a point to be determined upon by an election to be held for that and other purposes, after this act shall have become a law; that the parish of Acadia shall form a part of the Thirteenth Judicial District; that the judge of said district shall hold regular terms of his court for said parish of Acadia at the parish seat at such times as he may fix in accordance with law; that said parish of Acadia shall form part of the Third Circuit; that said parish of Acadia shall, until otherwise provided, form a part of the Twelfth Senatorial and the Sixth Congressional Districts of this State.

SEC. 3. Be it further enacted, etc., That in the house of Representatives,

21 *Crowley Daily Signal,* Oct. 4, 1937, Par. sec.,7

until otherwise provided, the parish of St. Landry shall have three (3) Representatives, and the parish of Acadia shall have one (1) Representative.

SEC. 4. Be it further enacted, etc., That within thirty days after this act shall have become a law, it shall be the duty of the Governor to appoint and commission for said parish of Acadia, five police jurors from the parish at large, who shall within ten days after the receipt of their commissions, meet at the town of Rayne, in said parish, and proceed to divide the parish into separate wards to be known as justice of the peace and police jury wards; and to designate in each of said wards a place for holding elections for State and parish officers; within thirty days thereafter, the Governor shall appoint a returning officer for said parish of Acadia, and shall order an election for all parish and ward officers according to law; that said police jury shall, in due time, make the necessary arrangements to provide the requisite public buildings, lots and offices, and the seals, books and appurtenances for the said parish of Acadia and the officers thereof; that the powers and duties of said police jurors herein provided for, shall be the same as other like officers throughout the State.

SEC. 5. Be it further enacted, etc., That immediately after the organization of the parish of Acadia and the election of qualification of its officers, it shall be the duty of the clerk of the District Court and ex-officio recorder of the parish of St. Landry to transmit to the clerk of the District Court and ex-officio recorder of the parish of Acadia, all petitions, answers and other documents and papers appertaining to suits wherein the defendant or defendants reside within the parish of its organization, and also a certificate copy of all orders made in any suits which are entered on the minutes of the court; and the fees allowed him for making a copy of such minutes shall be ten cents for every hundred (100) words, and twenty cents for each certificate, with seal attached; the same to be charged as costs in the case; and he shall also transmit to the clerk of the District Court of the parish of Acadia all criminal proceedings against persons charged with an offense or offenses alleged to have been committed in said parish of Acadia, and he shall also transmit to the clerk of the District Court for the parish of Acadia, all the petitions, orders, bonds and other papers relating to successions heretofore opened in the parish of St. Landry, which may be unsettled and in course of administration, when the deceased resided in that portion of the parish of St. Landry now embraced in the limits of the territory of the parish of Acadia by this act; and he shall transmit also to the clerk of the District Court of Acadia parish all papers relating to the tutorship of minors when they, or a majority of them, reside in the parish of Acadia, that all matters civil and criminal so transferred shall be proceeded with in said parish of Acadia, as if they had originated therein.

SEC. 6. Be it further enacted, etc., That as soon as possible after the organization of the parish of Acadia, it shall be the duty of the clerk of the District Court, and ex-officio recorder of the parish of St. Landry, to make a true and correct transcript, in a well bound book or books, to be furnished by the police jury of the parish of Acadia, in the order of dates as recorded in his office, after the adoption of this act, of all acts, mortgages, deeds, and title pages of records in said office relative to and affecting landed property situated within the limits of the parish of Acadia, accompanied by the certificate and seal of said clerk affixed at the end of each book; that when so completed the clerk of the parish of St. Landry shall immediately transmit said book or books to the clerk of the parish of Acadia, together with all the original acts, deeds, mortgages and title papers on file in his office, from which said transcript shall have been made; that the fees allowed said clerk of the parish of St. Landry for said transcript shall be six cents for every hundred words and one dollar for his certificate and seal in each book; and that said fees and the actual expenses incurred by said clerk in the transmission of papers and documents to the parish of Acadia, shall be paid by the treasurer of the parish of Acadia, on the warrant of the president of the police jury, when he is satisfied that the services have been performed, and the fees legally charged, a specific account of which shall accompany each warrant and be sworn to by said clerk as correct.

SEC. 7. Be it further enacted, etc., That no judgment, lien or privilege, or mortgages upon any property within the parish of Acadia, shall lose the effect of its inscription by the creation of the parish of Acadia by this act, if the same has been legally inscribed in the parish of St. Landry in such manner as to bind such property at the date of its inscription, and which is void for no other reason or legal cause, and the certificate of the proper officer of the parish of St. Landry relative to said property shall be received in all cases where such certificate is required by law.

SEC. 8. Be it further enacted, etc., That immediately after the organization of the parish of Acadia, it shall be the duty of the sheriff, and ex-officio tax collector of the parish of St. Landry to transmit to the sheriff and ex-officio collector of taxes of the parish of Acadia, a list of all unpaid taxes assessed upon property within the limits of the parish of Acadia, and the Sheriff of the parish of Acadia shall collect all taxes and pay over the parish tax to the parish treasurer, and the State tax to the State treasurer; and for any expenses incurred by the sheriff of St. Landry in the performance of the service required by this act; he shall be paid the amount which he may have actually expended, and no more; said amount to be paid by the treasurer of the parish of Acadia, on the warrant of the president of the police jury.

SEC. 9. Be it further enacted, etc., That the school fund of the said parish of Acadia shall be provided in the same manner as for other parishes of the State.

SEC. 10. Be it further enacted, etc., That the creation of the parish of Acadia shall in no wise impair the obligation of the people or property thereof, in favor of the public creditors of the parish of St. Landry as heretofore constituted; but the parish of Acadia shall assume pro rata the portion of the public debt due at the time this act shall become a law for that part of the parish of St. Landry as heretofore constituted; which is embraced in the territorial limits of the parish of Acadia; and the balance of said debt shall be assumed by the parish of St. Landry.

SEC. 11. Be it further enacted, etc., That it shall be the duty of the police jury of the parish of Acadia immediately after their first meeting, as provided in section 4, of this act, and of the police jury of the parish of St. Landry, at a meeting to be held by them within thirty days after this act shall have become a law, to select and agree upon three commissioners for each parish, who shall be residents, voters and real estate owners in their respective parishes, whose duty it shall be to convene in the town of Opelousas, in the parish of St. Landry, on a day to be fixed by the judge of the Thirteenth Judicial District, within twenty days after the appointment of the commissioners, who shall give to said commissioners due notice thereof; and at said meeting said commissioners shall proceed to ascertain the amount of indebtedness of the parish of St. Landry immediately preceding the adoption of this act and to apportion to the parish of Acadia and to the parish of St. Landry the apportionment and proportion of said indebtedness due from each parish respectively which amount shall be determined by said commissioners, and shall be in proportion to the relative value of the taxable property in each of said parishes, after having ascertained the amount of said indebtedness and made the said apportionment, said commissioners shall report the same to the police juries in both parishes; and said police juries shall each immediately proceed in their respective parishes to make suitable provisions for the payment of their proportion of said indebtedness, under such regulations as they may adopt. Should said commissioners, in the performance of their duties prescribed in this section, fail to agree, and be unable to settle such disagreement among themselves, they shall be empowered to elect by unanimous consent another person a resident of either one of said parishes, an owner of real estate, who shall act as umpire in the settlement in said disagreement. Should either of said commissioners herein designated, decline to serve, then and in that event the two remaining commissioners representing the parish of the commissioner so declining, shall be empowered to elect another resident of said parish, an owner of real estate who shall serve in his stead.

SEC. 12. Be it further enacted, etc., That immediately after the passage of this act by the General Assembly, it shall be the duty of the Governor to direct the proper officer of St. Landry parish to procure a registration of the legal voters of the parish of St. Landry, said registration to continue for at least sixty days; that immediately after said registration an election shall be held by the legal voters of the parish of St. Landry for the purpose of taking the sense of the people of said parish in regard to the creation of the new parish of Acadia; and it shall be the duty of the commissioners of election to receive the votes of all persons entitled to vote by reason of sufficient residence in said parish as required by law; and that at said election all who shall be in favor of the creation of the new parish shall deposit a ballot "For the creation of the Parish of Acadia;" all who are opposed shall deposit a ballot, "Against the creation of the Parish of Acadia." And the returns of said election shall be made and promulgated as now required by law in other elections; and if a majority of the votes cast at said election shall be in favor of the creation of the said parish of Acadia, the Governor shall issue his proclamation declaring that the said parish has been created, and the creation of said proclamation.

SEC. 13. Be it further enacted, etc., That all laws or parts of laws contrary to the provisions of this act, be and the same are hereby repealed.

H. W. OGDEN
Speaker of the House of Representatives
CLAY KNOBLOCH,
Lieutenant Governor and President of the Senate.
Approved June 30, 1886
S. D. McENERY,
Governor of the State of Louisiana
A true copy from the original:
OSCAR ARROYO,
Secretary of State.

Shortly after its introduction Opelousas people found fault with the Lyons bill. The bill was defective, the Courier editor said. There was certainly enough land for two parishes, but the public good should be considered. The editor expressed fear that the proposed division would affect the Democratic majority of St. Landry.[22]

A second mass meeting was called for May 30 at Rayne. The people of Rayne charged the people of Opelousas with violating their pledge by sending a committee to Baton Rouge to oppose the new parish. Opelousas denied the charges, saying that the Baton Rouge lobbyists objected to the parish boundaries, not its creation. Rayne, they said, was warned not to run boundary lines to Opelousas, so as to affect the Democratic majority of St. Landry, or to jeopardize its claims and rights to the parish site. Rayne had not consulted the people of Opelousas or the committee in laying the boundary lines, Opelousas averred, and such would now deprive St. Landry of 1,500 Democratic votes and make the parish Republican.[23]

Proponents of division had sound arguments that were difficult to put down. In addition to the obvious reasons advanced, the timing was perfect for current issues. For years newspapers of the state had been preaching immigration as an economic measure, urging communities to

---

[22] *Opelousas Courier*, May 29, 1886
[23] *Ibid*, June 5,. 1886

provide inducements to new settlers; the success of the German colonies at Fabacher and Robert's Cove was used as a prime example. A new parish would provide easier accessibility to the centers of government for both parishes, the old and the new; what better inducement to immigration? Also, Rayne had that new Titan of commerce and industry, the railroad.

Representative Lyons' bill passed the house on June 11, the senate on June 28, and was approved by Governor McEnery June 30.[24]

An event which was to shape the future for Acadia Parish took place two weeks after the governor signed the bill. The charter of the Southwestern Land Company was recorded in the St. Landry Parish courthouse.[25]

The charter, dated July 12, 1886, was notarized by Gilbert L. Dupre. The articles provided that the corporation "is established for the purpose of developing the agricultural resources of Southwestern Louisiana; the promotion of immigration thereto and the purchase and sale of lands as real estate so as to provide homesteads or farms to persons immigrating thereto . . . " The capital stock of the company was fixed at $250,000, represented by 2,500 shares at $100 each. Stockholders were G. W. Hudspeth, 10 shares; Joseph Bloch, 200 shares; C. C. Duson, 200 shares; Alphonse Levy, 200 shares; Julius Meyers, 200 shares; Henry L. Garland, 20 shares; W. W. Duson (per C. C. Duson) 200 shares.

Alphonse Levy was president of the board of directors, C. C. Duson was vice president. The other five stockholders constituted the remaining members of the board.

The president of the land company, Alphonse Levy, was an Opelousas banker and partner in a large mercantile firm with Julius Meyers. Joseph Bloch was also an Opelousas merchant. Hudspeth was the district judge, and Garland a prominent attorney. Gilbert Dupre was the attorney for the land company.[26]

As provided by the enabling act, in July Governor McEnery called an election to determine the will of the people of St. Landry Parish concerning parish division. The election was set for October 6, 1886.

Newspaper debates on the question continued. The St. Landry Democrat reminded the divionists that the new parish, if established, would owe the mother parish of St. Landry more than $20,000, besides other and unknown indebtedness which the new parish would have to share. The

24 *Crowley Daily Signal* 50th Anniv. Ed., 51
25 Mortgage Book No. 25, 776, St. Landry Parish
26 Perrin: *SW La.,* etc., Part II, 55, 7, 28

Rayne Signal came back with: "We thank the Democrat for its sweet and disinterested kindness but hope it won't worry about us." The editor said the people were not afraid of any special tax, and besides felt certain the debt of the parish would not exceed $17,000, and "the public buildings scarecrow don't fright us." The new parish could get along without a courthouse for some time, "as St. Landry and Vermilion parishes are now doing and we hope and think we won't need an expensive jail."[27]

Answering another Democrat anti-division editorial of July 24, the Signal compared the Democrat's position on division to "the arguments in England during the Revolutionary War. That is, that the colonists had always been in the habit of looking to London and England for support and assistance in government, and were therefore unable or unwilling to take care of themselves."[28]

The Democrat pointed out one of the disadvantages of division: the tremendous expenditure connected with transferring records of a half million acres of land which had been bought and sold and inherited for a hundred or more years. The Signal came right back and called attention to the wording of the enabling act, which specified that the records to be transferred would only be those which appeared after the enabling act, and those which appertained to pending suits, unsettled successions, etc.[29]

Rayne had its division machinery well oiled and organized by August 7. Meetings were held every Saturday at Duhon Hall to plan startegy for the coming election.[30] On the campaign committee were B. H. Harmon, William Sarver, J. D. Bernard, James Webb, M. Arenas, Fremeaux Istre, D. B. Lyons, George K. Bradford, Charles A. Perrodin, Joseph Trahan, Samuel Cart, J. M. Lyons, H. D. McBride, A. V. Johnson, Lewis Hayes, W. F. Stakes, James Ledoux, Thomas Bowden, Frank Brooks, R. A. Guidry, Andrew Henry, Rudolph Beer, R. J. C. Bull, Dr. G. C. Mouton, Raymond Richard.[31]

A committee of three, H. D. McBride, D. B. Lyons and George K. Bradford, was appointed to draft resolutions for the campaign committee. Five members, James Webb, J. M. Lyons, Thomas Bowden, George K. Bradford and M. Arenas, were to canvass Opelousas, Washington and other points in St. Landry for votes. Dates were set for barbecues and

27 *Rayne Signal,* July 24, 1886
28 *Ibid,* July 31, 1886
29 *Ibid*
30 *Rayne Signal,* Aug. 14, 1886
31 *Acadia Sentinel,* Oct. 23, 1886

political rallies at Church Point, Pointe-aux-Loups, Rayne, Prudhomme City and Mermentau to which "all prominent men of St. Landry" were to be invited to attend and express views "without regard to politics on the subject of creating the new parish of Acadia." Provided these men were willing, they would be asked to speak up for the cause by addressing public meetings at places and times to be agreed upon. Handling the finances for these activities were A. S. Chappuis, E. O. Bruner, Sam Wilder, J. E. Tolson and A. V. Lyons.[32]

Meanwhile the divisionists had found a staunch friend in the Opelousas Courier. Apparently satisfied that the proposed division no longer posed a threat to the Democratic majority of St. Landry, the Courier voiced support of the cause: "The lines of the new parish have been remodeled so as to remove these apprehended dangers . . . We feel that our citizens should ratify the protocol by voting for the new parish. To do otherwise would seem like bad faith on our part. Let us be sincere and generous."[33]

The St. Landry Democrat, continuing to oppose division, introduced an element of racism as an issue by stating that it was "difficult to find a white man in the parish of St. Landry this side of the line of the proposed parish of Acadia who is not opposed to division." There was speculation that Thomas Lewis, one of Sheriff Duson's most bitter political foes and organizer of the White League in St. Landry, had written the piece in the Democrat.[34]

The divisionists recruited more active campaign workers. Named to the executive committee for the creation of Acadia were R. C. Webb, chairman; R. T. Clark, G. K. Bradford, Thomas Bowden, Sidney Arceneaux, Homer Barousse, H. D. McBride, D. B. Hayes, W. N. Milton, Albert Guidry, James Webb, L. V. Fremaux, M. Doucet, R. B. Sloan and V. Maignaud.[35]

A delegation of five divisionists left Rayne about August 15 "to feel out the pulse in Opelousas, Washington and other points." In the Rayne Signal of August 21 the editor happily reported on the work of the touring delegation: "Latest advice by telephone from those quarters give us the gratifying intelligence that 'she's all right!'"

[32] *Rayne Signal*, Aug. 14, 1886
[33] *Ibid*, Aug. 14, 1886
[34] *Rayne Signal*, Aug. 21, 1886; Dupre: *Political Reminiscences*, 16, 67
[35] *Acadia Sentinel*, Oct. 23, 1886

The St. Landry Democrat denounced the division movement as "engineered by a few politicians of Opelousas and a few interested parties in Rayne." The Opelousas Courier came back with an immediate rebuttal: "It is too late now to say the thing was engineered by a few politicians of Opelousas and a few interested parties in Rayne . . . We had better consent to an agreed formulated plan which threatens less peril to Opelousas and to the present political status of the parish than some future plan which might not afford security on either one of these important considerations. We must look beyond purely personal motives in the matter and be willing to make sacrifices for our friends who desire a parochial government of their own."[36]

Gilbert Dupre, in his "Political Reminiscenses" credits Opelousas with making the concessions which led to parish division: "Instead of uniting, we agreed to disagree as to the formation of the new parish," he wrote. "Both sides wanted the lines drawn whereby to advance their respective fortunes. The Hudspeth-Duson combination wanted as much of Coulee Croche retained as would benefit it; the other side, very naturally, wanted Church Point to remain in the mother parish. Church Point . . . had fought Duson and supported Charlie Thompson. Its people wanted to remain in St. Landry."[37]

According to Dupre, Opelousas' fight to keep the courthouse brought on some high-powered wheeling and dealing, ending with concession to the divisionists: "Within the territory demanding a division of the parish resided John Crawford Lyons, a representative from the parish. In Washington resided M. D. Kavanaugh, one of our state senators. Kavanaugh stood for removal of the parish seat, Lyons for dividing the parish. Thus when we shunned Scylla, the senator, we fell into Charybdis, the representative. We were in the game to win. We simply had to. We had to make sacrifices, and we did. We gave up Acadia prematurely — it would in time have come, but the time had not been set . . . No one who was not a participant in this fight can appreciate what a battle we won, and how it was we broke the lances of our opponents. I was in the struggle, steeped in to the very lips, and am therefore qualified to speak. We made a deal with the divisionists whereby to secure Representative Lyons' sup-

[36] *Opelousas Courier*, Aug. 21, 1886
[37] Page 54

ATTENDS TO
Buying, Selling, Locating
—AND—
Homesteading Lands
—AND—
COLLECTING
CLAIMS.

OFFICE OF
W. W. DUSON,
Real Estate Agent and Notary Public,
RAYNE, LA.,

H. L. Garland, G. Oct 20 1884
Opelousas La.

Dear Capt;

You are correct in your inference, as per medium letter of 17th and if you will look at the succession of Anna Harding you will see that Josephine Harding wife of Patrick Crowley bought there ten in she being the only heir — and as Anna belie the whole affair was a fraudulent deal I went to leave it to you, I am no interested in the St Landry Lands but as I said I think we can compromise with Scott, he (Scott has no othe property w Crowley is responsible, but if I aseen a have but brought agent would do so. I told as you have it the form from Isaac Saml P, but I also hold a sale show it be best we (James d Cole of N.O. + myself own jointly the entire fourtee

Letterhead of the W. W. Duson real estate office at Rayne. The letter, written by Duson to H. L. Garland of Opelousas, was dated October 20, 1884.

port in the house. This would insure us a united delegation against parish seat removal."[38]

Approximately one month before the election, on September 1, 1886, the Rayne Signal was purchased by W. W. Duson for a price of less than $1,000.[39] The new owner offered a salutatory in his first issue. Promises, he said, were "easily given, more easily broken." The paper "would like to be judged by deeds rather than words." The main issue at hand, the division of St. Landry Parish, would be pursued "by all the power, reason, persuasion and other more potent means of politics that will toil and labor to this end." The new publisher stated that in politics the paper was Democratic, "however it is not to be ironbound even in that, for we can see defects even in the objects we love most. So must every true upright newspaper object at times to frailties and demagogism which are seen in party leaders. The greatest good for the greatest number is true democracy and true patriotism. That man who is not moved by this principle is not a true citizen. Such shall be the end and aim of this newspaper." The publisher promised "a good moral family newspaper . . . pure and moral, hightoned in its general makeup, worthy of your praise and support."[40]

Duson employed H. Bodemuller, who had been publisher of the St. Landry Democrat of Opelousas, to put out the Rayne Signal for him.[41] The Duson newspaper immediately espoused the cause for parish division. A short editorial appealed to voters to support the move: "We hear a good deal of talk about the dear old mother. But to be a good mother she should be generous enough to set her daughter up in the world and give her a good sendoff. Such that daughter expects and hopes for. To the promises of true men, to the honor of gentlemen, to the reason of thinking men and to all parties the majority of southwestern St. Landry appeals for a division of the parish. Let it not be postponed for it will create a dissension which will not be halted."[42]

Also, there were glowing reports of promotional barbecues given at Pointe-aux-Loups and Mermentau. The Pointe-aux-Loups meeting had been "presided over by that patriarch of Pointe-aux-Loups and landmark of Democracy, Mr. Antoine B. Cart, who with gray hair streaming in the wind, held the beautiful banner of Democracy in his hand, so proudly won

---

38 Pages 52-53

39 *Crowley Daily Signal,* Oct. 4, 1937, Signal sec., 6

40 *Rayne Signal,* Sept. 4, 1886

41 *Opelousas Courier,* Sept. 11, 1886

42 *Rayne Signal,* Sept. 4, 1886

by his people in their constant efforts to forward the cause of Democracy. Words cannot express the grandeur of the scene. May that good old Democrat hold it for years to come. Mr. Cart's son, Severien Cart, eloquently addressing the multitude, introduced Mr. F. F. Perrodin, who in his usual happy manner addressed the large crowd." The barbecue at Mermentau was also "largely attended." Andrew Henry presided, and introduced F. F. Perrodin, the speaker.[43]

Voter registration was said to be "in excess of what was considered a full registration last time. Men 70 years of age who had not voted before came out so as to be able to cast a vote for the new parish." The newspaper also quieted a rumor: "We are reliably informed that James O. Chachere, our accommodating clerk at Opelousas, and C. C. Duson, the sheriff, are heart and soul for the new parish and will fulfill their pledges. Therefore all reports to the contrary are base falsehoods, fabrications of their personal enemies."[44]

One week after the Rayne Signal changed hands, on September 11, 1886, a second newspaper, the Acadia Sentinel, began publication in Rayne. The proprietor was George K. Bradford, land attorney and Duson's competitor in the real estate business.

The Rayne Signal did not immediately acknowledge the existence of a rival newspaper. However, in the issue of September 25, 1886 an editorial entitled "Our Collaborater" extended a warm welcome to the new publication: "We gladly welcome into our midst an able assistant in this fight for the new parish, The Acadia Sentinel. With Mr. G. K. Bradford as proprietor and editor, all will expect strong blows and convincing arguments in favor of division, and the first issue is proof that the public will not be disappointed. We extend to our comrade in a common fight our earnest sympathy, and hope his more powerful arguments and more vehement calls may be far more effectual in impressing the northern part of our parish with the justness of our demands, and in arousing all our neighbors to the necessity of the hour — union of all action and singleness of purpose. We cordially and heartily commend this paper to the reading public. Competition is the life of publishing as of trade, and we can only demand the public patronage upon the excellence we achieve in the make-up of our paper — upon this we are to stand or fall. Though we are certain there is no need for competition in this case, for if our endeavors in awaking our

---

43 *Ibid*
44 *Rayne Signal,* Sept. 4, 1886

citizens to the importance of reading and being posted in the happenings of the day are successful, there is sufficient territory tributary to our town to amply support these two public enterprises. The same territory in the older States will support two papers readily. Why can it not do so here? But be that as it may, the opening of this paper gives promise of being strong in editorial matter and excellent in its general make-up. We again cordially commend it to our citizens, asking for it the support that is due a paper whose aim is so laudable, and whose presence in our midst can only be a source of benefit to the public, and of great power in the coming election. May the shadow of the Sentinel never grow less, nor its warning of the approaching enemies of our community cease to ring out with a clarion call."

Unfortunately for posterity and this history, there are no extant copies of the first six issues of the Acadia Sentinel, either in the original or on microfilm. Files of the Acadia Sentinel, owned by the Crowley Post-Signal, are from October 23, 1886 to September 10, 1887 and have been microfilmed. Publication of the paper was suspended in 1891. Copies of the Rayne Signal published by C. W. Felter and George C. Addison (March 13, 1886 to September 4, 1886) are owned by the Addison family of Rayne. Microfilmed copies of this first newspaper, available at Louisiana State University Library and Dupre Library, University of Southwestern Louisiana, cover the first year of publication, March 13, 1886 to February 26, 1887. Without these two publications, which cover a most crucial phase of Acadia's history, it would not be possible to reconstruct in any detail the major events of this important period. The Rayne Signal and the Acadia Sentinel constitute the only sources of information on the identity of the leaders in the campaign for parish division; except for a few fragmented items in other newspapers — which are virtually meaningless unless placed into the context of a broader background — these publications provide the only way to follow the steps of parish development.

One such step was reported in the Rayne Signal of September 11, 1886. This was the completion of a bridge over Bayou Plaquemine Brûlée, the construction of which was directed by a three-man committee: James Webb, L. V. Fremaux and W. W. Duson. The bridge, identified in the newspaper as the "Duson Bridge," was 225 feet long, having a span of 89 feet from bank to bank, and was 37 feet high from the bottom of the bayou. The span, costing $1,000, was designed by Webb and Fremaux; more than 26,000 feet of lumber and 3,000 pounds of rod iron were used in the construction. The location of the bridge was given as follows: "The bridge crosses the bayou at the old railroad grade, and parties who may not know where it is can find it by simply following the old grade down to the bayou." A barbecue, to celebrate the completion of the bridge, was held September 30, 1886; the public was invited to attend the barbecue, especially "the residents of Pointe-aux-Loups, Mammouth and Prairie Hayes."

This new bridge, the newspaper stated, "would greatly facilitate travel between Rayne and a large section of country on the other side of the bayou."[45] The bridge, which later came to be known as Long Bridge, was the first step towards the founding of the new town of Crowley.

About 400 persons attended the barbecue at the new bridge. "We are now fully convinced of the importance of the enterprise and feel doubly rewarded for the time and money spent in it," the Signal editor stated. Those from Rayne who attended the gala event included B. H. Harmon, A. S. Chappuis, J. D. Bernard, M. Arenas, R. T. Clark, R. Beer, Dr. Webb, Dr. Mouton, Dr. Leonards, Thomas Bowden and their families; from Opelousas were C. W. Duroy, Laurent Dupre, Sheriff Duson, James O. Chachere. The Pointe-aux-Loups delegation included "Zavia" Cart, Melon Doucet, John Regan, M. Pousson and Savinien Cart. The occasion was also used to promote the campaign for parish division; Duroy and Dupre made speeches for division, also a former New Iberia resident, who had located in Prairie Hayes, Capt. John T. White. The Pointe-aux-Loups guests "assured us that the bridge would be of untold value to them and their people;" the affair ended with the "trust that Duson's bridge will prove a blessing to the whole country."[46]

Meanwhile Sheriff Duson, one of the prime movers for parish division, had spent a month in the north and Canada. He returned September 6, "much improved in health."[47]

Voting precincts and election commissioners for the October 6 election were published in the Rayne Signal of September 25, 1886. Six of the precincts were located within the boundaries of the proposed new parish. These were at Church Point, at the Barousse store, with H. Barousse, H. D. McBride and D. B. Hayes commissioners; Plaquemine Brûlée, the H. M. Andrus store, Robert Sloane, Robert M. Andrus and

45 *Rayne Signal,* Sept. 11, 18, 25, 1886
46 *Ibid,* Oct. 2, 1886
47 *Ibid,* Sept. 11, 1886

Offutt Lyons, commissioners; the Rayne Town Hall, Thomas Bowden, B. H. Harmon and H. W. Anding, commissioners; Pointe-aux-Loups, at the S. Cart store, Y. Sensat, Louis Cart and M. Pousson, commissioners; Mermentau, at Maignaud's, Charles Duhon, L. V. Fremaux, Jean Pierre Frugee, commissioners; Prudhomme City, at T. C. Chachere's, E. H. McGee, Angelas Savoie and D. Courville Sr., commissioners. Two borderline precincts were at Faquetaique, at Honore Fuselier's, with David Courville Jr., H. Fuselier and W. R. Ashford commissioners; and Mallet, at Sullice's store, with Ed Dejean, Lucien Joubert and Jean Lejeune commissioners.

A final editorial, aimed at opponents of division, appeared in the October 2, 1886 issue of the Rayne Signal: " . . . Let every voter consider the question at leisure . . . There should be no consideration of factions or personal jealousies, but merely the justice of the demand . . . Remember the breach is made, it is not to be bridged, nor can any man weld us to the old parish again . . . "

The same issue revealed that a controversy had begun between the two Rayne newspapers: "Our confrere at the Sentinel had a strangely misrepresenting and impolitic piece in his last issue, headed '"Ante Up."' The gist of the piece was a rebuttal to the Sentinel editor's public challenge to the landowners in the proposed new parish, especially the non-resident landowners, to help in defraying the expenses of the division campaign. The Sentinel article, the Signal editor contended, implied that the division was the work of the large landowners. ". . . this demand is from the people and for them, not the land speculators," the Signal editor stated. "It is yet to be proven that the division will raise the value of land in the new parish, except where the courthouse may be located. It (the Sentinel article) misrepresents some of the stockholders of the Southwest Louisiana Land Company who have been personally working for the cause ever since the commencement of the struggle and paid their hotel bill at Baton Rouge without calling upon the campaign funds, and are now using their own money for the division privately without any public display . . . If this is a fight for land speculators and for their benefit as the Sentinel intimates, the sooner it is defeated the better. But it is not the battle of land speculators, but for the people alone."

The October 6 election resulted in 2,516 votes for the proposition and 1,521 against, a majority of 995 for parish division. Acadia, the 59th Louisiana parish, was created by the will of the people.

Election returns from precincts within the new parish were: Mermentau, 109 for, 6 against; German Settlement, 1 for, 31 against; Prudhomme City, 28 for, 96 against; Pointe-aux-Loups, 64 for, 34 against; Plaquemine Brûlée, 124 for, 9 against; Church Point, 28 for, 228 against; Rayne, 658 for, 1 against.[48]

Both Opelousas and Washington made good their promises to Rayne. The Opelousas vote was 507 for, 110 against; at Washington, 227 for, 29 against. Main opposition to division was at Church Point and at precincts in the north and northwest areas of St. Landry.[49]

After the vote was officially promulgated Governor McEnery proclaimed the parish of Acadia officially created as of October 11, 1886.[50]

St. Landry Parish had lost an estimated one fourth of its population. The population of the new parish of Acadia was said to be from 10,000 to 12,000;[51] The population of St. Landry Parish in 1880 was 40,000; Acadia Parish population in 1890 was 13,231.[52]

---

[48] *Opelousas Courier,* Oct. 9, 1886
[49] *Ibid*
[50] *Acadia Sentinel,* Oct. 23, 1886
[51] *Rayne Signal,* Oct. 16, 1886
[52] *Louisiana Almanac,* 1975-1976, 117; 1973-1974, 103

CHAPTER XV

The Courthouse Fight

The Rayne Signal, strong advocate of parish division, paid scant attention to the victory. Other than the returns, by precinct, in small print, the post-election issue of the newspaper carried only the vote totals in a three-line news brief. However, an article on the editorial page of the October 9 issue left little doubt about the newspaper's position. Under a heading of "Acadia's First Banner" a victory celebration was reported. After the polls were closed a committee of Rayne citizens, members of the executive and campaign committees "headed by the Acadia Funny Nine Brass Band went to the A. S. Chappuis home where the ladies presented the emblem of glorious victory, an elegant banner bearing the inscription 'Acadia'." Mrs. Chappuis made the presentation to the committee, the article stated. The name of the Rayne band had been changed "in honor of the new parish."

Several factors could account for the absence of victory headlines in the Rayne Signal. Communications being what they were, election returns were slow in coming in; even the Opelousas Courier, right at the parish seat, published incomplete returns in its October 9 issue. When the Courier went to press there were still two polls to hear from, Melville and Bayou Chicot, but "they will not materially affect the figures," the editor added.

Even had more information been readily available, there was also a time factor involved. There was a limit to the amount of work one typesetter could do, at a time when every line had to be set by hand. Be that as it may, lack of space was probably the main reason for the paucity of election news in the Rayne Signal. The entire front page was taken up with notices of final proof in support of homestead claims. The back page was likewise filled with legal advertisements and display ads of Rayne businessmen.

Soon after the election the Rayne Signal editor turned his attention to problems of parish organization. He felt that one of the immediate needs was the careful selection of police jurors; that the future of the parish depended upon the persons selected to sit on the governing body. In a second editorial he deplored the "innumerable aspirants for office" and found the situation "disgusting." Such, he stated, were "looking for fat salaries with no toil."[1]

It appeared to be a foregone conclusion that Rayne would be the parish seat. Ten days after the election Eugene Hockaday, a farmer of Prairie Hayes, a sparsely populated prairie area west and north of Plaquemine Brûlée, made an offer of $10,000 and land, providing the government building be located on his property. Hockaday announced a picnic at his residence for October 22, to which all persons, regardless of color, were invited. The picnic was to help get votes to locate the courthouse at Prairie Hayes. The Opelousas Courier commented that it appeared that Rayne "was not to get the courthouse without a struggle."[2]

In the issue of October 16 the Rayne Signal editor announced that he was not publishing the "proceedings of the so-called mass meeting at Duhon Hall after the dissolution of the executive committtee" because of lack of space in the newspaper. "We will publish the farce next week, with comments," he promised.

The promised report did appear in the October 23 issue. Dr. G. C. Mouton had served as temporary chairman of the "so-called mass meeting," and George K. Bradford the temporary secretary. The result was the formation of a parish committee on organization; the committee was to direct members in each ward to learn the choice of candidates for their respective wards. A committee of four, J. M. Lyons and William Chevis of Plaquemine Brûlée, M. Arenas and J. D. Bernard of Rayne, selected the following men to serve on the committee on parish organization: Robert Sloane, Wesley Stakes, from Plaquemine Brûlée; S. Cart and Yves Sensat, from Pointe-aux-Loups; Edgar Barousse and F. Brooks of Church Point; Ed Fremaux and Fremont Istre of Mermentau; H. Anding and William Sarver of Rayne. The Rayne Signal editor again termed the proceedings "a perfect farce;" he felt that the committee members named were presumptuous to speak for the parish and besides, no prior notice had been given of the meeting.

The Signal editor also found the Hockaday proposal "ridiculous." Rayne, he stated, was mainly responsible that the election had carried; it was "the most accessible and best established" place for the parish seat.[3]

---

1 *Rayne Signal*, Oct. 16, 1886
2 *Opelousas Courier, Rayne Signal*, Oct. 16, 1886
3 *Rayne Signal*, Oct. 23, 1886

Beginning with the issue of October 23, 1886 the files of the Acadia Sentinel reveal the other side of the coin. The committee on parish organization met at Rayne on October 27 at which time leaders from key points in the parish made known the choices of their respective communities to serve on the Acadia Parish Police Jury. S. Cart from Pointe-aux-Loups said that Zeno Huber was the unanimous choice from his section; D. C. Calkins had been a nominee, but had withdrawn in favor of Huber. Edgar Barousse nominated Homer Barousse as the unanimous choice of the people of Church Point, William Sarver presented the petition of Sidney Arceneaux for Rayne, and V. Maignaud of Mermentau was nominamed by J. D. Bernard. There was some difference about Maignaud's approval by the committee, but Maignaud's opponent "would not submit his case and claims." All nominees were unanimously approved.[4]

At about this time the editors of the two Rayne newspapers got into a bitter feud which was to continue unabated for several years. The end result was a challenge to a duel and the final departure of one of the participants.

On October 30, 1886 the Acadia Sentinel published an item under the usual heading of a public announcement, "A Card." The announcement read: "Some weeks ago, Mr. W. W. Duson became the proprietor of the Rayne Signal by a trick which was a disgrace to this business community. Since that time he has published offensive insinuations about certain reputable gentlemen in the old and the new parishes, and has lately directed his attention to me. In his recent issues of the Signal he broadly intimates that I have falsified facts. I, therefore, pronounce Mr. Duson to be what he has proven himself, a contemptible falsifier and an impudent ass. George K. Bradford, Editor Acadia Sentinel."

Editor Duson refuted Bradford's charges by stating that if Bradford could prove the "cheap trick" assertion before any committee of respectable gentlemen, he, Duson, would "present him the Signal and its fixtures." To the charge of having falsified facts, he stated that instead he had "corrected certain editorial statements." Duson also published a letter from E. I. Addison, former owner of the Signal: "Dear Sir: In answer to your letter, you nor any one got me under the influence of liquor to purchase the Signal office. While sitting in Mr. Bradford's office in conversation with Mr. Bennett, I was called out by Mr. David Bull and taken to your office where the sale was passed and I received my money. Possibly

---

4 *Acadia Sentinel,* Oct. 30, 1886

while under the influence of liquor I may have made some remarks which led the people of Rayne to believe there was a trick, all of which I retract."[5]

(The battling editors evidently did not let their personal feud interfere with business. A display advertisement for the W. W. Duson real estate business appears in every extant issue of the Acadia Sentinel)

Prior to the election there had been some open opposition to parish division on the part of at least two individuals. One of the first Duson editorials in favor of division was directed at Dr. William Childs, an opponent of the proposal. Another out-spoken citizen was S. Cart, who made known his position (and also revealed some sidelights on the election) in a letter to the editor of the Acadia Sentinel:

Cartville, La. October 18, 1886

Dear Sir: Rumors have reached me to the effect that some party or parties had reported to my friends of Rayne, that I had worked all day, on the day of the election, against the division of the parish. Such stories are erroneous and false from the beginning to the last. I am ready to prove by the most honorable and respectable men of Pointe-aux-Loups that said report is without foundation whatever.

Moreover, in vindication of the political standing and character of the voters of Pointe-aux-Loups, I will say that all the electioneering and whiskey drinking that was so freely offered the voters on that day, by supporters of division, did not make any change in the result of the day, for the reason that these honest voters had their opinions formed long before the day of the election, and no whiskey or flatteries could induce them to change their ideas. Consequently had there been no representative of the division to work on that day, the result would have been the same.

As for myself, everybody knows that I was opposed to division from beginning to end; I did not hide it, neither did I at any moment try or intend to hide it in any shape or form whatever; but, as I am always ready to submit to majority, I shall now stand to the banner of the Parish of Acadia. Very respectfully yours, S. Cart[6]

Early in November Governor McEnery appointed five parish citizens as members of the first police jury. Appointed were Dr. B. E. Clark of Plaquemine Brûlée, Homer Barousse of Church Point, B. H. Harmon, Rayne; Paul E. Fremaux, Mermentau, and Melon Doucet, Pointe-aux-

---

5 *Rayne Signal,* Nov. 6, 1886
6 *Acadia Sentinel,* Oct. 23, 1886

Loups. D. B. Lyons was appointed parish assessor.[7] The governor's action did not altogether please the Acadia Sentinel editor, who had this to say: "The men appointed are all good men so far as we know. But we object to governor's making appointments at the request or suggestion of one or two men as seems to have been the case. There was no expression of popular desire, so far as we ever heard, that this particular ticket should be appointed, but the people did endeavor in a perfectly legitimate way to select men who would be satisfactory to the majority. Their action was ignored. Acadia seems to be in the same box with most of the other parishes as regards executive appointments."[8]

The Rayne Signal declared its position on the selection of the parish seat in a lengthy editorial of October 30, 1886, titled "Where Shall the Courthouse Be Located?"

"The time has come when this question is the main topic for public consideration. The settlement of this question is now of pre-eminent importance. We have heretofore been quietly waiting the decision of the people as to whether there was to be division; since that is permanently determined we can enter into this weighty question, and state what we wished to say when the first issue of this paper was sent forth as having been transferred to us: namely, that we are for Rayne as the parish seat, first, last and forever.

"There have been insinuations and slanders, mysteriously noised abroad that the sale of this paper was for the purpose of working against the town of Rayne as the site for the courthouse, which we then denounced privately as a slander and wholly false, now we make public that denunciation reaffirming what there was said and adding that all such statements and insinuations are without foundation. It is true there are selfish interests which would prompt us to have it located at other places if it is to be sold, but as it is to be decided by the majority of the voters we are for Rayne. Some have declared that we were opposed to Rayne to injure us, and break down this paper, when the slander was first circulated we could only be silent till division was an assured fact, now we state that those were base fabrications, falsehoods pure and simple.

"Rayne is eminently suitable for the parish seat, its accessibility, its establishment as a trade center are facts that cannot be controverted. It is a town which is backed by a trade which is permanent, as it is the natural

[7] *Acadia Sentinel,* Nov. 13, 1886
[8] *Ibid*

outlet for that trade. This trade is independent of the location of the courthouse, in truth it will hold that trade if the courthouse is located somewhere else. The other places which may be put in competition with Rayne are wholly unsuitable, because inaccessible, and bare prairies, which would depend upon Rayne as their nearest railroad depot. That $10,000 proposition amounts to just SEVEN DOLLARS per capita, that is the voter would sell out his preferences as to the site of the courthouse for this paltry sum. The sequel would be this same voter would have to repay that SEVEN DOLLARS in the exorbitant costs in attending court sessions and the high prices for everything consumed in the town just being built would far exceed the paltry sum of SEVEN DOLLARS. We may be greatly mistaken in our voters, but at the present time we are firmly convinced that our voters are just a little above this price; if they are to be bought at all, seven dollars is too paltry to consider. There is but one objection which if offered against Rayne as the seat of the parish, and that it is not the geographical center which is really no argument, for the capitals of states and governments are made without regard to geographical center. To begin with, our own state capital, and that of our general government, are not geographical centers. Alexandria has long contended that it is nearer the center of the state than any other town, hence ought to have the state house, but all her efforts have been futile and without effects. Geographical centers are a secondary consideration. Commercial centers are of far more weight, which Rayne is now. It being the commercial center, controlling more votes, doing more business and having made the most strenuous efforts for division deserves the courthouse above any other point. Now, what are reasons for placing the courthouse on Mr. Hockaday's land? Absolutely nothing but that offer of $10,000 which is offering about seven dollars a head for voters in the parish, This is our task to try and get a majority of votes for Rayne as the parish seat. All who may believe, or imagine, or insinuate otherwise are assured by us that we shall talk for Rayne, work for her, write for her, then go up as our final act and vote for Rayne as the most suitable and best adapted place for the parish seat of Acadia."

By the first part of November some substantial support had developed for the Hockaday proposal to locate the courthouse in Prairie Hayes. At a meeting held November 6 the principals were T. C. Chachere, J. C. Lyons, R. C. Sittig, W. R. Hornsby and W. F. Brooks. Committees were named to consider what appeared to be two different proposals: Hocka-day's offer of money and land, and a proposal made by two other persons, identified only as Clements and Young, presumably landowners in the Prairie Hayes area.[9]

The main reason given for wanting the courthouse at Prairie Hayes was to place the seat of government in the geographical center of the new parish. The Acadia Sentinel editor, while conceding that a geographical center was desirable, contended that Rayne was the proper place, being the center of population. People, he said, came to Rayne to trade, to buy and sell, "and will continue to come, whether the courthouse be here or elsewhere." Locating the courthouse "in the wilds of Prairie Hayes" would be a burden to those who must go there to pay taxes, attend court, etc., whereas when those same people came to Rayne to sell cotton, corn, rice and cattle and to buy supplies they could attend to legal matters "all in one place." Editor Bradford allowed that he doubted "a town would spring up" as Prairie Hayes said it would. "Towns spring up where there is population to support a town." The editor pointed out that even if a town should develop at Prairie Hayes people wouldn't trade there because "no store 10 or 12 miles from the railroad . . . can buy and sell on as favorable terms as one on the railroad."[10]

Editor Bradford also advanced the argument that should Prairie Hayes be chosen, buildings necessary for parish government would have to be erected immediately. He pointed out the expense of hauling lumber and materials to the Prairie Hayes site. On the other hand, Rayne already had two good halls which could be rented; quarters for prisoners could be rented at the Lafayette jail. All that need be built was a fireproof record office, which could be erected 25% cheaper at Rayne than at Prairie Hayes.[11]

The date for the election to determine the parish seat was set by Governor McEnery for Tuesday, January 25, 1887, from 7 a.m. until 6 p.m.[12]

Meanwhile candidates for the various parishes offices had announced. The Sentinel right off endorsed Homer Daigle for sheriff, Thomas Bowden for clerk of court and Dr. R. C. Webb for coroner.[13] Other candidates

9 *Acadia Sentinel,* Nov. 13, 1886
10 *Ibid*
11 *Ibid*
12 *Ibid,* Nov. 27, 1886
13 *Ibid,* Oct. 30, 1886

were R. T. Clark and Charles A. Perrodin for clerk of court, Dr. J. A. McMillan for coroner and E. W. Lyons for sheriff. Perrodin later withdrew from the race. The Rayne Signal came out for Lyons for sheriff.[14]

The Acadia Parish Police Jury held its first meeting November 11, 1886 at Rayne. B. E. Clark was unanimously voted president of the body, and A. S. Chappuis as first clerk. The jury laid out five wards, and set up polling places as follows: Ward 1, Rayne Town Hall; Ward 2, Plaquemine Brûlée store of Kahn and Smith; Ward 3, Church Point, H. Barousse store; Ward 4, S. Cart store; Ward 5, E. C. Fremaux store.

Bradford went gunning again for Duson. In the November 20, 1886 issue of the Sentinel he charged that about 20 homesteaders, with witnesses, had "proved up" their claims in the office of a land agent in Rayne, in the presence of a deputy clerk, instead of in Opelousas before the judge or clerk, as required by law. This, he said, had been done before in Rayne, and was wrong; he claimed that such procedures injured the business of other land agents and attorneys.

Until the end of November it appeared to be taken for granted that Rayne would be the parish seat, despite Hockaday's offer. The New Iberia newspaper commented on the liberality of the Hockaday offer, but added "it is a foregone conclusion that Rayne will be the seat of justice."[15]

On December 14, 1886 Governor McEnery issued an amended proclamation changing the date of the election from January 25, 1887 to March 1, 1887. The reason for the postponement was given: " . . . whereas, the notice of registration by the assessor of said parish does not allow the time prescribed by said act for the registration of voters. Now in order to allow time to the assessor, ex-officio registrar of voters to publish, for seventy days before the date on which the election is to be held, a list of all the places where and the time when the office of registration will be opened at each place during the sixty days required by law for the registration of voters, etc ... "[16]

The required voter registration information was published immediately. Voters could register at the Rayne Town Hall, from Tuesday, December 28, 1886, through Thursday, January 6, 1887 inclusive. At Plaquemine Brûlée, on Friday, January 7, 1887, at the Kahn and Smith store. The registrar would spend two days in Church Point, January 10 and 11, at

14 *Rayne Signal*, Oct. 23, 1886
15 *Acadia Sentinel*, Nov. 27, 1886, from *New Iberia Enterprise*
16 *Acadia Sentinel*, Dec. 18, 1886

the Barousse store, to register votes. From January 12 to January 19, registration would take place, a day at a time, at the following places: Adolphe Miller's residence at Mallet; Z. Huber's residence at Faquetaique; Dennis Miller's store at Mammouth (Millerville); E. C. Fremaux store at Mermentau; L. Cart store at Pointe-aux-Loups, and the school house at Robert's Cove. After January 19, voters could register at the Rayne Town Hall until February 26, when the registration would close.[17]

In the issues of November 6, 13 and 27 the Rayne Signal carried editorial comment regarding the choice of a parish seat; the general tone of the short editorials was less pro-Rayne than they were anti-Prairie Hayes. The columns of the newspaper were largely devoted to legal notices of homesteaders establishing final proofs of claims. There were some items of local interest, in addition to a regular column entitled "Personal Mention."

During the fall and winter months short articles in the paper told of the increasing production of rice in Acadia Parish: "Mr. D. Miller will ship this season 10,000 sacks of rice . . . Maignaud, Castex and Fremaux together will ship 8,000 sacks . . . the floor of Kahn's rice warehouse fell through on Monday, from the heavy weight of the rice stored therein . . . N. J. Zaunbrecher shipped to New Orleans 360 sacks of rice which will net about $1,000, and he made about $200 threshing rice for other people. He bought a thresher and engine three months ago for $1,100 and expects to pay two third from proceeds this year."[18]

In the December 11, 1886 issue of the Acadia Sentinel the editor charged that politicians from St. Landry were interfering in Acadia's affairs. "It is currently reported and generally believed that in the approaching contest for offices in Acadia parish, considerable interference in local affairs will be practiced by the political factions of St. Landry. It is said that the meddling has already begun. Of course it is natural for politicians in St. Landry to be interested in our politics, even our local issues; but that they should so interest themselves as to take sides and electioneer for their favorite strikes us as being impertinent." St. Landry, the editor believed, should maintain a strict neutrality; in fact, "should mind their own business."

In the interim, while Rayne and Prairie Hayes were haggling over the courthouse like two chicks over one worm, a third chick was being

---

[17] *Acadia Sentinel,* Dec 18, 1886
[18] *Rayne Signal,* Nov. 13, 1886; Jan. 8, 1887

hatched in a new-made nest to the west. The Abbeville Meridional, late in November, made first mention of the third contender: "It was whispered in our ear a few days ago that while the citizens of Rayne and Prairie Hayes are discussing the question as to which place would be the most eligible point to build a courthouse for the new parish of Acadia, some parties in Opelousas are privately discussing the propriety and arranging a scheme of having it located six miles west of the former named place, and called the new town Parkersonville."[19]

There are no contemporary accounts of the establishment of the new town, or the formation and development of plans to build it. The Crowley Signal of August 25, 1888 re-printed, in part, an article which had appeared in the same newspaper of January 7, 1888, the first issue of the newspaper printed in Crowley.

The re-printed article reveals that the idea of building a new town was conceived in June of 1886, approximately four months before the new parish was established. The article does not say by whom the idea was conceived, but it is assumed that it was the brain child of W. W. Duson and/or his brother, C. C. Duson. In November of 1886, the month after Acadia Parish was established, "several gentlemen, having large interests in the Southwestern Louisiana Land Company," at the invitation of W. W. Duson, had a picnic dinner at the edge of a woodland about a half mile from the place later selected for the town site. The article indicates that some rather vague plans for building the town were discussed at the time. A month went by; "then came the request from the president of the company, Mr. Alphonse Levy, to Mr. W. W. Duson, the manager: 'go ahead and make the town; and draw on us for $10,000 as a starter.'"

The new town was given the name of Parkersonville, in honor of J. G. Parkerson, general agent of the Louisiana Western railroad. Parkerson declined the honor, and the town became Crowley, for Patrick Crowley, roadmaster for the railroad, who had charge of a spur-track called "the Crowley Switch" located one mile west of the town site.[20]

A brief item in the Acadia Sentinel of December 18, 1886 acknowledged the existence of the third contender for the parish seat: "The governor has put off the election in Acadia Parish to March 1. The prospects of Parkersonville for the parish seat loometh a little."

---

[19] Opelousas Courier, Dec. 4, 1886, from Abbeville Meridional
[20] Crowley Daily Signal 50th Anniv. Ed., 56

Two days before Christmas the Opelousas Courier took note of the new developments: "Sheriff Duson is back from New Orleans where he has been advertising the embryo town of Crowley on the Louisiana Western railroad between Rayne and Mermentau." The sheriff told the newspaper he had advertised in the New Orleans press, also in Galveston, Houston and Dallas; that 40,000 lithograph maps and descriptive circulars had been printed for distribution. A bridge, costing $1,200 had been built over Bayou Plaquemine Brûlée, lumber was being delivered for a hotel, a schoolhouse and a large store, the sheriff said.[21]

Little is known of the early history of the area selected as the site for the new town. Earliest known settler was James Miers, who came to Bayou Blanc in the 1820s and settled about two miles southwest of the present city of Crowley. His descendants were still living on the old place in 1888.[22] The John Laughlin family also lived in the vicinity. The public sale of the estate of John Laughlin and his wife Sarah Foreman was advertised in the Opelousas Courier of July 29, 1865. The estate included the plantation and residence, situated on Bayou Blanc, "in Plaquemine Brulee," about 30 miles southwest of Opelousas, bounded north by land "supposed to be" public domain, south by the same, west by the Antoine Blanc claim, and east by public lands. The inventory listed about 40 acres of land, buildings and improvements; a Creole horse, three unbroken studs, two unbroken horses, seven head horse creatures, about 25 head wild horned cattle, a branding iron figured thus: 5C; about 40 hogs, a plough, a loom, household furniture and kitchen utensils. The property of Sarah Foreman, wife of John Laughlin, was sold the same day at the residence. Her estate included one gentle horse, two unbroken horses, 10 horse creatures, 25 gentle horned cattle, three branding irons and household furniture. Milton Laughlin was administrator of the estate.

A post office was in operation at "Coulee Blanc" September 17, 1857, with James Mires as postmaster. The location of the post office is assumed to have been the Mires' residence, which was probably located on or near the Old Spanish Trail, designated on the official plat as "the road to Lake Charles," the main route of travel from east to west. The St. Landry Police Jury at its meeting of September 17, 1866 appropriated funds to repair the bridge across Bayou Blanc at James Myers' place.

21 *Opelousas Courier,* Dec. 23, 1886
22 *Crowley Signal,* Aug. 25, 1888

The feverish activity that must have gone on at the new town site has to be imagined; the founding went unheralded and unreported by the two newspapers of Rayne.

The "embryo town" had a railroad station by January 5. The depot at Estherwood, a building 37 by 70 feet, was moved to Crowley. The building was placed on two flat cars and moved by rail the seven and a half miles to Crowley. The moving was done in an hour and a half, and in another three hours the building was placed on a foundation. It was the largest building known to have been moved by rail and set a record for the railroad.[23]

Citizens of Rayne evidently became upset over the growing threat developing to the west. The Sentinel editor sought to quiet their fears. In an editorial of January 8, 1887 the editor wrote: "Just six miles west of Rayne is the spot selected for the projected little town of Crowley. The possibility of Crowley being a dangerous rival of Rayne for the parish seat has excited a number of our good citizens. It is true that if Crowley were a town or even a station, with an active, wealthy and energetic crowd of men backing it, it might become a rival. But the town exists on paper and a town is not built in a day or year either, especially in Louisiana, and it will be some years before the friends of this intended town will be justified in such an ambition. Rayne is at present the business center and center of population, and it is not natural to suppose that men will deliberately vote themselves to travel a long distance to the parish seat when they will trade at the nearest point, and might, by their votes be able to trade and attend to parish matters at the same time and place. At present, therefore, we see no danger in Crowley, and like every good citizen, we welcome the signs of progress on the west and heartily hope that some day Acadia may be populous and prosperous enough to satisfy half a dozen towns larger than Rayne."

Editor Bradford obviously did not know, at the time he wrote the editorial, that the Estherwood depot had been moved to the new town, nor could he have known that Crowley had progressed beyond the "paper" stage four days before his newspaper came out. Construction in the new town got underway on January 4, 1887. This date has since been observed as the birthday of Crowley.

The plan for the town, drawn by Leon Fremaux, called for the streets to be 80 feet wide and the avenues 115 feet wide. The streets, to run east

---

23 *Opelousas Courier,* Jan. 15, 1887

and west, were to be numbered; the avenues, to run north and south, were to be designated by the letters of the alphabet. Right angles were to be formed at the intersection of the streets and avenues. The one exception to this plan was Hutchinson Avenue, which was to run east and west, and Parkerson Avenue, which was to run north and south. At the point where Parkerson and Hutchinson Avenues intersected a circle was to be formed which would mark the center of the town.[24]

By the middle of January the new town was attracting state-wide attention. The New Orleans Times Democrat of January 16, 1887, under a heading of "The Crowley Boom," published the following: "Mr. Alphonse Levy, president of the Southwest Land Company of Crowley, La., was in the city yesterday, speaking of the new town of Crowley, in Acadia Parish. Mr. Levy, in conversation with a reporter of the Times-Democrat, had many encouraging things to say. He said he found the work of building, etc., progressing most satisfactorily. Sheriff Duson, vice president of the Southwest Louisiana Land Company, has charge of the improvements, which are numerous and of a most substantial character. The company are now completing a storehouse, hotel, livery stable and schoolhouse.

"The hotel is a handsome two-story frame building, and will be elegantly furnished, and when finished will accommodate fully 100 guests. The depot of the S. P. railroad is rapidly nearing completion, and the prospect generally is most encouraging. 'We have considerable demand,' remarked Mr. Levy, 'for lots in the new town, but have, thus far, declined all offers, our idea being that the sale, which occurs on the 10th of next month, should determine values. We have, however, donated lots to several people, who will, as soon as possible begin the work of improving them. The company is making arrangement for the establishment of a furniture factory.'

"They have ordered a road machine, which will be operated in putting the streets of the town in thorough order and to improve all the main roads leading into same. Judging from the great number of letters received daily from all parts of the country, the company expect a very large attendance at the sale of lots on the 10th proximo; and for this purpose excursion rates for the round trip have been secured. The round trip from New Orleans to Crowley can be made at the very low rate of $4.

---

24 Hair: "History of Crowley, La.," 7, reprinted from *Louisiana Historical Quarterly,* Vol. 27, No. 4

"Arrangements have been made with two lumber yards so that parties desiring can purchase building material at Crowley at extremely low rates.

"It is understood that Crowley will be made the parish seat of Acadia."

Editor Bradford re-printed the Times-Democrat article in full in the Acadia Sentinel of January 29, 1887. His reaction was to resort to a bit of humor to put down the publicity given Crowley. He wrote: "A friend suggests that Rayne do as New Orleans has done, and extend her limits so as to take in Crowley and any other embryo town, and thus settle the courthouse question. All parties might thus be satisfied."

The police jury met at Rayne January 15, 1887. The body adopted a resolution to prohibit certain animals from running at large, adopted a budget, elected a parish treasurer and 24 road overseers, considered printing bids and petitions concerning roads and drainage.

The legislation prohibited hogs, sheep, goats and geese from running at large in certain areas of the parish; the budget adopted amounted to $9,125, and H. W. Anding was elected parish treasurer. Road overseers named were Sidney Arceneaux, Jean Mauboules, Alexander Richard, D. E. Johnson, E. O. Bruner, James Baker, John Stewart, R. N. Lyons, Victor Richard, Jesse Andrus, Allen Rasberry, Anthony Bayer, Tom Roberson, R. B. Sloane, R. R. Lyons, Allen Laughlin, Rudolph Reed, Julien Gantt, Jules Clement, Alfred Reed, Angele Lejeune, Joseph Miller, Michel Roy and F. Istre. Petitions heard concerned better drainage for Prairie Hayes, a road from Rayne to Robert's Cove, and a change of the road running through W. B. Milligan's place to Coulee Croche.[25]

One paragraph in the minutes of that meeting reads: "The sealed proposals of the Signal and the Sentinel were handed to the jury, to do the public printing, the bid of the Sentinel being $25 for the privilege to be paid the parish, and the bid of the Signal of $50 for the privilege to be paid the parish. It was granted to the latter."[26]

This would seem to indicate that the newspaper paid the parish for the privilege of doing the public printing, instead of vice versa. Editor Bradford commented on the action: even though the Signal had the public printing, he would print the jury proceedings anyway, he said, "to keep the public informed."

The Sentinel called attention to the number of immigrants settling around Crowley; however, as the editor pointed out, these newcomers

[25] *Acadia Sentinel,* Jan. 22, 1887
[26] *Ibid,* Jan. 22, 29, 1887

"couldn't vote on the question." A letter to the editor, signed "Settler" from Mallet Cove, complained that he had come to Rayne to register, but had trouble finding the registrar. He said he looked for A. S. Chappuis at the hall, instead found him in the jail, where he was finally registered. The Sentinel provided an explanation: the so-called jail was the office of the justice of the peace "and is occasionally used to confine a boisterous Acadian. Fortunately we have never had use for a jail."[27]

First mention of the town of Crowley in the Rayne Signal was on January 29, 1887. The place name was used in a brief obituary: "DIED— Near Crowley, La., on January 25, Amelia, daughter of J. M. Steward and Leoncard Schexnaidre, age four years and 27 days." A second mention in the same issue was in the form of a poem, titled 'From Crowley, O!"

The first major crime in Acadia Parish was committed January 31, 1887. Thomas Laughlin, a farmer of the Long Point community, was shot and killed while crossing Long Point bridge. R. T. Clark conducted the inquest. Serving on the coroner's jury were M. Egan, H. J. Daigle, W. Gilman and Robert Sittig. Sheriff Duson conducted the investigation, remaining at the scene for three days, then took William Riley Jr. into custody. Riley, said to have been rejected as a suitor by one of Laughlin's daughters, was taken to Opelousas by sheriff's deputies and lodged in the St. Landry Parish jail. Both Rayne newspapers carried lengthy accounts of the murder, giving the details of the crime, the investigation, the suspected motive and citing Laughlin as "a sober and industrious citizen." The crime, it was stated, "caused a feeling of horror in the community," and one account said that Riley had been brought to the Opelousas jail for "safe-keeping," which indicated that officials may have feared the man might be lynched.[28] Riley was indicted for the crime, but was acquitted; his trial was held in Opelousas.[29]

The Crowley Auction

By the first of February, 1887, it appeared to be an accepted fact that Crowley was a serious contender for the parish seat. The contest, however, had its humorous angles, as revealed by the following item in

---

[27] *Acadia Sentinel*, Feb. 5, 1887
[28] Summary, *Acadia Sentinel, Rayne Signal*, Feb. 5, 1887; Acadia Parish Police Jury minutes, pub. *Acadia Sentinel* June 18, 1887
[29] *Opelousas Courier*, Oct. 29, 1887

the Sentinel: "One of Rayne's prominent merchants went electioneering for Rayne as the parish seat recently, and took with him two bottles of Rayne's best persuader. On the way he stopped at Crowley and there one of the sharp boys interested in that place for the courthouse, captured one of the bottles and emptying its contents into one of his own, filled the empty bottle with Crowley well water. A few miles farther west our friend discovered the state of affairs by pulling out his bottle to treat the crowd. He does not wish to be teased about it."[30]

The Opelousas Courier of February 5, 1887 reminded its readers of the forthcoming Crowley auction, set for February 10, 11 and 12. The newspaper reported that 75 men were at work building houses, planting trees and attending to other construction details. Fourteen miles of ditches had been dug, the principal streets had been made and leveled by machines, and the avenues ornamented with shade trees protected by "neatly constructed white-washed boxes." Some 4,000 trees were to be planted. Low excursion rates were to be in effect and arrangements had been made for train stops at all way stations between Lafayette and Crowley. Austin Lacombe "famous caterer of Opelousas," was to have charge of the cuisine at the Crowley House during the three days of the sale.

It was to be a day of pleasure as well as business, with roulette, chuck-a-luck, and a miniature lottery in evidence. A free barbecue was to be provided each day of the sale. Railroad fare for the round trip from Opelousas to Crowley was $1.50.[31]

Editor Bradford of the Acadia Sentinel attended the first day of the sale. His account of the event, published in the issue of February 12, 1887, read as follows: "On the 10th instant, a crowd of about 500 persons from this section and various outside places, brought (to Crowley) by idle curiosity or a desire to invest in town lots at auction. At about 3 p.m. Sheriff Duson took a stand on the depot platform and addressed the crowd, stating that every lot would be sold, whatever the offer. He described the country tributary to Crowley which should insure a bright future for the town. He stated that a called meeting of the police jury would be held in Crowley and a proposition submitted to them, offering $5,000 cash to be deposited with the parish treasurer as a bonus to be used by the parish, in case the voters, on the first of March, would locate the courthouse of Acadia in the public square prepared for it, at Crowley. He stated that

---

[30] *Acadia Sentinel*, Feb. 5, 1887
[31] Hair: "History of Crowley," reprint *LHQ*, 4, 8

the Company had spent $10,000 on Crowley and would spend $7,000 more in improving the roads leading to it. He said that it was determined to make Crowley a go-ahead business town like those so common in the West, and unknown in Louisiana. Parties bidding on one lot should have the privilege of two or more on terms accepted for the first.

"The first lot sold was No. 8 in block 24 and brought $50. After this the bidding became general and by 6 p.m. the hour of closing, 99 lots had been adjudicated to the various purchasers bringing nearly $10,000. We understand that the first 50 lots sold averaged $57.98 each, the last 49 averaged $140 each. The highest bid on one lot was by Mr. D. B. Lyons, $210.

"The Company certainly feels encouraged over the success of the first day's sale. We would say editorially to our friends of Rayne, that if they don't wake up, get to work and profit by the example set them, they will be dumbfounded about the second of March next. The work accomplished by this land company in six weeks and the fact that they are determined bidders for the parish seat, warns the people of this village to be up and doing if they would save their property from great loss in value and their business a great reduction in volume. Rayne can get the parish seat and should have it, but she will have to fight."

The Opelousas Courier also reported on the Crowley auction sale, using figures copied from the Times-Democrat of February 13, 1887. Figures for the final day of the auction showed 426 lots sold for $7,735. Total lots sold for the three days was 619, bringing a total of $30,000. Considerably less than one fifth of the town plot was sold, the Courier reported, and added "in five years this town plot will yield the company $150,000. Very good for a cow pasture."[32]

Even the Rayne Signal carried a brief report on the land sale, stating that the bidding had been spirited and the land had brought good prices. About three inches of column space was devoted to the article. Earlier in the month the newspaper had carried two small items concerning Crowley. One was the announcement that two new voting polls had been established, one at Crowley and one at the Jean Castille store at Coulee Croche. The second mention was obviously a joke of sorts: "Crowley has become the acknowledged pleasure resort for professional men of Rayne. On last Sunday evening two of them repaired to that place and

---

[32] *Opelousas Courier*, Feb. 19, 1887

enjoyed themselves by indulging in the most invigorating pasttime, a genu-ine school-boy foot race, for 5 cents a side."[33]

The proponents for "the Center" at Prairie Hayes re-doubled their politicking on February 8, two days before the Crowley auction. Some 200 persons attended a meeting at Prairie Hayes on that date. Principals at the meeting were W. F. Brooks, W. K. Hornsby, Homer Barousse, Zeno Huber, E. L. Harmon, N. Reed and S. Cart. A committee, formed to look after the interests of Prairie Hayes, unanimously accepted Eugene Hocka-day's offer of land and money to build the courthouse and parish buildings. Hockaday's proposal was to donate 80 acres of land "one fourth mile south of my residence," in Section 12, Township 8 Rayne 1 East, and $5,000. He also agreed to open necessary streets, provide drainage, and also to give land for churches "of all denominations, white or colored, also for schools of any color or religious faith."[34]

A correspondent for the New Orleans Picayune, Charles J. Kellogg, came to Rayne and wrote a lengthy report on the town. Kellogg said he had visited various businesses in Rayne, including the W. W. Duson real estate office, where he saw a stalk of cotton "by actual measurement 12 feet high" and ears of corn 11 inches long by 3½ inches in diameter. Already, he said, 55 carloads of rough rice had been shipped from Rayne, and "a remarkable shipment from this place was coops of bullfrogs, consigned to New Orleans." There were in Rayne six cotton gins, one of which had run day and night the past season, and a telegraph office. Rayne was the commercial center of the new parish, which had been created at the instigation of Rayne citizens, said Kellogg, and ended his letter with: "Asking Mr. A. S. Chappuis in regard to Rayne's chances for the seat of justice, he replied: 'Rayne is now virtually, and will be in fact, the county seat of the new parish of Acadia. You can just put that down as emanating from me, as I am in a position to know of what I am talking."[35]

The principal argument against placing the parish seat at Rayne was that the town was not centrally located. This the Sentinel editor refuted in an editorial of February 19, 1887. He pointed out that there were many Louisiana parishes with courthouses not situated in the geographical centers, and named 14 such parishes. He announced himself as "not in favor of the voters selling their votes for the money offered by parties

---

33 *Rayne Signal*, Feb. 12, Feb. 5, 1887
34 *Acadia Sentinel*, Feb. 12, 1887
35 *Ibid*

interested in either of these places," meaning Prairie Hayes and Crowley. "The mere fact that money is offered is good proof that the place offering the bonus is not fit for the parish seat. For why should a place while desirable, offer a bribe for the courthouse? Had the Land Company or Mr. Hockaday put up money to help create the new parish, we should feel lenient toward them, but as they did not assist that we know of, or put their shoulder to the wheel when we were struggling into existence, we think it consummate gall and cheek to now come forward and try to take from Rayne her well earned laurels." Editor Bradford strongly urged "an immediate organization and active canvass on the part of Rayne, and if it is found that there is any probability of Crowley getting the courthouse, then to vote solid and unanimously for a geographical center." The only conclusion to be drawn from this last statement is that Bradford, and perhaps other Rayne leaders, felt that the only way to beat Crowley was to join forces with Prairie Hayes. The strongest bid for the courthouse offered by Prairie Hayes, other than Hockaday's offer of land and money, was that the place was "the geographical center" of the new parish.

Other developments during the first half of February involved activities of the Southwest Louisiana Land Company. At a special meeting held in Rayne the Acadia Parish Police Jury considered a proposal by the land company to deposit $5,000 for the construction of a courthouse should Crowley be chosen the parish seat, plus a donation of a square of ground at the interesection of Parkerson and Hutchinson Avenues as the site. The proposition was accepted by a three-to-two vote; E. C. Fremaux, Melon Doucet and B. E. Clark voted for the proposition, B. H. Harmon and Homer Barousse voted against it. It was specified that the offer would be null and void unless Crowley was selected, and unless the courthouse would be built in 12 months.[36] At about this time the land company was advertising in the New Orleans Picayune for bids to construct 12 frame houses in the town of Crowley, the work to start immediately.[37]

Ten days before the election the Acadia Sentinel opened fire on the Rayne Signal with an implied charge that the rival newspaper had failed to support Rayne for the parish seat. For ammunition, the Sentinel reprinted in full the Rayne Signal editorial of October 30, 1886, in which Duson had proclaimed himself "for Rayne, first, last and forever." The editorial was reprinted under the headline "Then and Now," the editorial

---

[36] *Rayne Signal,* Feb. 19, 1887
[37] *Ibid*

placed under the "Then" and the "Now" column left totally blank. The Sentinel editor offered no comment on the Signal's three-and-a-half-months-old editorial, evidently feeling that he had made his point with the blank side of the column.[38]

The following week Editor Duson made answer: " . . . while we have been silent on the courthouse question, we have also been silent on Crowley, which is more than can be truthfully said of the Sentinel. In fact, we have repeatedly refused to boom the town, either by noticing it editorially, or publishing communications in regard to it, and some of these rejected articles were published in the Sentinel. The public can judge our position . . . " Duson averred that he had offered the parish treasurer a note or cash in the amount of $500, and, as agent for Mrs. Cunningham, had offered to deed a square of land two blocks from the depot worth at least $1,000, should Rayne be chosen as the parish seat, "while on the other hand there was being circulated a subscription list which was not legally binding and the parties signing it failed to accept my proposition and bind themselves according to law. Subscription or promises to pay are worthless in such an affair unless they are made so they can be collected by law. None of the parties on this list have as yet legally bound themselves, as the Editor of the Sentinel has neither subscribed anything or even signed any of these lists, that we ever heard of." Duson called on the public to decide which newspaper had done the most for Rayne — the Signal or the Sentinel. For every lot sold or new family located (by the Sentinel) he promised to show 25 to 50. "'A tree is known by its fruit,' he wrote, "and the value of a man to a community or town is judged by his success in building up the country. The prosperity and popularity of the Signal and its Editor is the real difficulty with the Sentinel."[39]

As further evidence of his concern for Rayne Editor Duson complained editorially about the railroad company. A construction crew, which had been working at Crowley, had been hauled off the job and ordered to a new station midway between Rayne and Scott. The new station, to be called Hutchinson, after the general manager of the railroad, was in an area where the railroad owned large acreage, and Duson ex—

---

[38] *Acadia Sentinel,* Feb. 19, 1887
[39] *Rayne Signal,* Feb. 26, 1887

pressed fear that should the new town be developed by the railroad it would damage business in Rayne.[40]

The subscription list referred to by the Rayne Signal included the names of 19 business and professional men of Rayne who inserted a public notice in the newspaper in which they agreed to give the necessary money and land to erect a courthouse "suitable for the seat of justice." The notice carried the names of J. D. Bernard, I. A. Smith, Thomas Bowden, A. S. Chappuis, F. Crouchet, M. Arenas, Auguste Perres, M. L. Melancon, G. R. Tolson, B. H. Harmon, J. E. Wimberley, D. B. Lyons, M. A. Cunningham, W. Brien, George H. Lagroue, A. Duclos, J. F. Morris, M. D., H. W. Anding and R. C. Webb, M. D.[41]

A group of backers for Crowley offered a similar proposition. A public notice, addressed to the president and members of the police jury, promised to pay specified amounts of money "to help defray expenses of the courthouse" should the parish seat be established at Crowley. The group pledged a total of $520 as follows: J. Frankel and Co., $100; United Implement Co., $100; M. Schwartz, 100; Henry Getel, $25; Charles Levy, $25; D. Bloch and Bro., $50; J. Meyers and Co., $100; B. M. Lambert, $20.[42]

In a final editorial before the election, Editor Bradford seemed prepared for the inevitable. In the February 26, 1887 issue of the Acadia Sentinel he wrote: "The next issue of this paper will doubtless chronicle the settlement of the vexed courthouse question — Rayne, Crowley, the Center or Hockaday, will come off victorious. We won't attempt to say which. The prospect is too clouded, and the question too mixed for us to decide. Now as ever, we are for Rayne, believing that the true interests of the people of Acadia Parish would be promoted by locating the seat of justice here." The editor warned the people of Rayne "not to be too sanguine." There were, he said, "active and popular enemies in the field." He urged Rayne citizens to get out and work the remaining days until the election, "or else this town will get left." He stated that while the people of Rayne had been "sleeping and dozing the time away your rivals have been hard at work for weeks, well organized, and spending money like water." The editor felt that Rayne still had a chance, provided the citizens would use "well directed work and argument," but cautioned

---

40 *Rayne Signal,* Feb. 26, 1887
41 *Ibid*
42 *Ibid*

them "to be vigilant and watchful on election day, as Rayne tickets will be hidden or smuggled away and Crowley tickets kept in view and worked into boxes through the ignorance of voters who can't read and write." He advised the posting of "good, sober, strong men at every poll; men who won't get drunk, or won't sell out, and who will stick to the polls until the returns are made."

Another item in the same issue of the Sentinel revealed that while urging citizens of Rayne to get out and work for the cause, the editor was critical of some of the methods which had been used to get votes. "There was a negro wedding in the vicinity of Rayne on Thursday night," he wrote, "and many of the elite of Rayne, white male society, attended, bent on electioneering business. Shame, gentlemen."

A total of 1,777 voters went to the polls on March 1. The final tabulation showed Crowley with 698 votes; Rayne, 560, and Prairie Hayes, 519. In less than a year after the St. Landry courthouse burned the parish had been divided and a new seat of government established in a place that had not existed at the time of the courthouse fire.

A breakdown of votes for the parish seat shows that Crowley even won some support at the Rayne precinct. First ward precincts were at Rayne and Crowley. The Rayne precinct vote was: Crowley, 32; Rayne, 414; Prairie Hayes, none. At the Crowley precinct the vote was: Crowley, 111; Rayne, 4; Prairie Hayes, none.

Second ward precincts were at Plaquemine Brûlée, Castille and Robert's Cove. Voting figures at the three precincts were, at Plaquemine Brûlée: Crowley, 119; Rayne, 7; Prairie Hayes, 42. Castille: Crowley, 48; Rayne, 18; Prairie Hayes, 5. Robert's Cove: Crowley, 52; Rayne, 28; Prairie Hayes, 1.

Third ward had only one precinct, Church Point. The voting was: Crowley, 33; Rayne, 9; Prairie Hayes, 226.

Fourth ward precincts were at Pointe-aux-Loups and Mammouth. At Pointe-aux-Loups the vote was: Crowley, 73; Rayne, 6; Prairie Hayes, 53. Mammouth: Crowley, 11; Rayne, none; Prairie Hayes, 56.

Fifth ward precincts were at Mermentau and Estherwood. The Mermentau precinct gave Crowley 70 votes; Rayne, 53; Prairie Hayes, 2. Estherwood: Crowley, 48; Rayne, 18; Prairie Hayes, none.

Sixth ward precincts were at German Settlement (Fabacher) and Prudhomme City. The German Settlement vote was Crowley, 55; Rayne,

2; Prairie Hayes, 26; Prudhomme City: Crowley, 46; Rayne, 1; Prairie Hayes, 108.

A further breakdown shows a total registration for the parish of 1,910; of this number, 1,777 voted on the courthouse location. First ward had 597 qualified voters; of this number, 561 voted. In second ward, with 345 registered voters, 239 voted. Third ward, with 294 registered, 268 voted. Fourth ward, 221 registered, 191 voted. Fifth ward, 215 registered, 191 voted. Sixth ward, 238 registered, 238 voted.

The new parish also elected its first slate of officers at the March 1 election: Elridge W. Lyons was elected first sheriff of Acadia, garnering 1,069 votes to H. J. Daigle 708. R. T. Clark won for clerk of court with 979 votes; his opponent, Thomas Bowden, had a total of 795.

Incumbent Representative John Crawford Lyons received 754 votes; his opponents were S. G. Reed, with 654, and W. R. Hornsby, 321. Dr. Rufus C. Webb won for coroner with an impressive 1,618 votes, to Dr. J. A. McMillan 74.

In the ward officer election, for first ward, the vote for justice of the peace was Archibald Hoffpauir, 315; O. E. Bruner, 291; R. J. C. Bull, 250. For constable, Abner Hoffpauir, 459; A. V. Lyons, 396.

Second ward, for justice of the peace: Tilford McClelland, 201; Ernest Cahanin, 76; W. H. Hornsby, 32; Orsamus Hayes, 1. Constable: J. M. Lyons, 192; John Laughlin, 119.

Third ward, for justice of the peace: H. D. McBride, 131; P. L. Guidry, 97; William Clavier, 39. Constable: Ernest Daigle, 157; Rodolphe David, 109.

Fourth ward, for justice of the peace: Sevigne Cart, 159; J. Regan, 40. Constable: Sam Cart, 105; Fremont Andrepont, 58; Raymond Reed, 38.

Fifth ward, justice of the peace: A. J. Vincent, 75; Addison Moore, 63; Andrew Henry, 56. Constable: Pinckney C. Smith, 89; E. D. Roy, 82; W. C. Whittaker, 21.

Sixth ward, justice of the peace, J. W. Young, 132; Joseph Copes, 55; Ben Goss, 52. Constable: S. M. Hundley, 55; Marius Amy, 32, James Ledoux, 49; C. T. Andrus, 34; Edmond Amy, 36; Matthew Little, 34.[43]

---

43 *Acadia Sentinel,* Aug. 20, 1887

The bearded gentleman at right is believed to be John Crawford Lyons, the Louisiana legislator who introduced the act to create Acadia Parish. At left is Albert J. Guidry, St. Landry representative; the man at center has been identified as A. L. Durio. The picture was taken in Baton Rouge prior to 1890. (From the original owned by Mrs. Eric Guilbeau, Sr.)

CHAPTER XVI

Aftermath

No sooner had the courthouse question been settled when Acadia was precipitated into another political controversy — one which was to create new dissensions and friction within the seven-month-old parish.

The Sentinel editor took the loss of the courthouse with fairly good grace. He congratulated Crowley, after a fashion, also the new parish officers, at the same time reminding Rayne: "I told you so!" An editorial published in the first issue of the paper after the election, on March 5, 1887, was as follows:

"On Tuesday the first instant, the first great election was held in the new parish of Acadia, and on that day was decided, probably forever, the location of the seat of justice. On the part of Crowley and the Land Company, it was a great victory, resulting from perfect organization, hard work and a free expenditure of money. The men who directed and worked the Crowley campaign were experienced and drilled politicians with everything at their backs except the votes. These they worked up, and it goes to show what well directed work in a campaign will effect. Without doubt Rayne was entitled to the courthouse because of her former good work for the creation of the parish and because at the beginning of the campaign she had the votes to back her. Her loss of these was owing to a lack of organization, even up to the day of the election. Crowley received 698 votes, Rayne, 560, a difference of 138 votes in favor of Crowley. These 138 votes and 200 more besides could have been cast for Rayne had the people interested in her success bent their energies to the fight, and realized who their opponents were. Even Prairie Hayes, which was a scattered and disorganized community, made a better fight comparatively than Rayne, and could have done better, had her various friends been united. Rayne has received a serious lesson and may profit by it. Her people may learn that the time has passed when an election can be carried by a few men on the very day of election; and further, the valuable lesson that in unity there is strength.

"We congratulate the parish and the newly elected officers. They are a good set of men, and will doubtless perform their duties satisfactorily. We should all bear in mind, however, that the parish is new and inexperi-

Schrock 161.56 acres	Barnes 161.86 acres	Abbott 161.90 acres	T. L. Cagneaux 161.90 acres	Dusenberg 162.51 acres	Pa 16 a
15		14		3	
Joel B. Stockwell 161.86 acres	James E. Portis 161.86 acres	Celathial Abbott 161.90 acres	Martin II Abbott 161.90 acres	Martina Rodigo 162.51 acres	Wille T Aye 16
Miss Mary Ann Kenny 161.20	Miss Eliza Kenny 161.20 acres	James K Killmer 162.15 acres	David H. Abbott 162.15 acres	Joseph Crossen 162.90 acres	Carl H 16 a
22		23		24	
George J. Tromp 156.04 acres	Ellery Wellman 161.56 acres	Joseph Thomas 162.15 acres	Peter J. Leonard 162.15 acre	Joseph Leonard 162.90 acres	Do Lo Meg 162 a
John K Snyder 160.52 acres	Miss. Rachel E Snyder 160.48	Leon Garot 161.20 acres	Wilhelm J Zaundrecher 161.20 acre	Lorenz J. Zaunb 148.28 acres	
27		26		25	N. Zaundrecher 141.30 ac
Ira E. Simpson 161.28 acres	Michel Bonreau 161.86 acres	Thomas Bee 161.20 acres	John Manion 16 acres	Nicholas	41 Antoine Blan 870.25 acre
Theodore J. Reumont 126.42 acres	T. P. Reumont 42.17 acres	John M. Bailey 110.48	John M. Bailey 40 Raphael Smith	Charles C. Thayer 154.28 acres	
	4		35	36	

Segment of Township 9 South Range 1 West, between Crowley and Egan. Landowners' names were written in at some time between 1886 and 1900. John P. Parsons was authorized to do the survey in 1881.

enced, consequently some mistakes and errors are unavoidable. Therefore, don't criticize to hastily."

The Opelousas Courier, long-time friend of Sheriff Duson and supporter of parish division, was jubilant: "The Crowley Boom which started a thriving village on an open prairie in a few days time, mainly through the liberal use of printer's ink and the determined energy of its projectors, bounced the embryo town into the staid dignity of a parish site last Tuesday. This gives the place a permanent habitation and a name which will not prove the evanescent bubble that many predicted it would be. As a matter of course its success is now assured and Crowley will take its stand among the sisterhood of the parish capitals and march on the road of rapid progress and prosperity."[1]

The reaction of the Rayne Signal to the election returns cannot be known; there are no extant copies of the newspaper after February 26, 1887.

The less than two-months-old "embryo town" which became the parish seat was little more than a hamlet. The 115 qualified voters who went to the Crowley poll March 1 were hardly representative of the population of the town; with only two precincts in first ward, the Crowley precinct certainly drew on voters from the countryside as well. On the other hand, the number of voters did not include the newer immigrant residents who had not had time to qualify as voters.

A Lake Charles newspaper circulated a bit of fun at the expense of the new town. The paper related a story about a traveler in Acadia Parish, who, while crossing the prairie, came upon some people who appeared to be preparing a field for planting. The traveler, curious about the work going on, asked one of the workmen: "Why are you making the corn rows so far apart?" The workman, speaking in a pseudo mid-western dialect, answered: "Them ain't corn rows, mister. Them air streets, and right now you're standin' on the corner of Parkerson and Hutchinson!"[2]

The feuding between the proprietors of the two Rayne newspapers got off to a fresh start after the election. In the March 5, 1887 issue of the Acadia Sentinel Bradford answered the charges directed against him in the Rayne Signal editorial of February 26. Bradford asserted the Signal had attacked him and his newspaper by "false insinuations and direct untruths." He said he didn't "care a snap for the proprietor of the Signal or his

1 *Opelousas Courier,* Mar. 5, 1887
2 *Acadia Sentinel,* May 14, 1887, from the *Lake Charles Commercial*

Advertisements from early issues of the Crowley Signal.

opinions," but did object to a "personal overhauling whenever that individual loses his temper."

The following week Bradford took issue with a statement which he said had appeared in the March 5 issue of the Signal alleging that "Rayne citizens tried to play the Acadians against the American portion of the community." Bradford said he didn't think the issue was raised; that Plaquemine Brûlée had voted for Crowley because many of her citizens had acquired property there, and it was to their interests to locate the courthouse in Crowley. "They voted for candidates elected because those candidates come from Plaquemine Brulee," he stated, and offered as proof

Businessmen of Rayne and Crowley used these advertisements in the "Immigration Number" of the Crowley Signal, August 25, 1888.

283

that the successful candidates received more "French-Creole votes and less of the stranger votes" than the defeated candidates.[3]

Judge G. W. Hudspeth, one of the directors of the Southwest Louisiana Land Company, died in New Orleans April 19, 1887. The respected district judge, who had lent his support to parish division, was reported near death on April 2, and his long-time friend, Sheriff Duson, was at his bedside.[4]

Six weeks after the courthouse election the Sentinel endorsed the candidacy of Francis T. Nicholls for governor of Louisiana, thereby adding fuel to the feuding fire between the two editors. In the issue of April 16, 1887 Editor Bradford made answer to certain statements made by the Signal wherein his endorsement of Nicholls was questioned. (Unfortunately, only one side of the controversy can be presented, since there are no existing copies of the Rayne Signal for this period) Bradford stated: "The people of Acadia need not be reminded of the bitter lesson so recently taught them by a few hard-working politicians." He then added: "We believe the parish officers were elected by a majority of the voters, but have yet to meet a man who believes that Crowley could have won the parish seat if the question had been left to a majority vote for a decision."

Fortunately for those interested in its early history, Crowley was not ignored by the Acadia Sentinel, the only available parish publication from March 1 to September 10, 1887.

The Sentinel carried several lengthy letters from a resident of Crowley who signed himself "Settler." One of these letters, couched in the grandiose language of the day, told of a problem with the railroad. "Settler" complained about freight trains blocking the crossing; he wrote about the time when the freight blocked a crossing while he waited, with two sick children in the wagon, while the engine uncoupled and "went all the way to the Mermentau River for water" leaving the freight cars blocking the crossing. "Again," he wrote, "as everyone knows, there are two lumber yards here, one at each end of the switch, and every time, without fail, they place the cars of lumber at the wrong place."[5]

A second letter from "Settler" provided something of a progress report on the new parish seat. "Look at the thriving little town of Crowley," he wrote, "with something over 40 houses, built and being erected, where

---

3 *Acadia Sentinel*, Mar. 12, 1887
4 *Acadia Sentinel*, Apr. 2, 23, 1887; *Opelousas Courier*, Apr. 2, 1887
5 *Acadia Sentinel*, Apr. 2, 1887

only a few months ago nothing but a broad and bleak prairie stood . . . a large and commodious hotel where the traveler can find everything that is to be enjoyed in a country hotel, two stores and one drug store."[6]

The anonymous reporter told of the first school, but neglected to mention the name of the teacher or the location of the school. "We have a school taught by a gentleman that seems to be predestined for that place inasmuch as he has gained the love and esteem of both parents and scholars."[7] There was also a Sunday School, with 33 members.[8]

One of "Settler's" letters reported on a mock election. "Inasmuch as we are growing so fast, we found it necessary to elect officers. Accordingly, an election was held for mayor in which the opponents were Hons. Wirt Collins and J. G. Medlenka. After the vote was taken and counted, it was found that Hon. J. G. Medlenka was duly elected; and there being some dissatisfaction, the election was contested, with Judge Clark on the bench and Alphonse Levy as clerk of court, and the jury being duly sworn and empanelled, the case was given a fair and impartial hearing, when it was found that fraud had been used to such an extent that the election was annulled and a new election ordered to be held within 30 days."[9]

The operation of parish business, which prior to the March 1 election had taken place in Rayne, was transferred to the parish seat. The Acadia Parish Police Jury held its first meeting in Crowley on April 11 and 12, 1887, convening for two days in the temporary courthouse. The first day of the meeting was given to appointing commissioners to lay out roads in various parts of the parish.[10]

The main business to come before the police jury was taken up at the April 12 session, when the jury proceeded to examine various plans and specifications for erecting a courthouse. The plan offered by Theodore Schaedel, to construct a frame building, for $6,000, was accepted. Appointed to the building committee were B. H. Harmon, James Webb, Dallas B. Hayes, Jasmin Breaux and W. F. Stakes. In other action the jury accepted the resignation of A. S. Chappuis as jury clerk and elected H. W. Carver in his stead.[11]

---

6 *Acadia Sentinel,* Apr. 30, 1887
7 *Ibid*
8 *Ibid,* May 14, 1887
9 *Ibid*
10 *Ibid,* Apr. 23, 1887
11 *Ibid*

Courthouse plans were reconsidered at subsequent meetings of the police jury. At a meeting on May 5, 1887 the jurors decided that the courthouse should be built of brick; the contract given Schaedel was abrogated, and a time period of 30 days set for receiving bids for a brick courthouse. The following month, on June 13, the police jurors met and awarded the building contract to Hannan & Voss, a Baton Rouge firm, at a cost of $11,000. The $5,000 donation from the Southwest Louisiana land Company would constitute the first payment.[12]

The first term of court was held in Acadia Parish May 9 to May 12, 1887. Judge E. D. Estillette and four attorneys from Opelousas came to Crowley by train. Thirteen civil cases and one probate were disposed of; there were four other cases on the docket which were not ready for trial.[13]

The probable basis of the fight going on between the two Rayne newspapers was revealed in the May 28, 1887 issue of the Acadia Sentinel: "In the last issue of the Signal appeared some forty or more notices of the intention to make final proof by homesteaders. Some months ago before the selection of the parish seat of Acadia, most of these notices appeared in the same paper, and ran for nearly 30 days when the Sentinel stopped the publication and knocked the bottom out of a fine scheme to defraud the government. The innocent homesteader was not to be blamed; it was his attorney or agent. This time the notices seem all right, but we raise a protest of the selection by the United States Land officers of the newspaper in which said notices appear . . . We object because the Signal is a ring newspaper and is supported in every way possible by the district and local rings, in other words, it will support and will be the organ here of that faction in state politics headed by Senator Eustis and Governor McEnery. Some of its job printing bills presented to the police jury should not, we think, have been approved. And all jobs which the parish has to pay for should be given the lowest bidder."

Abstracts from the Acadia Sentinel provide information on happenings in both Rayne and Crowley:

— "One day last week two young men, William Sarver and M. Morgan, got into a difficulty in the course of which Sarver's finger was so badly bitten it had to be amputated. It is very unfortunate that two gentlemen cannot settle a difficulty without thus mutilating each other. We wonder if wounded honor can be vindicated in such a manner."

12 *Acadia Sentinel*, May 7, June 18, 1887
13 *Opelousas Courier*, May 14, 1887

— The Acadia Homestead Loan Association of Crowley was organized May 23, 1887, with the following officers: W. Coleman Logue, president; H. W. Carver, vice president; A. P. Kip, secretary; J. Frankel, treasurer. Directors were Frankel, Logue, Carver, D. B. Hayes, J. T. Stewart, Wirt Collins, A. S. Chappuis, A. Levy and R. T. Clark. Capitol stock was $250,000.[14]

Other news briefs about Crowley told of movements to organize a fire company and a literary society; four houses were on the road to completion; an express office had been established, and the town would soon get a post office. Construction was slated to begin on "another large and commodious store" for A. Goldstein of New Orleans; Jac Frankel's residence was nearly completed "and is no doubt the handsomest in the parish," two other cottages, belonging to Pharr and Williams, and Kennedy and Foote, were reported almost finished.[15]

The Sentinel editor next turned his attention to progress for Rayne, at the same time reminding that the "Land Company" had not made good on its promises. In an editorial promoting a rice mill for Rayne, he stated that "the Land Company captured votes for Crowley by promising a rice mill, which will probably not be erected in our day." The need for a rice mill was self-evident, he said; thousands of barrels of rice were produced annually, and the freight saved on shipping clean rice would be considerable; the producers would derive the benefits. A rice mill in Rayne would pay well; it would be the only one in about 100 square miles — the mill should be built in Rayne, and should be owned by Rayne businessmen and farmers.[16]

Crowley received its first mail the first week of June, 1887. A news brief in the June 11, 1887 issue of the Acadia Sentinel read: "Crowley p.o. received, today, their first pouch of mail, much to the delight of everyone." The undated news item is presumed to have been written and submitted for publication several days prior to the newspaper's deadline. United States post office records show that a post office was established at "Crowleyville" February 26, 1887, with J. Frankel as postmaster, and discontinued as of May 16, 1887. A post office at Crowley was established May 14, 1887, with Jac Frankel as postmaster.

---

14 *Acadia Sentinel,* May 21, 28, 1887
15 *Ibid,* May 28, 1887
16 *Ibid,* June 4, 1887

Other news items carried in the June 11, 1887 issue of the Sentinel reveal more progress in the new town: "Fontenot's cottage being erected by the Acadia Homestead Loan will soon be completed. It is quite handsome, and the cheapest cottage in the parish . . . the brick yard of Andrus & Fontenot are molding on an average 9,000 bricks a day; they will burn their first kiln in time for building the Courthouse . . . genial Neil McDevitt was presented by Hon. D. B. Lyons, aspirant for the first executive office of the city of Crowley (to be), with a handsome Cleveland hat. The presentation speech was made by Hon. D. B. Lyons, and responded to by Major H. W. Carver, in behalf of Col. McDevitt. After speeches, glasses commenced rattling and champagne flowed quite freely."

The Crowley news column in the Sentinel also reported the death of a resident, Mrs. William Carlin, on June 4, and told of the organization of Crowley's first church: "A Methodist church was organized here last Sunday (June 5, 1887) by Rev. H. O. White, of Rayne, with 10 members. Those who were present had the pleasure of hearing a splendid sermon by Mr. White."[17]

News of the Rayne community included a report on a funeral of state arranged by the Rayne Hook and Ladder Co. No. 1, for a deceased member, F. E. Bailey. The members of the fire company met at the fire house dressed in uniform, an hour before the funeral on June 4. The hearse was the horse-drawn fire truck, draped in mourning. The firemen wore mourning badges, which were later deposited in the grave, and formed a procession and honor guard for the funeral cortege to St. Joseph's Church. Participating firemen were A. J. Guidry, A. D. LeBlanc, A. J. Besse, J. E. Cessac, G. E. Addison, F. J. Bernard, R. J. C. Bull, A. J. Christman, A. C. Poulet, E. Capel, A. Crouchet, H. Carlin, Laurent Pucheu.[18]

One of the adversaries in the newspaper conflict left the battle field in May of 1887. President Grover Cleveland appointed George K. Bradford, editor of the Acadia Sentinel, agent for the detection of fraudulent entries of public lands.[19] (The following year, on April 26, 1888, Bradford married Caroline Nicholls, eldest daughter of Governor Francis T. Nicholls)[20] Bradford's new duties as special detective for the federal government took him out of the state most of that summer, so he employed

[17] *Acadia Sentinel*, June 11, 1887
[18] *Ibid*
[19] *Abbeville Meridional*, May 21, 1887
[20] *Ibid*, May 5, 1888

an associate editor to publish the Acadia Sentinel. This was William C. Chevis, the fiery editor who continued the feud with the Rayne Signal, got into a hassle with the mayor of Rayne, and ended up challenging the editor of the Crowley Signal to a duel.

The Acadia Sentinel was cricital of the police jury's decision to build a more expensive courthouse. Earlier, the paper had commended the jury for choosing to build a frame building and not put the parish in debt by erecting a more elaborate building. Commenting on the jury's action in rescinding the first plan in favor of a more expensive structure, the editor said, in part: "The only objection raised was by Mr. Harman, member from the first ward, who did not favor the running of the parish in debt so deep at this critical time. Our views have been before expressed and coincide precisely with those of Mr. Harman . . . we need a jail much more than we need a Courthouse." The editorial stated that during the campaign for parish division "our people were promised by leading politicians that the immediate building of a Courthouse would not be necessary, and upon the faith of this promise most of our people voted for a division." In the editor's opinion, had the people known they would be taxed so soon for the additional $6,000 to finish paying for a courthouse, the issue of parish division would have been defeated.[21]

Another historic event in the chronicle of Acadia Parish took place July 11, 1887. The parish school board held its first meeting. William Sarver was elected president and D. W. Hoyt secretary. School districts were laid out in five wards: Sarver to supervise the district in first ward, Jean Castille, second ward, J. Wesley Young, third ward, D. C. Calkins fourth ward and D. W. Hoyt fifth yard.[22]

The summer of 1887 found the parish involved in a heated political battle triggered by the forthcoming gubernatorial election.

Notice of a mass meeting to be held at noon July 23, 1887 in the temporary courthouse at Crowley appeared in the July 16 issue of the Acadia Sentinel. Purpose of the meeting was to organize a Democratic Executive Committee and to name a delegate to the State Central Committee. The notice of the meeting was followed by a listing of 87 names: Joseph Trahan, Sidney Arceneaux, E. C. Fremaux, J. Miers, G. L. Boudreaux, F. Istre, F. B. Sloane, Emile Miers, T. J. Toler, J. M. Lyons, P. J. Manouvrier, B. M. Lambert, D. B. Smith, R. T. Clark, R. N. Lyons,

21 *Acadia Sentinel,* June 18, 1887
22 *Ibid,* July 16, 1887

J. W. Young, J. E. Barry, Louis Miers, E. D. Roy, R. Wainwright, V. Maignaud, P. Fremaux, L. V. Fremaux, T. McClelland, Stephen Clark, J. H. Rumpkins (Lumpkin?);

W. F. Stakes, J. M. McClelland, W. C. Chevis, J. E. Wimberley, J. P. Grant, W. C. Dunshie, E. O. Bruner, A. Hoffpauir, D. Derouen, D. K. Brazeale, I. A. Smith, E. Deputy, C. W. Foreman, A. S. Chappuis, D. B. Lyons, J. M. Harman, Joseph Harmon, E. W. Lyons, Benjamin Myers, Jean Castille, J. P. Fruge, Jean Castex, A. Dugas, E. Istre, John Stewart, J. B. Stewart, J. B. Clark, W. W. Duson, J. A. Williams, G. C. Mouton, M. D., A. V. Lyons, Edmond Clark, B. E. Clark, Eyeh Clement, E. L. Harmon, F. Quebedeaux, L. Broussard;

A. J. Vincent, Andrew Henry, L. Espergalier, M. D., M. Thibodeaux, R. B. Sloane, Milton Laughlin, W. A. McClelland, Henry Clark, H. M. Couch, A. Bonnet, H. Picard, R. C. Webb, M. D., A. V. Johnston, R. J. C. Bull, A. Hoffpauir, A. Duclos, H. W. Anding, G. F. Jones, Mervine Kahn, George W. Lagroue, B. H. Harman, D. B. Hayes and John C. Lyons.

The list of names included virtually everyone who had previously been identified with parish leadership. It appeared that for once the leaders of Acadia Parish would be united under the banner of the Democratic party. The apparent truce was to be short-lived.

On the date of the meeting, July 23, a broadside for Nicholls appeared in the Acadia Sentinel. The editorial writer brought the state contest down to the parish level: "Remember, citizens of Acadia, how your interests have been consulted in all the affairs that have pertained to your welfare, in which the Governor of Louisiana has been interested. We would submit the question, in all candor, to the people of Acadia: Who have controlled the appointments made in your parish since its organization? Have your interests been consulted, or rather, have they not been controlled by persons who do not represent the sentiments of the people, and in some instances even by persons who do not even reside in the parish?"

By "persons who do not even reside in the parish" readers could readily identify Sheriff Duson, one of the chief supporters of the incumbent governor, Samuel D. McEnery. The insinuation could have been provoked by an article, or letter, which had been published in the Signal. The Sentinel editor, in a separate part of the paper of the same date, makes reference to this: "In a recent issue of the Signal Mr. C. C. Duson makes use of some language unbecoming to a gentleman in making a most unwarranted attack upon the editors of this paper." Editor Chevis took full responsibility for whatever it was in the Sentinel which had evoked comment from the sheriff, adding that he had "full and complete charge of the paper during Mr. Bradford's absence." Chevis, who signed his name to the article as associate editor, said that he regretted that Sheriff Duson "saw fit to vent his spleen through the newspaper columns," and that he, Chevis, did not "propose to carry on a newspaper controversy."

A third pieces in the same issue (July 23), in the form of a letter to the editor, was written by E. T. Lewis, brother of Thomas Lewis and member of the anti-Duson faction of St. Landry Parish: "A card appeared in the last issue of the Rayne Signal, signed by C. C. Duson, in which, under pretext of answering an editorial of yours, he takes occasion to boast of his pretended efforts in behalf of the creation of the parish of Acadia, and to criticize my course in the Senate upon that question." Lewis said he refused to be drawn into any newspaper controversy, but called on Duson to explain "how it happened that his strenuous efforts in behalf of the creation of the parish of Acadia (of which he seizes this occasion to remind your people) ended in location of the parish seat, not in either Rayne or Prairie Hayes, as expected by everybody, but upon an uninhabited spot, not previously thought of, belonging to himself and his associate land owners." Also, "to explain through whose influence and for what purpose the election in Acadia was postponed," and further, "to explain some things connected with the performance of the duties of office." Lewis suggested the sheriff "turn his attention to the affairs of the office he holds in St. Landry."

This controversial issue of the Sentinel is dated the same day the mass meeting took place in Crowley. What effect, if any, the Chevis and Lewis insinuations had on the outcome of the meeting can only be conjectured. The meeting began at noon; Chevis conceivably could have distributed copies of his paper before the meeting started.

At an early hour on Saturday, July 23 every available hitching post in Crowley was taken up, and by noon the temporary courthouse building was filled to capacity.[23]

Chevis himself opened the meeting and nominated Homer Barousse for chairman. W. W. Duson nominated B. H. Harmon. The vote was taken, but couldn't be counted on account of the crowded condition of the courthouse. It was decided to continue the meeting outside; this was done, Chevis wrote, "at the suggestion of the McEnery faction." Chevis claimed

---

[23] *Acadia Sentinel,* July 30, 1887

that two thirds of the vote was for Barousse, and "when the McEneryites discovered they were in a hopeless minority, raised a most disgraceful howl, taunted and insulted the Nicholls men," and challenged Chevis to vacate the chair and "engage in personal combat."[24]

The Chevis report of the meeting states that the McEnery faction attempted to break up the meeting: "Finding that their attempts to either break the meeting, or force the Nicholls men to bolt were futile, they then dashed around to gain possession of the courtroom by the rear entrance. In this they were foiled, as no sooner did the Nicholls supporters see it, they rushed in by the front door and gained possession of the hall."[25]

The meeting was resumed inside the building and "the election of Mr. Barousse was then made unanimous." M. Pousson was elected vice president and S. Cart secretary. In his report Chevis added that while this business was being transacted "the McEneryites, were hissing and howling, as if the gates of pandemonium had been opened, and its inmates brought into the meeting." After the meeting, said Chevis, "they (the McEneryites) held a side show, composed of some fifty or sixty men who endorse the administration of Gov. McEnery and elected some members of a pseudo Democratic Committee."[26]

The minutes of that first Democratic Committee reveal that President Barousse called for nominations for members of the committee from the different police jury wards. Those elected were M. Arenas, first ward; E. L. Harmon, second ward; Homer Barousse, third ward; A. B. Cart, fourth ward; Jean Castex, fifth ward.[27]

The Opelousas Courier took note of the political comedy being enacted in Acadia Parish. In the issue of July 30, 1887 the editor commented: "A lot of St. Landry politicians went to Crowley last Saturday to teach the good people of Acadia how to 'run the machine.' Two Democratic committees were formed. Editor Bradford ought to be on hand now to protest against 'the interference of outside parties' in the local affairs of Acadia." The Courier gave the names of the anti-Nicholls committee appointed by the McEnery faction: Archibald Hoffpauir, R. B. Sloan, T. C. Chachere, A. B. Cart, A. J. Vincent, Joseph Trahan, Sidney

24 *Ibid*
25 *Ibid*
26 *Ibid*
27 *Ibid*

Arceneaux. W. F. Stakes was named delegate to the State Central Committee.

Four days after the meeting in Crowley the Democratic Executive Committee met again, this time at Duhon Hall, Rayne. President Barousse announced the members at large: Thomas P. Bowden, first ward; James M. Lyons, second ward; D. J. Jenkins, third ward; Andrew Henry, fifth ward. Chevis was the delegate to the state committee. There was no mention of a member at large from the fourth ward.[28]

There was no further mention of the activities of the democratic Executive Committee, either the McEnery or the Nicholls faction, in subsequent issues of the Acadia Sentinel, copies of which are available through September 10, 1887. A follow-up appeared in the Opelousas Courier of September 24, 1887, a re-print of a dispatch from Crowley to the Times-Democrat: "Politics are at fever heat in the Congressional contest. The Barousse committee, representing Nicholls, called a primary election for September 24, 1887. The Hoffpauir committee, representing the people, adopted the same day, the same commissioners and the same representatives, and both local papers published this in their issues following the meetings of the two committees. The Barousse committee met again and changed the date to September 23 and kept the day a secret from the people. The Acadia Sentinel, the organ of the pure and undefiled, was kept back from Friday evening until Monday to prevent the Hoffpauir Committee from getting the day of the primary, and names of the commissioners. The Hoffpauir committee secured a paper some 20 miles away and set the same day and commissioners."

The outcome of the controversy was reported in the New Orleans Democrat of October 1, 1887: "At the ward elections in the parish of Acadia last Saturday, the McEnery Democrats sought the fight. They seemed to be confident of victory, for their committee followed up the Nicholls or Barousse committee, and fixed their ward elections for the same day, so as to force a contest. Notwithstanding, as alleged by the Acadia Sentinel, 'that officials from St. Landry took an active part,' the McEnerites were overwhelmingly defeated."

Meanwhile, area newspapers considered the arrival of newcomers in Acadia Parish to be newsworthy. The Opelousas Courier of March 26, 1887, in an item copied from the Lafayette Advertiser, noted that Mr. D.

---

[28] *Acadia Sentinel,* July 30, 1887

Aleshire and J. A. Williams of St. Paul, Nebraska, were in Lafayette "looking at the country with a view of locating in southwest Louisiana." In its issue of April 2, 1887 the Courier reported, from the Rayne Signal, that "during the week over 25 parties have located in Acadia Parish;" Williams and Aleshire had "located claims." A week later, another excerpt from the Rayne Signal stated that Eugene B. Hunt, John Mang and wife and Joseph Thoman had located on a homestead near the Southwest Louisiana Land Company sawmill; M. Couch, from Hamilton County, Texas, had purchased the D. B. Lyons farm; J. H. Hamilton, also from Hamilton County, Texas, had bought an 80-acre farm from R. B. Sloane.[29]

The Courier of April 23, 1887 reported that S. B. Bird, who had bought a lot opposite the depot at the Crowley auction for $65, had subsequently sold the lot for $425. "At this rate of increase in value, lots sold the day of the sale for $30,000 are now worth $180,000. Brains, energy and printer's ink have wrought a remarkable change in the cow pasture of three months ago."

News columns of the Acadia Sentinel during August and the first part of September were mostly filled with excerpts from other newspapers praising General Nicholls or criticizing Governor McEnery. The paper did devote space to minutes of the school board meeting of August 27, at which time action was taken to open about 15 schools, a time was set to examine teachers, and teachers' salaries were fixed at $30 per month. The paper noted that the foundation had been laid for the rice mill at Rayne, also that the Prairie Hayes schoolhouse had burned, and that the fire was believed to have been the work of an arsonist.[30]

During this time a "cease fire" was observed by the rival newspapers. In the August 27 issue of the Sentinel Editor Chevis explained the armistice: "We must apologize to our readers for not producing the Tale of the Two Editors in this issue. We had a fine article prepared, but when we reflected that the fighting Editor of the Signal is recuperating in Canada and might come back and 'chaw us up' we were persuaded to desist."

Acadia Parish and the town of Rayne played hosts to a distinguished visitor on September 6 and 7, 1887. Brigadier General Francis T. Nicholls, on a campaign tour for the Democratic nomination for governor, spent

29 *Opelousas Courier,* Apr. 9, 1887
30 *Acadia Sentinel,* Sept. 3, 1887

two nights and a day in Rayne. Nicholls, a Civil War hero, had lost an arm and a leg in the war. He had earlier served a term as governor of Louisiana; his opponent in 1887 was the incumbent governor, Samuel D. McEnery.

General Nicholls arrived in Rayne on the afternoon train from Opelousas. In his entourage were F. F. Perrodin, former district attorney for St. Landry Parish, proponent of parish division and former friend and colleague of Sheriff Duson. His presence with the Nicholls party indicates that Perrodin and Duson were at that time on opposite sides of the political fence, at least so far as the governor's race was concerned. The Nicholls party also included John O. Ogden, district attorney for the 13th Judicial District of St. Landry and Acadia, and E. T. Lewis, arch enemy of the Dusons.

General Nicholls was greeted at the depot by "a large concourse of people" then helped into a buggy. Accompanied by Rayne Mayor Bull, he was driven to the Rayne Hotel, where more people had assembled to welcome him. He was the guest of honor that evening at an informal reception at the hotel.

At an early hour the following day "people began pouring into town in all manner of conveyances, from the weak, jaded creole pony, and the primitive wooden cart of the poorer classes to the elegantly liveried turnout of the fashionable and wealthy." At about 10:30 a.m. General Nicholls, escorted by Mayor Bull, M. Arenas and Homer Barousse, entered an open carriage and was driven to Mauboules Point, about a mile north of Rayne, where the rally and barbecue were held.

The procession of vehicles which followed the general's carriage was described as stretching from the crowded streets of the town to the woods at Mauboules Point. Many of the people walked, even though the sun was hot and the road dusty. By 11 a.m. some 2,000 persons, "of all ages and races" had assembled.

The distinguished guest made his address in French, "as many of his followers in the parish speak that language and were delighted to know that the General was able to address them in their vernacular." At the conclusion of his speech, General Nicholls was presented a bouquet by two little girls, Bessie Cunningham and Emma Hoffpauir. After the barbecue picnic, the general accepted an invitation to dine with the J. D. Bernard family. The next day he was accompanied to the train by a "large and enthusiastic delegation of citizens from all parts of the parish."[31]

(Acadia Parish supporters of General Nicholls were not disappointed in their candidate. He became the next governor of Louisiana, and after completing this second term was appointed Chief Justice of the Louisiana Supreme Court, a position he held until his retirement in 1911. At the time of his death in 1912 the Picayune wrote that "he was without doubt the most truly eminent, the most highly esteemed and the most deservedly honored citizen in Louisiana.")[32]

Rayne was also visited by Governor McEnery prior to the Democratic convention. The Opelousas Courier of November 26, 1887 carried a detailed account of the governor's visit; the newspaper reported that at least 2,000 people welcomed the chief executive, which proved that "Acadia was not solid for Nicholls." Judge Barry and Dr. G. C. Mouton presided at the meeting, and Leon Fremaux acted as secretary. The newspaper listed the names of a number of McEnery supporters, also the names of the ladies on the reception committee: Mrs. W. W. Duson, Mrs. R. C. Webb, Mrs. R. T. Clark, Misses Rosa and Olive Burton, Mrs. L. V. Fremaux, Miss Minerva Williams, Mrs. E. Bruner, Mrs. Sidney Arceneaux, Mrs. Omere Arceneaux and Mrs. J. B. Lyons.

Available copies of the Acadia Sentinel end with the issue of September 10, 1887; the Rayne Signal files end with the issue of February 26, 1887. Except for occasional news items used in neighboring newspapers, this leaves a blank of six months in the chronicle of Acadia Parish history: from September 10, 1887, to March 10, 1888, when the existing files of the Crowley Signal begin. There are no known copies of the Crowley Signal from January 7, 1888, the first issue published in Crowley, through March 3, 1888.

During the late summer of 1887 Sheriff Duson moved his family to Crowley. The Opelousas Courier of August 13, 1887 reported: "Sheriff Duson's family have taken up their residence at the 'future great' Crowley." An item in the September 17 issue of the newspaper stated: "Mrs. C. C. Duson, wife of our energetic and enterprising sheriff, now living in Crowley, was in town."

The W. W. Duson family continued to live in Rayne until January of 1888, when the newspaper plant was moved to Crowley. There are

---

[31] *Acadia Sentinel,* Sept. 10, 1887
[32] Davis: *Louisiana, a Narrative History,* 285

some indications that the decision to move to Crowley did not come about until the latter part of 1887. The Rayne Signal of March 20, 1886 carried this item: "Mr. W. W. Duson is having the grounds around his office beautifully adorned with shade trees. He intends, in a few years hence, to have a nice playground for his children." More than a year later, in the June 18, 1887 issue of the Acadia Sentinel, this item appeared: "Mr. W. W. Duson has just finished a beautiful cottage on Polk street. It is indeed an ornament to the town."

The first grand jury was called into session in Acadia Parish in September, 1887. Judge E. D. Estillette of Opelousas delivered an eloquent charge to the jury, concluding with: "Acadia is a new parish, with a bright destiny before it. It is beautiful to look at, and cannot fail to attract attention of the lovers of nature. It is for the most part settled by the descendants of those unfortunate Acadians who were dispersed and driven from their far distant homes after many days of wandering and suffering settled along the Teche and in the lovely Attakapas and Opelousas prairies. Poets have sung their praises, immortalized their noble traits of character; and their history is a heritage precious to everyone in whose veins courses the Creole blood. In old Acadia, if not distinguished by proficiency in the arts and sciences, our ancestors were noted for their kind disposition, their frugality, justice, their proverbial honesty and their strict observance of the laws of God and man; and besides being possessed of these virtues, they were a happy and contented people. Having accepted the name of that distant land, by which it was known to Evangeline and her companions, see that by a strict performance of the sacred duties now devolving upon you as the first grand jurors of this new parish you give to your fellowmen proof conclusive that law and order shall reign supreme throughout Acadia."[33]

---

[33] *Opelousas Courier*, Sept. 24, 1887

CHAPTER XVII

Acadia 1888 - 1900

Acadia's adolescent years — 1888 to 1900 — were paralleled by a similar period of burgeoning growth in the rice industry. For both the parish and the industry these were years of experimentation, uncertainty and disappointment on the one hand, and the confidence and courage to meet the challenge on the other.

The Courthouse

The first order of business for the new parish was the construction of a government building. Pleasant weather during the fall of 1887 facilitated work on the courthouse; by mid-October the foundation had been laid.[1]

Dimensions of the two-story structure were 42 by 56 feet, with wings on the east and west measuring 16 by 20 feet. The building, with brick walls and stone cement finish, had a mansard type slate roof. A bell tower, about 80 feet above the foundation, was surmounted by a brass spire.

The entrance, on the south side, gave into a wide hallway that extended the length of the building. On the right, the sheriff's department occupied the room on the southeast front. Across the hallway was the tax collector's office. Next to the sheriff's department was the police jury room, which was also used by the school board and grand jury. Across the hall was the assessor's office which connected with the tax collectors's office. The clerk of court's office, on the north end of the east side, extended into the right wing, and opposite was the recorder's office, extending into the west wing. The recorder's office was equipped with a fireproof vault.

Occupying the various offices were E. W. Lyons, sheriff; John G. Sloane, deputy sheriff; Martin J. Andrus, tax collector; D. B. Lyons, assessor and recorder; W. C. Logue, deputy assessor; R. T. Clark, clerk of court.

The second floor was reserved for the courtroom, the judge's chambers and the jury room. The courtroom ceiling, of hard pine finished with oil and varnish, was described as "very handsome." The parish jail occupied the northwest corner of the square. The jail was of brick and iron,

---

[1] *Opelousas Courier*, Oct. 15, 1887

The first Acadia Parish courthouse. Completed June 30, 1888, it was in use until May 1, 1902, when it was torn down to make way for the second building. (Freeland Archives photo)

Courtroom scene in the first Acadia Parish courthouse, about 1894. Hampden Story is at the judge's bench at far left; seated at left is Sheriff Eldridge W. Lyons. Standing with book in hand is Attorney Philip J. Chappuis, and at right, standing, is Charles L. Crippen. (Freeland Archives photo)

30 by 30 by 20 feet high, and contained four rooms and a corridor. One of the rooms was a security cell.

The courthouse square, which measured 250 by 250 feet, was planted with oak trees. A water well was sunk on the square and later a cistern was put up. The building was formally accepted by the police jury on July 23, 1888.[2]

The Editor's Feud

The feuding between the editors of the two parish newspapers was continued after the Signal was moved to Crowley. Duson had been no match for the invective heaped upon him by Chevis of the Sentinel; after the paper was moved to Crowley he acquired a partner in the business — A. R. Burkdoll, an experienced newspaperman from Minnesota — who could take care of himself very well in any battle of words. In the earliest issues of the Crowley Signal may be found innuendos and unflattering references to Chevis and the Acadia Sentinel; barbs and brickbats were flung over all public issues, especially politics.

The newspaper battle reached an explosive point during the spring and summer of 1889, when Governor Nicholls appointed Chevis assessor of Acadia Parish. On the heels of this the Acadia Parish Police Jury, on motion of Homer Barousse, appropriated $50 a year for the public printing and named both the Crowley Signal and the Acadia Sentinel as official organs.

Burkdoll castigated Governor Nicholls for his action, charging that the governor had ignored a petition, signed by a majority of the parish voters, which asked that D. B. Lyons be re-appointed assessor. Then he turned his verbal guns on Homer Barousse, whom he blamed for the police jury action.

The Acadia Sentinel evidently returned the abuse. Burkdoll wrote that the Rayne paper had published "a cowardly assault which is far beneath a gentleman's notice and is unworthy of even the vomiting curs who insult the good people of this community," then maintained that he had been personally attacked by the Rayne paper which had labeled him "a disreputable carpetbagger" and "a nondescript Republican."[3]

Burkdoll's reply to Chevis literally flung the gauntlet: "For some unaccountable reason these disreputable scalawags can find more time to devote to abusing us than they can to paying their honest debts and ful-

2 Summary, *Crowley Signal,* June 30, July 21, 28, 1888
3 Summary, *Crowley Signal,* Jan. 12, 26; April 13, June 29, 1889

CROWLEY SIGNAL.

Official Journal of the Parish of Acadia.

DUSON & BURKDOLL, Proprietors.

Subscription Price, $1.50 per Year.

SATURDAY, JULY 6, 1889.

Clubbing Rates.

We have made arrangements by which we are enabled to club the "SIGNAL" with either of the following newspapers, for one year at the price mentioned:

Wilke Collins, the noted novelist, is reported to be dying.

Thos. Ewing Sherman, eldest son of Gen. Sherman, is soon to be ordained a Catholic priest.

Baton Rouge, according to the Advocate is at present enjoying an unhealthy moral atmosphere, caused by the influx of a large number of vagrants, both black and white.

Mr. B. K. Whitefield, owner of the Acadia Nurseries in Lafayette parish, besides a large amount of other nursery stock now has 800 LeCompte pear trees and 500 Kelsey plum trees.

Gen. Wm. Pierce, superintendent of the public works department of New Orleans, committed suicide in the barroom attached to the Con-

THAT RETRACTION.

In last week's SIGNAL there appeared an article in which very strong language was used, perhaps much stronger than should appear in a respectable paper. This article, W. C. Chevis took exceptions to, and demanded a retraction. That in case of a denial of his request he called the writer to personal account and to meet him in a duel. This demand and challenge was brought to me by E. L. Wells, THE NEPHEW OF OUR DISTRICT JUDGE. It came four days after the article had appeared in print. It seemed to show premeditation. In an instant the situation was revealed to me, and the question was: shall I fight the Governor, the Governor's son-in-law, the Governor's appointee and the judiciary of this district? Beside this our own sheriff is a first cousin of Chevis, although one of the most honorable and warm-hearted gentlemen I have met in the South; yet kinship has its strong ties. Where in any case was I to look for well-tempered justice? In case that I should slay my adversary what kind of jury would my life be with? This trouble has grown out of a political matter and I would be tried by a Democratic jury which, although composed of good Southern men, all must admit, would not be partial to a Northern Republican. I therefore declined to sacrifice my life into the hands of enemies. I think that I am amply and fully justified.

Burkdoll's answer in part to W. C. Chevis' challenge to a duel in 1889.

filling the duties of their office. We have information which we feel it our duty to publish, showing the libelous skunks to the people in their true character. It has been our most honest endeavor to shun this personal fight, and the press of the State and the good people of this parish can bear witness to the fact. But there is a time when silence and forbearance cease to be virtues, even though your assailant would corrupt the worst qualities of a mongrel puppy. A self-confessed criminal and a picayune ingrate! A pretty brace of moralists. What is lying and libeling to them but a merry pasttime enjoyed with about the same degree of venal rapacity that impels the lowest order of animals to root among their own filth and enjoy its stench."[4]

Chevis answered with a demand for a retraction or a challenge to a duel. Burkdoll refused to make the retraction, or to meet Chevis in a duel.[5] An item in the Crowley Signal of August 10, 1889 wrote "thirty" to this particular phase of the feud: "A. R. Burkdoll and wife and little son Guy left for the north during the week."

The Election of 1888

Published accounts of the 1888 political campaign reveal some interesting developments in the Acadia Parish political picture. Two state senators for the district composed of Acadia and St. Landry were to be elected; the Democratic nominees were John Crawford Lyons of Acadia and Willis Prescott of St. Landry. Sheriff Duson, nearing the end of his 14th year as sheriff of St. Landry, and Louis Stagg of St. Landry announced as independent candidates. A controversy arose between Duson and Lyons, during which Duson charged that Lyons had been bribed to support the movement to get the parish seat of St. Landry moved to Washington, a charge which Lyons denied.

Prescott and Duson won the two senate seats. Returns of the April 17 election showed Prescott high man in the senate race, with 5,350 votes; Duson was in second place, with 4,452 votes, nine votes over Stagg. Lyons' name does not appear in the election returns, which were published in newspapers of the two parishes; the conjecture is that Lyons had withdrawn from the race and thrown his support to Prescott, his Democratic running mate.

Duson's slim margin over Stagg brought on another election contest, during the course of which Duson was accused of misappropriation of

---

4 *Crowley Signal,* June 29, 1889
5 *Crowley Signal,* July 6, 1889

funds in the sheriff's department. The state auditor issued Duson's quietus, which cleared him of these charges. The controversy over the election was resolved on June 8, 1888, when Stagg's claims were rejected by the Senate committee, which then recommended that Duson's seat in the senate be confirmed.[6]

Acadia Parish did not support Duson in his bid for the senate seat. He carried but three of the 13 parish precincts.[7] The parish was strongly

[6] Summary, *Crowley Signal,* April 21 through June 16, 1888; *Opelousas Courier,* April 14, 21, 1888
[7] *Crowley Signal,* April 21, 1888

A tabular statement of the votes cast in Acadia Parish April 17, 1888, in the handwriting of Newton Lyons. C. C. Duson, candidate for the state senate for the district composed of Acadia and St. Landry Parishes, was defeated in Acadia Parish but won the seat by the St. Landry vote. (Freeland Archives photo)

Democratic, and Duson's candidacy had been endorsed by the hated Republicans. This could have accounted for his loss of votes in the parish which owed its creation largely to his efforts. According to the Crowley Signal of April 21, 1888, "a combined fight against C. C. Duson was made by Rayne, Church Point, Prudhomme City and Pointe-aux-Loups . . . these places polled a solid vote of nearly eight hundred against him." Voting totals showed Duson with 658 votes in Acadia, 3,794 in St. Landry.

A close relative of the Dusons was defeated in the election. James Webb ran for state representative, was defeated by J. D. Bernard of Rayne by a majority of 322 votes. Webb's defeat brought some strongly worded criticism from the Crowley Signal; "The defeat of the Hon. James Webb is nothing short of a public calamity." It was, the editor added, "blindest folly for citizens of this parish to elect J. D. Bernard . . . a man wholly incapable and unfit . . . "[8]

In the race for parish officers the incumbent sheriff, E. W. Lyons, was victorious over Homer David by a majority of 325 votes; the incumbent clerk of court, R. T. Clark won over Thomas Bowden by 260. In the coroner's race the two candidates were G. E. Brooks and F. N. Condon; Dr. Brooks won by a majority of 106.

There were few changes in the list of justices of the peace and constables. The following were elected:

Ward 1, Rayne: E. O. Bruner, Joseph Falcon, justice of peace; A. V. Lyons, M. Arceneaux, constables.

Ward 2, Plaquemine Brulee, Westley F. Stakes, justice; Milton F. Laughlin, constable.

Ward 3, Church Point, H. D. McBride, justice; Ernest J. Daigle, constable.

Ward 4, Pointe-aux-Loups, Sevigne Cart, Samuel Cart.

Ward 5, Mermentau, Andrew Henry, John Duhon.

Ward 6, Prudhomme City, J. Wesley Young, S. M. Hundley.

Ward 7, Crowley, Alex C. Lormand and J. L. Atkinson, justices of the peace; Louis Mires, Alex Richard, constables.

Ward 8, Castille (Coulee Croche) J. W. Spears, Gerasin Meche.

District Judge E. T. Lewis and District Attorney John N. Ogden were unopposed in the election.

At this time Acadia Parish had 2,308 registered voters; of this number, 1,926 were of native birth, 382 of foreign birth. White voters

8 April 21, 1888

305

totaled 2,006, and colored, 302. The number of white voters who could write their names was given as 851; those who marked their ballots with an "x" totaled 1,155. Colored voters who could write, 87; colored who made marks, 215.[9]

Churches 1886 - 1900

Ten church buildings were erected in Acadia Parish between 1886 and 1900. With the seven churches already established, this gave the parish a total of 17 houses of worship.

---

[9] *Crowley Signal,* Apr. 21, 1888

The first church to be built in Crowley was the Methodist Episcopal Church South, erected in 1889. The church was built on land given by W. W. Duson.

Church buildings in existence when the parish was established were the Catholic churches of Church Point, Rayne and Pointe-aux-Loups; Methodist churches in Plaquemine Brulee and Rayne; Pilgrim's Rest Baptist in Prairie Hayes, and Maryland Chapel, C.M.E., of Plaquemine Brulee. (The Catholic church of Mermentau, built about 1882, was destroyed by fire in 1886)

Edifices constructed between 1886 and 1900 were the Methodist Episcopal Church, South, the Central Methodist, Baptist, Presbyterian, Episcopal, Catholic, Morning Star Baptist and Lutheran churches of Crowley; Methodist churches at Ebenezer and Church Point, and the Catholic church of Robert's Cove.

St. Michael's Catholic Church of Crowley, built in 1892. The land for the church was donated by W. W. Duson. (Reproduced from the Crowley Signal, Oct. 27, 1894).

Crowley's first church was the Methodist Episcopal Church South. Methodist services were held in the village as early as the spring of 1887;[10] the congregation was formally organized May 30, 1887 by Rev. H. O. White, pastor in charge of the churches of Rayne and Plaquemine Brulee.[11] A one-room school house, erected by W. W. Duson and R. T. Clark, was used for Methodist services (and also by other early church groups) until a church building could be built. Construction on the Methodist church was begun October 8, 1888 on land donated by W. W. Duson. The dimensions of the edifice were 36 by 60 by 20, and the plans called for a 70-foot spire.[12] The church was completed in the spring of 1889, the spire placed in position and the bell hung. During the last week of April services went on both day and night in the new church.[13]

[10] *Acadia Sentinel,* May 14, 1887
[11] *Ibid,* June 5, 1887
[12] *Crowley Signal,* Oct. 13, 1888
[13] *Crowley Signal,* Mar. 2, Apr. 13, May 4, 1889

Settlers from the north erected this church building for the Crowley congregation of the Methodist Episcopal Church, later known as the Central Methodist Church. (Reproduced from the Crowley Signal, Oct. 27, 1894)

A Baptist congregation was organized February 10, 1889 by Rev. T. B. Harrell. Plans to build a church on Avenue G between Fourth and Fifth streets were announced the following month.[14]

A second Methodist church, the Methodist Episcopal Church North, later known as the Central Methodist Church, was organized in 1889. A church was built in 1892.[15]

The Lutheran church, first established in the parish by Rev. H. Gellert, was organized in Crowley August 27, 1894 under Rev. F. W. Siebelitz. A church building was erected that same year, on land given by W. W. Duson.[16]

First services for members of the Episcopal faith were conducted in Crowley May 28, 1893, by Rev. William Hart, rector of the New Iberia church. The contract to build the first church was let February 1, 1900. The building was erected on lots on the courthouse square, on land given by George K. Bradford and W. W. Duson.[17]

Presbyterian ministers from Opelousas and Lake Charles held services in Crowley at intervals during 1887 and 1888. The church was formally organized August 3, 1890 by Rev. George Fraser, D. D., at the time pastor of the church in Lake Charles. Two years later Dr. Fraser moved to Crowley. Early services were held in the school house, in the chapel of Acadia College, and in the Methodist and Baptist churches. The first church, a frame building completed in 1894, served the congregation until 1929, when the present church was completed. Land for the church was purchased from Pat Crowley, the man for whom the town was named.[18]

Catholics of the Crowley area, like those of Rayne, Church Point, Iota and Mermentau, were served by Jesuit missionaries during the early years. The first Catholic chapel in Crowley, a frame building erected in 1892, was located in Block 131, between Avenues H and I, and Eighth and Ninth streets.[19] At the time the Crowley church was a mission of St. Joseph's Church of Pointe-aux-Loups (Iota), under the pastorate of Rev.

14 *Crowley Signal*, Mar. 2, 1889
15 Research by Rev. Paul B. Freeland, D. D.
16 *Crowley Daily Signal*, Aug. 25, 1954
17 *Crowley Daily Signal* 50th Anniv. Ed., 27
18 Freeland: *First Presbyterian Church of Crowley, Louisiana, A Brief History, 1890 to 1965*, 1-5
19 Oral history, 1975, Henry Duson

F. L. Gassler.[20] The church, named for St. Michael the Archangel, was consecrated on St. Michael's Day, September 29, 1895. Several members of the Catholic clergy attended the consecration rites, performed only when a church is free of debt. The steeple of the church had been re-built to accommodate a new thousand-pound bell, which was christened during the ceremonies. P. J. Chappuis of Crowley and Miss Mary Duggan of Pointe-aux-Loups served as sponsors for the bell. The choir was directed by Mrs. L. V. Fremaux.[21] Rev. W. F. Geens was first resident pastor, assigned in 1897.[22]

20 *Crowley Daily Signal* 50th Anniv. Ed. 7
21 *Crowley Signal,* Sept. 21, Oct. 19, 1895
22 *Crowley Daily Signal,* 50th Anniv. Ed., 7

Completed in 1894, this church served the Presbyterians of Crowley for 35 years, until it was replaced in 1929 by the present (1976) edifice. Land for the church was purchased from Pat Crowley, the man for whom the city was named. (Freeland Archives photo)

Morning Star Baptist Church was the first church for black people in Crowley. First efforts to organize a church was in August of 1889 when the colored people of Crowley and vicinity held a meeting in the grove south of town to plan for the building of a church. The meeting was well attended, and the sum of $29.35 collected for the building fund.[23] In 1892 W. W. Duson gave two lots to the church, and the recordation was done without charge by Gus E. Fontenot and R. T. Clark.[24] Appointed to accept the deed were Jarrett Perkins, Joseph Johnson and Albert Wilkerson, trustees of the church.[25] In May of 1894 colored preachers of the seventh district held a quarterly convention at Morning Star Baptist Church of Crowley.[26]

23 *Crowley Signal,* Aug. 24, 1889
24 *Ibid,* Dec. 3, 1892
25 Conveyance Book H, 754, Acadia Parish
26 *Crowley Signal,* May 19, 1894

Public school building in Crowley, reproduced from the Crowley Signal, Oct. 27, 1894. Several private schools were also operated in Crowley during the early years of the town.

Other than Maryland Chapel and Morning Star Baptist Church, there is no documented information concerning the building of churches for black people during this period.

Schools

Lack of funds hampered efforts to provide public education during the early years of the parish. Insufficient funds forced cancellation of the school board's plans to open 15 schools in the fall of 1887; the opening of parish schools was postponed until January of 1888.[27]

In April of 1888 representatives of the school board appeared before the police jury to ask for funds with which to operate the parish schools. The school board members reported that there were 3,200 educable youths, ages 6 to 18, in the parish. Acadia, they said, "had one township in sight of the parish seat with 94% illiteracy among the native population, and not one colored person living in the township."[28] Later that year the

[27] *Opelousas Courier,* Oct. 15, 1887
[28] *Crowley Signal,* Apr. 14, 1888

The Gum Point school building, from a photograph taken by Prof. J. H. Lewis about 1908. The hand-pumped water well, the outside privy and the teacher's horse and buggy were necessary adjuncts to the school house. (Freeland Archives photo)

school board reminded the police jury that 1½ mills of the 10 mill tax levied for 1889 should be put aside for schools, as provided by law.[29] In 1889 the Crowley Town Council levied a tax on dogs within the corporate limits of the town; dog owners paid $1 per dog, the tax earmarked for the school fund.[30]

The Crowley Signal of October 27, 1888 published a report on parish schools and listed the names of the teachers:

Ward 1 schools and teachers were: Crowley, teacher not yet assigned (R. H. Bagby was hired later, according to the Signal of November 3, 1888); Rayne, Miss Frances T. Greig; Perry Point, Miss Mildred Jester; Hoffpauir, William Shepherd; Rayne colored school, Mrs. Clara P. Thornton. There were 989 pupils in Ward 1.

Ward 2: Castille, Miss Susie E. Wilson; Stakes, Miss Minnie Williams; Sloane's, P. Leyden; Plaquemine Brûlée, J. Tomlinson; Long Point, O. Hayes; Daigle's, teacher wanted. Ward 2 pupils numbered 475. (Listed

---

[29] *Crowley Signal,* Oct. 13, 1888
[30] *Cdowley Signal,* July 6, 1889

Eighteen pupil and the teacher posed for this photograph of the Mc-Cain school, taken by Prof. J. H. Lewis. Prof. Lewis, third superintendent of schools for Acadia Parish, used the pictures in his crusade for better schools in the early 1900s. (Freeland Archives photo)

among the schools in Ward 2 was "Coulee Croche, St. Landry, ½ school." Since the land area known as Coulee Croche was divided by the boundary line between Acadia and St. Landry, the two parishes probably shared the cost of maintaining the school)

Ward 3: Prudhomme City, Bert W. Read; Church Point, Mrs. J. G. Brooks; Light and Tie, W. M. Hoyt; Fabacher, Joseph Kopp; Schamber, teacher wanted; new school wanted in Township 7, Range 1 East; 899 children in ward.

Ward 4: Evangeline, Milo Hunt; Millerville, W. J. Randolph; Cartville, teacher wanted; McCain's, Avery C. Wilkins; 391 children in ward.

Ward 5: Mermentau, G. D. Farrar; no teachers at Estherwood and Sensat; teacher also wanted for Cotswell or Webb's Cove; 446 children in ward.

Sessions for the 18½ schools in the parish began November 5 and closed December 31. The spring sessions, for two to four months, were set up at the January meetings of the school board.[31]

---

[31] *Crowley Signal*, Oct. 13, 1888; Jan. 12, 1889

An unidentified early school building, believed to have been the Freeland school in Prairie Hayes. The picture is one of the snapshots taken about 1908 by Prof. J. H. Lewis. (Freeland Archives photo)

By 1890 there were 25 public schools operating in Acadia Parish, with 31 teachers instructing 836 pupils. There were two private schools, Acadia College in Crowley, and one in Church Point, with a combined attendance of 140.[32] By the end of the decade three Catholic schools had been established in Acadia: in Rayne and Church Point in 1891, and in Crowley in 1900.[33]

The five-member school board was increased to nine members in September of 1888. Board members named were William Sarver, Jean Castille, James A. Williams, Samuel Cart, H. C. Wilkins, W. F. Brooks, L. V. Fremaux, J. Westley Young and D. W. Hoyt. Fremaux was elected president.[34] D. W. Hoyt was the first superintendent of schools for Acadia Parish. Hoyt died January 1, 1889; he was succeeded by James Edward Barry.

Names of other early teachers occur in news of the various communities of the parish. Some may have been teachers at private schools. Names of persons identified as teachers include Miss Ella Crippen, W. F. Hebert, William Woods, A. A. Murff, S. A. Davis, W. F. Humphreys, Miss Minerva Humphreys.[35]

The first public sale of school lands in Acadia Parish took place in November of 1888. School section 16 north of Crowley was sold to nine persons for a total of $1,330.70[36]

Newspapers 1886 - 1900

The Rayne Signal, the first newspaper in Acadia Parish, was established by C. W. Felter and George C. Addison and began publication March 13, 1886 in Rayne. The newspaper was purchased by W. W. Duson September 1, 1886. Publication of the paper in Rayne was continued until January of 1888, when Duson moved the newspaper and printing plant to Crowley and sold a half interest in the business to A. R. Burkdoll. Duson bought out Burkdoll in 1889 and continued the publication until June of 1896 when he sold the newspaper to L. S. Scott.

The Acadia Sentinel, established by George K. Bradford, began publication September 11, 1886 in Rayne. Later W. C. Chevis was taken in as associate editor. Publication was continued by Bradford and Chevis

---

32 *Crowley Signal*, Feb. 1, 1890
33 Baudier: *The Catholic Church in Louisiana*, 549, 487; OHLS booklet, 73
34 *Crowley Signal*, Sept. 8, 1888
35 *Ibid*, Mar. 3, 1888 to Feb. 1, 1890
36 *Ibid*, Nov. 17, 1888

until February, 1890, when the newspaper was purchased by Oscar L. Alpha, former editor of the St. Mary Herald.[37]

Several references occur in the Crowley Signal files concerning a newspaper being published in Church Point in 1894 and 1895. The name of the publication was either the Church Point Advocate or the Acadia Advocate.[38] T. C. Lewis was listed as the proprietor, and according to the Signal, Homer Barousse provided the financial backing. The conjecture is that the establishment of the paper was an outgrowth of the continuing political battle between Barousse and the Dusons; in 1894 Barousse was opposed by Gus Fontenot, brother-in-law of the Dusons, in his bid for the seat in the Louisiana Senate. A brief mention in the Signal of February 2, 1895 indicated that the Church Point newspaper had ceased publication. However, on May 4 of that year the Acadia Advocate was again mentioned.

Two or more newspapers were published in Rayne during the mid-1890s. The Crowley Signal of May 5, 1894 retorted to an article, or editorial, which had been published in the Rayne Ranger. The opinion published in the Rayne paper was, according to the Signal editor, "no more than the bray of an ass." Later that year, on October 13, the Signal reported that the first copy of the Rayne Herald had been issued; the paper, described as "a neat four-column folio" was edited and published by A. Lepeyre. The same issue of the Signal noted that R. N. May, formerly with the Chicago Tribune, had taken over the managership of the Rayne Tribune. In the Signal of December 8, 1894 mention was made that R. E. Cunningham was the proprietor of the Rayne Ranger.

A disastrous fire in Rayne's business district on February 7, 1895 caused a loss estimated at $30,000. Among the build'ngs destroyed was a two-story structure owned by P. F. Besse, the second flor of which was occupied by "the Ranger printing plant, used in the publication of the Rayne Herald."[40]

The Signal of October 5, 1895 reported that the Rayne News, edited by Besse and Cunningham, had begun publication September 28. Six weeks later, in the issue of November 16, a brief item stated that "the Rayne News died of heart failure."

---

[37] Crowley Signal, Feb. 15, 1890
[38] Ibid, Apr. 21, 1894; May 4, 1895
[39] Ibid, Dec. 23, 1893
[40] Crowley Signal, Feb. 9, 1895

The Crowley Signal also had local competition. The newspaper plant of the Creole American, published by M. L. Goolsby, moved from Lafayette to Crowley in 1895.[41] After some nine months of publication the Creole American was sold by Goolsby to M. J. Andrus, A. C. Lormand and P. S. Pugh of Crowley.[42]

Approximately one year later the Crowley Signal and the Creole American were merged. The Signal of July 3, 1897 under its own masthead showed "The Creole American Vol. II, No. 48."

At an undetermined time, presumably between July, 1897 and March, 1899, another newspaper began publication in Crowley. In the issue of March 11, 1899 the Signal announced that J. M. Taylor, formerly employed by the Signal, had accepted a position with the Crowley Mirror.

Banks

Acadia's first bank, the Crowley State Bank, was established in 1892 by P. S. Lovell and W. E. Ellis. Two years later, in 1894, Rayne State Bank was founded, and in 1898 Crowley's second banking institution, the Acadia Bank, was organized.[43]

Crime

The most sensational crime of Acadia's first decade was the murder of a peace officer. On New Year's Eve, 1894, Deputy Sheriff Americus Vespucius Lyons was fatally shot. Sylvestre Abshire of Vermilion Parish was arrested and charged with the crime. Abshire was convicted and sentenced to be hung on May 24, 1895. Four days before the execution was to take place Governor Murphy Foster granted Abshire a reprieve. The convicted man was given two additional reprieves, finally had his sentence commuted to life imprisonment.[44]

Ethnic Groups

Names that made news in the Crowley Signal were, for the most part, the names of northern settlers and/or the people of Anglo-Saxon ancestry. The Acadians and the black people figured little in the news; but these native inhabitants were there, and were multiplying. Their names may be found in final proofs of homestead claims, jury venires, listings of unclaimed letters, marriage licenses issued, delinquent tax lists and the like.

---

41 *Ibid,* Nov. 9, 1895

42 *Ibid,* July 25, 1896

43 *Crowley Daily Signal,* Oct. 4, 1937, Crowley sec., 4; *Crowley Signal,* July 28, 1894; Dec. 3, 1898

44 Summary, *Crowley Signal,* Jan. 5, 1895 to February, 1897

In a population summary published in the August 25, 1888 issue* the Signal writer stated: "The population is almost entirely of the Caucasian race. There are some Negroes in the eastern portion of the parish, but they are at no place numerous . . . less than ten percent are colored and these are almost exclusively along the extreme eastern boundary. They are generally a well behaved class of people, having their own schools and

* The Immigration Number

The "hanging" of Sylvestre Abshire. Convicted of murdering Marshal A. V. Lyons, Abshire was sentenced to be hung on May 24, 1895. Large crowds were expected. Crowley's enterprising photographer, E. K. Sturdevant, prepared this card for sale showing a photo of Abshire and the scaffold set up in the yard of the parish jail. The hanging never took place. (Freeland Archives photo)

churches. Of the white population, a very large number are French speaking people but are fast becoming acquainted with the English language."

A tribute to the French-speaking population is found in the same issue, in a letter to the editor signed "An Old Settler." The letter writer placed "the native Creole" at the top of his list of best people: "I place them first although lacking in educational facilities in the past which have been meagre, they have not forgotten their fellow man. In sickness better neighbors cannot be found. In distress, appeal to them and you get relief; and it matters not who you be, if honest and upright, the hand of friendship is cheerfully extended . . . because they have hearts, and although they cannot read books they know full well how to read men's souls."

The rapidly expanding rice industry brought black families into the Crowley area in the 1890s. Here a family travels atop a cart loaded with sacks of rice while a youngster rides one of the three horses hitched ahead of a yoke of oxen. (Freeland Archives photo)

319

In the "Prosperity Number" of 1898 the Signal writer compared the prosperous condition of the parish with what it had been 20 years before, using the Acadian people as examples of unprogressiveness, citing their lack of enterprise in order to play up the prosperity wrought by the settlers from northern states. In so doing the writer gives a contemporary, but somewhat exaggerated, picture of the life style of the Acadians after the Civil War:

> In the days gone by, before progress found its way into this portion of the state, it was inhabited almost solely by a simple folk known as the Acadians. The history of this people has been so often told that any repetition here is unnecessary. Suffice it to say that they are descendants from that

Typical Acadian farm house, Acadia Parish, 1892. The mud chimney, if it caught fire, could be pushed away from the house. The mother is hulling rice with a mortar and pestle. (Freeland Archives photo)

portion of the seven thousand persons, whom the English carried off from Nova Scotia in 1755, that was scattered along the coast of Louisiana. Here they lived for a century and a quarter, entirely cut off from the rest of the world and hearing only the faintest echoes of outside happenings. They built the same houses, used the same implements, and pursued the same manner of life that their fathers and grandfathers and great grandfathers had before them. So it was that, until the recent settlement of these prairie regions of Southwest Louisiana by English-speaking people, this folk had made absolutely no advancement over their ancestors of Nova Scotia.

The Acadians had their homes in the strips of timber that grow on the banks of the rivers and bayous. They believed that if a man moved out into the open prairie he would starve, and all these vast tracts that are now making fortunes for their owners, in fact the very land on which Crowley now stands, was regarded as worthless and would hardly have been taken as a gift. In consequence one could travel for miles across the prairies and not see a house or a fence, much less a human being. In fact the only thing to be met with suggestive of man's existence were the herds of roving cattle that fed on the rich prairie grass, and constituted the chief wealth of the people.

The houses were of as simple a style as can well be conceived, and every one was practically an exact likeness of every other. They were all but a single story high and generally about fifteen by twenty-five feet in dimension, with a gallery in front. Window glass was of course unknown, and the little square openings, which served the purpose of windows, were fitted with a rough wooden shutter which could be closed at night and in bad weather. The house was divided into two rooms, in one of which was a fire-place opening into the big mud chimney built beside the house without, and these two rooms served all the purposes of the largest family.

But if the houses were primitive, the manner of dress was not less so. The cloth was homespun and all the clothing was made at home, and, as may be readily judged, the fit and style were not all that a tailor or modiste of a more pretentious people could desire. Everybody went barefooted, year in and year out, except on state occasions. As would be expected, the fare of an Acadian family had little variety. It was limited to cornbread, meat, milk and vegetables in season. Wheat flour was almost an unknown luxury. Everything that was eaten was raised at home on the little patch of three or four acres that constituted the usual farm. All that the ordinary Acadian cared for was to live, and he was content to live in the simplest way. Consequently a few acres were all he cultivated, and these were tilled only in the poorest manner. The farmer broke his ground with a little six-inch plow, drawn by a yoke of oxen, and planted the little corn necessary for meal, the little cotton necessary for clothing, and the invariable patch of sweet potatoes. To say the least his method was anything but scientific farming; his plowing was but scratching, and he had never heard of the theories of fertilizing and crop rotation. Even had these people had the desire to farm on a large scale, and had they possessed modern implements, it would have been practically impossible since everything would have had to be hauled a distance of thirty to forty miles across the pathless prairie to a shipping point.

Harder for the average American to bear than the hardships of this simple life, would be the entire absence of all schools and churches. The idea of having a school probably never entered the head of the ordinary Acadian. But few could read or write, and little need of an education was felt. The nearest church twenty years ago was at Grand Coteau, forty miles away. Once or twice a year a priest from there would travel through the country and say mass at a private house in each neighborhood, for the people were nearly all Catholics, and perform all the religious ceremonies of the Catholic faith.

The foregoing has all been written in the past tense; what has been said of the country is no longer true, but a large part of what has been said of the people is unchanged. As a whole they are the same simple people, following the same simple fashion of life, although they have been almost crowded out of sight by a new and different population. However, they are beginning to change, to take on the ways of the new settlers, and the old people and their customs are rapidly passing.

Such, in brief, is a sketch of this country as it was twenty years ago, and even as it was at the time Acadia Parish was created and the idea conceived of building a town where Crowley now stands. Vacant prairies, no schools, no churches, no advancement over the condition of a century ago, a people simple, ignorant, unprogressive, living in a manner that was primitive even in the days of their grandfathers — these sum up the country as it was at that time. And had not a new people come with new spirit and new ways, a hundred years hence would doubtless find them just where a hundred years ago left them.

The Signal provides other evidence that the Acadian population resisted change. In the issue of September 1, 1888 the newspaper published a letter from Prairie Mammouth, signed "Beulah," which gave a northern woman's viewpoint of living in Acadia Parish. The letter read, in part: "The other element of Southern society, the Acadians, we have found a very inoffensive, simple and rather timid people. They need much civilizing and christianizing. Ignorant to an extent almost incomprehensible to a person from the section of free public schools, they are fully a century behind the times, and it will require years of patient toil and continued intercourse to awaken them to the realization of their condition, and the benefits to be derived from an education and more industrious habits. They are very conservative and cling to their old habits, especially the older people. The younger ones, women in particular, can see the superiority of a modern cook stove over their mud fireplaces, and wherever they can do so are using stoves in their kitchens."

Acadian farmstead in Acadia Parish, 1892. Many such homes and out-buildings on small farms were once scattered over the parish, each practically self sufficient. At right is a "moulin à gru," or grist mill, power-ed by a horse. (Freeland Archives photo)

The woman writer was of the opinion that the black people of the area were more interested in improvement and education than the Acadians. Her letter also indicated that French was the language spoken by the blacks: "The negroes are here of course, but in our section of the state we see but few of them and do not come in contact with them at all, any more than we did in Iowa. They do not care to mingle with the whites on terms of equality, but are more earnest and energetic about improving and educating themselves than the Acadians. They seem to learn the English language more readily, and use it more properly than the white people who speak French."

The serious racial problems that surfaced in south Louisiana in 1889 apparently did not spread to Acadia Parish. As a result of the "white supremacy" movement groups of whites banded together, identified themselves as "Regulators," and proceeded to terrorize black people who attempted to exercise their right to vote. Sheriff Lyons of Acadia was asked to bring a posse to Lafayette to help quell a race riot in May of 1889, "but court was in session and there were no trains," the Signal reported. Editor Burkdoll of the Signal published some scathing editorials directed against the Regulators and so-called "white caps;" he deplored the violence which took place in St. Landry, Lafayette and Vermilion Parishes.[45]

The Crowley newspaper, under Burkdoll and Duson, for the most part showed a sympathetic attitude toward black people. This attitude changed in later years, particularly under the editorship of L. S. Scott. The general treatment of news involving black people showed scorn and contempt for the race; fillers were Negro dialect jokes, usually pointless, which pointed up traits of shiftlessness, ignorance and superstition.

Acadia Parish owes a large debt of gratitude to a third ethnic group— whose members can be counted among its pioneers—the Jewish people. These include three Opelousas residents who were stockholders in the Southwest Louisiana Land Company, Alphonse Levy, Joseph Bloch and Julius Meyers; Crowley's early merchants, Daniel Blum, Joseph Blum, Jacob Frankel, Abrom Kaplan, Jefferson Davis Marks, William Marks, Jacob Mayer and L. Sternberger, and Mervine Kahn of Rayne, who established a business there in 1884, two years before the parish was created.

Rice

Within the first decade of its existence Acadia Parish came into

---

prominence as an agricultural center, brought about by technical improvements in the irrigation, cultivation, harvesting and milling of rice.

The German farmers had already demonstrated that rice could be grown successfully on high land. Following their example the prairie farmers threw up levees to retain rain water for irrigation purposes. The levee system worked quite well in a wet season; during times of severe drought entire crops were lost.

The first break-through in irrigation came in 1888, when David Abbott and his sons devised a unique but simple method of irrigating their rice field. The Abbotts constructed a water conveyance system of buckets on a continuous log chain, powered by a small engine, to bring water from Bayou Plaquemine Brûlée to a 12-acre field. The experiment was successful. The following year the Abbotts invented a device known as the Abbott pump to raise water from a stream, thereby introducing an entirely new concept of raising rice by artificial irrigation.[46]

Dodd Jenkins, a farmer in the northern section of Prairie Hayes, invested in machinery for pumping water in the spring of 1889, conveying water from Bayou Mallet to his field by means of a small canal. However, Jenkins and another Prairie Hayes farmer, Etienne Stagg, had to close down their pumping operations at a critical time — in mid-July. Due to a prolonged drought, Bayou Mallet had gone dry.[47]

Two farmers in the Fabacher area of Prairie Faquetaique turned to artificial irrigation. John Frey and Joseph H. Fabacher pumped water on their rice from a large reservoir. Frey ran the machinery in the daytime, and Fabacher took over the night watch.[48]

During the summer of 1889 the Duson brothers installed a 30-horse power engine and boiler and a 12-inch irrigating and drainage pump on their farm north of Crowley. The water, from Bayou Plaquemine Brûlée, was raised some 25 feet by the pump, then conveyed by an aqueduct and canal to the field.[49]

By 1900 rice irrigation had become big business. Construction on two large irrigating canals, the Abbott canal and the Duson canal, was

[46] Summary, *Crowley Signal,* Nov. 3, 1888; Post: *"The Rice Country of Southwestern Louisiana,"* 583; Hair: *"The History of Crowley, La.,"* 41-42
[47] *Crowley Signal,* May 18, July 20, 1889
[48] *Ibid,* Aug. 31, 1889
[49] *Ibid,* June 6, July 27, Aug. 10, 1889

begun in 1894.[50] By 1899 six such canals were providing irrigation for more than 40,000 acres of rice lands. The canals not only furnished water for the canal owners, but for other farmers as well. The rice planter who had no canal of his own could buy water.[51]

The aqueducts, or flumes, which conducted the water pumped from the streams into the canals and thence to the fields, were constructed of cypress or pine and placed on elevated trestles which often reached a height of 30 feet.[52]

In addition to irrigating from the streams by means of pumps and canals, many rice farmers put down artesian wells. Among the pioneer well-diggers were John M. Ware and L. H. Thompson, who sank deep wells in 1895.[53] Winston Jones of Mobile, Alabama, who owned several thousand acres of the Thomas Coopwood lands in the northern sector of the parish, put down a number of wells in 1897.[54]

New implements, introduced by settlers from the north and mid-west, began to replace the more primitive methods of cultivation and harvesting. In 1888 31 rice harversters and binders were sold in Acadia Parish; the following year 60 were sold.[55] Farmers who purchased new farm implements made news in the Crowley paper: Andrew Henry of Mermentau was one of the first to move his steam threshing equipment around the parish and thresh for other planters; M. Scanlan and son P. J. of Prairie Hayes purchased two riding plows, an Acme harrow, a disk harrow and a rice planter in the spring of 1889; in the fall of that year Johnson Hanks of Mermentau and Homer J. Daigle of Prairie Hayes bought steam-powered threshing machines.[56] A demonstration of a new rice thresher and wind straw stacker took place on the J. H. Robinson farm near Crowley in the fall of 1894. The new machinery was hailed as an implement that would do away "with one of the hardest and most laborious jobs of the harvest." The thresher, with the wind straw stacker attached to it, "stacked straw without the assistance of any men on the stack, blowing dust and litter far out into the stack."[57]

---

50 *Crowley Signal,* July 14, Nov. 17, 1894
51 *Ibid,* Feb. 2, 1899
52 *Ibid,* Oct. 6, 1900
53 *Ibid,* Jan. 5, 1895
54 *Ibid,* Aug. 21, 1897
55 *Ibid,* Sept. 2, 1888; Sept.21, 1889
56 *Ibid,* Oct. 23, 1888; Apr. 13, 1889; Sept. 28, 1889
57 *Ibid,* Dec. 1, 1894

An 1896 report on the rice industry stated that there had been but one self-binder in Acadia Parish in 1884, and by 1895 the number had increased to 4,000, the immense increase attributed to the utilization of canal irrigation for upland prairie lands.[58]

Until the establishment of mills in the parish rice was shipped to New Orleans for milling and marketing The first rice to be milled in Acadia Parish was in July of 1888 at the newly constructed rice mill in Rayne.[59] By the end of 1897 four rice mills were operating in the parish: one at Rayne and three in Crowley, and a fifth was being built. These were the Acadia mill in Rayne; the Crowley, the Eagle, and the People's Independent mills in Crowley. The fifth was the Southwest Louisiana mill, under construction on Crowley's west side.[60] Another Crowley mill, the J. D. Marks mill, was built in 1898.[61] Two of the Crowley mills, the Southwest Louisiana and the Eagle mills, were destroyed by fire early in 1899.[62] Another Crowley mill, the American, was completed in the fall of 1899,[63] giving the parish a total of five operating mills by the end of the century.

Crowley's first rice mill was the Pickett mill, chartered March 1, 1893. A small two-story building had been erected by Squire A. Pickett and equipped with the necessary machinery, some of which was invented and patented by Pickett himself. The engine for this first mill served a double purpose: the 50-horsepower unit was used at a pumping station during the irrigation season, then moved to the mill in time for milling. The initial enterprise was not a success.[64]

The erection of rice storage warehouses was another step forward for the industry. Farmers who had access to storage facilities could hold their grain for better prices. The first storage warehouse was put by W. W. Duson in 1889; the building, 32 by 80 feet, was a two-story structure. The first consignment of rice, 121 sacks raised by Lemuel Hoffpauir, was brought to the warehouse late in September of 1889.[65]

There were three main shipping points for rice in Acadia Parish: Crowley, Rayne and Mermentau. Of the three, Crowley was shipping

58 *Ibid*, Jan. 25, 1896
59 *Ibid*, July 14, 1888
60 *Ibid*, Dec. 25, 1896
61 *Ibid*, Oct. 1, 1898
62 *Ibid*, Feb. 18, 1899
63 *Ibid*, Nov. 13, 1899
64 *Crowley Daily Signal*, Oct. 4, 1937, Industrial sec., 1, 4
65 *Crowley Signal*, Aug. 24, Sept. 28, 1889

about half of the total crop in 1892.[66] The rough rice was brought to the railroad shipping points in the early days by ox cart; these primitive vehicles were eventually supplanted by mule-drawn wagons. A great deal of the rice grown in the Mamou and Faquetaique prairie areas was transported by barges and tugboats down the Nezpique to Mermentau. The most noted of the tugboats was the "Little Susie" which hauled rice and other products for many years beginning in 1888.[67]

A comparison of shipping statistics shows the tremendous increase in rice production from 1888 to 1892. In 1888 the total number of sacks shipped from Acadia Parish was 26,195; this total had almost trebled by 1889, and by 1890 the figure had reached 118,139 sacks. An increase of almost 100,000 sacks over the previous year was recorded in 1891; in 1892 the total amount shipped stood at 489,464 sacks, almost 20 times the amount shipped in 1888.[68]

This spiraling success of the rice industry in Acadia Parish was' not achieved without some set-backs and failures. The perennial problems of weather and market plagued the planter, then as now; the great hurricane of August 19, 1888 destroyed half the crop and damaged the rest; the enormous production of 1892 paralyzed the rice market to the extent that many planters were driven out of the business.[69] Only three varieties of seed rice were available — Japan, Honduras and Carolina — none of which were disease — or weather-resistant. During the experimental stages of canal construction some were found to be inadequate for the acreage planted, and it was only after several years of trial and error that the early mills became solvent.[70]

---

66 *Crowley Signal*, Aug. 26, 1893
67 *Ibid*, Dec. 8, 1888
68 *Ibid*, Aug. 26, 1893
69 *Ibid*, June 2, 1894
70 Summary, *Crowley Signal*, 1888 - 1899

Early rice threshing scene, about 1890, on the Spurgeon farm si: miles from Crowley. Primitive machinery was being used, the "tinke boiler" running the thresher, which had a hayloader, instead of an ai blower, to stack the straw. (Freeland Archives photo)

329

Scene on a rice farm near Crowley in September, 1892. The shocked rice in background was being loaded on wagons to haul to the thresher. (Freeland Archives photo)

330

Five binders at work cutting rice in 1892. Binder at right was "oxen-powered." Sacks of rice in the foreground were left in the field for three weeks to allow the grain to dry before being threshed. (Freeland Archives photo)

Harvesting rice on the P. S. Lovell farm, 3½ miles east of Crowley, about 1900. By this time rice farmers had learned that mules made better work animals than oxen and horses. (Freeland Archives photo)

Threshing rice on the Ridgeway farm near Iota, in 1900. The wood burning engine powered the threshing machine, which had an air blower stacker. (Freeland Archives photo)

A long leather belt, criss-crossed between the steam powered tractor at right and the threshing machine at left, transferred the power to separate the rice from the straw and send each in a different direction. This threshing scene was on the A. Kaplan rice farm, Prairie Hayes, about 1900. (Freeland Archives photo)

334

The grain, after being separated from the straw, was sacked then taken to the mill. This scene, a familiar one until rice combines came into general use after World War II, was on the A. Kaplan rice farm about 1900. (Freeland Archives photo)

335

The Duson rice farm near Rayne, 1892. W. W. Duson, in grey suit in front of binder at right, was giving visitors from the north a tour of the rice field at cutting time. (Freeland Archives photo)

336

..., 1900. One of the earliest in the area, the plant continues in operation today (1976). Joseph R. Roller, the organizer, in white shirt and ...enders, is shown at right. (Freeland Archives photo)

337

The Acadia canal relift near Iota, 1900. Rice irrigation water flows by gravity from the pump over the nearly flat prairie land, but when its momentum slows down relifts are necessary to force the water still further over the many miles it must travel. (Freeland Archives photo)

338

Cannes is raised by the pumping plant, seen in the distance, into the flume and canal. This plant continues in operation at this time, 1976. (Freeland Archives photo)

339

Railroad box-cars being loaded with rice in Crowley in November, 1894. At left is the Duson warehouse, at right the Southern Pacific depot. Ox-carts in foreground have been unloaded, others are waiting their turn at the warehouse. (Freeland Archives photo)

The rice harvest season of 1892. Wagons loaded with sacks of rough ri and drawn by teams of yoked oxen are shown here waiting to be u loaded at the warehouse, which was located along the Southern Paci railroad tracks. (Freeland Archives photo)

341

Wagons lined up at the American mill in Crowley in 1900 wait their turn to be unloaded. Improved roads in the parish made it possible for farmers to use horses and mules instead of oxen to haul heavy loads to market. (Freeland Archives photo)

342

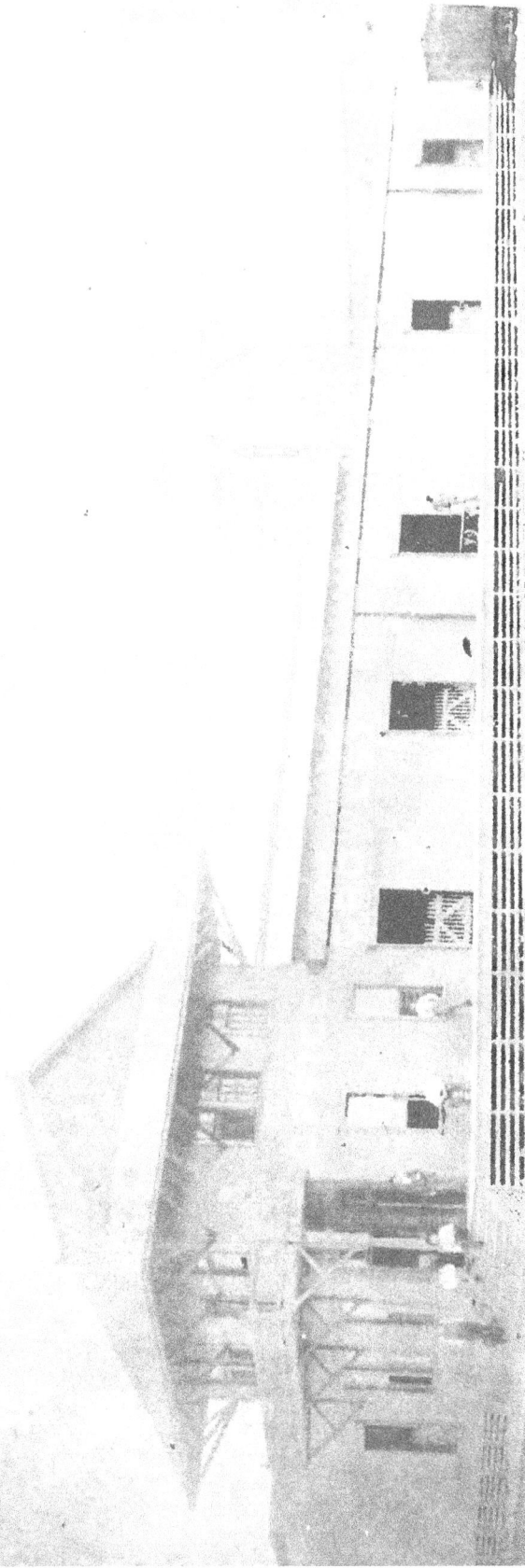

The Crowley Rice Milling Company plant as it appeared about 1897. This was the successor to Pickett's Mill. This and other mills originating in the late 1890s benefitted the local rice industry by processing rice in Crowley instead of sending it to New Orleans to be milled. (Freeland Archives photo)

The first rice mill in Crowley, Pickett's mill, was built in 1893 to test the patent issued in 1890 to Squire A. Pickett for a new method of cleaning rice. The experiment was successful, but the mill had a short life. Using its machinery the company was reorganized in 1895 as the Crowley Rice Milling Company. (Freeland Archives photo)

Crowley

Crowley began its second year by electing a mayor and town council members. The first officials, elected by acclamation on January 6, 1888, were Dr. D. P. January, mayor; J. Frankel, H. W. Carver, D. B. Lyons, A. R. Burkdoll, J. T. Stewart. The council prepared and offered for adoption a town charter, which was accepted on February 17. F. B. Grayson was the first marshal and ex-officio tax collector. Burkdoll resigned his position on the council in March, and C. W. Foreman was elected to fill the vacancy.[71]

During its early years Crowley had trouble keeping a mayor. During the 12-year period 1888-1900 seven mayors served: Dr. D. P. January, J. T. Stewart, A. R. Burkdoll, Gus E. Fontenot, D. R. January, P. J. Chappuis and Judge James E. Barry. Mayor January resigned after serving 10 months; he was succeeded by Stewart, who served four months then resigned to return to Opelousas. Burkdoll served five months, then tendered his resignation and left town as a result of the trouble between him and W. C. Chevis. Fontenot, the fourth mayor, resigned after serving 10 months; the governor appointed D. R. January, son of the first mayor, to replace Fontenot. Chappuis, elected in 1894, served two two-year terms prior to 1900. Judge James E. Barry served from 1898 to 1900.[72]

The enthusiastic predictions about Crowley becoming a boom town did not materialize. Despite the courthouse victory, the town struggled during its early years. This becomes evident through a careful reading of the early issues of the Crowley Signal, dedicated though that newspaper was to the propaganda of prosperity. Some businesses failed, some promising newcomers returned to their former homes, or sought greener pastures. "Crowley's growth is slow but steady," the Signal editor wrote in the April 7, 1888 issue, and again on May 26, 1888: "There is no great boom but a constant and increasing growth." Weekly reports on new construction and the arrival of newcomers helped to maintain the brave front.

There can be no doubt that W. W. Duson and the Crowley Signal were responsible for the improvements effected during that second year and for several years following. Duson donated land for schools and churches; he put up the money, and/or solicited for funds, for public improvements. The newspaper constantly prodded the city fathers into

[71] *Crowley Signal*, Aug. 25, 1888
[72] Research by Rev. Paul B. Freeland, D.D.

undertaking civic projects, such as laying sidewalks, beautifying the courthouse grounds, repairing the streets and bridges, securing a cemetery, offering inducements to new settlers and business enterprises.[73]

By mid-summer of 1888 Crowley boasted three general stores, one grocery, two drug stores, a livery stable, three hotels, a lumber yard, two meat markets, two blacksmith shops, three saloons; a barber shop, bakery, cypress cistern factory, tin shop, real estate agency and newspaper.[74]

Among Crowley "firsts" were Dr. D. P. January, physician and mayor; Jac Frankel, merchant and postmaster; T. C. May, grocer; D. R. January, druggist; R. T. Clark, livery stable; D. B. Lyons, butcher; J. T. Stewart, cistern maker; Ernest Capel, tinner; P. W. Cheney, barber; J. S. Bailey, blacksmith and wheelwright; J. E. Barry, attorney; Dr. J. A. Hines, dentist; Neil McDavitt, saloon keeper; F. B. Driskill, house painter; Miss Ella Crippen, milliner; William Davidson, bricklayer; B. Harrington, drayman; J. G. Medlenka, station agent.[75]

Improvements in the town during its second year included laying sidewalks on both sides of Parkerson Avenue, from the depot to the courthouse. The sidewalk, of wood planks, was extended from Parkerson to the north side of Third street, where Crowley's first church, the Methodist Episcopal Church South, was under construction.[76] The Southern Pacific put up a large water tank, to supply the locomotive engines, and painted it red; the railroad company, spurred by the Signal, also built a stock yard and livestock loading chute near the depot. Prior to this it had been impossible to load livestock for shipping, and northern settlers coming in to Crowley were obliged to unload their stock on the depot platform.[77] The loading chute was used for the first time in late September, when J. W. Smith shipped out two carloads of cattle to the Chicago market. People gathered at the depot to see the loading take place; some of the wild cattle got out of hand and caused some excitement.[78]

One of the major improvements, which affected other areas of the parish as well as Crowley, was the re-building of the Duson bridge over Bayou Plaquemine Brûlée. The approaches to the much-used bridge had become so bad that farmers could no longer use it to come to Crowley to

73 Summary, *Crowley Signal*, Mar. 10, 1888 to Jan. 5, 1889
74 *Crowley Signal*, Aug. 25, 1888
75 Summary, *Crowley Signal*, Mar. 10 to Aug. 25, 1888
76 *Crowley Signal*, July 7, 1888
77 *Ibid*, Aug. 18, Sept. 1, 1888
78 *Ibid*, Sept. 29, 1888

market their produce, attend to court business and buy supplies.[79] Nudged by complaints in the Signal, the police jury appropriated $1,800 to build a new bridge; Crowley businessmen, realizing the importance of the bridge to local trade, put up an additional $500.[80] The new bridge was opened to traffic November 10, 1888, in time for the prairie farmers to haul their rice into Crowley. The bridge, 1,815 feet long, was said to be the longest in southwest Louisiana.[81]

Other news items published during 1888 which reflect the life and times, as well as the growth and development of the parish, included: A new police jury, appointed by Governor Nicholls in June; three of the McEnery appointees were re-named to the body: B. H. Harmon, Homer Barousse and B. E. Clark; the new members, replacing Paul Fremaux and Melon Doucet, were Dennis Miller and Charles T. Duhon . . . in August a telephone line was installed between Rayne and Crowley . . . a new bridge was completed over Bayou Mallet a mile east of the Fabacher post office in November . . . *pieux* fencing was giving way to barbed wire; during September the Signal editor reported: "Several wagon loads of cypress *pieux* were hauled through town this week. At one time in the history of this section the *pieux* was an important factor in everyday trade and as staple an article of commerce as a barrel of flour or shoulder of meat" . . . in December W. W. Duson bought a new road grader, drawn by three pair of oxen, which could plow and grade at the same time . . . George Faulk donated to the police jury the west one half of Faulk Bridge over Bayou Queue de Tortue.

The Signal issued its first special edition on August 25, 1888. This "Immigration Number," designed especially to draw newcomers to the parish, was widely circulated in the north and mid-west. The front page of the eight-page paper was devoted to a historical sketch and an outline of the geographical advantages of the area, and illustrated with a five-column map of Acadia showing the location of the 10 post offices: Rayne, Crowley, Mermentau, Evangeline, Plaquemine Brulee, Church Point, Prudhomme City, Fabacher, Pointe-aux-Loups and Millerville.

The inside pages of the "Immigration Number" carried information about the various communities, illustrated with 11 woodcuts of business places and residences. The buildings pictured included the courthouse,

---

79 *Ibid,* Apr. 14, 1888
80 *Ibid,* June 2, 1888
81 *Ibid,* Nov. 10, 1888

the Crowley House, the Duson real estate office and Crowley Signal plant, the Rayne rice mill, and the Catholic church and rectory at Church Point, this last evidently the most handsome church property in the parish at the time.

The listing of churches included Catholic church buildings at Rayne and Pointe-aux-Loups; Methodist churches (South) at Plaquemine Brûlée and Rayne, and one under construction at Crowley, and a Baptist church "about four miles south of Prudhomme City." Other denominations holding services at various points in the parish were the Quakers and the German Lutherans, both of which originated in the vicinity of Evangeline.

Several columns of the special issue were devoted to the agricultural advantages and the salubrious climate of the region. Other information included brief biographical sketches of the leading business men of the parish. Among the advertisements, inserted mostly by Crowley and Rayne merchants and professional men, was a two-column, page-length ad by the W. W. Duson agency, in which Duson claimed to have settled "over one hundred northern families in Acadia Parish during the past twelve months."

The Southwest Louisiana Land Company held a second town lot sale on March 20, 1889. A total of 424 lots sold for $16,025; the lots averaged $25 each and were sold on terms of half cash, the balance to be paid in 12 months at 8% interest. The sale had been widely advertised in the Signal and other newspapers, and low train fares were in effect for the one-day sale. C. C. Duson auctioned the lots from the depot platform. Visitors, the Signal stated, "were well pleased at the well graded and beautifully laid out avenues, the substantial sidewalks. and the beautiful timber that fringes our southern side." Sale day visitors were told about the special bonuses being offered by the land company: $1,000, grounds, side track, for a rice mill; the same and $200 for a cotton gin; grounds and $250 for a cannery; $100 cash for a dairy of 25 or more cows; grounds, side track and $250 for a sash, blind and door factory; a building site and $500, or $1,000 cash, for a bank; grounds, side track and $250 for a factory and the same for an ice factory.[82] Apparently there were no takers for the bonus offers; if there were, no mention of them appeared in the Signal.

A third land sale was scheduled for May 22, 1889. The land company chartered a special train to bring visitors in, but the attendance was

---

[82] *Crowley Signal,* Mar. 23, 1889

so poor that the auction was postponed until the fall.[83] The land sale was apparently cancelled; no further publicity concerning the auction appeared in subsequent issues of the Crowley newspaper.

The Signal covered the news fronts of Crowley and the parish in remarkable fashion, considering the limitations of the time. Courthouse cases of primary interest were given in detail; births, marriages and deaths were reported, attention was given to social events; unusual weather, such as severe drought or cold, brought comment. Prizes were offered to news correspondents in other communities of the parish to stimulate regular and efficient reporting. Top priorities were immigration, farming and politics, in that order.

The newspaper files also reflect the growth of Crowley as a town, and the effectiveness of the prodigious publicity campaigns staged by the Dusons to lure newcomers, particularly northern and mid-western people, to the area. Scarcely a week went by that the Signal did not report on the arrival of new settlers. The columns of virtually every issue contain names of newcomers from Kentucky, Missouri, Montana, Illinois, Minnesota, Indiana, Michigan and other northern states. The largest party of immigrants to come in at one time was reported in the Signal of February 1, 1890. A party of 25, which included five families, all from Dalton City, Illinois, arrived on January 25. Their possessions were shipped to Crowley in five railroad cars; besides furniture and household goods the immigrants brought 22 head of mules, a brood mare, hogs, chickens, a threshing machine and traction engine, wagons and plows; "in fact, they have a complete outfit of everything necessary for commencing farming," the Signal noted.

In the party from Illinois were Charles J. Freeland Sr., Thomas B. Freeland, Margaret E. Freeland, Eugenia E. Freeland; John W. Roller, his wife, the former Alice Freeland and their son Iral; Mr. and Mrs. Joseph R. Roller and son Harry; Dr. John F. Naftel, Mr. and Mrs. Will Naftel and children, Charles, Frank, Harry and Ethel; Mr. and Mrs. Wilbur Gibson and son Vernon; Mr. and Mrs. Moist W. Marshall and daughter Viola; John Cole and Lon Shelton.[84]

In less than a decade four of the men from Illinois — the two Rollers and the Freeland brothers — were to become giants of the rapidly de-

[83] Ibid, May 25, 1889
[84] Crowley Signal, Feb. 1, 1890

veloping rice industry of Acadia Parish. In addition to their farming interests, the four invested in the early rice mills and irrigation canals; the Freelands built the American rice mill, later acquired a controlling interest in the Louisiana Irrigation and Milling Company, then the First National Bank, first chartered in 1899. Another newcomer, whose name, like those of the Rollers and Freelands, was destined to make history in the rice industry, arrived in Crowley the same week as the party from Illinois. This was A. Kaplan,[85] who began as a merchant but soon turned his energies and business acumen to the development of the rice industry.

---

[85] *Crowley Signal,* Feb. 1 ,1890

The Duson land office building served as quarters for Crowley's first bank, organized in 1892. Shown in front of the original building are, from left, John M. Pintard, Guy S. Norton and William E. Ellis, cashier. (Freeland Archives photo)

The Crowley Signal put out three more special editions which were widely circulated: a 24-page, profusely illustrated special on October 27, 1894; the "Prosperity Number" of May 10, 1898, and the "Commercial and Industrial Number" of October 6, 1900.

The success of these publicity campaigns is evidenced in population figures. In 1890 the federal census listed Acadia with a population of 13,186; Crowley's population was given as 399, and Rayne, 599.[86] By 1900 Crowley's population was 4,214, and Rayne's stood at 1,007. The population of Acadia Parish had climbed to 23,483 — an increase of more than 10,000 in 10 years.[87]

The new century found Acadia, Louisiana's 59th parish, facing the future with the confidence born of experience and maturity — and standing proud "among the sisterhood of parishes."

---

[86] *Crowley Signal*, Sept. 6, 1890
[87] *Louisiana Almanac*, 1973-1974

One of the earliest photographs of Crowley, about 1890, shows Parkerson avenue, looking north from the Southern Pacific railroad. The first courthouse is visible in center background; at right is the Crowley House, at that time being used as quarters for the Acadia College. (Freeland Archives photo)

Panoramic view of Crowley, 1897, looking northeast from the railroad. The Southern Pacific depot is in left foreground, the Crowley House, center, the Crowley State Bank to its left, and the old courthouse down Parkerson avenue in the distance. Spires at right are the Methodist Church, South, on the right, and the Presbyterian Church at left. (Freeland Archives photo)

The Crowley House, Crowley's first hotel, served as quarters for Acadia College in 1890. The college was a co-educational school or academy established in 1889. The Crowley House, one of the oldest buildings in Crowley, built in early 1887, was a landmark until 1972, when i was condemned and torn down. (Freeland Archives photo)

353

The W. W. Duson home in Crowley, at the corner of Second street and Avenue H, in 1894. Mr. and Mrs. Duson are standing on the porch. (Freeland Archives photo)

...ourthouse, at extreme right is ... Francis Jensen ... next is the "Flag Store," then a grocery. Building with twin roof peaks, an approximate center of picture, is the Thomas building, standing today 1976). (Freeland Archives photo)

355

Scene on Parkerson avenue at Third street about 1894. Favre's Opera use with J. D. Marks's general merchandise store on the ground floor is left; across Third street is H. W. Carver's store, with Dr. J. F. Morris' g store on the right. (Freeland Archives photo)

356

Outing on the "Agnes T. Parks" down the Mermentau River to Lake Arthur, about 1893. W. W. Duson and his wife, Clara Thayer Duson, are at extreme left. C. C. Duson is at right, leaning on the rail. Others are friends and relatives. (Freeland Archives photo)

357

W. W. Duson's land office in Crowley, 1892, on the corner of Parkerson avenue and Second street. W. W. Duson is standing at the rear on the right of the entrance. This building is presently (1976) being used as a dwelling at 418 north Avenue B. (Freeland Archives photo)

ACKNOWLEDGEMENTS

The authors wish to acknowledge, with deep gratitude, the assistance given by a number of friends (other than those cited in the bibliography) in the preparation of this work. These include: Elizabeth Lyman Barnett, Paul Letz, Paul Mayne, Otis Hebert, Wade O. Martin, Jr., Mrs. B. W. Spell, Charles Leon Redlich, Jr., Anna Jane Marks, Myrta Fair Craig, Marie Cook, Judge Joseph E. LaHaye, Jan Lewis, Donald Doga, Anna Mae Menard, Dennis Gibson, Juana Roche, Dr. Claude Oubre, Lee Veillon, Glenn Conrad, Marjorie Johnson Lyons, Judge A. Wilmot Dalferes, John Thistlethwaite, James Forrester, Milo Nickel, Malva Huson Brown, Shirley McGrath, Kathleen Toups, Henry Bolden, Maude Addison, Judge Denald Beslin, Lindsay Baur, Miriam Dezauche, Congressman John Breaux, Sen. Edgar Mouton, Helen Olivier, Mr. and Mrs. Frank Nixon, the late H. I. "Red" Mitchell, the late Max Thomas, Catherine Frey, Vincent Riehl Sr., Lee Riehl, Helen Richard, Pearl Segura, Paul DeClouet, Vivian Mayes Smith, Rita Anderson Young, Zenon Joubert, Jr., Jerry Veltin, Goldie Young, Oscar Lormand, Sheriff Elton Arceneaux.

Mary Alice Fontenot
Rev. Paul B. Freeland, D. D.

BIBLIOGRAPHY

PRIMARY SOURCES

ACADIA PARISH RECORDS:
    Abstracts U. S. Land Entries, No. 1
    Conveyance Books
    Donation Books
    Mortgage Books
    Official Township Survey Plats
    Successions
AMERICAN STATE PAPERS — PUBLIC LANDS, Vols. II and III Washington, 1832-1861
BRAND BOOK for the Districts of Opelousas and Attakapas, 1739-1888, Jefferson Caffery Louisiana Room, Dupre Library, University of Southwestern Louisiana
CENSUS RECORDS:
    Rencensements General des Oppeloussa du 4th Mai, 1777 (Archivo General des Indias, Sevilla, Cuba, 2358)
    Third Census of the United States, 1810, Louisiana.

CHURCH RECORDS (marriages, births, burials):

St. John Catholic Church, Mermentau, La.

St. Joseph Catholic Church, Iota, La.

St. Joseph Catholic Church, Rayne, La.

St. Landry Catholic Church, Opelousas, La.

Our Lady of the Sacred Heart Catholic Church, Church Point, La.

Sacred Heart Catholic Church, Grand Coteau, La.

Maryland Chapel, C. M. E. Rayne, La.

LOUISIANA ARCHIVES AND RECORDS SERVICE:

Copy of Enabling Act to create Acadia Parish

Correspondence concerning act to create St. Joseph's Parish

NATIONAL ARCHIVES AND RECORDS SERVICE, WASHINGTON, D. C.:

Register of Appointments of Postmasters, St. Landry and Acadia Parishes, 1832-1900

RAYNE, LA. TOWN COUNCIL:

Minutes, 1883-1890

ST. LANDRY PARISH RECORDS:

Conveyance Books

Donation Books

Mortgage Books

Official Township Survey Plats

Police Jury Minutes, 1811-1819, 1862-1886

Sheriff's Deeds, 1811-1887

Successions

U. S. GEOLOGICAL SURVEY, FEDERAL CENTER, DENVER, COLORADO:

Basile Quadrangle

Eunice Quadrangle

BOOKS

ARSENAULT, Bona, *Histoire et Genealogie des Acadiens* Tomes I, II, (Quebec, 1965) *History of the Acadians* (Quebec, 1966)

ARTHUR, Stanley Clisby, *Jean Laffite Gentleman Rover* (New Orleans, 1952)

ARTHUR, Stanley Clisby, and KERNION, George C. H., *Old Families of Louisiana* (New Orleans, 1931)

BARDE, Alexandre, *Histoire de Comites de Vigilance aux Attakapas* (St. Jean Baptiste, La.) translation by Henrietta Guilbeau Rogers, Louisiana State University thesis, 1936

BAUDIER, Roger, *The Catholic Church in Louisiana* (New Orleans, 1939)

BODIN, Rev. George Anthony, *Selected Acadian and Louisiana Church Records,* Vols. 1 and II (special publications of the Attakapas Historical Association, St. Martinville, La., 1968, 1971)

BOOTH, Andrew B., *Records of Louisiana Confederate Soldiers and Their Commands* (New Orleans, 1920)

COX, I. J., "Daniel Clark," *Dictionary of American Biography* (New York, 1928-1947)

DARBY, William, *A Geographical Description of the State of Louisiana and the Southern Part of Mississippi and the Territory of Alabama* (New York, 1817)

DAVIS, Edwin Adams, *Louisiana A Narrative History* (Baton Rouge, 1965)

DEVILLE, Winston, *Opelousas* (Cottonport, 1973)

DEVILLE, Winston and VIDRINE, Jacqueline, *Marriage Contracts of the Opelousas Post, 1766-1803* (Ville Platte, La. 1960)

DEVILLIER, Gladys, *The Opelousas Post* (Cottonport, 1972)

DISMUKES, J. Phillip, *The Center: A History of the Development of Lafayette, Louisiana* (Lafayette, La. 1972)

DUPRE, Gilbert L., *Political Reminiscences, 1876-1902* (Baton Rouge, 1917)

DU PRATZ, Antoine Simon Le Page, *History of Louisiana* (Paris, 1758)

FORTIER, Alcee, *A History of Louisiana* (New York, 1904)

FREELAND, Rev. Paul D., D.D., *The First Presbyterian Church of Crowley, Louisiana, A Brief History, 1890-1965* (Crowley, La., 1965)

GRIFFIN, Harry Lewis, *The Attakapas Country, A History of Lafayette, Louisiana* (New Orleans, 1959)

HAIR, Velma Lea, *The History of Crowley, Louisiana,* reprinted from *Louisiana Historical Quarterly,* Vol. 27, No. 4, Oct., 1944 (master's thesis in history, Louisiana State University, 1941)

HARMON, Nolan B., *The Famous Case of Myra Clark Gaines* (Baton Rouge, 1946)

HARPER, Robert Henry, D. D., *Louisiana Methodists* (Washington, 1949)

HEBERT, Rev. Donald J., *Southwest Louisiana Records,* Vols. I, II, III (Eunice, La., 1974-1975)

JONES, Rev. John G., *A Complete History of Methodism* (Baton Rouge, 1966)

LeBLANC, Dudley J., *Acadian Miracle* (Lafayette, 1966)

_____*Louisiana Almanac,* 1973-1975; 1975-1976, James Calhoun, editor, (Gretna, La.)

_____*Louisiana, A Guide to the State* (American Guide Series, New York, 1941)

_____*Louisiana Territorial Papers,* U. S. Department of State, Territorial Papers of the United States, compiled and edited by Clarence Edwin Carter (Washington, 1934)

MARTIN, Francois Xavier, *The History of Louisiana from the Earliest Period* (New Orleans, 1882)

_____*Mississippi Provincial Archives,* 1701-1743, collected, edited and translated by Dunbar Rowland and A. G. Sanders (Jackson, Miss., 1927-1932)

PERRIN, William Henry, *Southwest Louisiana Biographical and Historical* (New Orleans, 1891)

POST, Lauren C., *Cajun Sketches* (Baton Rouge, 1962)

READ, William A., *Louisiana-French* (Baton Rouge, 1931); *Louisiana Place Names of Indian Origin* (Baton Rouge, 1927)

ROBIN, Claude C., *Voyage to Louisiana, 1803-1805,* translated by Stuart O. Landry (New Orleans, 1966)

ROBINSON, James Alexander, *Louisiana Under the Rule of Spain, France and the United States, 1785-1807,* Vol. II (Cleveland, 1911)

SANDERS, Mary Elizabeth, *Records of the Attakapas District, 1739-1811,* Lafayette, 1962); *Records of the Attakapas District, St. Mary Parish, La.,* Vol. II (Lafayette, 1963); *Annotated Abstracts of Successions, St. Mary Parish, La., 1811-1834* (Lafayette, 1972) *Annotated Abstracts of Marriage Book 1, St. Mary Parish, 1811-1829* (Lafayette, 1973)

SAXON, Lyle, *Lafitte the Pirate* (New York and London, 1930)

SIBLEY, John Ashley, *Louisiana's Ancients of Man* (Baton Rouge, 1967)

SWANTON, John R., *Indian Tribes of the Lower Mississippi Valley and the Adjacent Coast of the Gulf of Mexico* (Washington, 1911)

WHITFIELD, Irene Therese, *Louisiana French Folk Songs* (Baton Rouge, 1939)

BOOKLETS

BAUDIER, Roger, *History of Our Lady of the Sacred Heart Catholic Church, Church Point, La.,* (from Jesuit records, Church Point, La., 1954)

LOUISIANA DEPARTMENT OF AGRICULTURE, *Louisiana Products, Resources and Attractions,* (New Orleans, 1881)

POST, Dr. Lauren C., *The Rice Country of Southwestern Louisiana,* reprinted from the *Geographical Review,* Vol. XXX, No. 4, Oct., 1940

ARTICLES

BURNS, Frances P., "Henry Clay Visits New Orleans," *Louisiana Historical Quarterly,* Vol. 27

CASSIDY, Vincent H., editor, "Attakapas Country, Cabeza de Vaca," *Attakapas Gazette,* Vol. 2, No. 1

CASSIDY, Vincent H. and ALLAIN, Mathe, "Simars de Belle-Isle Among the Attakapas, 1719-1721" *Attakapas Gazette,* Vol. III, No. 3

COKER, William S., "Luke Collins Senior and Family," *Louisiana History,* Vol. XIV

DEUTSCH, Eberhard P., "Myra Clark Gaines vs. New Orleans," *Louisiana Bar Journal,* Dec. 1971

FONTENOT, Mary Alice, "History of Eunice, Mrs. Duson's Namesake, Opelousas *Daily World* supplement, Nov. 3, 1955; "Houses Over Graves Unique Burial Custom," Lafayette *Daily Advertiser,* May 25, 1975

GINN, Mildred K., "A History of Rice Production in Louisiana to 1896," *Louisiana Historical Quarterly,* Vol. XXIII

POST, Lauren C., "Some Notes on the Attakapas Indians of Southwest Louisiana," *Louisiana History,* Vol. III, No. 3

PRITCHARD, Walter; KNIFFEN, Fred B.; and BROWN, Clair A., "Southern Louisiana and Southern Alabama in 1819: The Journal of James Leander Cathcart," *Louisiana Historical Quarterly,* Vol. 28

STAHL, Annie Lee West, "The Free Negro in Ante-Bellum Louisiana," *Louisiana Historical Quarterly,* Vol. 25

WALL, Jerry, "Louisiana Family Claims Old Debt, *Beaumont Enterprise,* Aug. 22, 1975

NEWSPAPERS

Abbeville Meridional, May 21, 1887

Acadia Sentinel, Oct. 23, 1886 to Sept. 10, 1887

Crowley Post-Signal, Aug. 10, 1975

Crowley Signal, March 10, 1888 through February, 1899

Crowley Signal "Immigration Number," Aug. 25, 1888

Crowley Signal "Prosperity Number," May 10, 1898

Crowley Signal "Commercial and Industrial Number," Oct 6, 1900

Crowley Signal "Rice Number," Jan. 30, 1904

Crowley Daily Signal Golden Jubilee Edition, Oct 4, 1937

Crowley Daily Signal 50th Anniversary Edition, 1899-1949

Daily World, Opelousas, special supplement, "Some History of St. Landry Parish from the 1690s," Nov. 3, 1955   —

Morning Star, 1911

New Orleans Times-Democrat, Jan. 16, 1887, Oct. 1, 1887

Opelousas Courier, 1852-1860; 1862-1887

Opelousas Gazette, Nov. 20, 1841 to Sept 14, 1844

Rayne Signal, March 13, 1886 to Feb. 26, 1887

St. Landry Democrat, Jan. 3, 1880 to Dec. 31, 1887

St. Landry Whig, Sept. 5, 1844 to Aug. 28, 1845; July 18, 1846

INTERVIEWS, ORAL HISTORIES

ARCENEAUX, Thomas J., Ph.D., Dean College of Agriculture (ret.), University of Southwestern Louisiana

BIBB, Clyde L., Branch, La.

BRUNER, Walter, Branch, La.

CHACHERE, Lloyd, Eunice, La.

COURVILLE, Bessie Richard, Eunice, La.

DUHON, Mrs. Edna B., Mermentau, La.

DUSON, Henry T., Crowley, La.

EDMONDS, David C., associate professor of economics, University of Southwestern Louisiana

GIBSON, Jon L., associate professor anthropology, chairman social studies, University of Southwestern Louisiana

GUIDRY, Owen, Church Point, La.

KAHN, Leo H., Lafayette, La.

LANDRY, Ourelie, Carencro, La.

MAIGNAUD, Leonie, Mermentau, La.

NcNEIL, Hugh "Buck," Iota, La.

OHLENFORST, Rev. William, Morse, La.

ROSINSKI, Charles, Rayne, La.

STUTES, Sweeny, Crowley, La.

ZAUNBRECHER, Rev. Charles, Lafayette, La.

UNPUBLISHED

FREELAND, Rev. Paul B., "Early Mayors of Crowley;" "History of Crowley Churches;" "Index to Crowley Daily Signal Golden Anniversary Edition, Oct. 4, 1937"

McCORD, Stanley Joe, "A Historical and Linguistic Study of the German Settlement at Robert's Cove, Louisiana," Louisiana State University dissertation, 1969

MOUTON, Alexandre, "Memoirs, 1853-1936," Southwestern Archives, Dupre Library, University of Southwestern Louisiana

POST, Dr. Lauren C., material not included in *Cajun Sketches,* San Diego, Calif., 1973

ROGERS, Henrietta Guilbeau, "History of the Committees of Vigilance of Attakapas," Louisiana State University master's thesis, 1936

ZAUNBRECHER, Rev. Charles, "History of the German Settlement at Robert's Cove, La."

GENEALOGY RECORDS

ANDRUS, Sybil Parrott, Rayne, La.

BREAUX, Huey Henry, Lafayette, La.

D'AVY, Mrs. A. D., Opelousas, La.

CART, Mrs. Robert, Rayne, La.

CHRISTOPHER, Virginia Terrell, Crowley, La.

DESHOTEL, C. Kenneth, Opelousas, La.

FONTENOT, Ruth Robertson, New Orleans, La.

FREELAND, Rev. Paul B., D. D., Crowley, La.

HAMILTON, Dr. C. E., Lafayette, La.

OLIVIER, Mrs. Oscar, Grand Coteau, La.

PHARR, Henry Newton, New Iberia, La.

PIERREL, Mrs. Thelma, Washington, La.

SPELL, Judge Carrol L., Abbeville, La.

INDEX

367

371

Pousson, Mathieu, 160, 163, 252, 253, 292
Prairie Cottereau, 23, 68; location of, 68
Prairie Faquetaique, 27, 29; location of, 68; origin of name of, 68
Prairie Hayes, location of, 40, 192; origin of name of, 192; bid for courthouse, 256-276; school house fire, 294
Prairie Mammouth (Mamou), 61
Prairie Soileau, 43, 71
Presbyterian Church, Crowley, 307, 309, 352
Prescott, Willis, 303; Wills (Willis?) 236
Province of Picardy, France, 62
Provost, Joachim, 114; Magdalene, 64
Prudhomme City, post office, 26, 89; location of, 189; polling places of, 189, 190; sawmill at, 190; school district, 190, 314; Chachere family reunion, 192; early physicians, 192
Prudhomme, Celeste, 55; Marie, 49; Michel, 21 22, 24, 25, 55, 68, 77, 79; Michel, Jr., 21, 24, 79, 188; William, 188
Prudhomme house, 24, 25
Pucheu, Donat, 139; Laurent, 288
Pugh, P. S., 317

Quakers (Society of Friends), of Evangeline, 197, 199
Quarentin, Evelina, 144
Quebec, bishop of, 27
Quebedeaux, F., 290; Frank, 174, 199; Marguerite, 113, 114
Quebedeaux Cemetery, 199
Quefray, Ann Stephan de, 33
Quinteros, Manuel, 38
Quirk, Thomas, 49

Raiternauer (Rayter), Marie, 23
Randolph, W. J., 314
Raper, Henry, 21, 38
Rapides District, 49
Rasberry, Allen, 268
Ravet, Gustave, 175
Rayne, B. W. L., 123
Rayne, town of, 111-141; early names for, 111, 117; election precinct of St. Landry Parish, 111; site of Vigilante activty, 111-115; early populaton of, 117, 119; first post office of, 92; first church of, 118, 184; post office reestablished, 119; post office location, 119; founding of, 123; incorporation of, 124; first officials of, 124; social activities of, 124; first newspaper of 128; early business firms, 124, 128, 132, 137, 139, 141; fatal shooting at, 130; town council records, 132-137; first rice mill, 137; brass band of, 128; first bank of, 125, 317; fire company of, 130, 288; frogs shipped from, 272
Rayne Drop Saloon, 139, 237
Rayne Herald, 316
Rayne Methodist Church, 140, 307, 348
Rayne News, 316
Rayne Ranger, 316
Rayne schools, 128, 136, 313
Rayne State Bank, 125, 317
Rayne Tribune, 316
Rayter, Miguel, 29, 50; Theresa, 29
Read, Burt W., 314; William, 70

Rectangular System of Surveys, 20
Redlich, Julia, 90; post office, 90
Redtop post office, 92
Reed, Alfred, 268; N., 272; Raymond, 277; Rudolph, 268; S. G., 277
Reese, William, 174
Regan, John, 92, 252, 277; post office, 92
Regan family, 199
Regulators ("White Caps"), 324
Reiners family, 180
Rhea, John, 21, 45
rice, as "Providence" crop, 180, 181; harvest methods of, 182; upland rice first grown, 184; first rice shipped, 184; improvements in irrigation, 325, 326; early rice mills, 137, 327
Richard, Alexander, 268, 305; Clearance, 205; Dominic, 188; Fabien, 21, 22, 29, 30, 70, 159; F., 167; Francois, 79; Jean, 118; Jean Baptiste, 51; Joseph, 51; Julien, 216; Louis, 21, 22, 29, 30, 38, 70; Louis Theogene, 118; Marguerite, 29; Mathurin, 57; Olivier, 29; Philippe, 29; Pierre, 22, 29; Pierre Louis, 150; Placede, 159; Raymond, 245; Theogene, 195; Victor, 21, 22, 51, 268
Richard Consolidated School, 195
Richard settlement, name origin of, 195; another name for, 195; post offices of, 92
Riders, Marie, 27
Ridgeway farm, 333
Riley, William, Jr., 269
Rippy, Samuel, 166, 212
Ritchie (Fabacher), 179
Ritter, Madelone, 26
riverbank system, advantages of, 20
Roach, Henry, 205
Robert, Benjamin, 21, 42, 52; Sarah, 52; Susanne, 42
Robert's Cove, name origin, 42; founding of settlement, 179; customs preserved, 184-187; church of, 184, 307
Roberson, Tom, 268
Robin, C. C., 5, 6, 85
Robinson, Frank E., 92; J. H., 326
Roccofort, Rev. Aloysius L., S.J., 144
Rochat, Susanna, 33
Roger, Jean, 170
Rogers, John H., 163
Roller, Harry, 349; Iral, 349; John W., 349; Mrs. John W., 349; Joseph R., 337, 349; Mrs. Joseph R., 349; brothers, 350, pumping plant, 337
Romero family, 201
Ronkartz family, 180
Roosevelt, Pres. Theodore, 222
Rose, George J., 89; Joseph, 92
Rousseau, Louis, 219, 220
Roy, Edgar W., 128, 139; Eugene D., 90; E. D., 277, 290; Joseph, 50, 65, 90, 169; Joseph R., 169; Michel, 268; Susanna, 50; Yphamie, 65
Rozas (Rozat), Alexander Joseph, 24; Bartholemy, 63; Caroline, 24; Delphine, 24; Francois, 21, 24, 68, 69, 83; Pierre, 24
Rule, Nancy Ann, 38
Rumpkins (Lumpkin?) J. H., 290
Ruppert, Christian, 177
Russ, J., 50; Sophie, 50

www.ingramcontent.com/pod-product-compliance
Lightning Source LLC
Chambersburg PA
CBHW050225270326
41914CB00003BA/571